Defending Civil Resistance Under International law

by
Francis Anthony Boyle

TRANSNATIONAL PUBLISHERS INC.
Dobbs Ferry, New York

This 1988 paperback edition is published by
The Center for Energy Research, 333 State Street,
Salem, OR 97301.

Reprinted by permission of Transnational Publishers, Inc.

Library of Congress Cataloging-in-Publication Data

Boyle, Francis Anthony, 1950—
  Defending civil resistance under international law.

  Includes index.
  1. Trial practice—United States. 2. Civil rights
(International law) 3. Passive resistance—United States. 4. Antinuclear
movement—United States.
5. United States—Foreign relations—1981 -
I. Title.
KF8925.C5B69   1987   342.73'085'0269   87-5825
ISBN 0-941320-43-X   347.302850269

© Copyright 1987 by Transnational Publishers, Inc.

Manufactured in the United States of America

IN MEMORY OF MY FATHER

TABLE OF CONTENTS

Acknowledgements   vii
Preface by Alex Miller, Executive Director,
    The Lawyers' Committee on Nuclear Policy   ix
Foreword by Sean MacBride, S.C.   xiii
Introduction by Richard Falk   xvii
Open Letter to Pro Se Protesters   xxiii

Chapter 1. Recognizing a First Amendment Right of
                Nonviolent Civil Resistance to Prevent
                Violations of International Law   1

Chapter 2. Rules for Defending Nonviolent Civil
                Resistance Under International Law   13

Chapter 3. The Relevance of International Law to the
                Paradox of Nuclear Deterrence   51

Chapter 4. Trial Materials on Nuclear Weapons and
                International Law   107

Chapter 5. Trial Materials on Central America and
                International Law   155

Chapter 6. Trial Materials on South Africa and
International Law   211

Chapter 7. The Hypocrisy and Racism Behind the
Formulation of U.S. Human Rights Foreign
Policy   283

Appendices   317
Bibliography   359
Index   371
Afterword from the Publisher   379

ACKNOWLEDGEMENTS

I would like to express my deep gratitude to all my colleagues from The Lawyer's Committee on Nuclear Policy. In particular, Richard Falk and Sean MacBride have provided an enormous source of inspiration, guidance and support for my work. I also want to express my great appreciation to my beautiful wife, Betsy, for the patience, kindness and understanding she has always shown during the past six years of the Reagan administration despite my many trips away from home around this country and abroad. However, unless otherwise specifically indicated to the contrary, I alone am responsible for the contents of this volume.

This book is dedicated to the memory of my father, a trial lawyer:

> ". . .
>
> Two roads diverged in a wood, and I —
> I took the one less traveled by,
> . . ."

F.A.B.
December 18, 1986

PREFACE

Nonviolent, symbolic political speech has a long tradition in American political life. One need look back only a few years to the civil rights demonstrations of the 1960s to recall the important impact which civil resistance can have on the political process. And in the 1980s, perhaps more than ever before, this form of speech is being used by a diverse group of individuals across the country. Increasingly disenchanted with the foreign policy of their government, and deeply concerned with their obligations as citizens to register disapproval of conduct which violates international law, a growing number of Americans have been engaging in a variety of nonviolent protests.

For the past several years, members of the Board of Directors and the Consultative Council of the Lawyers' Committee on Nuclear Policy have volunteered their time and resources to the cause of helping provide quality legal defense to citizens engaged in nonviolent protest against prevailing nuclear weapons policies and the nuclear arms race. Initially, the Committee provided advice on an ad hoc basis, offering information on the relevance of international law to antinuclear protest. Later, as more and more cases moved to trial, Francis Boyle and other legal scholars served as expert witnesses and counsel to the defendants.

As the requests for information and assistance multiplied with the number of cases nationwide, toward the end of 1985 it became clear that there was an urgent need for a comprehensive set of materials which would assist defendants in preparing for trial and articulating the legal rationale for their actions. Without hesitation, Professor Boyle agreed to take on the task of assembling the relevant material and tying it together in a clear and concise fashion. What follows is a practical legal manual for use in preparing the defense of citizens protesting to uphold international law in the nuclear context, and also in protest actions related to Central American and South African policy (other areas in which Professor Boyle has had extensive experience as a consultant and expert witness).

The need for a legal manual such as this is apparent. At present, many -- if not most -- nonviolent protesters go into the courtroom underprepared. Often they represent themselves. Frequently, when they do receive advice from a lawyer, their counselor is working on a pro bono basis and is not familiar with the use of legal arguments based on international law. As a result, the quality of legal defenses being mounted by these protesters has varied greatly, contributing to wide discrepancies in their treatment by the courts. Consider, for example, the cases of the *Plowshares*, a group of religious anti-nuclear protesters arrested in the course of eighteen separate actions since 1981. Sentences for similar actions undertaken by different members of their group in the past two years have ranged from suspended sentences to eighteen-year prison terms.

It is essential, if these disparities are to be discontinued, that the courts involved be given a clear understanding of the motivations and legal justifications underlying protest actions. It was our hope in asking Professor Boyle to write this book that we would contribute to that process. Indeed, as a consultant and expert witness in a number of recent cases, Professor Boyle has already been successful at helping to guide the court through the often complex international legal issues that form the background to these cases. The materials gathered in this book should help bring the courts another step toward a greater understanding that -- rather than representing disorder and political nihilism -- individuals involved in nonviolent protest undertake their actions in the highest spirit of patriotism and respect for law, consistent with the U.S. Constitution and the law of nations.

With regard to all three political issues dealt with in this book, nonviolent protest in recent years has become a more and more prominent element of broader political movements. The daily arrests at the South African embassy and consulates across the country two years ago; the numerous arrests in the past year of large groups at the Nevada Nuclear Test Site (one of which included the scientist Carl Sagan); and the massive Pledge of Resistance Movement op-

posing intervention in Nicaragua are all testimony to this phenomenon. In fact, reliable estimates say that each year during the past
several years there have been approximately 5,000 arrests for cases
of nonviolent anti-nuclear weapons protest alone. This broad-based
movement has received increasing attention in the national media
as a legitimate and important form of political expression.

In this resistant political environment, a book like Professor Boyle's
is both practical and necessary. It gives the Lawyers' Committee a
chance to help support a greater number of these protesters more
effectively, based on Professor Boyle's unique experience and skills.
And more importantly it gives the protesters -- and the lawyers who
defend them -- an opportunity to plan and conduct their cases using
the best knowledge available.

Alex Miller
Executive Director
The Lawyers' Committee on Nuclear Policy
New York: December 16, 1986

FOREWORD

by
Sean MacBride, S.C.

The vast political, social and economic upheavals that followed the two world wars led to a realization that the principles of the Rule of Law required clearer definition and were indeed of universal application. On 26 June 1945 the Nations of the world, meeting in San Francisco, adopted the Charter of the United Nations. It is, I think, necessary in this period of international chaos to keep on remembering what had been decided then:

"WE THE PEOPLEs
OF THE UNITED NATIONS
DETERMINED
>   to save succeeding generations from the scourge of war, which twice in our lifetime has brought untold sorrow to mankind, and
>   to reaffirm faith in fundamental human rights, in the dignity and worth of the human person, in the equal rights of men and women and of nations large and small, and
>   to establish conditions under which justice and respect for the obligations arising from treaties and other sources of international law can be maintained, and
>   to promote social progress and better standards of life in larger freedom,

AND FOR THESE ENDS

> to practice tolerance and live together in peace with one an-
> other as good neighbours, and
>
> to unite our strength to maintain international peace and se-
> curity, and
>
> to ensure, by the acceptance of principles and the institution
> of methods, that armed force shall not be used, save in the
> common interest, and
>
> to employ international machinery for the promotion of the
> economic and social advancement of all peoples,

HAVE RESOLVED TO COMBINE OUR EFFORTS TO ACCOMPLISH
THESE AIMS"

Then, in more detail, the first two Articles provide for the maintenance
of international peace, the removal of threats to peace, and for the
suppression of acts of aggression. They also provide for respect of
the right of national self-determination of peoples and in Article 2,
paragraphs 3 and 4, specifically provide that all members shall settle
their international disputes by peaceful means in such a manner that
international peace and security are not endangered.

> "All Members shall refrain in their international relations from the
> threat or use of force against territorial integrity or political inde-
> pendence of any state, ..."

I have tremendous affection for the people of the United States and
for the contribution which Americans have made in the fields of arts
and science which have benefited the world. It is because of this
admiration that I now look on with horror at the actions of the in-
dustrial-scientific-military complex of American scientists and military men. Not only do they appear to be preparing for a world nuclear
holocaust, but they are also assisting in the destruction of the International Rule of Law, and the Principles upon which the United
Nations was founded.

We are passing through a period of universal terrorism and a disregard
for morality. While undoubtedly there has been a substantial amount
of individual acts of terror perpetrated by ethnic, or nationalist revolutionary organizations throughout the world, the greatest acts of
terrorism in recent years have been carried out under the aegis of
some of the major powers. Several attempts have been made to

assassinate the President of Cuba. President Allende of Chile was successfully overthrown and assassinated with the results we know. In pretty well every country of the Middle-East, the Americans and the Israeli secret service have carried out extensive covert operations which have promoted armed conflicts in that area. The American fleet bombarded Druze villages in the Lebanon for no ascertainable reason. The Lebanon was invaded by the Israelis with the concurrence of the United States. Palestinians in refugee camps were systematically killed. American planes were sent into Tripoli with the mission of assassinating Colonel Ghadaffy and his family; successfully killing his two-year old daughter!

The CIA mined the Nicaraguan coastal waters and flew arms and armed forces into Nicaragua. Just now it has transpired that the U.S. has been secretly selling arms to Iran and using the vast sums of money thus illegally obtained for secret operations in Central America. The French secret service sent their agents to blow up the Greenpeace ship *Rainbow Warrior* in New Zealand and killed a man during the course of that operation. The British secret service have mounted several covert murderous operations in Ireland to add to our difficulties. England, the United States and West Germany have been systematically supporting South Africa in her covert actions against Mozambique, Angola and Namibia.

I have detailed this long and unpleasant list of crimes for which governments are responsible. I am sure there are many, many more and the countries I have mentioned are not the only ones to have been involved in such criminal activities. I have done so to emphasize the need to restore the Rule of Law in international affairs and in the hope that governments may realize the highly damaging effect of these crimes against peace in the world and on their own self-respect and image in the world.

I am sure that many Communist regimes have also been responsible for many violations of the Rule of Law. But, two wrongs do not make a right; their violation of humanitarian law is as reprehensible.

I am glad Professor Francis Boyle has had the initiative and the courage to write this analytical book which will awaken and guide lawyers throughout the world. I am happy that Professor Richard Falk by his introduction has joined our colleague Professor Francis Boyle in his clarion call for a return to the Rule of Law based on morality.

There has been a near total breakdown in all standards of public and private morality in the world. This in my view is in no small degree due to the bad example which governments have given. It should be the task of the lawyers in the world to try to rebuild standards of moral responsibility which should form the base for the Rule of Law.

INTRODUCTION

by
Richard Falk

   George Delf in his important, yet little known, book *Humanizing Hell: The Law v. Nuclear Weapons* (Hamish Hamilton, London, 1985), concludes his discussion of lawyers with this indicting sentence: "As long as lawyers feed off rather than uphold the law they will continue to undermine their professional integrity by obstructing what they claim to serve." (p. 85). Delf had in mind the refusal of international law professionals to uphold notions of legal accountability for government leaders based on principles set forth at the Nuremberg trials after World War II. His concern was animated by a sense of radical incompatibility between continuing preparations for nuclear war and the inhibitions of international law.
   With some overgeneralization it seems accurate to admit that the legal profession has crystallized in recent decades around the ideal of rendering competent services to holders of official power and to those with the ability to pay. But it is more than crass material interests and less than crude Marxist imagery of government in a capitalist society as a committee of the ruling class. There is an inarticulate assumption that legitimated power is at the center of the governmental bureaucracy, and that deference to its claims, especially on matters of national security, is virtually synonymous with what it means to be a good citizen. In effect, the executive branch is given a free rein, even on such vital matters as nuclear weapons policy. It is this free rein, and its incompatibility with prevailing legal doctrine, that so

distresses Delf, and inspires the pathbreaking book by Francis Boyle.

Fortunately, the urgency of bringing law to bear on the foreign policy process is beginning at long last to arouse even lawyers, and helping to establish a more constructive image of professionalism. Such collective ventures as the Permanent Peoples Tribunal, the Lawyers' Committee on Nuclear Policy, and the Center for Constitutional Rights give expression to the view that law is above all an instrument to secure justice for society as a whole, and that the implementation of international law even against one's own government is an essential aspect of constitutional process in a political democracy. This dynamic is being played out here in the United States because the government is a superpower engaged in a nuclear arms race and pursuing an interventionary diplomacy in the Third World, while at the same time sustaining the forms of constitutionalism. As Americans, we are challenged at this time both by the illegality and criminality of several foreign policy initiatives, but also by the continuing availability of constitutional avenues of challenge, especially courts.

The legal profession cannot by itself assure a return to legality in foreign policy. The active collaboration between most judges and national security managers needs also to be identified for what it is, and repudiated. The fundamental constitutional commitment to the separation of powers has never been carried out by courts with regard to foreign policy, and instead a virtual blank check has been given to the Executive Branch, jeopardizing the foundations of popular sovereignty virtually from the outset of the Republic. As the constitutional bicentennial descends upon us it is a matter of highest priority to challenge this Hamiltonian reading of the Constitution and remind the judiciary that it is their overwhelming duty to assure that the governing process is constrained by the basic mechanism of checks and balances, which means an independent *judicial* construction of legal rights and duties, including in settings where argumentation arises from international law. At present, a few courts are beginning to acknowledge these long suppressed responsibilities, and cast aside such fallacious notions as the irrelevance of international law in domestic courts or the inability to adjudicate international law issues because of their alleged character as political questions. It is also evident that many judges are straining to exclude international law testimony in cases involving prosecution of symbolic, non-violent political crimes, where the intent of the defendants was motivated by their conviction that it was necessary to commit trivial violations of law to call into question gross violations of international law by the government. An encouraging sign is that where juries of ordinary Americans get the chance to take account of international law arguments, they seem impressed, almost regardless of their political predilections. Jurors seem ready to acknowledge that their duty as citizens is to apply the law, including international law, not merely to defer blandly to the government. Patriotism in the nuclear age is beginning to express itself as an oppositional force!

No one has done more to guide these new forces of legality, and to nourish their expression, than Francis Boyle. As scholar, as international law specialist, as citizen Professor Boyle has developed the theory and practice of a new constitutionalism in which every American has the right and duty to insist upon a lawful foreign policy. This book embodies the fruit of his labors to date, and it facilitates the spread of this new professionalism among lawyers, judges, and citizens generally. *Defending Civil Resistance Under International Law* is the only book so far that sets forth both the legal theory of civil resistance in foreign policy settings and provides lawyers with a practical guidebook that enables the optimal legal defense to be developed for prisoners of conscience invoking law as defense and rationale. In carrying out this vital endeavor, Professor Boyle not only displays erudition, but he illustrates through his own notable experience, that these international law arguments can be made to succeed in American courts.

We are at a strange paradoxical moment in our history. We march on toward Armageddon, our elected representatives voting further billions for the Pentagon each year, while seeming to ignore several extraordinary possibilities for nuclear disarmament in the Gorbachev era. And yet there are more and more among us who stand up to be counted as saying "No," being reinforced in this stance of secular resistance by the guidelines of organized religion and by shows of solidarity on the part of leading clerics. Crucial statements by mainstream churches on nuclear weaponry, on *apartheid*, on sanctuary for those threatened with persecution if forcibly returned to their countries of origin are suggesting that a new vision of justice, security, and order is being generated, and that courts are an important theater of ideas by which to work out the transition from the old to the new.

Underlying this transition are three central ideas that are all present in Francis Boyle's interpretation of the situation. There is, to begin with, a widespread acknowledgment that the normal procedures of representative democracy (elections, political parties, legislative action) are not adequate to challenge illegal undertakings in foreign policy. Extraordinary initiatives are needed and justified on grounds of normative gravity, as well as political expediency. Symbolic, non-violent resistance to government, including violations of its laws, is an appropriate, and if correctly understood, *legally* justified method of resistance. Such justification is especially persuasive in relation to nuclear weapons policy, as well as to challenges directed at uses of armed force and interventional tactics and in response to gross abuses of human rights overseas or at home.

It should be remembered that social progress throughout American history has consistently depended on resistance to official policies. From the Boston Tea Party to the Civil Rights Movement Americans have celebrated, in retrospect, those who stood up to oppose unjust and oppressive policies of government. More widely in Western civilization, we celebrate those who stood for justice in their often lonely vigil against state power: Antigone, Socrates, Jesus, Thoreau, Gandhi, Dieterich Boenhoffer, Martin Luther King. Our whole edifice of constitutionalism rests on the militant struggle of the English barons to check the absolutism of the king, a movement for reform culminating in the Magna Carta, reluctantly signed in 1215 by royal authority to avert civil war. Resistance and the growth of constitutionalism are everywhere intertwined in the history of Western democracy.

Such a reality is reinforced by the peculiar character of impending nuclear doom. Unlike other wrongs and catastrophes that leave victims behind to reconstruct the world, the occurrence of nuclear war threatens our capacity to recover, even to survive. The preparation for nuclear war is the only evil that we can usefully address, as only by its effective rejection can we sustain the capacity to provide for our security. If we wait for the breakdown of deterrence through nuclear warfare, we have waited too long, no matter what happens subsequently. In this regard, the reasonableness of assessing now the legality of these weapons and their range of possible applications, seems beyond question. Congress and the electoral process has been coopted by nuclearism, and thus it is only by an insistent recourse to normative criteria of morality and law that such a challenge can be mounted out of the bosom of civil society. Courts and judges are currently being given a series of opportunities to open up these portals to survival by civil resisters. If they remain bolted, then a conscientious citizenry will have to adopt yet more drastic means.

There is a final element present here. Since 1945 when the Nuremberg and Tokyo Judgments were reached, holding surviving German and Japanese leaders individually responsible for their violations of international law in the area of war and peace, a new element has been introduced into the relations between citizen and state. At the time, the victorious governments promised that the principles being set forth to make the leaders of the defeated countries accountable were generally applicable, including to the governing processes of the victorious countries. A resolution to this effect was introduced by the United States in the United Nations General Assembly and unanimously approved. In post-Nuremberg settings, a government that flagrantly violates international law is engaged in criminal behavior even on a domestic plane, and as far as internal law is concerned, its policies are not entitled to respect. To disobey is no longer, as with Thoreau, to engage in "civil disobedience," an initiative designed to point up the discrepancy between "law" and "morality," and the priority of the latter for a person of conscience. Such a tension no longer exists. To resist reasonably a violation of international law is a matter of legal right, possibly even of legal duty if knowledge and a capacity for action exists. Our resisters who properly invoke the authority of Nuremberg stand on firm legal ground, and should not be sent off to jail, but should be exonerated. Or better, the courts should lend the weight of their authority to the claim that a given direction of foreign policy or national security doctrine are incompatible with international law, and that its principal executors are subject to criminal prosecution. We should seek an Attorney General who understands that his responsibility includes securing compliance of government with international law. It would be helpful to signal the acceptance of this mandate by the designation of an Assistant Attorney General for Foreign Policy Matters.

In essence, what is at stake is the birth process of a new stage of constitutionalism. It took more than a century of political challenges and judicial practice to translate the promises of equal protection and due process into a system of rights and practices that included minorities and women, and even then only imperfectly and partially. We have far less time to embody the constitutional promise of the supremacy of international law into authoritative doctrine. Francis Boyle's book is so important because it provides us with an excellent repertoire of techniques for accelerating the pace of struggle. And it yet may be, that the outcome of this struggle will significantly determine the destiny of the planet for ourselves and others.

Princeton, New Jersey
December 27, 1986

PREFACE TO THE PAPERBACK EDITION
An Open Letter to All Pro Se Protesters

Dear Pro Se Protester:

Due to the gracious efforts of a courageous anti-nuclear protester, Martin Hird, and my publisher, Heike Fenton, we have been able to produce a paperback edition of this book at a cost that is readily affordable to almost anyone. I would strongly recommend that any individual contemplating an act of civil resistance read *beforehand* Chapter 1, together with the relevant subsequent chapters depending on the type of protest involved, whether anti-nuclear (Chapters 3 and 4), anti-U.S. intervention in Central America (Chapter 5), anti-South African apartheid (Chapter 6), pro-Jewish emigration from the Soviet Union (Appendix 5), etc. This minimum effort will put you in a much better position from which to defend yourself at trial if necessary.

When asked to write this book by the Lawyers' Committee on Nuclear Policy, I was requested to do so for the express purpose of explaining to *lawyers* how to defend those who have engaged in nonviolent civil resistance activities by using principles of international law. For this reason, then, the book has been written primarily as if it were addressed to trial lawyers. Nevertheless, it has been successfully used by pro se defendants acting without the assistance of a lawyer.

If you are a pro se defendant, do not be intimidated by Chapters 2 and 3. Rather, immediately read Chapter 1, and then Chapter 4 or Chapter 5 or Chapter 6 or Appendix 5, depending upon the subject matter of your protest. You should pay particular attention to the sample expert witness testimonies that I have prepared concerning the rules of international law with respect to nuclear weapons, Central America, and South Africa, which can be found, respectively, in Chapters 4.2, 5.2 and 6.3. Based upon my experience, you do not need to be even a college graduate, let alone a lawyer, in order to comprehend and articulate the international law issues at stake in these cases.

Of course, for a variety of reasons explained in Chapter 2, I would prefer that you give serious consideration to allowing yourself to be represented by a trial lawyer. But in the event you have firmly decided as a matter of principle that such an approach is not for you, then it is your constitutional right to represent yourself at trial. I will be more than happy to assist you in whatever way you desire—within reason. Please feel free to telephone me as soon after your arrest as possible, and we can attempt to work out a strategy of defense based upon international law with particular reference to the facts of your case. There is no charge to you for my professional services in such cases.

Despite our best efforts, however, sometimes the judge will decide to strip you of all your international law defenses as well as of all your expert witnesses. In my professional opinion, this would constitute a clearcut violation of your constitutional rights. Nevertheless, it happens all too often in American courts, and especially in federal courts. Many federal district court judges operate under the erroneous assumption that they possess some inherent right to play God with your life. *Do not be discouraged!* For there is still one other way to defend yourself by using principles of international law.

At trial you will usually have an opportunity to explain what you did and why you did it in your testimony-in-chief. You should prepare this statement with a great deal of care. While in the process of doing this, you should consult the sample direct testimony I have already prepared with respect to the particular issue at trial in your case. You can use that testimony in order to prepare your courtroom statement.

In other words, you should attempt to present *some* of the international law arguments presented in the relevant chapters of this book during the course of your statement. This does not mean that you should simply commit my testimony to memory and repeat it by rote in front of the jury. That tactic would be too artificial and readily transparent for all to see. Rather, you should make a good-faith effort to convey to the jury the meaning and content of some of the most important international law principles that have motivated you to protest: typically, these would include the Nuremberg Principles, the Genocide Convention, the Geneva Conventions, the United Nations Charter, and the Supremacy Clause of the United States Constitution.

In the event that there is more than one defendant in your trial, then you can divide up my sample testimony among the defendants so that each basic international law point would be covered by at least one defendant during the course of your respective statements. Please remember, however, that you must not attempt to sound as if you are experts on international law. Rather, you are simply explaining the relevance of international law to your protest in a simple manner to the members of the jury as one group of concerned human beings and American citizens to another.

Your objective in doing this should be to attempt to convince at least one juror that your protest was motivated by a good-faith belief that such conduct was justified by basic norms of international law that have been fully subscribed to by the United States government. Hopefully, that one juror would be prepared to hold out for your acquittal. If convincing enough, you should at least be able to produce a hung jury in those jurisdictions where unanimity is required for conviction. In another case I worked on, this tactic by a pro se defendant resulted in an outright verdict of acquittal with respect to a less serious charge. Of course this same tactic can also be used even if you are being represented by an attorney at trial.

Finally, in the event that the judge has stripped you of all your defenses, rejected your expert witnesses and then gone so far as to indicate that he will not even allow you to mention considerations of "international law" during the course of your testimony-in-chief, then you might wish to consider pursuing the following strategy as a last ditch effort: When it comes time for you to take the witness stand, stand up in open court and politely but firmly inform the judge that you renew your request to have two experts (one on the facts, the other on the law—both mentioned by name) testify on your behalf; and that otherwise, you choose to exercise your constitutional right to remain silent. Then respectfully sit down, indicating that you intend to produce no further evidence whatsoever on your behalf. At that point the judge will find himself in the difficult position of risking a reversal on appeal because he will have so obviously denied your constitutional right to put on a defense if he does not accede to your renewed (and reasonable) request for only two experts. He will also look pretty unfair in the eyes of the jury if there is one.

When faced with such a joint strategy pursued by ten anti-nuclear protesters in a sequential fashion, a federal district judge realized that he could very well be overruled on appeal for committing reversible error if he did not allow the defendants to produce at least one expert on U.S. nuclear weapons policies and another expert on international law. I would not, however, recommend this tactic to a defendant who could face a considerable period of time in jail or a substantial fine if convicted. Most probably, you should employ this fairly drastic technique only if you would be facing an inconsequential penalty upon conviction for a misdemeanor-trespass or other minor infraction. If you are charged with any type of felony I would strongly recommend that you give serious consideration to being represented by an attorney.

Please rest assured that there are many other individuals in the United States who have successfully represented themselves by using principles of international law as set forth in this book. This assurance, however, is not intended to provide any type of guarantee that you will be successful. *You very well might not.* Rather, it is our hope that the paperback edition of this book can provide you with whatever ammunition you need to mount a credible defense of yourself during the course of a criminal prosecution.

I wish you the best of luck! And please keep in touch: Others can benefit from your experience.

Yours very truly,
Francis A. Boyle

(217) 333-0931
Champaign, Illinois
November 2, 1987

Chapter 1.

Recognizing a First Amendment Right of Nonviolent Civil Resistance to Prevent Violations of International Law

Since January of 1981, the people of the world have witnessed a government in the United States of America that demonstrates little if any respect for fundamental considerations of international law and organizations, let alone appreciation of the requirements for maintaining international peace and security. What we have watched instead is a comprehensive and malicious assault upon the integrity of the international legal order by a group of men and women who are thoroughly Machiavellian in their perception of international relations and in their conduct of both foreign and domestic affairs. This is not simply a question of giving or withholding the benefit of the doubt when it comes to complicated matters of foreign affairs and defense policies to a U.S. government charged with the security of both its own citizens and those of its allies in Europe, the Western Hemisphere and the Pacific. Rather, the Reagan administration's foreign policy represents a gross deviation from those basic rules of international deportment and civilized behavior that the United States government has traditionally played the pioneer role in promoting for the entire world community. Even more seriously, in several instances, specific components of the Reagan administration's foreign policy have constituted ongoing criminal activity under well-recognized principles of both international law and U.S. domestic law.[1]

In direct reaction to the Reagan administration's wanton attack upon the international and domestic legal orders, large numbers of American citizens have engaged in various forms of nonviolent civil resistance activities to protest against distinct elements of the Reagan administration's foreign policy. These citizen protests have led to numerous arrests and prosecutions by federal, state, and local government authorities around the country. Most regrettably for all concerned, many individuals involved in these nonviolent protests have been prosecuted, convicted and sentenced in a particularly harsh and vindictive manner.

For example, the Reagan administration's offensive nuclear weapons buildup has generated protests by numerous groups and individuals against U.S. nuclear weapons installations, facilities, programs and personalities around this country and abroad. In this regard, the Greenham Common Women and the Catholic nonviolent civil resistance group known as Pax Christi are two of the most prominent movements. In addition, much outstanding work in the nuclear area has likewise been performed by the numerous groups of individuals who have protested the production of plutonium triggers for U.S. hydrogen bombs at the PUREX facility before the Hanford Site in the state of Washington, as well as at the U.S. government's nuclear weapons test facility in Nevada. Of course the Nuclear Freeze Movement has served as the fountainhead for much of the organizational and intellectual activities in the anti-nuclear arena today.

Similarly, the Reagan administration's disingenuous policy of so-called "constructive engagement" toward the criminal apartheid regime in South Africa has spawned a nationwide campaign against apartheid and U.S. governmental complicity therein. Protests have been mounted before the South African Embassy and consulates, business establishments that sell krugerrands, IBM for selling computers to the South African police, and other economic targets. On American college campuses, students are vigorously demanding that their administrators divest university portfolios of all stock held in

---

1. *See* Boyle, "The American Society of International Law: 75 Years and Beyond," 75 *Am. Soc'y Int'l L. Proc.* 270 (1981), *reprinted in* Appendices *infra*; Boyle et al., "Conclusions and Judgment of Brussels Tribunal (Sept. 30, 1984)," *N.Y. Times*, Oct. 7, 1984, at 77, *and in* International Progress Organization, *The Reagan Administration's Foreign Policy* 459 (H. Kochler ed. 1985), *reprinted in* Appendices *infra*.

American companies that do business in South Africa. These citizen protests have led to numerous arrests and prosecutions for several types of nonviolent civil resistance activities designed to produce official and unofficial condemnation and sanction of apartheid. To a great extent, the anti-apartheid protest movement has been successful at producing a marked change toward the adoption of more aggressive policies against South African apartheid at the national, state, local and university levels.

The Reagan administration's illegal military intervention in El Salvador, Honduras, Costa Rica, and Nicaragua has probably been responsible for the greatest number and degree of nonviolent civil resistance activities in America today. First comes the so-called Sanctuary Movement, which consists of approximately 300 American church and synagogue communities that are providing sanctuary to refugees fleeing the conflicts of Central America in dire fear for their lives. In explicit violation of the requirements of both the 1967 Protocol to the U.N. Convention Relating to the Status of Refugees[2] and the U.S. Refugee Act of 1980,[3] the Reagan administration refused to give these refugees political asylum so as not to undercut the pseudo-legitimacy of the military dictatorships that actually rule El Salvador and Guatemala with the active political, economic and military support of the United States government. To sustain this reprehensible policy the Reagan administration launched a vicious vendetta against the church people who organized the Sanctuary Movement as an expression of their deeply-held religious convictions. The latter have been prosecuted to the absolute limit of the law, if not beyond, despite the protection afforded their activities by the First and Fourth Amendments to the U.S. Constitution.[4]

Last, but not least, comes the self-styled Pledge of Resistance Movement, whose 80,000 members have taken a vow that in the event the Reagan administration decides to launch an invasion of Nicaragua, its membership will engage in a nationwide campaign of nonviolent civil resistance activities designed to terminate such internationally lawless behavior. The Pledge of Resistance Movement

---

2. *See* Protocol Relating to the Status of Refugees, *opened for signature* Jan. 31, 1967, 19 *U.S.T.* 6223, *T.I.A.S.* No. 6577, 606 *U.N.T.S.* 267.
3. *See* Refugee Act of 1980, Pub. L. No. 96-212, 94 *Stat.* 102 (codified at 8 *U.S.C.* § 1101 (1982)).
4. *See* Boyle, "A Legal Analysis of the Resolution Declaring Oak Park, Illinois a Sanctuary Village," *reprinted in* Chapter 5 *infra*.

has already called out its members on more than one occasion to demonstrate against the repeated votes by Congress to provide military and so-called humanitarian assistance to the contra mercenary bands which, at the Reagan administration's behest, are illegally attacking the legitimate government of Nicaragua in violation of the U.N. Charter, the O.A.S. Charter, and the Geneva Conventions of 1949, inter alia. These resistance activities consisted of sit-ins and other forms of nonviolent protest conducted at federal military installations and the offices of U.S. congressional representatives and senators who voted in favor of such aid. In significant part these courageous individuals have been motivated to protest by the firm conviction that the Reagan administration's foreign policy toward Nicaragua violates fundamental principles of both international law and U.S. domestic law.

It is probably the case that on a day-in and day-out basis there are thousands of people in the United States of America who are either planning, preparing, committed to, or actively participating in nonviolent civil resistance activities directed against some aspect of the Reagan administration's foreign policies. In the opinion of this author, these activities represent a positive development for the future role of democratic government in the United States of America with its historical commitment to the rule of law both at home and abroad. Due to the personal popularity of President Reagan, Congress has proven to be completely pusillanimous when it comes to the enforcement of respect for its own laws on the part of the executive branch of government.

The courts are essentially powerless to prevent or impede the gross international lawlessness of the Reagan administration. Even when given a rare opportunity to exercise some small degree of restraint on executive branch excesses in foreign affairs, federal judges have generally decided to defer to presidential lawlessness under the so-called doctrines of "political question" or "judicial restraint." For the most part, the members of the federal judiciary have completely, and in my opinion quite inappropriately, abnegated any constructive role they might have played in support of the widespread public demand that American foreign policy be conducted in a manner consistent with the requirements of both international and U.S. domestic law.

Thus we have witnessed a total breakdown of the constitutional doctrine of separation of powers when it comes to the illegal and oftentimes criminal conduct of foreign policy by the Reagan administration. In light of this breakdown, large numbers of American citizens have decided to act on their own cognizance in order to demand that the Reagan administration adhere to the principles of international law, of U.S. domestic law, and of our own Constitution in its conduct of foreign affairs. Mistakenly, however, such actions have been popularly defined to constitute classic instances of nonviolent "civil disobedience" as historically practiced in the United States. And the traditional admonition for those who knowingly engage in nonviolent civil disobedience has always been that they must meekly accept their punishment for having performed a prima facie breach of the positive law as a demonstration of their good faith and moral commitment. In my opinion, nothing should be further from the truth.

Here I would like to suggest a different way of thinking about nonviolent civil resistance activities that are specifically designed to prevent or impede ongoing criminal activity by members of the Reagan administration under well-recognized principles of international and domestic law. Such civil resistance activities represent the last constitutional avenue open to the American people to preserve their democratic form of government with its historical commitment to the rule of law, and thus the last hope we have to prevent the Reagan administration from moving even further down the path of lawless violence in Southern Africa, military intervention in Central America, and nuclear warfare with the Soviet Union. For reasons more fully explained in the next chapter, such measures of "civil resistance" must not be confused with, and indeed must be carefully distinguished from, acts of "civil disobedience" as traditionally defined.

Under the First Amendment to the United States Constitution, civil resistance protesters are exercising their right "peaceably to assemble, and to petition the Government for a redress of grievances." Note that the First Amendment does not require their assembly to be "lawful" in a positivist technical sense, but only that it be peaceable. Similarly, ongoing criminal activity committed by officials of the government itself is certainly the type of grievance the people should have a right to petition for redress against by means of nonviolent civil resistance. Therefore, we must recognize that the First Amendment includes within its scope the right for the American people to engage in acts of nonviolent civil resistance specifically intended for the purpose of preventing or impeding ongoing criminal activity in the conduct of foreign policy on the part of this or any other government.

The First Amendment to the Constitution also provides for and protects the free exercise of religion. Based upon my involvement in a fairly large number of civil resistance cases over the past several years, I have been struck by one factor that seems to be fairly constant throughout many of them. Namely, at the heart of most civil resistance activities in America today are religious people acting with the support of their local church communities out of a sense of strong moral and religious commitment. This country's mainstream religious groups such as Catholics, Presbyterians, Methodists, Friends, and Jews, are the only organized sources of opposition to the Reagan administration's gross international lawlessness that are operating in America today.

A classic struggle between Church and State over the proper conduct of American foreign policy is now being waged without the general public having any clear indication that this is going on. The most graphic result was of course the persecution of the founders of the Sanctuary Movement, though similar prosecutions of religious people have occurred all over the country. From this author's secular perspective, the religious peoples in our country constitute the primary groups providing true moral leadership and guidance for the rest of America on foreign affairs issues. To be sure, there are many Americans who are actually doing something about the Reagan administration's gross international lawlessness. But the religious people seem to be in the vanguard, and certainly the primary ones who are fully prepared to go to jail for what they believe in. Many of them have actually done so. As my friend and colleague Ramsey Clark is reported to have said: "Our jails are filling up with saints."

Despite the publicity received by the Sanctuary case, there has basically occurred a "conspiracy of silence" by the news media with respect to its failure to report on the amount and extent of civil resistance activities in America today. Indeed, this country's so-called Fourth Estate has, for the most part, debased itself into becoming the Reagan administration's compliant lapdog. Until the outbreak of the Iran/contra affair toward the end of 1986, American news media served as uncritical transmission belts for the conveyance of whatever

6

propaganda line the Reagan administration concocted that day in order to justify its unremitting attacks on the international and domestic legal orders.

Hence, the final arbiter of the constitutionality, technical legality and overall legitimacy of such acts of nonviolent civil resistance becomes the American people themselves. In particular, under the Sixth and Fourteenth Amendments to the U.S. Constitution, those individuals who have been indicted for alleged prima facie breaches of positive law by engaging in acts of nonviolent civil resistance are generally entitled to a trial by a jury of their own peers. Thus it is the American criminal jury system that shall prove to be the last bastion of democracy and law against the Reagan administration's pernicious assault on both. I would submit that under the existing political conditions in the United States of America, our criminal jury system has now become a long-overlooked but vital independent institution within the separation of powers arrangement created by the Founding Fathers of our Constitution.

Of course, the American jury system consists of common, everyday, ordinary citizens. Most Americans consider themselves to be law-abiding and peaceful, and strongly believe that their government should be law-abiding and peaceful as well. The fate of those prosecuted for nonviolent civil resistance has thus been committed by the Constitution to the common sense of decency, justice, fair play, and peaceableness, so characteristic of the members of an American jury. It is my personal opinion that if the members of American juries are made aware of the Reagan administration's gross international lawlessness, there is no way they will convict those who engage in acts of nonviolent civil resistance for the express purpose of stopping it.

If the juries refuse to convict these protesters, then it is obvious that the latter have committed no crimes. In other words, they are completely innocent of any wrongdoing at all. In essence, the jury would have ratified sub silentio the argument that such protesters were merely engaged in the exercise of their First Amendment rights to peaceably assemble, to petition their government for a redress of grievances, or to freely exercise their religion.

It is in this fashion, then, that I believe we must distinguish acts of nonviolent "civil resistance" from acts of "civil disobedience." The former are not crimes, and the people who engage in them are not criminals—at least until they have been proven to be guilty of an offense beyond a reasonable doubt to the satisfaction of twelve men and women sitting on a jury in accordance with all the requirements of due process of law. Thus it is not true that we should expect those who have performed acts of nonviolent civil resistance to meekly accept any punishment for having committed an alleged prima facie breach of a positive law. Rather, we must actively work to obtain their acquittal because they were courageously exercising their constitutional rights specifically for the purpose of restoring to the United States of America a democratic government with a commitment to the rule of law both at home and abroad.

Over the past several years of the Reagan administration, I have been involved in giving advice, counsel, and assistance to individuals and groups who have engaged in acts of nonviolent civil resistance directed against various aspects of the Reagan administration's foreign policy. In one capacity or another, I have worked with the Nuclear Freeze Movement, the Sanctuary Movement, the Anti-Apartheid Movement, and the Pledge of Resistance Movement, among others. I have also participated in the defense of individuals who are not part of formal movements but nevertheless have resorted to nonviolent civil resistance to protest the Reagan administration's foreign policies toward nuclear weapons, Grenada, Central America, Southern Africa, and the Middle East.[5]

Throughout these six years of opposition to the Reagan administration's gross international lawlessness, we have experienced many disappointments, setbacks, and failures in the defense of those engaged in nonviolent civil resistance. Too many brave, courageous and principled people have gone to jail or otherwise been vindictively prosecuted and punished simply for opposing the ongoing commission of international and domestic crimes by the Reagan administration in its daily conduct of foreign affairs. Many of the very best and most admirable people produced by contemporary American society have been treated as if they were common criminals, and sometimes prosecuted and punished more severely than murderers, robbers, and rapists.

That is until now. Just recently, two criminal cases have produced

---

5. *See* Boyle et al., "Violations of International Law," *Middle East International*, Sept. 3, 1982, at 11, *reprinted in* Appendices *infra*.

a major breakthrough for the defense of those engaged in nonviolent civil resistance against the Reagan administration under international law: *People v. Jarka*, No. 002170 in the Circuit Court of Lake County, Waukegan, Illinois; and *Chicago v. Streeter*, No. 85-108644, in the Circuit Court of Cook County, Chicago, Illinois. In both cases, the defendants were acquitted by invoking the traditional common law defense known as "necessity," which was incorporated into the Illinois Criminal Code. According to Chapter 38, § 7-13 of the Illinois Revised Statutes (1983), conduct which would otherwise be an offense is justifiable by reason of "necessity" if the accused was without blame in occasioning or developing the situation and reasonably believed such conduct was necessary to avoid a public or private injury greater than the injury which might reasonably result from his own conduct.

In the *Jarka* case, the defendants were protesting U.S. military intervention in Central America and the Reagan administration's offensive nuclear weapons buildup before the Great Lakes Naval Training Center on November 14, 1984. The defendants were charged with the fairly serious crimes of mob action and resisting arrest despite the fact that they had merely linked arms and sat down in the middle of the road in front of the base. After a three-and-one-half-day courtroom trial in which defense attorneys produced eight expert witnesses (including this author) on nuclear weapons, Central America, and international law, the defendants were acquitted of all charges on April 15, 1985.

In *Jarka* the greater public and private injury with respect to Central America was successfully argued to be crimes against peace, crimes against humanity, war crimes, grave breaches of the Geneva Conventions, violations of the U.N. Charter, the O.A.S. Charter, and the International Court of Justice's 1984 Interim Order of Protection on behalf of Nicaragua that the Reagan administration had committed on a daily basis. But the *Jarka* case was an even more significant precedent for the defense of anti-nuclear protesters under international law. To the best of my knowledge, for the first time ever in the annals of American jurisprudence, the judge in the *Jarka* case actually instructed the jury that the threat or use of nuclear weapons violated international law. To quote the exact language of this pathbreaking instruction as read to the *Jarka* jury by Judge Alphonse F. Witt: "The use or threat of use of nuclear weapons is a war crime or an attempted

war crime because such use would violate international law by causing unnecessary suffering, failing to distinguish between combatants
and noncombatants and poisoning its targets by radiation." Judge
Witt's courageous decision to issue this instruction represented the
successful culmination of four years of vigorous efforts by the members of The Lawyers' Committee on Nuclear Policy, which had been
publicly arguing this position since its foundation in 1981.[6]

The stunning victory in *Jarka* was immediately used as a precedent
for establishing the defendants' right to the necessity defense with
respect to international law in the *Streeter* trial, which was held
approximately one month later in Chicago. There was close cooperation between the respective teams of defense attorneys in *Jarka*
and *Streeter*, and this author served as a consultant to both groups
of attorneys on questions of international law.[7] In the *Streeter* case,
the defendants attempted to meet with the South African Consul at
his office in Chicago to discuss that country's policy of apartheid.
When he refused to do so, the defendants refused to leave the cor-
ridors of a building outside the consulate offices, and were eventually
arrested and prosecuted for violating a provision of the City of Chicago Municipal Code prohibiting "unlawful trespass." To substan-
tiate their defense of necessity, the defense attorney team presented
at trial several expert witnesses who testified to the effect that the
government of South Africa has been committing international crimes
by its policies of apartheid and that the defendants acted reasonably
in their efforts to prevent the continuation of these crimes. Once
again, in this case too, the jury acquitted the defendants of all charges
brought against them.

As a direct result of the *Jarka* and *Streeter* acquittals, numerous
attempts have since been made around the entire country by defense
attorneys seeking to invoke these cases as precedents for the defense
of other individuals who have engaged in acts of nonviolent civil
resistance protesting against the Reagan administration's illegal policies toward Nicaragua, El Salvador, South Africa, and nuclear weap-

---

6. *See* The Lawyers' Committee on Nuclear Policy, *Statement on the Illegality of Nuclear Weapons, reprinted in* Appendices *infra.*

7. *See* Neely, "Legal Necessity and Civil Disobedience: Preventing the Greater Harms of War and Apartheid," 12 *Ill. Bar J.* 596 (1986); Aldridge and Stark, "Nuclear War, Citizen Intervention, and the Necessity Defense," 26 *Santa Clara L. Rev.* 299 (1986). *See also* Campbell, "The Nuremberg Defense to Charges of Domestic Crime: A Non-Traditional Approach for Nuclear-Arms Protestors," 16 *Cal. West. Int'l L.J.* 93 (1986).

ons, inter alia. There have now occurred several such nonviolent civil resistance cases in which criminal charges have been dismissed, or the defendants acquitted, because of *Jarka*-type defenses founded upon principles of international law. The attorneys in all these cases have used mimeographed materials developed by this author for the successful defense of their civil resistance protester clients. This book collects these materials into one volume for the purpose of explaining to other attorneys how they can defend civil resistance protesters using principles of international law. The book is also designed to inform such protesters and their supporters why such civil resistance is fully consonant with basic principles of international law, U.S. domestic law, and our Constitution.

It is crucial for preserving the future of our democratic system of government with its historical commitment to the rule of law both at home and abroad that we conscientiously and systematically pursue analogous trial strategies for the defense of such protesters under international law that will eventually result in a series of dismissed charges, acquittals or at least hung juries in these cases. If properly publicized, each dismissed charge, acquittal or hung jury will encourage other private citizens to engage in similar nonviolent civil resistance activities. In the case of an acquittal, a jury of their peers would have already determined that the protesters' actions were definitely not criminal behavior but rather perfectly lawful conduct under both international and U.S. domestic law. In the case of a dismissal or hung jury, the presumption of innocence with respect to such activities would still remain undisturbed.

An extended series of acquittals, or hung juries, or dismissed charges in such nonviolent civil resistance cases will send a strong message to the power elite of this country that the ordinary people of America who comprise juries will no longer tolerate their government's pursuit of patently illegal foreign policies that constitute ongoing criminal activity under well-recognized principles of international and domestic law. Indeed, this author has now been informed by more than one attorney that due to the success of *Jarka*-type defenses in their jurisdictions, there is no way a prosecutor can obtain a conviction for an act of nonviolent civil resistance protesting the Reagan administration's foreign policies on nuclear weapons, Central America or South Africa. In these jurisdictions, state and local government authorities are now in a quandary as to how they should proceed, while the civil resistance protesters carry on with their activities.

For example, in one student divestment protest case I worked on concerning a university located near a major metropolitan area, the trial judge granted our motion in limine to allow a necessity defense with respect to international law. Shortly thereafter the city's prosecutor announced that he was dropping criminal charges against the defendants on the following grounds: Because of the judge's ruling, the city would be placed in a position of having to defend the university's refusal to divest itself of stock in corporations doing business in South Africa. But in light of the terrible events that were then occurring in that country as a result of its government's imposition of a state of emergency, the city did not want to be in the position of having to defend the university's refusal to divest. I predict that ultimately this university will have to divest because it has now been shorn of the coercive powers of the state to repress internal dissent and protest by its students and faculty because of our successful invocation of international law on behalf of the latter.

* * * *

This author once received an unsolicited telephone call from a woman who, in an unnecessarily self-deprecating tone of voice, identified herself as an ordinary middle-class, middle-aged housewife living in a typical suburb near Denver, Colorado, wanting to discuss the following matter: She and a group of similarly-situated friends had an appointment in a few days with the director of the Rocky Flats nuclear arsenal, and at that time they planned to place him under citizen's arrest in his own office for the commission of crimes against international law! Unless and until the ordinary people of America rise up to challenge the elemental lawlessness of the Reagan administration, the future of the human race will be determined by those Machiavellians who occupy positions of power and influence in America's government, its sycophantic think-tanks, and its prostituted universities. We must mobilize the common people to save humanity from these so-called experts. Only then can we expect to see some fundamental changes in the nature of the predicament created by the Reagan administration's gross international lawlessness that confronts America and the world today.

Chapter 2.

Rules for Defending Nonviolent Civil Resistance Under International Law

Because of the aforementioned experiences, The Lawyers' Committee on Nuclear Policy has asked me to sit down and draw up a short manual for criminal defense attorneys who seek to defend those engaged in acts of nonviolent civil resistance by utilizing considerations of international law. Since The Lawyers' Committee on Nuclear Policy is primarily concerned with the illegality of nuclear weapons, my remarks in this chapter will be oftentimes directed toward the defense of anti-nuclear protesters under international law. However, the rules that I will be discussing below and the general thrust of my analysis are equally applicable to the defense under international law of those who have engaged in nonviolent civil resistance activities directed against U.S. military intervention in Central America, U.S. support for the apartheid regime in South Africa, U.S. foreign policy in the Middle East, Jewish rabbis protesting Soviet human rights violations,[1] etc. The principles set forth here can be used anytime individuals are subjected to governmental prosecution for protesting matters related to questions concerning international relations. If you are presented with such a problem that has not been covered here, please feel free to contact me and I am sure we can work out a suitable strategy for the defense of your clients so long as I personally support their cause.

1. *See* Anderson & Verr, *Draft Motion on Behalf of Washington Rabbis, reprinted in* Appendices *infra.*

In this book I do not have the space to develop a scholarly analysis of the substantive legal issues relating to any one of the above areas except to the extent necessary to facilitate the development of the procedural suggestions presented below. But a succinct statement of the substantive legal merits concerning many of these matters can be found in Part Three of my book *World Politics and International Law*, published by Duke University Press in 1985. In addition, those of you defending anti-nuclear protesters will, at a minimum, want to read the next chapter of this book entitled *The Relevance of International Law to the Paradox of Nuclear Deterrence*, since it has provided the intellectual foundation for such a defense.

At the outset, let me state that I am not a litigator, and I suspect that trial lawyers deem it presumptuous for anyone who is a non-litigator to give them advice on how they should conduct their trials. But just because I am not a litigator does not mean that I am thoroughly devoid of knowledge relevant to the actual practice of law. For the past eight years, I have taught substantive criminal law at the University of Illinois College of Law in Champaign. For this reason, I think I have a somewhat better comprehension of how principles of international law should be related to the defense of those engaged in nonviolent civil resistance activities than some of my more erudite international law professor colleagues who do not have such specialized training and expertise. So please bear with me when you discover that the rules and principles I am about to discuss below are obviously being written by someone who has never conducted a trial himself.

Take the international law arguments seriously

Most regretfully, in my extensive dealings with criminal defense attorneys on civil resistance cases, I have sometimes received the distinct impression that many of them do not take the international law arguments very seriously. Invariably it is the case that the international law arguments are at the very bottom of the list of grounds upon which they intend to defend their clients. In order of priority, attorneys usually strongly prefer any type of argument based on the United States Constitution (e.g., the First Amendment, the Fourth Amendment, the Fifth Amendment, the Fourteenth Amendment, etc.); then traditional substantive and procedural criminal law defenses; and finally, principles of international law. It is quite understandable why they should seek to defend their clients on the strongest grounds possible. And of course this means that if a defense is available under well-recognized principles of constitutional law or criminal law, then it should be made.

Yet in their search for such defenses, trial attorneys oftentimes ignore or short-change the international law defenses. Generally they seem to treat the latter as if they were throw-away arguments that would be nice if they could be successful, but are not really critical or even central to their "real" defense precisely because in their opinion they probably will not be successful. Such a subliminal attitude usually produces a self-fulfilling prophecy.

I believe this unwarranted assumption constitutes a grievous tactical error. If properly prepared and presented, an international law defense can be just as effective as a constitutional attack upon a criminal charge against those involved in nonviolent civil resistance activities. In many cases, principles of international law will be the only defense available to such protesters.

As stated above, it is my personal opinion that if the international law arguments against the validity of the Reagan administration's foreign policies around the world are presented to a jury consisting of twelve ordinary men and women who consider themselves to be peaceful and law-abiding, there is absolutely no way the government would be able to convict such defendants. Either the jury would acquit them outright, or else you stand a good chance of getting a hung jury, or better yet, charges dismissed before or during trial. The real task, then, is to reorient your thought as a litigator toward the effectiveness of the international law arguments. Conversely, if you do not take the international law arguments seriously, then it will be difficult if not impossible to convince the judge that he should take the international law arguments seriously enough to allow you to present them to the jury.

Contact your international law expert right away

The second point that must be kept in the forefront of your mind is that when your client comes in and states that he or she has engaged in nonviolent civil resistance activities directed against some aspect of the Reagan administration's foreign policy, you should contact an international law expert immediately. It never ceases to amaze me the number of phone calls I receive from criminal defense attorneys one or two days before the trial date asking me for advice on international law as it relates to the defense of their clients, or to appear as an expert witness at trial, or both. Of course, I know that litigators work by the seat of their pants and oftentimes do not have the opportunity to worry about such matters until the very eve of trial when the prospect is imminent. On the other hand, I submit that the tardy approach by litigators to international law experts is simply part of the problem that they do not really take the international law arguments very seriously. There is little if anything an international law expert can do for you 24 to 48 hours before trial, though I have done my best under such difficult circumstances in many cases.

The effectiveness of your international law arguments will increase directly in proportion to the earliest stage at which your expert is brought into the case. Consultation with an international law professor immediately after agreeing to represent such clients will be invaluable in terms of developing a proper theory or theories of defense, preparing any motions or briefs that must be submitted to the court before trial, determining and obtaining other necessary expert witnesses, convincing the judge to consider the international law arguments seriously, and laying the proper foundation necessary for their introduction into evidence before the jury at trial. By contrast, it has been my general experience that if the international law expert is brought into the case on the very eve of trial, the odds in favor of successfully mounting an international law defense for your clients are negligible. Such lackadaisical behavior is oftentimes characteristic of trial attorneys who do not take the international law arguments seriously in the first place.

This is not a civil disobedience case

Whenever a defense attorney contacts me to serve as his consultant on international law, one of the most important preliminary conceptual tasks I have is to convince him that this is not a civil disobedience case, but rather a civil resistance case. Many attorneys automatically adopt a defeatist attitude toward such civil resistance cases because they unconsciously assume that these are similar to the civil disobedience cases that arose out of the Civil Rights Movement in the United States of America during the 1950s and 1960s. But by doing this, they subliminally endorse the status quo oriented teaching that civil disobedience defendants should be prepared to accept their guilt and punishment as some indication of their moral purity.

Individuals who engage in nonviolent civil resistance activities to protest various aspects of American foreign policy are not engaged in civil disobedience activities as classically defined. In such civil resistance cases, what we have are individuals attempting to prevent the ongoing commission of international crimes under well-recognized principles of international and U.S. domestic law. This is a phenomenon very different from the classic civil disobedience case where individuals were purposely violating a domestic law for the purpose of changing it.

The distinction between civil resistance and civil disobedience must be made crystal clear to your clients, to the news media, to the judge, and ultimately to the jury. Indeed, one of the most difficult tasks you will have is getting them all to comprehend and understand the fundamental importance of maintaining this distinction. Therefore, you must never refer to your case as one of civil disobedience since such a characterization assumes the guilt of your clients.

Your clients are presumed to be innocent until proven guilty beyond a reasonable doubt to the satisfaction of a jury in accordance with the substantive and procedural requirements of due process of law. People who engage in nonviolent civil resistance have a constitutional right to rely upon whatever statutory and common law defenses are generally made available to every other criminal defendant in the jurisdiction concerned. They are also entitled to receive the most vigorous defense you can mount on their behalf. After all, alleged murderers, robbers and rapists are entitled to the presumption of innocence, a vigorous defense, and all the protections of due process of law. Your standards and expectations should be no less for those who have engaged in nonviolent civil resistance activities designed to prevent the ongoing commission of international and domestic crimes by members of the Reagan administration.

Preserve your right to a jury trial

On a procedural basis, one of the most important things to remember from the very outset of the case is the need to preserve your
right to a jury trial. Of course this assumes that you have a constitutional right to a trial by jury under either the federal or state constitution within the jurisdiction where you are defending. I should
point out that the federal government has been quite smart in this
matter by generally charging those engaged in nonviolent civil resistance activities directed against various aspects of the Reagan
administration's foreign policy with minor infractions the penalty for
which is less than six months in jail. This tactic usually precludes a
jury trial and leaves your clients with only a bench trial before a
federal judge or magistrate. It has been my experience that the members of a jury will be far more sensitive and receptive to the international law arguments than a judge or magistrate.

If the government has been foolish enough to indict your clients
for a crime that will give them a right to a jury trial, you should be
very cautious about engaging in any type of preliminary procedural
maneuvering which might defeat that right. Once again, the litigator
will prefer a good constitutional argument in order to strike one or
more of the charges against his clients before trial. But if successful,
this tactic might result in the removal from the case of the one charge
that gives your clients a right to a jury trial.

For example, in one anti-nuclear case I worked on the defendants
had prayed on a federal reservation despite a bar-order prohibiting
their re-entry, and were charged with a variety of crimes under the
Federal Criminal Code and the Federal Assimilative Crimes Act. Their
attorney filed a motion to dismiss the most serious charge against
them because the bar-order was "void for vagueness" and thus prosecution on those grounds would have been a violation of due process
of law—a good constitutional argument. Although agreeing with his
analysis on that substantive point, I observed that if he was successful
on this motion, he might lose his right to a jury trial because this was
the only serious offense among the group for which his clients were
indicted. Realistically, he did not believe he had any chance to
convince this federal judge to acquit his clients on the grounds of
international law during a bench trial.

I suggested that he withdraw his motion and then explain to the judge and the United States Attorney that he intended to make international law arguments with respect to all charges in the indictment—which he did. Less than one week later, the government dropped all charges against these defendants. Of course, we were never told the exact reason why the charges were dropped. But I have always had a suspicion that the government did not want this case to go to trial before a jury under the particular circumstances involved.

If you do not have a right to a jury trial, unless your federal judge is extraordinarily open-minded, I would suggest that you consider whether your clients should negotiate a plea-bargain rather than go through with a bench trial whose outcome is almost predetermined. You could explain to them that this is a purposeful strategy adopted by the Reagan administration, so there is no good reason why they should foolishly play into the government's hands. It might be far more helpful for the advancement of the cause they believe in to accept a plea-bargain rather than to run a substantial risk of obtaining the maximum penalty at the hands of a federal judge or magistrate.

Typically, many such protestors fully intend to engage in nonviolent civil resistance activities again if the particular foreign policy abuses continue. You could explain to them that negotiation of a plea-bargain in this non-jury prosecution would preserve their options for the future as best as possible under the circumstances. The government very well might decide to indict them for renewed activities in a manner that would provide a constitutional right to a jury trial. At that point, then, it would be worthwhile for them to go through the time, effort, expense, and emotional drain of a full-fledged courtroom proceeding.

Stay out of federal court if at all possible

The same type of considerations should be taken into account with respect to a bench trial before a state or municipal court judge. However, on this local level of prosecution it is oftentimes the case that the defendants are entitled to a trial by jury no matter how insignificant the charge under the state constitution. It has been my experience that state and municipal court judges are far more receptive to the international law arguments than their federal counterparts.

The attitude of the former group seems to be that the defendants are entitled to their day in court and therefore to put on whatever type of evidence they want so long as it fits within a liberal interpretation of the state's rules of evidence and does not exceedingly prolong the proceedings. By contrast, federal judges are prone to constrictly construe the Federal Rules of Evidence and the definition of "relevance" to exclude evidence of international law violations by the Reagan administration that could exercise a decisive impact upon the jury's determination of the guilt or innocence of the defendants. This is precisely what happened during the federal government's persecution of the founders of the Sanctuary Movement in Tucson, Arizona.

This observation has special significance for attorneys who are consulted by individuals or groups who are planning to commit nonviolent civil resistance activities. Of course as an officer of the court you are under an obligation to tell such individuals that they must obey the law. That being said, you should certainly explain to them the significant differences between a state and a federal prosecution, especially when it comes to the right to a jury trial. If at all possible, the prospective protesters should design their civil resistance activities so that they will not be in violation of federal law: e.g., instead of entering a federal military reservation, they should sit down upon the state road leading into it. That way, if they are arrested, prosecuted and tried, it will be done by state or local prosecutors and judges who are more sensitive to the concerns of their constituents that justice not only be done, but also that justice appear to have been done.

Remember that a U.S. Attorney and a federal judge are beholden to the Office of the President of the United States of America, who nominated them for these positions. They also receive their usually exclusive means of economic support from the United States Treasury. As one state court judge is reported to have commented: "I don't get my paycheck from the federal government."

It is also a well-established fact that the Reagan administration has purposefully sought to pack the ranks of the federal judiciary at all levels with ideological soulmates. Perhaps these factors can account in part for the reason why many federal judges have bent over backwards to be deferential to the position of the executive branch of the federal government in these civil resistance protest cases, whereas their counterparts in the state and local judiciary oftentimes do not.

Although the federal judiciary has reason to be proud of its constitutional independence in the domestic legal sphere, when it comes
to criminal or even civil cases involving foreign affairs, defense policies, national security, international terrorism, counter-intelligence,
etc., many federal judges seem to become just as subservient as
everyone else in this country to the wishes of an imperial president.
Under the guise of one legal artifice or another, they usually find
grounds not to interfere with whatever the executive branch of the
federal government has decided to do in foreign affairs no matter
how illegal, immoral, unconstitutional, criminal, or reprehensible.

This is not a show-trial

So long as you have a jury trial, there is always a good chance of
winning the case. On the other hand, even if it is a bench trial where
you might not have a snowball's-chance-in-hell of winning, there
might be extremely good reasons for rejecting a plea-bargain (if one
is offered) and going ahead with the trial anyway. Here the first and
foremost consideration would be the publicity value of such a trial
in the community where the civil resistance activities occurred.
Greater public awareness of the issues produced by courtroom generated publicity could create a significantly changed environment in
the local community that is more conducive to obtaining your clients'
overall objectives. Even a particularly harsh and vindictive prosecution of your clients could redound to the advantage of their cause
by engendering public sympathy for them. Once again, this is precisely what happened during the federal government's persecution
of the founders of the Sanctuary Movement in Tucson.

Assuming you adopt this strategy and go forward with the trial,
such a decision does not mean that you should approach this civil
resistance case with the attitude that you are going to put on a "show-
trial." As a matter of principle, I refuse to participate as an expert
witness in courtroom proceedings that the attorney himself describes
to me as being a "show-trial." An attorney who has already resigned
himself to losing the case does not need my help to do so.

By contrast, I have been more than happy to work on a case with
a non-existent probability of victory so long as the defendants and
their attorneys have thought through a coherent strategy of what they

intend to accomplish by going through with the case instead of plea-bargaining, and do whatever is necessary to win the case if at all possible. Your overall objective must always be to win the case by using principles of international law at trial to the best of your ability no matter how difficult the circumstances or how insignificant the charge. Occasionally, we have been pleasantly surprised by winning such cases for one reason or another.

Tell your clients why they must be represented in court by a lawyer

Oftentimes it is the case that those who engage in nonviolent civil resistance activities directed against various aspects of American foreign policy will state a preference to represent themselves during the trial, even though they would like to receive a lawyer's assistance on procedural matters and his advice on trial strategy beforehand. It is your obligation to dissuade them from this course of action in the strongest terms possible. The defense of civil resistance protesters under international law requires a skilled trial attorney working from the very outset of the case with an expert on international law to lay the proper foundation for getting the international legal considerations submitted into evidence before the jury.

Civil resistance protesters should be told that if they wish to successfully raise considerations of international law during the trial, they must allow themselves to be represented by an attorney during the proceedings. It will be difficult enough for that attorney to convince the judge to allow the international law considerations to be brought to the attention of the jury in the first place. And, given the technical rules of evidence, it would be almost impossible for a non-lawyer to lay the proper evidentiary foundation for their admissibility.

Consequently, civil resistance protesters must be educated to set aside what might be their personal preferences to represent themselves at trial. Instead, they must subordinate their personal wishes to the higher good by allowing their defense to be conducted by a trial attorney with the assistance of an international law expert. They will not perform any positive service for the goals they believe in by getting convicted because of their innate legal incompetence. But they could accomplish a great deal of good for their cause by allowing a trial attorney to attempt to obtain an acquittal, hung jury, or dismissed charges on their behalf. A conviction would only discourage other peaceable and law-abiding Americans from following their example, whereas an acquittal, hung jury, or dismissed charges will establish a precedent for others to emulate.

This is not to deny that I am prepared to work on a case where the protester plans to represent himself at trial. I have in the past and will continue to do so in the future, especially when I am convinced that the individual is dedicated to this course of action as a matter of moral principle. Some of the most admirable people I have ever met have insisted upon representing themselves at trial. My only regret is that they would not allow their attorneys and me to do all we possibly could to obtain their acquittal. It is a monumental tragedy for all of us in the United States of America when such courageous people are sent to jail.

Don't just argue an international law defense per se

In my dealings with criminal defense attorneys, it never ceases to perplex me that when I ask them on what grounds they intend to defend their clients, they go through a laundry list of one or two constitutional law arguments, then two or three traditional criminal law defenses, and then tack on at the end what they call a "general defense under international law." Such a recitation simply indicates to me that they really have not thought through the problem of mounting a defense under principles of international law for those involved in nonviolent civil resistance activities directed against specific components of American foreign policy. As a professor of criminal law for many years, I can state my personal opinion that it would be a tactical mistake only to argue for the existence of a separate and independent defense under international law. Indeed, sometimes you will only confuse the judge if you simply try to argue that there is something known as a "general international law defense" or a "Nuremberg Defense" that is different and apart from the traditional common law and statutory defenses recognized in your jurisdiction.

To be sure, you should certainly argue that there does indeed exist such a thing as an "international law defense" that has been incorporated into the common law or criminal statutes of the jurisdiction in which you are defending. Nevertheless, such a general defense should be supplemented by relating principles of international law to those traditional common law and statutory defenses already available within that particular jurisdiction against ordinary crimes. These substantive criminal law defenses typically include but are not limited to the defense of self, defense of others, defense of property, duress, compulsion, necessity, choice of evils, prevention of a crime, prevention of a public catastrophe, mistake of fact or law, measures otherwise authorized by law, reliance upon governmental authorization, etc.

Criminal defense attorneys should draw up an exhaustive list of all such statutory and common law defenses recognized in their jurisdiction, together with a brief analysis of the elements of the defenses as defined. If so, you will be surprised to discover the number and types of obscure, exotic, and generally helpful defenses you might be able to use to mount a defense for your clients under principles of international law. For example, in Illinois we found a late nineteenth century case recognizing a common law right to prevent the commission of a crime. As explained below, we then related it to the defense of our anti-nuclear clients using principles of international law.

When you have completed this comprehensive list of both statutory and common law defenses recognized in your jurisdiction, submit it to the international law expert for his evaluation. He should be able to tell you how principles of international law can be related to which if any of these defenses in an effective way. For example, with respect to defending those who have engaged in acts of non-violent civil resistance directed against U.S. nuclear weapons policies, principles of international law would be relevant to establishing the defenses of compulsion, necessity, choice of evils, prevention of a crime, prevention of a public catastrophe, measures otherwise authorized by law, and defense of self and others. Similarly, with respect to defending those who are protesting to stop attacks by the U.S.-supported bands of contra mercenaries against innocent civilians and private property in Nicaragua, principles of international law would be relevant to establishing the defenses of defense of others, defense of property, prevention of crime, etc.

No point would be served here by producing an extended analysis of how international legal considerations actually should be related to these traditional criminal law defenses, since the precise elements of each defense would depend upon the relevant state or federal law under which your clients are prosecuted. Trial attorneys representing civil resistance protesters are simply advised to submit this detailed and comprehensive analysis of available statutory and common law defenses to their international law expert for his advice on how this should be done. Without the careful establishment of this interconnection long before trial, the odds are fairly good that the judge will never allow the international legal principles to be brought to the attention of the jury since the proper legal and evidentiary foundation will not have been laid for their admission and consideration. As judges often say when they deny defense counsels' requests to allow international law experts to testify in such prosecutions: "International law has nothing at all to do with this case!"

Pay attention to the formal rules of evidence in your jurisdiction

Your basic objective will be to develop a theory or theories of defense that will convince the judge to allow you to introduce international law evidence at trial before the jury, including your expert's testimony. This can be most effectively accomplished by relating your international law evidence to one or more elements of the defense or multiple defenses that you have selected. For example, in the previous Illinois case invoking a common law right to prevent the commission of crime, we argued that the international law evidence should be admitted on the grounds that it was relevant to establishing what crime or crimes our clients were trying to prevent when they performed their nonviolent civil resistance activities.

Depending upon the jurisdiction involved, each common law or statutory defense could have three or four elements, and evidence of international law violations should be related to each element of all defenses made to whatever extent possible in order to get the evidence admitted under some theory. In this regard, you should pay special attention to the evidentiary rules for the allocation of the burden of proof with respect to affirmative defenses prevalent in your jurisdiction. For example, Illinois Criminal Code Chapter 38, § 3-2 provides that so long as the defense (or the state) presents "some evidence" with respect to the existence of an affirmative defense (other than insanity), then the state must sustain the burden of proving the defendant guilty beyond a reasonable doubt as to that issue together with all the other elements of the offense charged.

In a jurisdiction following this Illinois evidentiary rule—which is fairly common—you can argue to the judge that your proffered evidence as to the requirements of international law constitutes "some evidence" with respect to an element or elements of whatever affirmative defense or defenses you are relying upon. Hence, according to the statute itself, the judge must allow your introduction of "some evidence" of the international law violations to be submitted at trial for consideration by the jury. Otherwise, to refuse your request would impermissibly shift the burden of proof on the affirmative defense off the state and onto the defendant, thus committing an unconstitutional violation of due process of law under the Fifth and Fourteenth Amendments to the U.S. Constitution and analogous provisions of the concerned state constitution.

Be sure to distinguish elements of an affirmative defense from elements of the offense charged

As a general rule, many of the aforementioned traditional criminal law defenses are what professors of criminal law call "affirmative defenses." According to the holding of the United States Supreme Court in *Patterson v. New York*, 432 U.S. 197 (1977), it would be constitutionally permissible for a state to put the burden of proof upon the defendant to establish by a fair preponderance of the evidence that he is entitled to claim the benefit of such affirmative defenses. To be sure, however, not all jurisdictions do so. Some jurisdictions follow the Illinois practice that if the issue involved in an affirmative defense (other than insanity) is raised by "some evidence," then the state must sustain the burden of proving the defendant guilty beyond a reasonable doubt as to that issue "together with all the other elements of the offense" charged.

Notice that the Illinois evidentiary statute also requires that the state prove all elements of the "offense" beyond a reasonable doubt. According to the holding of the United States Supreme Court in *Mullaney v. Wilbur*, 421 U.S. 684 (1975), the state has the burden of proof with respect to establishing the existence of all elements of the crime beyond a reasonable doubt. This basic requirement of due process of law is in addition to the statutory requirement that the state must disprove the affirmative defense beyond a reasonable doubt so long as "some evidence" related to it has been presented at trial. Hence special care must be taken to distinguish elements of an affirmative defense from elements of the offense charged.

International law evidence should be offered not only for the purpose of establishing an affirmative defense, but also for the purpose of creating a "reasonable doubt" as to whether the state has proved all elements of the offense charged. Here a simple example would be a request to introduce international law evidence with respect to establishing the defendant's state of mind at the time he committed the civil resistance activity (i.e., general mens rea). For the judge to deny the admission of international law evidence relevant to an element of the offense charged would constitute a violation of due process of law, since it would impermissibly shift the burden of proof on this matter off the state and onto the defendant.

Distinguish the specific intent crimes from the general intent crimes

Many civil resistance protesters have been charged with crimes that criminal law professors denominate "specific intent crimes." That is, in addition to the general mens rea requirement that the defendant acted intentionally, these criminal statutes oftentimes require an additional mental element: for example, that the defendant also acted knowingly, willfully, maliciously, or for an unlawful purpose. A trial attorney would be well advised to establish whether or not any of the crimes for which his civil resistance clients have been charged are specific intent crimes, and if the matter has not yet been authoritatively decided, to determine that issue before trial. These specific intent crimes should be distinguished quite clearly and consistently from the other offenses charged against your clients during all phases of the prosecution, as well as from the affirmative defenses that you have chosen to rely upon.

As stated above, *Mullaney v. Wilbur* mandates that the state must prove all elements of a crime beyond a reasonable doubt. In the case of trespass for an unlawful purpose, the state must prove beyond a reasonable doubt not only that the defendant intentionally trespassed, but also that he did so for an unlawful purpose.

Defense counsel should argue that although his civil resistance client might have intentionally trespassed, nevertheless he did not do so for an unlawful purpose. Instead his client believed he was acting for the purpose of upholding the requirements of both international law and U.S. domestic law which specifically incorporates international law. This argument would then provide the basis upon which the testimony of an expert witness on international law could be introduced into evidence for consideration by the jury.

The expert's testimony as to the complete illegality of nuclear deterrence under international law would be relevant to the question of the defendant's specific intent—in this case, establishing the lawfulness of the purpose for which he intentionally trespassed. All that would be required is for the anti-nuclear protester to testify that he generally believed something known as international law, or the Nuremberg Principles, or the Genocide Convention, or the Geneva Conventions, or the Hague Regulations, or the U.N. Charter, etc. prohibited the threat or use of nuclear weapons and therefore that he was acting in order to uphold the standards of international law. The testimony of the expert witness should then be admitted for the purpose of corroborating the reasonability of the defendant's belief as to the requirements of international law. If not, the trial attorney should make an offer of proof to this effect so that the issue would be preserved for appeal.

This litigation strategy would be analogous to criminal trials in which psychiatrists have been permitted to testify as to the defendant's mental condition in so-called "diminished capacity" cases. As a criminal defense, diminished capacity was historically derived from the common law defense of voluntary intoxication,[2] which, although

---

2. *United States v. Brawner,* 471 F.2d 969 (D.C. Cir. 1972), explains the link between voluntary intoxication and diminished capacity as follows:

> Neither logic nor justice can tolerate a jurisprudence that defines the elements of an offense as requiring a mental state such that one defendant can properly argue that his voluntary drunkenness removed his capacity to form the specific intent but another defendant is inhibited from a submission of his contention that an abnormal mental condition, for which he was in no way responsible, negated his capacity to form a specific intent, even though the condition did not exonerate him from all criminal responsibility.

Id. at 999.

not traditionally recognized as a defense to general mens rea crimes, was nevertheless permitted as a defense to negate the specific intent element in a specific intent crime.[3] For example, in the case of common law larceny a voluntarily intoxicated defendant was nevertheless permitted to argue to the jury that he was so intoxicated that he could not have formulated an intention to permanently deprive the owner of the property at the time of the theft, which is the specific intent element of that crime.[4]

This rationale was subsequently extended to permit criminal defendants to argue that although their mental incapacity, disease or defect was not substantial enough to fulfill the requirements for the legal definition of insanity recognized in their jurisdiction and thus to negate general mens rea, nevertheless expert psychiatric testimony about their mental condition could be admitted and considered by the jury with respect to the issue of whether or not it negated the existence of a specific intent element necessary to constitute the crime.[5] For example, although a defense of diminished capacity would not generally be permitted to negate malice aforethought and thereby reduce second degree murder to voluntary manslaughter, it would be allowed to negate "premeditation and deliberation" and thus operate to reduce a first degree murder charge to second degree murder.[6] Expert psychiatric testimony would be admissible on the question of whether or not the defendant possessed the necessary mental capacity to premeditate and deliberate, and the burden of proof would be upon the state to establish beyond a reasonable doubt that the defendant had actually premeditated and deliberated before he committed the murder.

Criminal trespass is usually a specific intent offense

Most civil resistance protesters are invariably prosecuted for some type of criminal trespass offense, among other charges. A criminal of a specific intent crime, this requirement would include the need to prove beyond a reasonable doubt not only general mens rea but also the specific intent element necessary to constitute the crime. For example, in the prosecution of an anti-nuclear protester for the crime

3. *See, e.g., United States v. Nix*, 501 F.2d 516 (7th Cir. 1974).
4. *See, e.g., Edwards v. United States*, 172 F.2d 884 (D.C. Cir. 1949).
5. *See, e.g., People v. Wells*, 33 Cal.2d 330, 202 P.2d 53, *cert. denied*, 338 U.S. 836 (1949).
6. *See, e.g., People v. Wolff*, 61 Cal.2d 795, 40 Cal. Rptr. 271, 394 P.2d 959 (1964).

trespass charge usually provides you with a good wedge to get your international law arguments admitted into evidence at trial before the jury. At common law, intentional trespass was not a crime, but only a tort that was compensable by the payment of monetary damages to the plaintiff. Hence criminal trespass statutes typically require the presence of an additional mental element beyond mere intentionality, which will constitute the specific intent element of the trespass offense charged: e.g., "for an unlawful purpose," or "without lawful authority," or "for no legitimate reason," etc. Thus most criminal trespass statutes are either specific intent offenses on their face alone, or else must be construed to create specific intent offenses unless their respective legislative histories expressly indicate to the contrary.

After explaining these matters to the judge, you must argue that it was not at all criminal for your defendant to have intentionally trespassed—only tortious. Therefore, the state must prove beyond a reasonable doubt not only that he intentionally trespassed (i.e., general mens rea), but also that he intentionally trespassed "for an unlawful purpose," or "without lawful authority," or "for no legitimate reason," etc. (the specific intent). And even though the judge might decide that your international law evidence is not relevant to the question of whether the defendant trespassed intentionally, such evidence is certainly relevant to the question of whether your defendant intentionally trespassed "for an unlawful purpose," or "without lawful authority," or "for no legitimate reason," etc. For this reason, your international law evidence must be admitted because it is relevant to negating the specific intent element of the criminal trespass offense charged. To refuse to admit such evidence under these circumstances would constitute a violation of due process of law since this would shift the burden of proof on the specific intent element of the criminal trespass charge off the state beyond a reasonable doubt and onto the defendant.

If the judge allows the international legal considerations to go to the jury with respect to the question of whether or not the civil resistance protester actually possessed the specific intent element necessary to constitute the offense charged (whether criminal trespass or some other specific intent crime), defense counsel can then always argue that the government has not established beyond a reasonable doubt that the defendant acted with the specific intent required because of his reasonable belief—as corroborated by the international law expert—that both international law and U.S. domestic law prohibited the commission of crimes against peace, crimes against humanity, war crimes, genocide, grave breaches of the Geneva Conventions, as well as the inchoate crimes incidental thereto such as planning, preparation, conspiracy, attempt, aiding and abetting, complicity, etc. Depending on the quality of the defense counsel and the expert witness, the civil resistance protester might stand a good chance of obtaining an acquittal or at least a hung jury because the former have created a "reasonable doubt" on this issue.

For example, in oral summation at the end of trial you should certainly point out to the jury that in light of the expert testimony on international law by "the learned professor," it is clear that the state has not proved all the elements of the offense (e.g., intentional trespass *for an unlawful purpose*) for which your clients have been charged "beyond a reasonable doubt." Or, if you are dealing with an affirmative defense the burden for which is upon the state to disprove (e.g., necessity), you should certainly argue there must exist at least a "reasonable doubt" that your clients are entitled to the benefit of that affirmative defense, and therefore they must be acquitted. In any event, it would be a heedless and callous jury that would not have some serious doubts and scruples in its collective mind as to your clients' guilt when it is confronted with expert witness testimony along the lines of that found in the sample direct examinations on nuclear weapons, Central America, and South Africa that are presented in Chapters 4, 5, and 6, respectively.

International law is a part of U.S. domestic law

In order to better relate international law to your theory or theories of defense, the trial attorney should point out to the judge and later to the jury that U.S. domestic law has expressly incorporated international law by means of article 6 of the U.S. Constitution (i.e., the so-called Supremacy Clause) with respect to treaties, as well as by the famous decision of the United States Supreme Court in *Paquete Habana*, 175 U.S. 677 (1900), with respect to customary international law. Furthermore, in *United States v. Belmont*, 301 U.S. 324 (1937) and *United States v. Pink*, 315 U.S. 203 (1942), the Supreme Court held that other types of international agreements concluded by the United States government which have not received the formal advice and consent of the Senate are nevertheless entitled to the protection of the Supremacy Clause. Defense counsel should argue that international treaties and agreements must be accorded the benefit of the Supremacy Clause with respect to state criminal law statutes, and of the rule "last in time prevails" with respect to federal criminal statutes,[7] if applicable.

Likewise, counsel can also argue that since customary international law is a part of both federal and state common law, federal or state criminal statutes must be construed in a manner that would be consistent with the requirements of international law. Therefore the testimony of an expert witness on this subject should be admitted into evidence at trial for consideration by the jury for this purpose. A similar argument could be made with respect to relevant international treaties or agreements to the effect that the jury should be permitted to consider expert testimony on their contents in order to interpret federal or state criminal statutes in a manner that would be consistent with these U.S. obligations under international law.

The point of this exercise is to get the judge and later the jury to understand that international law is not simply some amorphous collection of rules adopted by some nebulous foreign entity, but rather is a living body of law that has been fully subscribed to by the United States government and, even more importantly, expressly incorporated into United States domestic law. Moreover, it should be argued that the president of the United States has taken an oath required by article 2, section 1, clause 7 of the U.S. Constitution to "preserve, protect and defend the constitution of the United States," which expressly includes international treaties and agreements by virtue of article 6. Similarly, article 2, section 3 of the U.S. Constitution requires the president to "take care that the laws be faithfully executed." This admonition clearly includes international treaties and agreements as well as customary international law.

These provisions of the Constitution can be invoked to establish yet another line of argument in favor of admitting your expert's testimony on the requirements of international law. Under the First Amendment to the U.S. Constitution, your clients had a right to petition the government for a redress of grievances being committed

7. *See, e.g., Diggs v. Schultz*, 470 F.2d 461 (D.C. Cir), *cert. denied*, 411 U.S. 931 (1972).

on a daily basis by the president and his executive branch of the federal government. These grievances consist of the latter's gross violation of the basic rules of international law, U.S. domestic law (both civil and criminal) and the president's recognized obligations under the terms of the Constitution. Your expert's testimony should be admitted for the purpose of establishing precisely what these constitutional grievances were that your clients were petitioning for redress against when they engaged in nonviolent civil resistance activities.

Submit a motion in limine to permit your expert to testify

It is crucial for the proper preparation of a defense for those who have engaged in nonviolent civil resistance activities using international law that long before trial you submit to the judge a motion in limine outlining your theory of defense, together with an explanation of why your international law expert's testimony is necessary to establish that defense, and then make a specific request that he be allowed to testify at trial. I have sometimes had trial attorneys reject this advice on the alleged grounds that they do not want to "tip their hand," as they put it, to either the judge or the prosecution before trial. As a tactical matter, this lackadaisical approach to establishing the interconnection between international law and criminal law will oftentimes fail.

It has been my experience that if the judge is first presented with a defense of this nature on the day of trial, there is a good chance he will deny the request by the defense counsel to allow the international law expert to appear and testify before the jury because the judge really does not understand the relevance of international law to the defense of his clients. Of course, this is not the judge's fault. On the other hand, in many instances where the international law arguments have succeeded, a motion in limine was prepared by the attorney in cooperation with an international law expert and submitted to the judge before trial precisely so that the latter could readily comprehend the relevance of international law to the defense that would be presented and why it was necessary for an international law expert to appear and testify before the jury.

Let me be honest and forthright about this point. In some of those cases where defense attorneys have rejected my advice to submit a motion in limine to the judge, I have received the distinct impression that the real reason was that they could not be bothered to put one together. This might have stemmed from the fact that they were litigating these cases on a pro bono basis and thus had decided to mount a pro forma defense, or that they did not really believe the international law defense was worth much effort, or both. Whatever the reason, if the defense attorney is not willing to do the minimum amount of preparatory work necessary to properly raise the international law arguments at trial, then I see no point in spending my precious time flying around the country on the offhand chance that I might be allowed to testify as an expert witness at his trial. There have been several instances where I have traveled somewhere to testify as an expert witness, only to discover when I arrived that the trial attorney had not really worked this matter out in advance with the judge, and for one reason or another, the judge would not allow me to testify. Nothing is more inconsiderate, frustrating, and a bigger waste of time, especially when I request no fee for my professional services in these cases.

For that reason, I have adopted a policy that normally I will not agree to testify as an expert witness at a trial unless defense counsel has already secured some understanding on this matter with the judge. The simplest way to accomplish this objective is to submit a motion in limine to the court explaining your theory of defense and the relevance of international law principles to it, together with a resumé detailing your international law professor's credentials. It will then be possible for the judge to decide before trial whether or not he is going to allow your expert to testify in court, either before the jury, or at least on an offer of proof.

For the sake of convenience, your motion in limine can draw upon the trial materials found in Chapters 4, 5, and 6 that have actually been used in the defense of anti-nuclear, Central America, and South African apartheid civil resistance protesters, respectively. But you must not automatically replicate the contents of these materials for the drafting of a motion in your own case. An international law expert should prove to be of invaluable assistance to you in drafting a motion in limine along the suggested lines for the purpose of articulating whatever theory of defense you have decided upon in your particular nonviolent civil resistance case. It must be the product of a joint and cooperative endeavor drawing upon his substantive expertise and your trial experience that is brought to bear upon the particular facts and legal issues of your clients' unique case.

To be sure, throughout all stages of these motion in limine proceedings, it is crucial to keep in mind that your motion is limited solely to the question of whether or not your international law expert will be allowed to testify at trial. Your motion must never request the permission of the court to allow you to put on evidence of the requirements or violations of international law by other means. Nor should you ever request the permission of the judge to put on a defense of self-defense, necessity, prevention of a crime, or any other affirmative defenses you have selected to rely upon. These affirmative defenses have been given to your clients by the statutes or common law rules generally available within your jurisdiction for anyone who has been charged with a crime, no matter how heinous. Therefore, you do not need to ask the judge's permission to put on any of these defenses or international law evidence related to them by means other than your expert's testimony at trial.

Indeed, for the judge to rule that you have no right to put on such defenses and evidence would constitute a violation of due process of law—an obvious reversible error. Hence, it must be made perfectly clear that your motion in limine amounts essentially to nothing more than an offer of proof on the part of an international law expert. In the event this motion is denied, you have not prejudiced your position with respect to any of the affirmative defenses you intend to raise at trial, nor your ability to introduce international law evidence with respect to those defenses by means of your clients' own testimony or otherwise.

I realize, of course, that similar arguments can be made in favor of not requesting the prior permission of the judge to allow your international law expert to testify at trial. Strategically, it might be the case that for a variety of sound reasons you have decided it would be preferable simply to put your international law expert on the stand without requesting prior permission. If there are very good reasons for proceeding in this manner, I have no objections to doing so as long as the defense attorney and I have discussed this tactic at length before trial and he has adduced some pretty convincing reasons why I should take time off from my busy schedule in order to fly out to his trial for no fee when there is a good chance that I will not be allowed to testify.

You owe an explanation beforehand to your expert as to why you are going to pursue this strategy, and a discussion of the risks involved that he could not be allowed to testify. With such full and prior disclosure your expert can then decide for himself how he wants to proceed. Thus, if something goes wrong at trial, it will not be due to anyone's fault or negligence.

If an attorney has been diligent and conscientious at pursuing in good faith my advice throughout the pre-trial proceedings, I am more than happy to give serious consideration to his judgment-call that it would be preferable not to tip *our* hand in advance. By contrast, if an attorney has not so conducted himself, I will probably adhere to the general rule enunciated above to the effect that I will not appear to testify at trial without obtaining the judge's prior acquiescence. In the latter case, however, I would still be happy to offer whatever advice I can over the telephone or by correspondence either before, during or after the trial.

Why should your international law expert be entitled to testify at trial?

According to Rule 702 of the Federal Rules of Evidence, if scientific, technical, or other specialized knowledge will assist the trier of fact to understand the evidence or to determine the fact in issue, a witness qualified as an expert by knowledge, skill, experience, training, or education may testify thereto in the form of an opinion or otherwise. Many states follow a similar rule in their respective state codes of evidence. You should certainly argue in your motion in limine that your international law expert's testimony at trial will serve the afore-mentioned purposes and that his qualifications will meet the required standards.

Sometimes, however, judges will respond that the testimony of an international law expert is not necessary to inform either the court or the jury of the requirements of international law since those tasks can be performed by submitting a trial memorandum to the judge and by your requesting international law instructions from the judge to the jury—as is oftentimes done in a case with respect to any other question of law at issue. The proper response to this question as to why your case should be treated differently is a bit complicated. But succinctly stated, the reason for such differential treatment can be justified on the following grounds.

The Statute of the International Court of Justice is an integral part of the United Nations Charter, which is a treaty that has received the advice and consent of the United States Senate. Therefore the ICJ Statute is entitled to the benefits of the Supremacy Clause of the United States Constitution, and is thus binding upon any state or federal court in the United States whenever questions of international law are presented for determination thereunder. ICJ Statute article 38(1) specifically designates the universally-recognized sources of international law to be applied by the World Court itself:

> a. international conventions, whether general or particular, establishing rules expressly recognized by the contesting states;
>
> b. international custom, as evidence of a general practice accepted as law;
>
> c. the general principles of law recognized by civilized nations;
>
> d. subject to the provisions of Article 59, judicial decisions and the teachings of the most highly qualified publicists of the various nations, as subsidiary means for the determination of rules of law.

ICJ article 38(1) essentially creates a choice-of-law rule for the determination of the rules of international law. It is applied not only by the International Court of Justice but also by any international or domestic tribunal seeking to determine the rules of international law. Routinely it has been the case in the United States that both state and federal courts have invoked this ICJ article 38(1) choice-of-law rule to determine the rules of international law when questions related thereto are involved in cases before them.

ICJ Statute article 38(1)(d) specifically states that "the teachings of the most highly qualified publicists of the various nations" are a "subsidiary means for the determination of rules of law." In other words, the teachings/writings/opinions of international law professors are explicitly recognized as being an authoritative source for the determination of the rules of international law. This characterization has been universally agreed upon by all state parties to the U.N. Charter/ICJ Statute, including the United States. Hence this U.N. Charter/ICJ Statute choice-of-law rule attributing special importance to the opinions of international law professors binds all U.S. federal and state courts under the terms of the Supremacy Clause of the U.S. Constitution.

Article 38(1)(d) attributes just as much significance to the opinion of an international law professor as to a judicial decision as a subsidiary means for the determination of the rules of international law. You should certainly point out to the judge that this equivalence in the degree of authoritativeness of international law professor opinions with judicial decisions is not true for any other area of the law. Indeed, it has always been the case that when it comes to determining the rules of international law, international tribunals and U.S. domestic courts have invariably attached great weight, respect and deference to the opinions of international law experts.

For example, in the aforementioned case of the *Paquete Habana*, 175 U.S. 677, 700 (1900), the Supreme Court of the United States expressly ruled as follows:

> International law is part of our law, and must be ascertained and administered by the courts of justice of appropriate jurisdiction as often as questions of right depending upon it are duly presented for their determination. For this purpose, where there is no treaty and no controlling executive or legislative act or judicial decision, resort must be had to the customs and usages of civilized nations, and, as evidence of these, to the works of jurists and commentators who by years of labor, research, and experience have made themselves peculiarly well acquainted with the subjects of which they treat. Such works are resorted to by judicial tribunals, not for the speculations of their authors concerning what the law ought to be, but for trustworthy evidence of what the law really is.

This, then, provides the reason why the judge should permit your international law expert to testify at trial even though this might not be the practice with respect to other areas of the law. In your case, the rule enunciated in FRE Rule 702 must be interpreted by reference to ICJ Statute article 38(1)(d) and *Paquete Habana* to permit your international law expert to testify at trial.

What if your international law expert is not permitted to testify?

Sometimes the judge might rule that your international law expert will not be allowed to testify. Such a ruling, however, does not mean that you cannot put on your affirmative defenses and international law evidence at trial anyway. In the event your expert is not allowed to testify, simply have your defendants bring out considerations of international law in their own words during your direct examination of them at trial. In addition, you should also prepare and request jury instructions dealing with the major substantive international law issues relevant to your case. Several examples of sample jury instructions concerning the requirements of international law with respect to nuclear weapons, Central America and South Africa can be found in Chapters 4, 5, and 6, respectively.

In the meantime, your clients' international law testimony can be easily prepared by having them sit down and read the relevant chapters of this book concerning the type of civil resistance activities they have engaged in. Chapters 4, 5, and 6 contain expert witness testimony I have actually given in nuclear protest cases, Central America protest cases, and South African apartheid cases, respectively. You should attempt to get introduced into evidence as many of these substantive legal issues that you believe your clients can reasonably present during your direct examination of them at trial. Obviously, there is no way your clients can speak very technically about these complicated matters of international, criminal, and constitutional law. But they can certainly get across to the jury the major international law violations that have been committed by the Reagan administration in pursuit of whatever governmental policies your clients were protesting by their civil resistance activities—e.g., the Nuremberg Principles, the Geneva Conventions, the U.N. Charter, the Genocide Convention, war crimes, etc.

You can plan in advance to get your international law evidence admitted

Indeed, it is now the case in more than one jurisdiction that before individuals have engaged in nonviolent civil resistance activities to protest the Reagan administration's foreign policies on nuclear weapons, Central America, or South African apartheid, the prospective protesters have read substantive materials developed by this author (some of which appear in this book) before they went out to protest. In these circumstances, it should arguably be even easier to get the international law violations admitted into evidence at trial by means of the defendants' own testimony on the grounds that what they read motivated them to protest and is thus admissible because it directly bears upon their general mens rea and/or specific intent at the time of their alleged offense. Furthermore, it would even be possible to argue to a judge that the concerned international law expert should be allowed to testify at trial on the grounds that the defendants were motivated to protest because of his writings. The same result could be accomplished by having an international law professor come out to give a public lecture or hold a teach-in on the substantive legal issues involved before individuals engage in acts of nonviolent civil resistance. One of the greatest accolades I have ever received was to have been told by a civil resistance defendant that she had been motivated to protest (to be sure, in part) by something I had written.

For example, if the prospective protesters read or hear international law arguments before they engage in their civil resistance activities, it could then set the stage for a defense of reasonable mistake of law. You could try to get your international law evidence admitted on the grounds that your defendants reasonably relied upon the opinion of a professor of international law when they conducted their civil resistance activities. This would then better prepare the grounds for you to call to testify at trial the very expert whose writings motivated your clients to protest.

In such a case, his testimony should be admitted, not for the general purpose of serving as a source for the determination of the rules of international law as explained above; but rather, for the more limited purpose of establishing the contents of his writings and the grounds for his conclusions as to the requirements of international law. You should argue to the judge that these defendants acted reasonably when they relied in good faith on the writings of an international law professor, and therefore that they should certainly be entitled to examine him at trial in order to corroborate the reasonability of their beliefs and the basis for his opinions. Once again, your primary objective is to get that international law evidence submitted for consideration by the jury under whatever theory or for whatever limited purpose possible. That being said, the rest of this chapter will assume that the judge has granted your motion to allow the international law expert to testify at trial.

Lay the proper foundation for the admission of your expert's testimony

When you finally put the defense's case on trial, it will be extremely important for you to call at least one defendant to testify as a witness on the stand before your expert witness in order to lay some foundation testimony with respect to international law. This should be easy enough to do. It is generally the case that most individuals engaged in nonviolent civil resistance activities have heard of something known as international law, the Nuremberg Principles, the Genocide Convention, the Geneva Conventions, the Hague Regulations, or the U.N. Charter, etc. Moreover, it is probably the case that your defendants believed that their activities were either permitted or even required by principles of international law or the numerous treaties and conventions mentioned above.

All that would be necessary, therefore, is for one civil resistance protester to get on the stand and testify that he generally believed something known as international law, the Nuremberg Principles, etc. prohibited the threat or use of nuclear weapons, U.S. foreign policy toward Central America, or South African apartheid, and therefore that he was acting to uphold the principles of international law when he protested. This testimony would then provide the basis upon which the testimony of an expert witness on international law could be introduced into evidence for consideration by the jury. The testimony of the expert witness should be admitted for the purpose of establishing the reasonability of the defendant's belief as to the requirements of international law.

In this regard, it might very well be the case that your clients acted in the sincere belief that they were *obligated* to do something about the situation in accordance with the requirements of international law. Nevertheless, it will be much easier for you to argue only that they were *privileged* to act under principles of international law. I cannot understand why defense counsel insist upon arguing for the existence of a duty to act when the establishment of a privilege to act would be just as effective and much easier to prove. Of course it might be true that your jurisdiction actually recognizes a defense based upon "other *obligations* of law." If so, then you should certainly present the "duty" argument with respect to that defense alone. Otherwise, no point will be served by making your job any more difficult than it already is going to be.

Prepare the testimony of your expert witness

Long before your expert witness on international law appears in the courtroom, you should have submitted to him a list of questions that you will be asking him during the course of your direct examination. The first part of these questions should deal with his qualifications as an expert. One of the cardinal rules that I am sure is well known to litigators is not to stipulate to the qualifications of your expert. Usually it is the case that an international law professor possesses all sorts of fancy degrees, impressive qualifications, prestigious committee assignments, distinguished public service activities, etc. For that reason, it is extremely important for you to take time on the stand to go through the complete academic and professional background of your expert witness.

The purpose of this exercise is to convince the jury that your expert witness is not motivated by any type of political considerations or personal animosities, but is simply appearing as an objective and detached scholar who is genuinely concerned about the gravity of the Reagan administration's violations of international law. The best evidence for this is the fact that normally the expert will receive no fee for his testimony, just out-of-pocket expenses. You should certainly emphasize this point for the jury at the end of your direct examination to qualify the expert.

In this regard, I should also point out that it would prove to be very difficult for the prosection to locate an international law expert willing to testify on its behalf for no fee who is not or has never been on the U.S. government's payroll. In the unlikely event that you are confronted with an international law expert for the other side, be sure to impeach his credibility in front of the judge and the jury by extensively inquiring into his economic, political and career connections with the U.S. government, and in particular whether he has received any form of compensation or reimbursement for his appearance and from whom. I regret to report that the number of U.S. international law professors who could pass such questions with flying colors are few and far between. If you conduct such a stringent cross-examination of him before qualification, you would have a good chance of winning any "battle of the experts" in the collective mind of your jury.

The great bulk of the proposed questions you should submit to your expert witness before trial will deal with the substantive issues of international law involved in the case. The expert witness will be able to point out any substantive problems with the questions as stated; any difficulties in phraseology; a proper sequence for asking the questions; any potential for damaging cross-examination on certain issues; and any questions that you left out that should be put in. In Chapter 4 of this book you will find a sample direct examination of an expert witness on nuclear weapons and international law. This sample is drawn from direct examinations of me actually conducted by two attorneys in different anti-nuclear protest cases. I have simply taken the better questions and answers from each case and edited them together.

Likewise, Chapter 5 contains a sample direct examination of an expert witness on Central America and international law taken from the testimony I gave in the *Jarka* case. And Chapter 6 contains an edited version of expert witness testimony I actually gave in court and in university disciplinary proceedings concerning the University of Illinois Student Divestment Protest Case. You can use these materials as a basis for developing the international law expert's testimony in your own case, subject of course to any modifications, amendments, or additions he believes to be necessary or desirable.

Any international law teacher can use this book to prepare expert testimony for trial

As a matter of fact, other international law professors have already reviewed these materials before they gave their own expert witness testimony at trial in civil resistance cases. So in a pinch it is not essential that this author be the expert to testify. This book is structured in a way so that any international law teacher can rely upon its contents in order to prepare his or her own expert witness testimony on short notice.

All you have to do is find someone who can be qualified as an expert on international law. This task should not be too difficult since most American law schools and departments of political science have at least one professor who teaches their basic course on international law. He or she might not be the leading expert in the field—or anywhere near it. But this one teaching credential should be enough to get him or her qualified.

Federal Rule of Evidence 703 provides that the "facts or data in the particular case upon which an expert bases an opinion or inference may be those perceived by *or made known to him at or before the hearing.*" Your expert's reading the relevant portions of this book the night before trial would certainly fulfill that requirement. FRE 703 further provides that if of a type reasonably relied upon by experts in the particular field in forming opinions or inferences upon the subject, such facts or data need not be admissible in evidence. The materials in this book have already been "relied upon by experts in the particular field in forming opinions or inferences upon the subject."

Finally, according to FRE 705, the expert may testify in terms of opinion or inference and give his reasons therefore without prior disclosure of the underlying facts or data, unless the court requires otherwise, though of course subject to such disclosure on cross-examination. In this regard I should point out that the cross-examinations to which I have been subjected in all these civil resistance protest cases by the prosecution have been routinely abysmal. Therefore, even an inexperienced international law teacher whose only preparation for the case is to read this book before trial should be able to mount a fairly credible presentation before the jury.

The expert witness should present his testimony as if it were a seminar

Once on the witness stand, the operative assumption of the expert witness should be that he is there for the purpose of educating a group of men and women who are basically well-intentioned, law-abiding, patriotic and peaceable Americans, but who are probably not very well informed about the underlying substantive issues involved in the case. He should proceed to testify with the objective of educating the jury on the nature of the international crimes being committed by the Reagan administration so that they can come to understand and sympathize with the sentiments that motivated the defendants to act in their comparatively restrained manner. To do this, the expert witness should conduct his testimony as if it were a private seminar or tutorial he was holding for the members of the jury on whatever the substantive legal issues are from the defense's point of view.

Consequently, when you direct questions toward him, he should answer while looking at the members of the jury, not you. He should adopt a colloquial form of talk. He should not use technical terms of art; or, if he finds it absolutely necessary to do so, he should first apologize for sounding "so much like a professor," and then proceed to explain the term to the jury. Likewise, he should engage in a repetition of concepts and definitions as often as he thinks necessary for their meaning to become clearly understood by the jury.

In the event your expert uses a term that is too technical without adequate explanation, you should interrupt him and ask him to define or further explain the term. Moreover, you should tell him beforehand that you are going to do this whenever you feel that he has lost contact with the jury for any reason; that he should expect this to occur, and thus not show any irritation on the stand over your interruptions. As is true in the classroom, the demonstration of patience, sincerity, simplicity and respect by the professor for his student-jurors will produce the most rewarding results.

The expert witness must also remember that, unlike a seminar, he only has a relatively short period of time in which to educate the jury to the defendants' point of view on a very complex subject. I would recommend that you allow at least one hour for the expert's substantive testimony, not including time for his qualification. If you believe your direct examination will take longer than that, then you should schedule the expert testimony so that it can be broken up by lunch in order to avoid taxing the jury's attention span. Even an outstanding group of bright and dedicated law students can rarely focus on complicated classroom lectures in a meaningful way for more than one hour at a time.

Before trial, the criminal defense attorney should have obtained authentic copies of any treaties, conventions, documents, or other sources of international law that his expert will be referring to during direct examination, as well as the aforementioned provisions of the U.S. Constitution. These copies should be prepared as exhibits for formal introduction into evidence during the course of the expert's testimony. Thus, when the trial attorney first mentions a particular treaty, agreement, convention, resolution, etc., he should pick up his copy of the document, ask the expert witness to identify it, and then move that it be introduced into evidence. It will help immeasurably if the attorney can also prepare a packet containing xerox copies of the most crucial excerpts from these documents so that the jury can have them on hand when they retire to consider their verdict.

Establish a pattern of ongoing criminal activity by the U.S. government

I cannot overemphasize enough the importance of this point to whatever theory of defense you eventually adopt. The ordinary man or woman sitting on the jury believes that the United States government is essentially peaceable and law-abiding. So it is up to you to convince them that this just is not true by means of the international law evidence and expert testimony that will be adduced at trial. You must argue not simply that the government is committing violations of international law, but in addition that these violations constitute ongoing criminal activity that creates personal criminal responsibility for members of the Reagan administration under well-recognized principles of international and U.S. domestic law as fully subscribed to by the United States government.

Depending upon the substantive issues involved, these international crimes would include but not be limited to crimes against peace, crimes against humanity, war crimes, grave breaches of the Geneva Conventions, genocide, apartheid, torture, assassination, as well as the inchoate crimes incidental thereto—planning, preparation, solicitation, incitement, conspiracy, complicity, attempt, aiding and abetting, etc. Here it would be worthwhile for your expert witness to explain to the jury the historical origins of the Nuremberg Principles as a direct reaction to the genocidal horrors inflicted by the Nazi regime of Adolph Hitler before and during the Second World War, as well as the leading role played by the United States government in the establishment of the Nuremberg Tribunal. Of course the great irony is that today's U.S. government officials are currently committing or planning to commit international crimes for which their predecessors successfully sought to put Nazi government officials to death!

As if that were not enough, your expert should mention to the jury that U.S. Army Field Manual 27-10, *The Law of Land Warfare* (1956) prescribes the appropriate standards of international criminal law applicable to such situations that have been long recognized as valid by the United States Government. According to paragraph 498 thereof, any person, whether a member of the armed forces or a civilian, who commits an act that constitutes a crime under international law is responsible for it and liable to punishment. Such offenses in connection with warfare comprise crimes against peace, crimes against humanity, and war crimes. Here the Manual basically incorporated the triumvirate of international crimes recognized by the Nuremberg Charter, Judgment, and Principles.

Paragraph 499 defines the term "war crime" to be the technical expression for a violation of the law of war by any person or persons, military or civilian. Every violation of the law of war is a war crime. Pursuant to paragraph 500, conspiracy, direct incitement and attempts to commit, as well as complicity in the commission of international crimes are similarly punishable as international crimes in their own right.

Paragraph 501 of the Manual recognizes the existence of and standard for vicarious criminal responsibility on the part of commanders for acts of subordinates. Any U.S. government official, whether civilian or military, who had actual knowledge, or should have had knowledge, through reports received by him or through other means, that troops or other persons subject to his control were about to commit or had committed international crimes and who failed to take the necessary and reasonable steps to insure compliance with international criminal law or to punish violators thereof is similarly guilty of an international crime. This test of vicarious criminal responsibility is based upon the seminal decision of the United States Supreme Court in *Application of Yamashita*, 327 U.S. 1 (1946).

Field Manual paragraph 509 denies an alleged international criminal the defense of superior orders, whether military or civil, unless the individual did not know and could not reasonably have been expected to know that the act ordered was unlawful, though superior orders may be considered in mitigation of punishment. Furthermore, Field Manual paragraph 510 denies the defense of "act of state" to such alleged international criminals by providing that the fact a person who committed an act which constitutes an international crime acted as the head of state or as a responsible government official does not relieve him from responsibility for his act. On these as in other matters, the U.S. Army Field Manual once again generally incorporated the terms of the Nuremberg Principles.

Hence, according to the U.S. Army Field Manual itself, all high-level civilian and military officials in the Reagan administration who either knew or should have known that civilians or soldiers under their control have committed or were about to commit international crimes, and they failed to take measures necessary to stop them, or to punish them, or both, are likewise personally responsible for the commission of international crimes. This category of officialdom who actually knew or at least should have known of the existence of substantive or inchoate international crimes and failed to do anything about them would typically include the secretary of state, secretary of defense, director of central intelligence, the national security adviser, the attorney general, and presumably the president and vice president. These Reagan administration officials, among others, are personally responsible for commission or at least complicity in the commission of crimes against peace, crimes against humanity and war crimes as specified by the U.S. Army Field Manual and the Nuremberg Principles.

Forty years ago at Nuremberg, representatives of the U.S. government participated in the prosecution and punishment of Nazi government officials for committing some of the same types of heinous international crimes that members of the Reagan administration are today inflicting upon innocent people around the world. The American people must reaffirm our commitment to the Nuremberg Principles by holding our government officials fully accountable under international law and U.S. domestic law for the commission of such grievous international crimes. We must not permit any aspect of our foreign affairs and defense policies to be conducted by acknowledged "international criminals" according to the U.S. government's own official definition of that term. The American people must insist upon the impeachment, dismissal or resignation of all U.S. government officials guilty of such international crimes. This is precisely what your clients were doing when they exercised their First Amendment right to petition the government for redress of grievances by engaging in their nonviolent civil resistance activities.

This approach to conducting the direct examination of your international law expert shifts the focus of the jury's attention away from an exposition of abstract principles of international law, to a discourse upon the grievous nature of the government's conduct. This latter point should prove to be a gut-level issue that the peaceable and law-abiding members of an American jury can readily understand, abhor, condemn and oppose by acquitting your clients. Such expert testimony will then set the stage for presenting to the jury your defenses of necessity, choice of evils, prevention of crime, prevention of a catastrophe, measures otherwise authorized by law, etc. during the subsequent course of the trial. The main point you want to drive home is that your clients were privileged to act as they did in order to prevent the ongoing commission of internationally recognized criminal activity by members of the United States government on an everyday basis. When you compare the minor nature of the crime for which the defendants have been charged (typically trespass) against the monstrous nature of the international crimes being committed, supported, condoned, or threatened by U.S. government officials, clearly the defendants should be entitled to whatever defenses you are claiming.

Oftentimes I think (or at least hope) it is true that the American people are basically unaware of the gross violations of international law being perpetrated in their name by their own government on a day-to-day basis; and that once they are informed, they would clearly be outraged and do something to stop the elementally lawless behavior of the Reagan administration around the world. For example, in the *Jarka* case I testified on the witness stand for approximately two hours as an expert with respect to the illegality of the Reagan administration's policies on nuclear weapons and Central America. After forty-five minutes of deliberation, the jury acquitted the defendants of all charges, and were then interviewed by representatives of the local news media. Several members of the jury stated that they were "shocked" to discover that the United States government was committing such gross violations of international law, and that this factor had led them to acquit the defendants. Moreover, some of the jurors stated that they had been so "radicalized" by the trial that they thought they themselves should go out and start to protest in order to do something about the situation! It is precisely this type of revulsion and reaction that you should strive to engender within the hearts and minds of all your jurors.

Conclusion

Quite obviously, in the limited space of this brief chapter, I cannot even begin to deal with all the problems that will arise in the defense of those who have engaged in nonviolent civil resistance activities under international law. If after having digested the contents of this book you still have any questions, please feel free to get in touch with me. Or else, if you prefer, The Lawyers' Committee on Nuclear Policy will be happy to do its best to secure another international law expert who will consult with you on a pro bono basis, subject of course to a reimbursement for out-of-pocket expenses.

If you have any advice, comments, criticisms or suggestions to make about the analysis, rules, and materials set forth in this book, please communicate them directly to me. I am certain this book will need to be put through another edition on the basis of further experience. Finally, in return for my assistance, I would appreciate being kept informed of the progress you make on your case, its ultimate disposition, and receiving any documents or pleadings you and the prosecution might file. That way The Lawyers' Committee on Nuclear Policy can serve as a central depository and resource center for all lawyers who nobly seek to defend those who have engaged in nonviolent civil resistance activities to terminate the Reagan administration's malicious attack upon the integrity of the international legal order, the U.S. domestic legal order, and the sacrosanct words of our own Constitution.

Chapter 3.

The Relevance of International Law to the Paradox of Nuclear Deterrence

Quite recently a substantial number of articles have been written on the subject of the legality or illegality of using nuclear weapons under international law.[1] Certainly the main impetus to this expanding body of literature has been the cavalier nuclear war-fighting rhetoric propounded by the Reagan administration since its ascent to power in the aftermath of the 1980 election.[2] Understandably, therefore, many of these articles have taken the counteractive position that the use of nuclear weapons is completely prohibited by international law, and consequently, that there exist serious legal problems related even to the threat to use nuclear weapons under a variety of circumstances.[3] In other words, these writings have either directly or indirectly called into question the very legitimacy of America's

---

A Dutch translation of this chapter has been published in 11 *Recht En Kritiek*, No. 3 (1985). A substantially revised and edited version of this chapter will be published by *Northwestern University Law Review*.

1. *See, e.g.*, Fried, "The Preparation for Nuclear War in the Light of International Law," Statement for the International Nuremberg Tribunal, Feb. 1983; Kennedy, "A Critique of United States Nuclear Deterrence Theory," 9 *Brooklyn J. Int'l L.* 35 (1983); Meyrowitz, "Are Nuclear Weapons Legal?," *Bull. Atomic Sci.*, Oct. 1983, at 49; Weston, "Nuclear Weapons Versus International Law: A Contextual Reassessment," 28 *McGill Law J.* 542 (1983). *See also* Brownlie, "Some Legal Aspects of the Use of Nuclear Weapons," 14 *Int'l & Comp. L. Quart.* 437 (1965).

2. *See* Halloren, "50 in Congress Protest Policy on Protracted A-War," *N.Y. Times*, Jul. 22, 1982, at A6, col. 3; Halloren, "Weinberger Angered by Reports on War Strategy," *N.Y. Times*, Aug. 24, 1982, at B8, col. 3.

3. *See* R. Falk, L. Meyrowitz, J. Sanderson, *Nuclear Weapons and International Law* 52, 78 (Oct. 1981).

strategic nuclear weapons deterrence policy, though few if any of these articles have ventured into a systematic examination of the so-called "paradox of deterrence" from an international law perspective.

Namely, if article 2(4) of the United Nations Charter prohibits both the threat and use of force except in cases of legitimate self-defense under article 51, and if it is also clear that the actual use of nuclear weapons would grossly violate the international laws of humanitarian armed conflict under most conceivable circumstances, how can the United States government nevertheless lawfully threaten to use nuclear weapons in accordance with any theory of nuclear deterrence without violating international law? Furthermore, if the Nuremberg Principles absolutely proscribe crimes against peace, crimes against humanity and war crimes,[4] how can the United States government nevertheless lawfully establish a threat to commit such heinous offenses as the very basis of its theory for nuclear deterrence? Finally, does not the very articulation of these extremely serious reservations about the overall legality of U.S. nuclear deterrence policy weaken the credibility of the deterrent itself and therefore render the risks of war with the Soviet Union at least somewhat more probable than would be the case with the present resounding affirmation of the essential legitimacy of the U.S. nuclear deterrent under international law?

Critique of the "Positivist" Approach to Analyzing the Legality of Nuclear Weapons

Most of the literature takes what the author will call a "positivist" approach to analyzing the question of the legality or illegality of nuclear weapons. Namely, the threat or use of "nuclear weapons" is said to be either "legal" or "illegal." Yet international life and historical fact are rarely so clear-cut, so susceptible to such dogmatic assertions and the automatic derivation of foreign policy recommendations therefrom. According to this "positivist" approach, no attempt is made to break down the concept of "nuclear weapons" into its constituent elements: in particular, what the weapons are, how they function, what their destructive capabilities are, what are the

---

4. *See* The London Agreement, Aug. 8, 1945, Charter, 59 *Stat.* 1544, *E.A.S.* No. 472, 82 *U.N.T.S.* 279.

actual contingency plans for their targeting and use, and under what particular circumstances. If any progress is to be made concerning the debate over the legality or illegality of nuclear deterrence, the author submits that such discriminations must be made from an international law perspective and placed within their factual context. It is fine for a legal positivist to declare that the *use* of nuclear weapons is illegal under all circumstances. But how useful is such a declaration to a government decision-maker actually dealing with issues related to the *threat* of using nuclear weapons in time of peace, in time of international crisis, or in time of war?

The existence of such a "positivist" argument affirming the complete illegality of using nuclear weapons under international law might very well be useful to a prosecutor at some future international war crimes trial similar to the Nuremberg Tribunal that is established in the aftermath of a nuclear holocaust for the purpose of trying both U.S. and Soviet government officials and military officers who launched or waged a nuclear war for the commission of crimes against peace, crimes against humanity, war crimes, grave breaches of the Geneva Conventions, and genocide, among other international crimes. The fact that many responsible legal commentators in the United States, the Soviet Union, and around the world were arguing that the use of nuclear weapons was illegal under international law long before they were actually so used could very well exercise a decisive bearing upon the culpability of such defendants.[5]

The author submits that at any such future war crimes tribunal held after a nuclear holocaust the judges would rule unanimously that as of today the use of nuclear weapons was absolutely prohibited under all circumstances by both conventional and customary international law. Therefore, all Soviet and American government officials and military officers who either launched or waged a nuclear war would be guilty of war crimes, crimes against humanity, crimes against peace, grave breaches of the Geneva Conventions, and genocide, at a minimum, and would not be entitled to the defenses of superior

---

5. I.C.J. Stat. art. 38, para. 1 provides in relevant part:

    1. The Court, whose function is to decide in accordance with international law such disputes as are submitted to it, shall apply:

. . . .

    d. subject to the provisions of Article 59, judicial decisions and the teachings of the most highly qualified publicists of the various nations, as subsidiary means for the determination of rules of law.

orders, act of state, duress, necessity, etc. They could thus be quite legitimately and most severely punished as war criminals, up to and including the imposition of the death penalty.

This prediction, which the author states with a high degree of confidence, provides little solace, comfort or guidance for foreign affairs and defense policy decision-makers today. The real purpose of public international law is not to punish violators on an ex post facto basis, but rather to prevent, forestall, or deter war, and a nuclear war in particular. Consequently, it must be the purpose of professional academics to produce an analysis of the legality or illegality of the threat to use nuclear weapons by breaking that subject down into its constituent elements in a manner that could be made relevant and useful to real world government decision-makers in the design of U.S. nuclear weapons policies for today and tomorrow.

From the decision-makers' perspective, the major defect of the "positivist" approach to analyzing the legality *vel non* of the threat and use of nuclear weapons becomes its inability to comprehend and operationalize the undeniable fact of international political life that in real-world situations government decision-makers must oftentimes choose the least bad as good.[6] A legal positivist approach prevents an analyst from making any discriminations between degrees of legality or illegality for the purpose of evaluating the propriety of a particular foreign affairs or defense policy decision and, consequently, from discerning any gradual improvement in or deterioration of the policy during the course of its development. From a legal positivist perspective, a foreign affairs or defense policy decision is essentially either legal or illegal, once and for all time. But interna-

---

6. *Cf.* American Law Institute's Model Penal Code § 3.02 (1962):
   Justification Generally: Choice of Evils.

   (1) Conduct which the actor believes to be necessary to avoid a harm or evil to himself or to another is justifiable, provided that: (a) the harm or evil sought to be avoided by such conduct is greater than that sought to be prevented by the law defining the offense charged; and (b) neither the Code nor other law defining the offense provides exceptions or defenses dealing with the specific situation involved; and (c) a legislative purpose to exclude the justification claimed does not otherwise plainly appear.

   (2) When the actor was reckless or negligent in bringing about the situation requiring a choice of harms or evils or in appraising the necessity for his conduct, the justification afforded by this Section in unavailable in a prosecution for any offense for which recklessness or negligence, as the case may be, suffices to establish culpability.

See also N. Machiavelli, *The Prince* 191 (M. Musa trans. & ed. 1964) (prince must choose the least bad as good).

tional political decision-making cannot realistically hope to be conducted on the basis of such a completely dichotomous and static viewpoint of the world, especially when it comes to the critical issue of nuclear deterrence.

No matter how regrettable it might be, for the immediate future U.S. government decision-makers must learn how to discriminate among the various nuclear weapons policies they have under consideration from an international law perspective in order to promote those policies which are more lawful, when possible, or at least less illegal, when necessary, over those which are less lawful or more illegal, respectively. In this manner U.S. nuclear decision-makers could select that policy or combination of policies which would move U.S. nuclear deterrence doctrine in a direction that is less objectionable under the rules of international law than the one the U.S. government currently pursues. In contrast to the traditional legal positivist approach to international relations, such a "functionalist" analysis of the legality or illegality of threatening to use nuclear weapons could prepare the way for incremental improvements in U.S. nuclear deterrence doctrine and practice.[7] A functionalist approach to this subject can provide an analytical mechanism for generating progressive movement out of the so-called "paradox of deterrence" that now confronts U.S. foreign affairs and defense decision-makers.

After all, that is the traditional role considerations of international law are supposed to play. It is oftentimes the case in foreign affairs decision-making that a policy based upon sound considerations of international law typically represents a good and eventually successful strategy. However, it is almost invariably the case that a policy which violates fundamental principles of international law is an unsound and unworkable approach that is usually counterproductive in the short term and ultimately self-defeating over the long-haul course of international relations. The author submits that such is and historically has been the case with U.S. nuclear deterrence policies and practices. If current U.S. nuclear deterrence doctrine is not progressively brought into some degree of accordance with the rules of international law, it will ultimately fail to prevent a nuclear war because of its own intrinsic contradictions, inconsistencies and in-

---

7. *See generally* Boyle, "International Law in Time of Crisis: From the Entebbe Raid to the Hostages Convention," 75 *Nw. U. L. Rev.* 769 (1980).

congruities. It is the purpose of this chapter to focus considerations of international law upon U.S. nuclear deterrence doctrine and practice. Not in the expectation that nuclear weapons are going to be abolished in the near future, but in the belief that the pursuit of deterrence policies which pay attention to considerations of international law are more conducive to the maintenance of international peace and security and thus to the prevention of a nuclear war.

To be sure, the alternative argument has been made by some academic international political scientists that the world would be a lot safer place if every state possessed a secure second-strike strategic nuclear weapons capability, or in the alternative that a "moderate amount" of nuclear proliferation throughout certain regions in the world should purposefully be encouraged by the current nuclear weapons states.[8] Such notions are naive and fatally dangerous to the future of mankind. No time will be spent here attempting to refute these speculative hypotheses since they have gained few adherents among either the scholarly community or government officials, let alone the professional military and intelligence establishments. The U.S. government's vigorous support for the 1968 Treaty on the Non-Proliferation of Nuclear Weapons[9] still remains the only viable alternative to the instigation of some future regional nuclear war with potentially global catastrophic consequences.

The U.S. Government's Argument for the Legality of Using Nuclear Weapons

Despite the above criticisms, however, this new spate of literature on the legality *vel non* of using nuclear weapons has proven to be most useful because it has opened up a debate on a subject that had long been considered well-settled. The official position of the United States government asserting the permissibility of using nuclear weapons for the purposes of legitimate self-defense has historically been based on the rationale enunciated in paragraph 35 of the 1956 De-

---

8. *But cf.* M. Kaplan, *System and Process in International Relations* 50 (1957) (unit veto system).

9. Treaty on the Non-Proliferation of Nuclear Weapons, July 1, 1968, 21 *U.S.T.* 483, *T.I.A.S.* No. 6839, 729 *U.N.T.S.* 161.

partment of the Army Field Manual 27-10 on *The Law of Land War-fare*:[10]

> The use of explosive "atomic weapons," whether by air, sea, or land forces, cannot *as such* be regarded as violative of international law in the absence of any customary rule of international law or international convention restricting their employment. [Emphasis added.]

To the same effect is paragraph 613 of the 1955 Department of the Navy Field Manual NWIP 10-2 on *The Law of Naval Warfare*:[11]

> There is at present no rule of international law expressly prohibiting States from the use of nuclear weapons in warfare. In the absence of express prohibition, the use of such weapons against enemy combatants and other military objectives is permitted.[8] [Footnote in the original.]

According to the United States government, if the actual use of nuclear weapons is permissible in legitimate self-defense under article 51 of the United Nations Charter, then a fortiori it is certainly lawful merely to threaten their use in order to deter an offensive nuclear or conventional attack by the Soviet Union upon America or the European members of the NATO alliance.

Although there exist substantial differences between these two formulations of the American rationale purporting to justify both the use of nuclear weapons and, by implication, the threat of their use (which will be analyzed below), these phraseologies are motivated by the same underlying conception of international law and its relationship to state sovereignty. Namely, that state conduct which is not expressly prohibited by a positive norm of international law is therefore per-

---

10. Department of the Army, *Field Manual 27-10: The Law of Land Warfare* 18 (1956).

11. Office of the Chief of Naval Operations, Department of the Navy Field Manual NWIP 10-2: The Law of Naval Warfare (1955). Footnote 8 then qualifies this bold assertion in the following way:

> The employment, however, of nuclear weapons is subject to the basic principles stated in Section 220 and Article 221. Also, see Articles 621 and 622, as well as Note 2 above. Nuclear weapons may be used by United States forces only if and when directed by the President.

After diligently threading through these cross-references and the cross-references in these cross-references, the reader is left with the distinct impression that footnote 8 is the proverbial exception that swallows the supposed rule of paragraph 613 permitting the use of nuclear weapons.

mitted. This doctrine is known in the international legal studies profession as the "prohibitive" theory of international law. It stands in contrast to the diametrically opposed "permissive" theory, which holds that a state is free to do only that which it is expressly permitted to do by a positive norm of international law.

By definition, adherence to the "prohibitive" theory creates an almost irrefutable presumption in favor of state sovereignty at the expense of international law whenever the latter is silent, and thus concedes an enormous degree of freedom and discretion to governments in their conduct of international relations. Whereas the "permissive" theory is purposefully intended to severely restrict the scope of state sovereignty within the presumably well-defined boundaries of international law. Quite predictably, therefore, for reasons of national self-interest the member states of the international community have generally subscribed to the "prohibitive" theory of international law as the correct approach, and have repudiated the "permissive" theory as utopian speculation by academic theorists that is at gross variance with the facts of international life. In recognition of, or perhaps in deference to, this well-nigh universal sentiment espoused by the governments of the world community, the Permanent Court of International Justice long ago adopted the "prohibitive" theory and expressly rejected the "permissive" theory as the proper formulation of the relationship between international law and state sovereignty in the famous case of the *S.S. Lotus* (1927).[12]

These two quite peremptory statements by the U.S. Army and the U.S. Navy have been routinely trotted out and cited by government lawyers, governmental apologists among international lawyers in academia or private practice, and other supporters of U.S. nuclear weapons policy to justify whatever was (and currently is) the then fashionable U.S. nuclear deterrence doctrine as being essentially consistent with, or at least not in violation of, the requirements of international law. By successfully propagating the general belief that American nuclear deterrence policy creates no serious problems under international law, these two statements have either directly or indirectly exercised a profound influence upon international lawyers, government officials, professional academics, the military establishment, and through the medium of these elite groups, upon U.S.

---

12. *S.S. "Lotus"* (Fr. v. Turk.), 1927, *P.C.I.J.*, Ser. A, No. 9.

public opinion. Even more insidiously, these two statements have contributed to the development of the facile yet erroneous opinion among such elite groups that U.S. nuclear deterrence policy is a matter concerning the highest national security interest of America and thus the entire "Free World," and which therefore must exist as some metaphysical entity above and beyond the domain of international law. In other words, international legal considerations are incorrectly deemed to be essentially "irrelevant" when it comes to any evaluation of the propriety of the threat to use nuclear weapons by the United States government.[13]

Moreover, despite all the various evolutionary stages U.S. nuclear deterrence doctrine has proceeded through since 1955, the purported legal justification has remained the same. America's rationale for the legitimacy of its threat to use nuclear weapons has remained untouched by time and uninfluenced by technological advances in nuclear weaponry, strategy, and destructiveness for over three decades. These unilateral and self-serving policy pronouncements by two branches of the U.S. armed services have essentially been spared from systematic examination and authoritative critique from the time of their original promulgation during the Eisenhower administration operating under its doctrine of "massive retaliation;"[14] to the Kennedy administration and its doctrine of "mutual assured destruction" (MAD);[15] through the Johnson administration and its doctrine of "flexible response" for NATO;[16] and the Nixon administration with its "Schlesinger Doctrine;"[17] until the Carter administration's Presidential Directive 59[18] (that naively contemplated the possibility of America "fighting" a "limited" nuclear war), which was, in turn,

13. *Cf.* Boyle, "The Irrelevance of International Law," 10 *Cal. W. Int'l L. J.* 193 (1980).

14. *See, e.g.,* L. Freedman, *The Evolution of Nuclear Strategy* 76-91 (1981); P. Peeters, *Massive Retaliation: The Policy and its Critics* (1959).

15. As United States Secretary of Defense from 1961 to 1968, Robert McNamara was the primary architect of "mutual assured destruction," "flexible response", and other nuclear strategies developed during that period. *See* Freedman, *supra* note 14, at 227-44. *See generally* Martin, "The Role of Military Force in the Nuclear Age," in *Strategic Thought in the Nuclear Age* 4-7 (L. Martin ed. 1979); D. Snow, *Nuclear Strategy in a Dynamic World* 57-58 (1981).

16. Flexible response was formally adopted by NATO in 1967. *See* Freedman, *supra* note 14, at 285-86. *See also* Harvard Nuclear Study Group, *Living with Nuclear Weapons* 85, 92 (1983); Stanford Arms Control Group, *International Arms Control* 205-07 (C. Blacker & G. Duffy eds. 1984).

17. *See* L. Freedman, *supra* note 14, at 377.

18. For a discussion of Presidential Directive 59, see R. Scheer, *With Enough Shovels: Reagan, Bush & Nuclear War* 11-12 (1982). *See also* President Carter's Remarks at the Annual Convention of the American Legion, 16 *Weekly Comp. Pres. Doc.* 1549, 1553 (Aug. 21, 1980).

essentially endorsed and embellished upon by Secretary of Defense Caspar Weinberger's 1982 Five-Year Defense Guidance Statement, that boldly proclaimed the objective of America "prevailing" in a "protracted" nuclear war.[19] Common sense dictates that over three decades of history demand a reexamination of the rationale behind the alleged legality of U.S. nuclear weapons deterrence policy.

For example, in another pathbreaking decision rendered just before *Lotus*, the Permanent Court of International Justice held in the case of the *Tunis-Morocco Nationality Decrees* (1923) that as the strength of the international legal order develops and improves over time, the domain of state sovereignty necessarily diminishes in direct proportion.[20] In recognition of this dynamic relationship between international law and state sovereignty, paragraph 35 of the U.S. Army Field Manual astutely left open the possibility that developments in the legal, organizational and political relationships between the states of the international community after 1956 could very well have created a "customary rule of international law" that by 1986 expressly prohibits both the threat and use of nuclear weapons *"as such"* under all circumstances, including for the alleged purpose of legitimate self-defense. There have been a fairly large number of developments in the field of international law between then and now that cast serious doubt on the continued validity of these two seminal statements uttered in the mid-1950s.[21] But putting these developments of the past thirty years aside for the time being, was the basic proposition that the use of nuclear weapons, and a fortiori the threat of their use, were not *"as such"* illegal when enunciated by the U.S. government in 1955-1956 really an accurate statement of international law as it stood at the time?

---

19. For a discussion of the Five-Year Defense Guidance Plan, see R. Scheer, *supra* note 18, at 8, 32. *See also* Bethe, Gottfried & Currey, "The Five Year War Plan," *N.Y. Times*, June 10, 1982, at A31, col. 1; *N.Y. Times*, May 30, 1982, at A1, col. l.

20. *Tunis-Morocco Nationality Decrees* (Fr. v. Eng.), 1923 *P.C.I.J.*, Ser. B, No. 4, at 24 (Judgment of Feb. 7):

The question whether a certain matter is or is not solely within the jurisdiction of a State is an essentially relative question; it depends upon the development of international relations. Thus, in the present state of international law, questions of nationality are, in the opinion of the Court, in principle within the reserved domain.

For the purpose of the present opinion, it is enough to observe that it may well happen that, in a matter which, like that of nationality, is not, in principle, regulated by international law, the right of a state to use its discretion is nevertheless restricted by obligations which it may have undertaken towards other states.

21. *See* Falk, Meyrowitz & Sanderson, *supra* note 3, at 44-62.

The Relevance of the Nuremberg Principles to Nuclear Deterrence

No point would be served here by the production of yet another comprehensive catalogue of all the numerous violations of customary and conventional international law that might arise from the use of nuclear weapons, as of either 1955 or today, since that task has been most competently discharged elsewhere.[22] But it would be worthwhile to discuss the relevance of one seminal source of customary international law to the issue of the legality *vel non* of U.S. nuclear weapons deterrence policy. This preliminary objection to the validity of the position taken by the Army and Navy with respect to the legality of using nuclear weapons was just as valid in 1955 as it is today.

Article 6(a) of the 1945 Charter of the International Military Tribunal subsequently established at Nuremberg to prosecute and punish Nazi war criminals defined the term "crime against peace" to mean "planning, preparation, initiation or waging of a war of aggression, or a war in violation of international treaties, agreements or assurances, or participation in a common plan or conspiracy for the accomplishment of any of the foregoing." Nuremberg Charter article 6(b) defined the term "war crime" to include "murder, ill-treatment or deportation to slave labour or for any other purpose of civilian population of or in occupied territory, murder or ill-treatment of prisoners of war or persons on the seas, killing of hostages, plunder of public or private property, wanton destruction of cities, towns or villages, or devastation not justified by military necessity." Article 6(c) of the Nuremberg Charter defined the term "crime against humanity" to include "murder, extermination, enslavement, deportation, and other inhumane acts committed against any civilian population."

Article 6 also provided that leaders, organizers, instigators, and accomplices participating in the formulation or execution of a common plan or conspiracy to commit crimes against peace, crimes against humanity, and war crimes are responsible for all acts performed by any persons in execution of such plan. Article 7 of the

---

22. *See, e.g.*, G. Schwarzenberger, *The Legality of Nuclear Weapons* (1958); Rubin, "Nuclear Weapons and International Law," 1984 *Fletcher Forum* 45; Weston, "Nuclear Weapons Versus International Law: A Contextual Reassessment," 28 *McGill L. J.* 542 (1983).

Nuremberg Charter denied the applicability of the "act of state" defense to them by making it clear that the official position of those who have committed such heinous crimes "shall not be considered as freeing them from responsibility or mitigating punishment." Finally, article 8 provided that the fact an individual acted pursuant to an order of his government or of a superior shall not free him from responsibility, but may be considered in mitigation of punishment if justice so requires.

The principles of international law recognized by the Charter of the Nuremberg Tribunal and the Judgment of the Tribunal[23] itself were affirmed by a unanimous vote of the United Nations General Assembly in Resolution 95(I) on December 11, 1946.[24] Since that time, the Nuremberg Principles have universally been considered to constitute an authoritative statement of the rules of customary international law dictating individual criminal responsibility for crimes against peace, crimes against humanity, and war crimes.[25] Under the general principle of customary international law creating "universality" of jurisdiction for the prosecution and punishment of those alleged to have committed such heinous offenses,[26] all U.S. government officials and members of the U.S. military forces who might order or participate in a strategic nuclear attack upon the Soviet Union could lawfully be tried by any government of the world com-

---

23. XXII *Trial of the Major War Criminals Before the International Military Tribunal* 411-589 (1948).

24. G.A. Res. 95(I), U.N. Doc. A/236, at 1144 (1946).

25. *See* I. Brownlie, *International Law and the Use of Force by States* 154-213 (1963). *See also* R. Woetzel, *The Nuremberg Trials in International Law* 232-35 (1962).

26. *See, e.g., Attorney General of Israel v. Eichmann,* Criminal Case No. 40/61, District Court of Jerusalem, Judgment of Dec. 11, 1961, *reprinted in* 56 *Am. J. Int'l L.* 805 (1962), 36 *I.L.R.* 5 (1962). In the *Eichmann* case, the District Court of Jerusalem held that the power of the state of Israel to punish war criminals is based on the universal character of the crimes:

> The abhorrent crimes defined in this law are crimes not under Israeli law alone. These crimes which afflicted the whole of mankind and shocked the conscience of nations are grave offenses against the law of nations itself ("*delicta juris gentium*"). Therefore, so far from international law negating or limiting the jurisdiction of countries with respect to such crimes, in the absence of an International Court the international law is in need of the judicial and legislative authorities of every country, to give effect to its penal injunctions and to bring criminals to trial. The authority and jurisdiction to try crimes under international law are *universal*.

56 *Am. J. Int'l L.* at 808, 36 *I.L.R.* at 26.

The four Geneva Conventions of 1949 also recognize universal jurisdiction by obliging each contracting party to bring those who have committed "grave breaches" before the party's own courts, regardless of the offender's nationality. *See. e.g.,* Geneva Convention Relative to the Protection of Civilian Persons in Time of War, Aug. 12, 1949, art. 146, para. 2, 6 *U.S.T.* 3516, 3616, *T.I.A.S.* No. 3365, 75 *U.N.T.S.* 287, 386. *See also* Cowles, "Universality of Jurisdiction Over War Crimes," 33 *Calif. L. Rev.* 177 (1945).

munity that subsequently obtains control over them for crimes against peace, crimes against humanity and war crimes, inter alia.

The very existence of such heinous offenses and of personal criminal responsibility for the commission thereof is expressly recognized and affirmed by paragraph 498 of that same 1956 U.S. Army Field Manual on *The Law of Land Warfare*.[27] Yet simultaneously and quite inexplicably the Manual allegedly asserts the non-illegality of using nuclear weapons during wartime in paragraph 35! Furthermore, paragraph 500 thereof expressly provides that: "Conspiracy, direct incitement, and attempts to commit, as well as complicity in the commission of, crimes against peace, crimes against humanity, and war crimes are punishable."[28]

Does not contemporary U.S. nuclear deterrence policy constitute planning, preparation and conspiracy to commit crimes against peace, crimes against humanity, and war crimes? Are not the nuclear decision-makers of the Reagan administration thus subject to personal criminal responsibility and punishment under the Nuremberg Principles for currently pursuing the development of a U.S. "protracted nuclear war-prevailing" capability? In any event, does there not exist an incredible inconsistency if not a serious incompatibility between paragraph 35 of the 1956 U.S. Army Field Manual, on the one hand, and paragraphs 498, 499,[29] 500, and 501,[30] inter alia, on the other?

---

27. Paragraph 498 of the Field Manual defines "crimes" under international law to be as follows:

   Any person, whether a member of the armed forces or a civilian, who commits an act which constitutes a crime under international law is responsible therefor and liable to punishment. Such offenses in connection with war comprise:
      a. Crimes against peace
      b. Crimes against humanity
      c. War crimes.
   Although this manual recognizes the criminal responsibility of individuals for those offenses which may comprise any of the foregoing types of crimes, members of the armed forces will normally be concerned only with those offenses constituting "war crimes."

The Law of Land Warfare, supra note 10, ¶ 498, at 178.

28. *Id.*, ¶ 500, at 178.

29. Paragraph 499 of the Field Manual defines the term "war crime" to mean "the technical expression for a violation of the law of war by a person or persons, military or civilian. Every violation of the law of war is a war crime." *Id.*, ¶ 499, at 178.

30. Paragraph 501 of the Field Manual imposes criminal responsibility on commanders for the acts of subordinates in the following way:

   In some cases, military commanders may be responsible for war crimes committed by subordinate members of the armed forces or other persons subject to their control. Thus, for instance, when troops commit massacres and atrocities against the civilian population of occupied territory or against prisoners of war, the responsibility may rest not only with the actual perpetrators but also with the commander. Such responsibility arises directly when the acts in question have been committed in pur-

If so, what are the ramifications of this gross discrepancy for both the validity and the effectiveness of the contemporary U.S. nuclear deterrent in theory and practice?

At the very minimum, under the Nuremberg Principles, the U.S. nuclear destruction of Soviet civilian population centers would be absolutely prohibited under all circumstances.[31] This proposition would be true even if such a countercity attack was undertaken as a measure of retaliation in response to a prior nuclear attack against U.S. population centers by the Soviet Union.[32] But if the actual destruction of civilian population centers is prohibited under all circumstances, how can a theory of strategic nuclear deterrence that threatens to destroy cities be justified under international law?

The simplistic answer to this objection would be that the Nuremberg Principles apply only to the actual use of nuclear weapons during wartime. Hence, arguably, it is perfectly lawful for a state in peacetime to threaten to do something that would be completely unlawful to do in wartime, especially if the purpose of the peacetime threat is to prevent a nuclear or conventional war in the first place. This proposition is the cornerstone of the alleged "paradox" concerning the legality *vel non* of strategic nuclear deterrence.

Of course this rationale fails to account for the existence of the inchoate crimes incidental to war crimes, crimes against peace and crimes against humanity (viz., planning, preparation, conspiracy, incitement, attempt, complicity) that can be committed by government officials during peacetime and can thus create individual criminal responsibility for the commission thereof even before the outbreak of war. The primary purpose for recognizing the existence of such inchoate crimes with respect to war crimes, crimes against

suance of an order of the commander concerned. The commander is also responsible if he has actual knowledge, or should have knowledge, through reports received by him or through other means, that troops or other persons subject to his control are about to commit or have committed a war crime and he fails to take the necessary and reasonable steps to insure compliance with the law of war or to punish violators thereof.

Id., ¶ 501, at 178-79. *See also Application of Yamashita*, 327 U.S. 1 (1946).

31. The Nuremberg Charter includes as a war crime the "wanton destruction of cities, towns, or villages, or devastation not justified by military necessity." Nuremberg Charter, *supra* note 4, art. 6(b). The Charter also provides that murder and extermination of any civilian population are crimes against humanity, whether committed before or during a war. *Id.*, art. 6(c).

32. *See, e.g.*, Falk, Meyrowitz, and Sanderson, *supra* note 3, at 30-32, 45, 50-51, 63-71; Rubin, *supra* note 22, at 53-57; Weston, *supra*, note 22, at 585.

peace and crimes against humanity was to deter, prevent, or forestall the commission of the substantive offenses in the first place.[33]

Once again, the simplistic response to this objection would be that the recognition of such inchoate crimes with respect to nuclear deterrence is counterproductive to maintaining a credible nuclear balance between the two superpowers that is supposedly necessary to preserve world peace from nuclear Armageddon. According to this rationale, the application of the concept of inchoate crimes from the Nuremberg Principles to the issue of nuclear deterrence would weaken the credibility of the deterrent itself and therefore increase the risks of war. In other words, this argument reduces itself to the bald-faced and reprehensible Machiavellian proposition that the ends justify the means. Yet the rules of international law have been formulated precisely for the purpose of evaluating the propriety of both the ends and the means of international behavior pursued by governments and foreign policy decision-makers alike. That point was made quite clear by the Nuremberg Tribunal to the Nazi war criminals after World War II. It would also be made quite clear by a Nuclear Holocaust Tribunal to any surviving American and Soviet civilian and military leaders after World War III.

Conversely, however, if the U.S. government actually relies upon this instrumentalist argument in order to justify its current doctrine of nuclear deterrence under international law, then it would have to concede that in the event the Soviet Union ever used nuclear weapons or conventional forces against the United States of America or NATO members, the United States could not under any circumstances respond with the use of nuclear weapons against Soviet population centers. According to strategic theory, the nuclear deterrent has been developed in order to deter, not to be used. Once deterrence has

33. The following argument by Justice Jackson, Chief Prosecutor for the United States at Nuremberg, emphasized the importance of punishing inchoate crimes in order to avoid periodic wars:

> The case as presented by the United States will be concerned with the brains and authority back of all the crimes. . . . We want to reach the planners and designers, the inciters and leaders without whose civil architecture the world would not have been so long scourged with the violence and lawlessness, and wracked with the agonies and convulsions, of this terrible war.

II *Trial of the Major War Criminals Before the International Military Tribunal* 104-05 (1948).

Justice Jackson also argued that "[i]f aggressive warfare in violation of treaty obligation is a matter of international cognizance the preparations for it must also be of concern to the international community." *Id.* at 127. Similarly the Nuremberg Tribunal recognized that conspiracy should be included as an international crime because "[p]lanning and preparation are essential to the making of war." XXII *id.* at 467.

actually failed, the supposed justification for the threat to use nuclear weapons disappears, and the actual use of nuclear weapons in a countercity mode would still remain absolutely prohibited. Clearly this has not been the policy of the United States government since at least the time of the Eisenhower administration and its doctrine of "massive retaliation."[34]

A threat to do that which is illegal under any circumstances where it is almost inevitable that the threat will be carried out under a variety of circumstances is a materially different phenomenon from such a threat uttered in the abstract. If it was clear that once deterrence had failed the United States government would never use nuclear weapons against Soviet population centers, then some doctrine of strategic nuclear deterrence might theoretically be able to be justified under international law. But when a countercity threat has historically been implemented as the basis for the entirety of the U.S. strategic nuclear weapons establishment for the past thirty years, such a threat becomes presumptively illegal. And it is the presumptive illegality of that threat to use nuclear weapons against Soviet population centers under any circumstances that lies at the heart of U.S. strategic nuclear weapons deterrence doctrine in theory and practice both today and in the past.

Here there exists an enormous incongruity between the requirements of international law and the current status of U.S. strategic nuclear weapons deterrence theory. A somewhat more lawful policy would at least proclaim that although the United States government might be able to threaten to use nuclear weapons during peacetime, in the event of a nuclear or conventional attack upon the United States or NATO members by the Soviet Union, America would not under any circumstances actually use its nuclear weapons against Soviet population centers. Yet would not the mere public articulation of this policy weaken the credibility of the deterrent itself and thus invite a Soviet nuclear or conventional attack upon the United States or NATO?

Proponents of contemporary U.S. nuclear deterrence doctrine have

---

34. In his historic address before the Council of Foreign Relations on January 12, 1954, Secretary of State John Foster Dulles stated that "local defenses must be reinforced by the further deterrent of massive retaliatory power." J. Dulles, *The Evolution of Foreign Policy* (Jan. 12, 1954), *reprinted in* 30 *Dep't. St. Bull.*, Jan. 25, 1954, at 107, 108. *See generally* P. Peeters, *Massive Retaliation: The Policy and its Critics* (1959). The policy of "massive retaliation" was formally promulgated by the U.S. Government on October 30, 1954 in National Security Council Paper (NSC-162/2) on Basic Security Policy, *reprinted in* I Pentagon Papers 412-29 (Gravel ed. 1971).

answered this question in the affirmative, and have thus concluded that such a distinction must not be drawn. Yet basic requirements of international law dictate to the contrary: "Mutual assured destruction" (MAD) and all its essential accouterments and contemporary refinements must be abandoned as the heart of America's strategic nuclear deterrence policy. The overarching question then becomes, however, whether or not the United States government should move in the direction of the "protracted nuclear war-prevailing" doctrine advocated by the Reagan Administration, together with its so-called Strategic Defense Initiative (SDI), as desirable substitutes for MAD in accordance with international legal prescriptions. Those issues will be analyzed in more detail below and at the end of Chapter 4, respectively.

The *Lotus* Case Versus the Martens Clause

There are even more serious problems of a jurisprudential nature that have not been addressed in the 1955-1956 statements by the U.S. government concerning the legality of using nuclear weapons during wartime. As mentioned above, both the Army and the Navy Field Manuals' justifications for using nuclear weapons are based upon a similar rationale, which in turn is premised upon a metaphysical speculation concerning the relationship between international law and state sovereignty. Essentially the government's argument reduces itself to the jurisprudential proposition that since the use of "atomic weapons" during wartime is not specifically by name prohibited by the rules of international law, states remain presumptively free to use them. This particular formulation of the "prohibitive" theory of international law and its relationship to state sovereignty is derived from the famous case of the *S.S. Lotus* decided by the Permanent Court of International Justice (PCIJ) in 1927. In that case the PCIJ gave the classic formulation to the prohibitive theory of international law in the following terms:[35]

> International law governs relations between independent States. The rules of law binding upon States therefore emanate from their

35. *S.S. "Lotus"* (Fr. v. Turk.), 1927 *P.C.I.J.*, Ser. A, No. 10, at 18 (Judgment of Sept. 7).

own free will as expressed in conventions or by usages generally accepted as expressing principles of law and established in order to regulate the relations between these co-existing independent communities or with a view to the achievement of common aims. Restrictions upon the independence of States cannot therefore be presumed.

The *Lotus* Court came down decisively on the side of the prohibitive theory of international law, and therefore in favor of state sovereignty whenever international law is not expressly applicable. Nevertheless, as mentioned above, the PCIJ had already indicated in the *Tunis-Morocco* case of 1923 that as the rules of international law developed, so too the sovereignty of states would be proportionately diminished and restricted. Hence, applying the rationales of both *Lotus* and *Tunis-Morocco* to the matter of the legality of using nuclear weapons, it can be said that even though their use might not have been explicitly prohibited as of 1955, nevertheless their use could very well be prohibited as of today because of numerous developments in the field of international law and organization during the interim. And the same could be said for the threat to use nuclear weapons under a variety of circumstances.

The main problem with the Army/Navy application of the *Lotus* case to the use of nuclear weapons is that the *Lotus* rationale was never intended to have any applicability to the international laws of humanitarian armed conflict. At the time the *Lotus* case was decided, international law recognized a clear-cut bifurcation into two mutually exclusive international legal orders: the laws of peace and the laws of war.[36] This bifurcation was due to the fact that before the promulgation of the United Nations Charter in 1945 there was no absolute prohibition upon a state from going to war, or threatening or using force in international relations.[37]

---

36. A 1931 study of international law, for example, concluded that "the relations of international law can, according to their very nature, be divided into relations of *peace* and relations of *war*. A distinction can also be made between the *normal* relations of states and the extraordinary, which arise in conflicts between states, partly between the conflicting parties themselves and partly between these and other states." A. Moller, *International Law in Peace and War* (1931). *See also* J. Risley, *The Law of War* 40-48 (1897) (discussing the rules of peace as distinguished from the rules of war).

37. Under the United Nations Charter, "[a]ll Members shall refrain in their international relations from the threat or use of force against the territorial integrity or political independence of any state, or in any other manner inconsistent with the Purposes of the United Nations." U.N. Charter art. 2, para. 4. Article 2(4) is recognized as an unconditional prohibition on the threat or use of force in international relations that goes beyond any prior law. *See* A. Ross, *The United Nations: Peace and Progress* 99-104 (1966).

The Covenant of the League of Nations did not prohibit a state from going to war, but simply set up a procedure that members of the League had to follow and exhaust before they could go to war with another member of the League. Under the regime established by League of Nations Covenant articles 11(1), 12(1), 13(4), and 15(6), states retained their primordial right to resort to war to protect and advance their own interests, but only upon the fulfillment of the conditions specified therein.[38] Moreover, the Covenant had no such requirement for relations between League members and non-members, or a fortiori for relations between non-members among themselves. Since the United States never became a member of the League, Germany did not join until 1926,[39] and the U.S.S.R. until 1934,[40] this yawning gap in the Covenant's coverage was quite substantial.

To be sure, shortly after the *Lotus* decision was rendered, the states of the world community concluded the Kellogg-Briand Peace Pact of 1928, by means of which they agreed to renounce war as an instrument of national policy.[41] However, during the negotiation of the Pact, several parties made it quite clear that they reserved to themselves the right to resort to war in self-defense in accordance with their own determination of the necessity to do so.[42] In deference

38. Under the Covenant of the League of Nations, member states only agreed to submit disputes to arbitration, judicial settlement, or inquiry by the Council, League of Nations Covenant art. 12, para. 1, and they agreed not to go to war against a party to a dispute that had complied with an arbitration award, judicial decision, or unanimous report of the Council. *Id.* at art. 13, para. 4; art. 15, para. 6. Members that were parties to a dispute themselves only agreed not to resort to war until three months after the award, decision, or report had been made. *Id.* at art. 12, para. 1. Should a member disregard the covenants under articles 12, 13, or 15, the member was deemed to have committed an act of war. *Id.* at art. 16, para. 1. In that event, however, the Council was merely authorized to recommend what effective armed forces should be contributed by other states, and no real enforcement system was provided in the Covenant. *Id.* at para. 2.

Indeed, the League recognized the problems with the Covenant's system for peaceful settlement, and attempted to resolve the matter by providing a system for compulsory settlement of disputes in the Geneva Protocol of 1924. Although adopted by the League Assembly, the Protocol failed to come into force. *See* R. Russel & J. Muther, *A History of the United Nations Charter* 284-85 (1958).

39. 1 F. Walters, *A History of the United Nations* 316-27 (1952). Germany was admitted to the League of Nations on Sept. 8, 1926 by a unanimous vote of the Assembly. *Id.* at 326.

40. 2 F. Walters, *supra* note 39, at 579-85. The admission of the U.S.S.R. on Sept. 18, 1934 was a direct consequence of Hitler's rise to power in Germany, *id.* at 579, and came after Germany had resigned from the League in 1933.

41. Kellogg-Briand Pact, Aug. 27, 1928, art. I, 46 *Stat.* 2343, 2345-46, T.S. No. 796, 94 *L.N.T.S.* 57, 63, *reprinted in* 1928 (I) *Foreign Relations of the United States*, 153, 155: "The High Contracting Parties solemnly declare in the names of their respective peoples that they condemn recourse to war for the solution of international controversies, and renounce it as an instrument of national policy in their relations with one another."

42. *See, e.g.,* 1928 (I) *Foreign Relations of the United States* 15, 17-18 (France); *id.* at 42, 43-44 (Germany); *id.* at 66, 67 (Great Britain). France unsuccessfully proposed a draft anti-

to the fundamental principle of international law and politics recognizing the sovereign equality of states, according to the legal doctrine known as "reciprocity of reservations"[43] other parties to the Kellogg-Briand Pact that had not specifically made such a reservation were entitled to invoke it against any state party which had. So even the Kellogg-Briand Pact did not on its face expressly preclude the right to go to war, let alone threaten or use force, in self-defense as unilaterally determined by the state itself. Of course, however, after the Second World War the Judgment of the Nuremberg Tribunal decisively repudiated this self-judging element of the self-defense exception to the Kellogg-Briand Pact when it was invoked by the Nazi war criminals.[44]

Lotus was decided in an era when it was well recognized that the laws of peace and the laws of war were completely different entities that represented two separate and independent legal orders. And although the *Lotus* rationale (i.e., that which is not specifically prohibited is presumptively permitted) applied throughout the operation of the international laws of peace, that was not necessarily the case when it came to the application of the international laws of human-

war treaty specifically providing for the recognition of the right of legitimate self-defense within the framework of existing treaties. *Id.* at 32-34.

In his desire to keep an express recognition of self-defense out of the text of the treaty, Secretary of State Kellogg also conceded that self-defense was reserved under the Pact:

> There is nothing in the American draft of an antiwar treaty which restricts or impairs in any way the right of self-defense. That right is inherent in every sovereign state and is implicit in every treaty. Every nation is free at all times and regardless of treaty provisions to defend its territory from attack or invasion and it alone is competent to decide whether circumstances require recourse to war in self-defense.
>
> If it has a good case, the world will applaud and not condemn its action. . . .

American Note of June 23, 1928, *reprinted in* D. Miller, *The Peace Pact of Paris* 213 (1928).

The state right of self-judgment could only be defeated by the unanimous agreement of League Council Members other than representatives of parties to the dispute. League of Nations Covenant art. 15, para. 7, *reprinted in Basic Documents of the United Nations* 295, 300 (L. Sohn ed. 1968).

43. The doctrine of reciprocity of reservations provides that a reservation to a treaty applies reciprocally as between the state making the reservation and each of the other parties to the treaty. Therefore, when a particular state attempts, by a reservation, to relieve itself of treaty obligations, other parties to the treaty are relieved of those same obligations when dealing with the reserving state. *See, e.g., Aerial Incident of 27 July 1955* (U.S. v. Bulg.), 1960 *I.C.J.* 144, where Bulgaria applied the doctrine of reciprocity of reservations to defeat the World Court's exercise of compulsory jurisdiction by invoking a United States reservation to such jurisdiction. For a discussion of the case, see Gross, "Bulgaria Invokes the Connally Amendment," 56 *Am. J. Int'l L.* 357 (1962).

44. The Nuremberg Tribunal rejected the defense that Germany alone could decide conclusively, in accordance with the reservations made by the parties to the Kellogg-Briand Pact, whether preventive action was a necessity. The Tribunal held that "whether action taken under the claim of self-defense was in fact aggressive or defensive must ultimately be subject to investigation and adjudication if International Law is ever to be enforced." XXII *Trial of the Major War Criminals Before the International Military Tribunal* 450 (1948).

itarian armed conflict. The *Lotus* case itself made no attempt at all to apply the prohibitive theory of international law to a wartime situation.

Any attempt to apply the *Lotus* rationale to the laws of war runs up against an implacable and fatal obstacle: the so-called Martens Clause.[45] The Martens Clause essentially established a diametrically opposed presumption when it came to the employment of new weapons in conditions of warfare. Namely, that a state was not free to use any new weapon it wanted to use so long as it was not specifically prohibited from so doing by a positive norm of international law. Rather, the burden of proof was upon the state itself to justify the use of the new weapon under the existing norms for the international laws of humanitarian armed conflict. To quote from the Martens Clause as found, for example, in the Preamble to the Fourth Hague Convention of 1907, Concerning the Laws and Customs of War on Land,[46] which in turn the Nuremberg Tribunal subsequently held to be binding upon all states as a matter of customary international law at the time of the outbreak of the Second World War:[47]

> Until a more suitable code of laws of war can be drawn up, the high contracting parties deem it expedient to declare that, in cases not covered by the rules adopted by them, the inhabitants and the belligerents remain under the protection and governance of the general principles of the law of nations, derived from the usages established among civilized peoples, from the laws of humanity, and from the dictates of the public conscience.

Thus it is the permissive theory of international law, not the prohib-

45. For a discussion of the Martens Clause, see G. Schwarzenberger, *The Legality of Nuclear Weapons* 10-11 (1958); J. Scott, *The Hague Conventions and the Declarations of 1899 and 1907*, at 102-03 (1915); N. Singh, *Nuclear Weapons and International Law* 60-62 (1959).
46. Convention Concerning the Laws and Customs of War on Land (Hague IV), Oct. 18, 1907, 36 *Stat.* 2277, T.S. No. 539, 1 Bevans 631, *reprinted in* 2 Am. J. Int'l L. 90 (1908). *See also Report to the Hague Conferences of 1899 & 1907*, at 509 (J. Scott ed. 1917).
47. In response to the Nazi argument that Hague Convention No. IV of 1907 did not apply, the Tribunal held:
   The rules of land warfare expressed in the convention undoubtedly represented an advance over existing international law at the time of their adoption. But the convention expressly stated that it was an attempt "to revise the general laws and customs of war," which it thus recognized to be then existing, but by 1939 these rules laid down in the convention were recognized by all civilized nations, and were regarded as being declaratory of the laws and customs of war which are referred to in Article 6(b) of the charter.
XXII *Trial of the Major War Criminals Before the International Military Tribunal* 497 (1948).

itive theory as articulated by *Lotus*, that applies when it comes to determining the propriety of using new weapons during warfare.

Applying the rationale of the Martens Clause to nuclear weapons, one would have to conclude that the only possible use of nuclear weapons that might in an abstract and totally theoretical sense be "justifiable" is one that would, at a minimum, be completely consistent with the conventional and customary international laws of humanitarian armed conflict (i.e., the jus in bello). Yet it is extremely difficult to imagine what such circumstances might be. And whatever these exceedingly rare circumstances conceivably justifying the use of nuclear weapons might possibly be (e.g., a so-called "battlefield" nuclear war in Europe, to be discussed below), it is clear that the current U.S. strategic nuclear deterrence doctrine and practice are neither limited by nor confined to them. If nuclear weapons cannot be used in a manner that does not violate the humanitarian laws of armed conflict, then they cannot be used even during a war of legitimate self-defense. And the same can be said for the threat of their use against cities for the alleged purpose of deterring aggression. The rationale of the *Lotus* case is simply irrelevant to the question of whether or not the threat or use of nuclear weapons is lawful during peace or war.

The Precedential Significance of America's Response to Germany's Policy of Unrestricted Submarine Warfare During the First World War

The fundamental importance of the Martens Clause to the conduct of international armed conflict is not simply a matter of scholarly or pedantic interest alone. For the United States of America ultimately intervened and fought in the First World War precisely in order to vindicate the principle of international law enunciated therein. Namely, that new weapons of warfare, and especially instruments of indiscriminate mass destruction, are subject to the traditional laws of humanitarian armed conflict.[48] During the period of formal American neutrality from 1914 to 1917, it was generally believed within

---

48. This section of the chapter is derived in substantial part from Boyle, "American Foreign Policy Toward International Law and Organizations: 1898-1917," 6 *Loy. L.A. Int'l & Comp. L.J.* 185, 239-51 (1983).

the United States that the quality and quantity of violations of both customary and conventional international law committed by the Allied Powers were of a nature and purpose materially different from and far less heinous than those perpetrated by the Central Powers (i.e., destruction of property versus destruction of life and property, respectively). Of decisive impact upon American public opinion and governmental decision-making processes was Germany's wanton and indiscriminate destruction of innocent human life (American, neutral, and enemy civilian) by institution of its policy of "unrestricted" submarine warfare against merchant vessels and passenger ships. Such behavior was in express violation of several provisions of the unratified Declaration of London (1909) that were generally considered not only to state the customary international law of maritime warfare but, moreover, to embody rudimentary norms of humanitarian conduct for any civilized nation during wartime.

Tactically, German submarine warfare could only partially compensate for the preponderant surface naval supremacy fielded by Great Britain and her allies, who were then quite successfully imposing an economic stranglehold on all neutral commerce that could possibly be destined for Germany and her allies. It was extremely dangerous for a submarine to forego the security afforded by undetected submersion in order to surface and comply with the rules for interdiction of enemy or neutral merchant vessels suspected of transporting contraband that were applicable to surface warships as set forth in the unratified Declaration of London. Indeed, it had become standard British practice to arm its merchant vessels with defensive weapons sufficient to destroy a thin-hulled submarine should it surface, and also to fly neutral flags on British merchant vessels in order to deceive enemy submarine commanders. Under these circumstances, application of the laws for maritime warfare described in the Declaration of London to the conduct of hostilities by submarines would in effect have essentially precluded this new device for waging war for most practical purposes, and thus have provided Great Britain and her allies with a virtually uninterrupted stream of military and commercial products purchased from merchants in neutral states, most particularly the United States, for the duration of the war.

Legally, of course, the German government justified its policy of unrestricted submarine warfare as a legitimate measure of reprisal for the grievous and repeated British violations of the unratified Declaration of London and generally recognized rules of international law, both of which Germany alleged it had been strictly obeying. In addition, Germany complained that the neutral powers, and especially the United States, had been either unable or unwilling to exert enough pressure upon Great Britain to secure its compliance with customary and conventional laws of maritime warfare and neutrality in order to guarantee the continuation of their nationals' recognized right to trade with Germany and her allies. The neutral states' collective failure to effectively prosecute their rights against Great Britain or, in the alternative, their refusal to at least diminish proportionately the free flow of weapons, munitions and supplies to Britain by their own merchants, worked to the substantial military and economic detriment of Germany.

Notwithstanding the validity of some of these German objections, as far as American public and governmental opinion were concerned, if this new instrumentality of warfare could not be effectively utilized without violating international law, then Germany must jettison the submarine, not the humanitarian laws of armed conflict. Germany's persistent refusal to relent and its consequent sinking of merchant ships with large loss of life directly precipitated the U.S. decision to intervene into the war against Germany and later Austria-Hungary, which had endorsed the German practices. As President Woodrow Wilson succinctly phrased it in his April 2, 1917 request to a joint session of Congress for a declaration of war against Germany: "The present German submarine warfare against commerce is a warfare against mankind."[49] America's decision to abandon its neutrality and enter the war ineluctably spelled defeat for the Central Powers. This proved to be the definitive and most effective "sanction" for Germany's egregious violation of the international laws of humanitarian armed conflict by employing this new and quite effective weapon of indiscriminate mass destruction.

Just as the United States government adamantly insisted that the laws of humanitarian armed conflict applied to German submarines during the First World War, so too the same rationale would apply to the threat and use of nuclear weapons. Just as America argued that the fact the submarine could not be effectively used in a manner that

---

49. Address of the President of the United States Delivered at a Joint Session of the Two Houses of Congress (Apr. 2, 1917), *reprinted in* 11 *Am. J. Int'l L.* 143, 144 (Supp. 1917).

was not violative of international law was not sufficient to justify its use, so too the same rationale would apply to prohibit the threat and use of nuclear weapons today. Although international law did not specifically prohibit submarines "as such" then and does not specifically prohibit nuclear weapons "as such" now, nevertheless if these novel instrumentalities of indiscriminate mass destruction could not or cannot be used in a manner that does not violate international law, then they could not or cannot be used. Based upon the legal and political precedent established by the U.S. government with respect to submarines from 1914 to 1917, the correct response to this dilemma is not, as some international lawyers have recently suggested, to declare that nuclear weapons have made the laws of war obsolete. Rather, the solution to the "paradox of deterrence" is the realization that the international laws of humanitarian armed conflict require nuclear weapons to be rendered obsolete as soon as possible.

Paragraph 35 of the U.S. Army Field Manual Reconsidered

The 1955-56 statements by the U.S. Navy and Army do not attempt to grapple with any of these issues or even allow them to interfere with their automatic application of the *Lotus* rationale to allegedly justify the use of nuclear weapons in wartime. Furthermore, they seem to blithely ignore both the Martens Clause and the Nuremberg Principles. Is this defect attributable to faulty analysis on the part of the drafters of these statements? At least in regard to paragraph 35 of the 1956 U.S. Army Field Manual, the answer to that question must clearly be in the negative. The 1956 U.S. Army Field Manual on *The Law of Land Warfare* was drafted anonymously by the late Richard R. Baxter, then professor of international law at the Harvard Law School, and subsequently judge of the International Court of Justice.[50] One thing that all his fellow international law colleagues would agree upon is that Richard Baxter was a meticulously precise drafter of international legal documents. For several years Professor

---

50. Conversation with Waldemar Solf, Adjunct Professor of Law, Washington College of Law, American University. For a succinct account of Professor Baxter's career, see 1979-1980 *I.C.J.Y.B.* 30-31 (1980); 7 *Who Was Who in America* 37 (1977-81).

Baxter taught the course on International Legal Drafting at the Harvard Law School.

Therefore, in deference to the memory and prodigious talents of Professor Baxter, we have to go back and reread the language of the 1956 Army statement quite carefully. If so, we can discern that paragraph 35 of the 1956 Army Field Manual never really supported the standard interpretation accorded to it by government lawyers and their private-sector apologists to the effect that nuclear weapons can permissibly be used during wartime. Referring again to paragraph 35 as quoted above, particular attention should be paid to the words "as such":

> The use of explosive "atomic weapons," whether by air, sea, or land forces, cannot *as such* be regarded as violative of international law in the absence of any customary rule of international law or international convention restricting their employment. [Emphasis added.]

A close reading of this paragraph would indicate that all Professor Baxter intended to say was that the use of atomic weapons cannot be regarded as violative of international law solely because they are "atomic" as opposed to "conventional" weapons. In other words, there is no one conventional or customary rule of international law that specifically prohibits the use of "atomic" weapons by that name—for example, similar to the international conventions specifically prohibiting the use of poison,[51] expanding bullets,[52] or poison gas, bacteriological weapons, toxins,[53] etc. Arguably, of course, the use of atomic weapons might be prohibited by implication from the terms of the Geneva Protocol of 1925.[54] But the United States did not become a party to this convention until 1975, almost twenty years after Professor Baxter drafted the U.S. Army Field Manual.

The interesting part of this particular formulation is what Professor

---

51. Fourth Hague Convention of 1899 Regulations, art. 23, 32 *Stat.* 1803, *T.S.* No. 403, 187 *Parry's T.S.* 429 ("In addition to the prohibition provided by special Conventions, it is especially forbidden: (a) To employ poison or poisoned weapons. . . .").

52. Declaration (IV,3) Concerning Expanding Bullets, July 29, 1899, *reprinted in The Laws of Armed Conflict* 103-05 (D. Schindler & J. Toman eds. 1981).

53. Protocol for the Prohibition of the Use in War of Asphyxiating, Poisonous or other Gases, and of Bacteriological Methods of Warfare, *opened for signature* June 17, 1925, 26 *U.S.T.* 571, *T.I.A.S.* No. 8061, 94 *L.N.T.S.* 65, *reprinted* in 14 *I.L.M.* 49 (1975).

54. *See* Meyrowitz, "Nuclear Weapons Policy: The Ultimate Tyranny," 7 *Nova L.J.* 97, 98 (1982).

Baxter left out. Paragraph 35 never states that the actual use of atomic weapons would not be in violation of the international laws of humanitarian armed conflict and the laws of war. Professor Baxter was too good a draftsman and an international lawyer ever to attempt to make such a specious. and reprehensible argument. Also, the 1956 Army statement so carefully drafted by Professor Baxter purposefully did not repeat the grievous error committed by the 1955 Navy statement, which boldly proclaimed: "In the absence of express prohibition, the use of such weapons against enemy combatants and other military objectives *is permitted.*" (Emphasis added.) And whatever its defects, even this 1955 Navy statement never went so far as to assert that nuclear weapons could lawfully be used against civilian population centers, as opposed to legitimate military targets.

In contrast, Professor Baxter never said that the use of atomic weapons is permitted under any circumstances. He simply stated that their use is not violative of international law simply because they are "atomic" as opposed to "conventional" weapons. Furthermore, Professor Baxter never intended to imply that atomic weapons were exempted to any extent from the application of the customary and conventional international laws of humanitarian armed conflict. To a lawyer who selflessly devoted a substantial part of his professional career to the improvement of this "somewhat exotic field of law" (to use his own appellation), it would have been an apocryphal and highly offensive statement.

Finally, Professor Baxter's 1956 formulation of the problem referred only to "atomic weapons," whereas by contrast the Navy's 1955 manual employed the term "nuclear weapons." The latter term could be interpreted to include within its scope both atomic and thermonuclear devices; while Professor Baxter's terminology could be interpreted to exclude thermonuclear devices. By failing to adopt the Navy's pre-existing terminology on this point, Professor Baxter was perhaps attempting to draw a very subtle distinction between atomic weapons and thermonuclear devices. Because of their enormous destructive power, thermonuclear weapons were originally intended by the United States government to serve as weapons of mass and indiscriminate destruction. For this reason, inter alia, thermonuclear weapons were and still are inherently genocidal and thus absolutely illegal and prohibited.

Hence, the "atomic weapons" mentioned by Professor Baxter in

1956 probably did not refer to any of the thermonuclear bombs that were then part of the U.S. Strategic Air Command's "nuclear" arsenal. In any event, the "atomic weapons" language found in paragraph 35 of the 1956 U.S. Army Field Manual could not be invoked even purportedly to exonerate the threat or use of modern intercontinental ballistic missiles, submarine launched ballistic missiles, theater/intermediate nuclear forces, long-range cruise missiles etc., all of which are armed with thermonuclear warheads. Indeed, according to I *Nuclear Weapons Databook* 38-80 (T. Cochran, W. Arkin, & M. Hoenig eds. 1984), almost two-thirds of the current U.S. nuclear weapons arsenal is armed with thermonuclear devices.

I was privileged enough to have taken Professor Baxter's course on The Laws of War at the Harvard Law School in the Spring Semester of 1975. At that time an entire two-hour class session was devoted to analyzing the legality or illegality of using nuclear weapons under international law. I was struck by the precision with which Professor Baxter dissected the meaning of paragraph 35. He never said that the use of nuclear weapons was permitted under the international laws of humanitarian armed conflict. Nor did he say that the use of nuclear weapons fell outside their reach. To the contrary, the thrust of his analysis seemed to be that the traditional laws of war applied to the use of nuclear weapons, and that "as such" the actual use of nuclear weapons would be in violation of the customary and conventional international laws of humanitarian armed conflict.

As Professor Baxter phrased the dilemma quite succinctly in a written question posed for class discussion: "Would it be possible to frame *any* workable rules on the employment of nuclear weapons falling short of an outright prohibition?" (Emphasis added.) In my opinion, Professor Baxter never answered that question in the affirmative because he found it exceedingly difficult to conceive of any such circumstances where the use of nuclear weapons that was then realistically contemplated by the United States government could be permissible under the international laws of humanitarian armed conflict. It seemed pretty clear from the class discussion that Professor Baxter did not believe it possible to formulate such rules because the use of nuclear weapons simply could not be justified under international law.[55]

55. *Cf.* Baxter, "The Role of Law in Modern War," 47 *Am. Soc'y Int'l L. Proc.* 90, 91-92, 120 (1953).

I would submit, therefore, that paragraph 35 of the U.S. Army Field Manual as drafted by Richard R. Baxter was never intended to imply that the use of nuclear weapons would not violate the international laws of humanitarian armed conflict, whether customary or conventional. Hence government lawyers and their academic apologists are completely incorrect to cite paragraph 35 in support of the dubious proposition that the threat or use of nuclear weapons would be permissible by the United States government in legitimate self-defense during peace or war. Indeed, at the very time Professor Baxter was busy drafting the U.S. Army Field Manual, the Eisenhower administration was promulgating its strategic nuclear deterrence doctrine known as "massive retaliation" upon Soviet population centers in the event of a prior nuclear or conventional attack by the Soviet Union upon the United States or members of the NATO alliance. Quite obviously the doctrine of "massive retaliation" represented the exact antithesis of Professor Baxter's cherished notion that there existed such a phenomenon known as the jus in bello.

The Illegality of U.S. Nuclear Deterrence Doctrine Promotes Military Insubordination

The statement that there actually exists such an entity known as the international laws of humanitarian armed conflict seems to represent a contradiction in basic terms to many people who are ignorant of international law. A fortiori this would appear to be the case when it comes to the threat or use of nuclear weapons, which by definition seem to repudiate the very idea of the laws of war. Those who scoff at the international laws of humanitarian armed conflict, however, are usually academic political scientists or civilian government officials who operate upon the hard-nosed "realist" premise that war is hell, and thus there must be no rules when it comes to warfare, especially involving the use of nuclear weapons. Yet the primary reason behind the historical development of U.S. nuclear deterrence doctrine to the current point of imminent human extinction has been the completely antinomian prescriptions offered by academic think-tank theorists operating on the basis of such Machiavellian assumptions.

Nevertheless, most of these civilian officials or theorists will not be directly involved in the execution (though certainly some will be involved in the planning and ordering) of any nuclear weapons attack by the United States government against the Soviet Union. Rather the plans will be carried out by professional members of the United States military establishment. It is a truism to state that the officers and enlisted men of the United States military represent the strongest group of individuals in this country who give their full-fledged and unequivocal support to the humanitarian laws of armed conflict precisely because these rules were originally and primarily designed to protect them.[56] Any U.S. civilian government official or academic theorist who believes to the contrary is dead wrong and acts at his peril in contradistinction to this basic fact. Whether they like it or not, therefore, civilian nuclear decision-makers must take considerations of international law into account because their military counterparts have been trained, and indeed ordered to do so.

It is a requirement of the Geneva Conventions of 1949 that all U.S. military personnel be indoctrinated into the international laws of humanitarian armed conflict.[57] Part of this indoctrination includes the admonition that they must not carry out any order that they know to be illegal.[58] Moreover, the Nuremberg Tribunal went even one

---

56. *See* F. Lieber, General Order No. 100, Adjutant-General's Office, Instructions for the Government of Armies of the United States in the Field, *reprinted in The Laws of Armed Conflict, supra* note 52, at 3. *See generally* Davis, "Doctor Francis Lieber's Instructions for the Government of Armies in the Field," 1 *Am. J. Int'l L.* 13 (1907).

57. *See* Geneva Convention Relative to the Protection of Civilian Persons in Time of War, Aug. 12, 1949, 6 *U.S.T.* 3516, *T.I.A.S.* No. 3365, 75 *U.N.T.S.* 287:

Article 144. The High Contracting Parties undertake, in time of peace as in time of war, to disseminate the text of the present Convention as widely as possible in their respective countries, and, in particular, to include the study thereof in their programmes of military and, if possible, civil instruction, so that the principles thereof may become known to the entire population.

Any civilian, military, police or other authorities, who in time of war assume responsibilities in respect of protected persons, must possess the text of the Convention and be specially instructed as to its provisions.

58. Members of the armed forces are bound to obey only lawful orders. *See* Uniform Code of Military Justice art. 90, 10 *U.S.C.A.* § 890 (1982) (assaulting or willfully disobeying superior commissioned officer). Paragraph 509 of *The Law of Land Warfare, supra* note 10, at 182 provides as follows:

509. Defense of Superior Orders

a. The fact that the law of war has been violated pursuant to an order of a superior authority, whether military or civil, does not deprive the act in question of its character of a war crime, nor does it constitute a defense in the trial of an accused individual, *unless he did not know and could not reasonably have been expected to know that the act ordered was unlawful.* In all cases where the order is held not to constitute a defense to an allegation of war crime, the fact that the individual was acting pursuant to orders may be considered in mitigation of punishment.

b. In considering the question whether a superior order constitutes a valid defense, the court shall take into consideration the fact that obedience to lawful military step further by establishing personal criminal responsibility for participation by military subordinates in the commission of crimes against peace, crimes against humanity and war crimes so long as there can be said to exist a "moral choice" for them to refuse to obey clearly illegal orders to that effect:[59]

> It was also submitted on behalf of most of these defendants that in doing what they did they were acting under the orders of Hitler, and therefore cannot be held responsible for the acts committed by them in carrying out these orders. The Charter specifically provides in Article 8:
>
>> "The fact that the defendant acted pursuant to order of his Government or of a superior shall not free him from responsibility, but may be considered in mitigation of punishment."
>
> The provisions of this article are in conformity with the law of all nations. *That a soldier was ordered to kill or torture in violation of the international law of war has never been recognized as a defense to such acts of brutality, though, as the Charter here provides, the order may be urged in mitigation of the punishment. The true test, which is found in varying degrees in the criminal law of most nations, is not the existence of the order, but whether moral choice was in fact possible.* [Emphasis added.]

Thus, according to the Nuremberg Principles as well, all U.S. military personnel assigned to nuclear missions would be obligated to refuse to perform any such illegal orders for waging strategic nuclear warfare against the Soviet Union upon pain of suffering personal criminal responsibility, punishment and perhaps execution as war criminals.

To be sure, it is not absolutely certain that members of the U.S. military establishment might not carry out orders given to them by civilian officials that are egregiously illegal such as a nuclear first-strike or countercity attack. But there does exist a distinct probability that some soldiers might exercise their moral choice to refuse to do

---

orders is the duty of every member of the armed forces; that the latter cannot be expected, in conditions of war discipline, to weigh scrupulously the legal merits of the orders received; that certain rules of warfare may be controversial; or that an act otherwise amounting to a war crime may be done in obedience to orders conceived as a measure of reprisal. *At the same time it must be borne in mind that members of the armed forces are bound to obey only lawful orders* (e.g., UCMJ, Art. 92). [Emphasis added.]
See also United States v. Calley, 48 C.M.R. 19, 22 U.S.C.M.A. 534 (1973).

59. *See* XXII *Trial of the Major War Criminals Before the International Military Tribunal* 466 (1948).

so. And the distinct probability that some members of the U.S. military might refuse to obey egregiously unlawful orders given by civilian officials to wage a nuclear war against the Soviet Union provides the most compelling reason why U.S. nuclear deterrence theory and practice must be reexamined in light of the rules of international law.

To frame this problem in a more concrete manner: How should U.S. civilian government officials deal today with the fact that there exists a distinct possibility that the U.S. military officer routinely assigned to accompany the president at all times with the code for launching U.S. nuclear weapons—contained in that infamous attaché case handcuffed to his wrist—might someday in the future refuse to allow the president access to the code when so ordered because he believed he was obligated by both international law and U.S. domestic law not to become an accomplice to the commission of crimes against peace, crimes against humanity, and war crimes?

A strategic nuclear deterrence policy that is totally inconsistent with international law, to which the U.S. military establishment fully subscribes, is militarily counterproductive and thus politically unworkable because it lacks credibility, consistency, and staying power. Deterrence as a theory can not succeed for the United States over the long run (which it must) if it is premised upon egregiously illegal and/or immoral assumptions that are totally unacceptable to the American people, to the civilian government officials in charge of its design, and especially to the members of the United States military forces who would be in charge of its execution. In particular, any U.S. nuclear deterrent doctrine must take into account the legal and moral training, beliefs, and convictions of the members of the U.S. military establishment.

For example, there have been reported instances in which U.S. nuclear missile control officers have refused to fire under a mock nuclear attack. There have been other instances in which U.S. nuclear missile control officers have asked to be relieved of their positions because they believed that their assigned missions were completely inconsistent with the laws of war training they had received when they were indoctrinated into the military. There is another instance where an ICBM missile control officer was trained to engage in first-strike scenarios and subsequently left the military rather than continue to do so because he believed such training to be illegal and immoral.[60]

This author suspects that there exists a fairly large number of professional military officers and enlisted men assigned to nuclear missions who possess enormous doubts as to the legal and moral legitimacy of their delegated tasks. If that is the case, how reliable are any of them? Men and women are not robots. They are going to question whatever order that might be given to them for the use of nuclear weapons in any event, especially when it is highly probable that they will perish as a result of the process. As Professor Alfred Rubin from the Fletcher School of Law and Diplomacy has aptly put it, a missile control officer who has been ordered to turn the key will think long and hard about it when he realizes that he himself will probably be meeting his creator in less than fifteen minutes.[61] He might decide that it is better to do so with a clean conscience rather than have to bear responsibility for the deaths of millions of people.

The Nuremberg Tribunal expressly endowed such moral considerations with an international legal significance when it established the appropriate standard of personal criminal responsibility for participation by subordinates in the commission of crimes against peace, crimes against humanity, and war crimes. Hence, human morality—whether premised upon religious, ethical, or humanistic grounds—becomes both legally and therefore politically relevant to determining the validity and thus the effectiveness of nuclear deterrence. Whether or not there is a heaven, it is certainly true that many, if not a majority of people in the U.S. military services are religious, have faith in God, and believe in an afterlife. If so, then the United States government cannot effectively assign to them nuclear missions which, in their opinion, might put their souls in eternal jeopardy. According to the holding of the Nuremberg Judgment, they would be not simply entitled but indeed obligated to exercise their moral choice in this matter by refusing to obey clearly illegal orders given by their military superiors or civilian government officials to wage strategic nuclear warfare against the Soviet Union.

---

60. *See, e.g., Washington Post* (Parade), Aug. 14, 1983, at 10-11; Day, "Captain Coleman's Challenging Job and Why He Decided to Leave It," *Progressive,* Aug. 1981, at 27; *N.Y. Times,* Nov. 29, 1981, at A57, col. 1.

61. 76 *Am. Soc'y Int'l L. Proc.* 345 (1982).

Launch on Warning

The above argument is not intended to serve as an exoneration of the U.S. military establishment from any degree of legal and political responsibility for the development of the world's nuclear predicament to the current point of impending extinction for the human race. Nor is it intended to recommend the abolition of the constitutionally mandated system for civilian control over the military establishment throughout the United States government. In the event U.S. civilian government officials some day order their military subordinates to launch and wage a nuclear war against the Soviet Union, substantial numbers of U.S. military personnel will undoubtedly do their utmost to discharge their appointed tasks, and the devastation will be truly catastrophic for the entire planet. But any notion that a counterforce nuclear war can be kept "limited" assumes, among other imponderables, that most if not all U.S. military personnel assigned to nuclear missions can and will do precisely what they are told. This will certainly not be the case during a future nuclear crisis or war.[62]

Even more immediately, however, the fundamental illegality of U.S. nuclear deterrence doctrine and practice exercises a most profoundly corrosive effect on the internal fiber of the U.S. military establishment. It has done the same to the nature of the U.S. constitutional system of government purportedly operating under the rule of law. The essential lawlessness of nuclear deterrence not only promotes military insubordination, but also encourages both violent and nonviolent civil resistance actions by concerned U.S. citizens to bring their government into compliance with the requirements of international, domestic, and constitutional law.

Meanwhile, the inescapability of this former dilemma—whereby the fundamental illegality of nuclear deterrence inevitably promotes military insubordination—has led some academic think-tank theorists to conclude that the human element must be removed from the U.S. nuclear command system. Of course that would be impossible and unconstitutional to do completely. Nevertheless, it has been suggested that the United States government must move to what is known as a "launch on warning" nuclear response doctrine instead of the second-strike scenario it now supposedly adheres to. According to

---

62. *Cf.* G. Allison, *Essence of Decision* (1971).

this frightening concept, once U.S. satellites have sensed the launch of Soviet ICBMs, the retaliation by U.S. ICBMs would be almost automatic, triggered by computer. The definitive objection to this theory, however, is that the U.S. government has witnessed too many instances in which its computers related to the sensing and ordering of a nuclear attack have malfunctioned.[63] If that has been the case for the United States, it must certainly be true for the Soviet Union operating under the restraints of its far less sophisticated satellite and computer technology.

Overwhelming considerations of human survival should ineluctably compel the United States government to propose to the Soviet Union the conclusion of an international agreement expressly prohibiting their respective civilian government officials and military officers from ever adopting a "launch on warning" policy, as well as the testing and deployment of any technological measures or facilities ancillary thereto. Yet today the Reagan administration is rapidly deploying offensive, first-strike counterforce strategic nuclear weapons systems such as the MX, Trident 2/Delta 5 warhead, Pershing 2, and Minuteman 3/MK-12A warhead. These new American weapons systems make it extraordinarily difficult for the Soviet Union to refrain from formally or informally adopting a "launch on warning" policy, whereupon the United States government would feel compelled to respond in kind. Mutual adoption of "launch on warning" policies by both superpowers would create an enormous, almost inexorable incentive for either one to strike first in the event another critical geopolitical crisis breaks out between them along the lines of the Berlin Airlift, the Cuban Missile Crisis, or the Yom Kippur War.

There exists no conceivable justification under international law for the deployment of any one of these offensive, first-strike counterforce strategic nuclear weapons systems, let alone all four simultaneously.[64] The only argument in their favor is the Reagan administration's Machiavellian assertion that it is necessary for the U.S. government to develop the capability to "prevail" in a "protracted nuclear war"—not in the realistic expectation that a counterforce strategic nuclear war can actually be fought and won, but

---

63. During an 18 month period, NORAD experienced 151 false alarms, four of which were considered to be serious enough that B-52 crews and ICBM units were placed on increased alert. *N.Y. Times*, Oct. 10, 1980, at A10, col. 1.

64. *See* Boyle, "Nuclear Weapons and International Law: The Arms Control Dimension," 4 *N.Y.L. Sch. J. Int'l & Comp. L.* 257, 267-76 (1983).

in the misguided belief that obtaining the apparent capability to do so will more effectively deter a nuclear or conventional attack by the Soviet Union upon the United States or NATO than could either MAD or "flexible response." But if that premise is invalid, then the supposed need for the deployment of this new and unprecedented generation of U.S. first-strike counterforce strategic nuclear weapons systems disappears. These complex issues of nuclear and conventional deterrence will be addressed in the following sections of this chapter.

Analyzing the Legality or Illegality of the Reagan Administration's "Protracted Nuclear War-Prevailing" Deterrence Doctrine

Quite recently and most insidiously, members of the U.S. foreign affairs and defense establishment have been invoking the sentiment behind the international laws of humanitarian armed conflict in order to manipulate some people into supporting the proposition that the Reagan administration's announced intention to develop the capability to "prevail" in a "protracted nuclear war" is somehow more "humane" and therefore "more lawful" or at least "less illegal" than preceding theories of strategic nuclear deterrence pursued by the United States government such as MAD or "flexible response."[65] This specious argument maintains that by creating for the president the option of ordering a "limited" nuclear strike against Soviet ICBM silos and hardened command centers by means of the prior deployment of new counterforce strategic nuclear weapons systems such as the MX, Pershing 2, Minuteman 3/MK-12A warhead, and the Trident 2/Delta 5 warhead, in the event of a Soviet first-strike against U.S. ICBM silos the president could at least initially avoid ordering an all-out strategic nuclear attack upon Soviet population centers and therefore, hopefully, avert global nuclear suicide. According to this rationale, when analyzed from the perspective of the humanitarian laws of armed conflict, such counterforce nuclear weapons become preferable to extant strategic nuclear weapons systems which do not possess the requisite combination of survivability, reliability, speed,

---

65. *See, e.g.,* C. Builder & M. Graubard, *The International Law of Armed Conflict: Implications for the Concept of Assured Destruction* 34-37 (1982).

accuracy, ability to penetrate defenses, and explosive power necessary to be used in a counterforce as opposed to their traditional
countercity mode.

Superficially, therefore, considerations of international law might
at first glance seem to support the Reagan administration's shift from
MAD to developing a "protracted nuclear war-prevailing" capability
because, somewhat paradoxically, the latter's underlying counterforce philosophy seems to more closely comport with the general
prohibition against indiscriminate bombardment of civilian population centers than does the former's countercity philosophy. Surely,
the Reagan administration apologists argue, it would be far better
from a humanitarian, legal, moral, or ethical perspective to provide
the president with such new weapons now, because they would
enable him to fight a "limited counterforce" instead of an "all-out
countercity" nuclear war. Of course this entire line of argument
assumes that what starts out as a "limited counterforce" nuclear war
would not ineluctably and quite rapidly escalate into an "all-out
countercity" nuclear war. Most civilian government officials and
military experts believe to the contrary: There is no way a counterforce nuclear war between the United States and the Soviet Union
could be kept "limited." The general consensus of opinions held by
responsible political and military leaders (as opposed to academic
professionals or think-tank theorists) on both sides of the "balance
of terror" is that a "limited" nuclear war cannot be fought without
running an unacceptable risk of escalation into strategic nuclear warfare between the two superpowers.[66]

Putting aside this inherent escalatory potential into nuclear Armageddon, we must directly address the question whether or not the
Reagan administration's "protracted nuclear war-prevailing" doctrine can be justified on the grounds that it is more lawful or at least
less illegal than MAD or "flexible response." This argument seems
to constitute the primary legal-moral-ethical justification propounded
by the Reagan administration for its alleged decision to formally
abandon "mutual assured destruction" as the bedrock of American
strategic nuclear deterrence theory, as well as to pursue its so-called

---

66. *See, e.g., N.Y. Times,* Nov. 7, 1981, at A6, col. 3 (Soviet Defense Minister Dmitri
Ustinov); *N.Y. Times,* Oct. 21, 1981, at A5, col. 1 (Leonid Brezhnev); *N.Y. Times,* Oct. 25,
1981, at A3, col. 4 (Michael Foote); *U.S. News & World Rep.,* Apr. 26, 1982, at 17 (George
Kennan).

Strategic Defense Initiative (SDI) of attempting to create a seemingly effective land-based and spaced-based defense for U.S. ICBM forces, hardened command centers, and maybe some civilian population concentrations against incoming Soviet nuclear warheads.[67] Hence determining the correct answer to this question goes to the very heart of the Reagan administration's massive nuclear and conventional weapons buildup, together with its correlative lack of any genuine commitment to the negotiation of realistic nuclear arms control and reduction agreements with the Soviet Union.[68]

The Theory Versus the Reality of U.S. Strategic Nuclear Deterrence

Although the above rationale might be the theory behind the justification for the Reagan administration's development of a U.S. protracted nuclear war-prevailing capability, the practice of strategic nuclear deterrence is something totally different. And although the theory might be superficially justifiable as an abstract proposition, such a justification becomes meaningless if the theory has little material bearing upon the actual practice of strategic nuclear deterrence. Throughout any analysis of the legality or illegality of the threat to use nuclear weapons it becomes critical to distinguish between U.S. strategic nuclear deterrence doctrine in theory and in practice. This distinction is important because there exists an enormous difference between the two.

Historically I have divided the evolutionary development of U.S. nuclear weapons deterrence theory into the periods of: (1) massive retaliation; (2) mutual assured destruction; (3) flexible response; (4) the Schlesinger Doctrine; and (5) Presidential Directive 59. These were the theories that the United States government propounded in public as to what motivated the planned use of its nuclear weapons deterrence systems. Yet the truth of the matter was that these theories

---

67. In a televised speech aimed at defending a 10% increase in military spending in 1984, President Reagan appealed to modern technology to develop a program of defense measures for the future whereby deterrence would be based not upon the Soviet Union's fear of immediate U.S. retaliation to a nuclear attack but, rather, upon the capability of the U.S. to "intercept and destroy strategic ballistic missiles before they reached our own soil or that of our allies." *N.Y. Times*, Mar. 24, 1983, at A20, col. 5.

68. *See* Boyle, *supra* note 64, at 277. *See also* S. Talbot, *Deadly Gambits* (1984).

were used essentially for two purposes: either (1) to win election or re-election by certain presidential candidates; and/or (2) to justify the acquisition or non-acquisition of new nuclear weapon systems or conventional military forces, as well as the expenditure or non-expenditure of funds incidental thereto.[69] In essence these theories bore some relevance to the actual practice of U.S. nuclear weapons deterrence, but the theories were never determinative of the practices. For the latter can only be found in the U.S. government's currently existing plans for the actual *targeting* of its strategic nuclear weapons forces.

The actual practice of U.S. strategic nuclear weapons targeting consists of what is known as the Single Integrated Operational Plan (SIOP).[70] The SIOP contains the actual list of and priority among military, political, economic, and civilian targets in the Soviet Union that will be destroyed in the event of a nuclear war. Very little if anything is revealed about the SIOP in the public record because its exact contents are highly classified. As of today, however, we do know that the SIOP has supposedly gone through several distinct phases, in theory at least along the lines of the evolution of the different stages outlined above.[71]

In fact, however, the general consensus seems to be that irrespective of any changes in the publicly declared theory, what actually happened was that as these theories were used to justify the acquisition of new nuclear weapons systems, more targets were simply added to the list.[72] Since the United States now possesses approximately 10,000 strategic nuclear warheads designated for use on the Soviet heartland,[73] it is probably the case that every Soviet city of even a minor size, every economic and industrial complex of even minor size, all military bases and installations, every airfield and even auxiliary airfields in the Soviet Union, are currently listed on the SIOP for destruction in a prearranged order of priority,[74] with many targets scheduled to be destroyed several times over. And as the United States government moves forward to acquiring thousands of more

69. P. Pringle & W. Arkin, *SIOP: The Secret U.S. Plan for Nuclear War* 108-09, 189 (1983).
70. *See, e.g.*, P. Bracken, *The Command and Control of Nuclear Forces* 74 (1983); Pringle & Arkin, *supra* note 69; Powers, "Choosing a Strategy for WWIII," *Atl. Monthly*, Nov. 1982, at 82, 92-95.
71. *See, e.g.*, Bracken, *supra* note 70, at 85, 91.
72. Pringle & Arkin, *supra* note 69, at 169-79, 186, 188-89.
73. *Id.* at 37.
74. *Id.*

nuclear weapons systems such as ground, sea and air launched cruise missiles, Bl and Stealth bombers, Pershing 2s, the MX, Midgetman, and Trident 2, targets that are even more insignificant will simply be added to the SIOP.

What is most likely to occur is that once the president of the United States is given these new weapons systems, no alteration in the SIOP will be made to reflect Reagan's allegedly more humanitarian theory of "counterforce" nuclear targeting. Rather, all that will probably happen is that the newer weapons systems will be assigned to destroy the higher priority targets, the older systems will be assigned to destroy lower priority targets, and some even more infinitesimally insignificant targets will be added to the bottom of the SIOP and targeted by the oldest systems. So, although the Reagan administration's "counterforce" doctrine might at first blush appear to be somewhat justifiable in an abstract and totally theoretical sense, the fact of the matter is that the doctrine will not be implemented in the practice of strategic nuclear targeting, which is all that really counts.

The Counterproductivity of the Reagan Administration's SIOP

The highly classified nature of the SIOP does create a serious methodological problem for any study of the legality or illegality of strategic nuclear deterrence. Namely, we simply do not have access to it and can only make our best estimate of what it might contain. In an ideal situation we would be able to examine the records of the Joint Strategic Target Planning Staff (JSTPS) in order to determine whether or not they have added, allocated, and prioritized targets for the SIOP in accordance with any theory that takes into account considerations of international law.[75] To the contrary, I suspect that most probably the SIOP is totally lawless and completely unjustifiable in accordance with any standard of international law, political and personal morality, or human sanity whatever the publicly proclaimed theory as to the contemplated use of nuclear weapons. And this has

---

75. *See generally* Ball, "Targeting for Strategic Deterrence," *Adelphi Papers* No. 185 (1983); Ball, "U.S. Strategic Forces: How Would They Be Used?" 7 *Int'l Security* 31 (1982/83); Carter, "The Command and Control of Nuclear War," 1985 *Sci. Am.* 32; Mariska, "The Single Integrated Operational Plan," *Mil. Rev.*, March 1972, at 33; O'Malley, "JSTPS: The Link Between Strategy and Execution," *Air U. Rev.*, May-June 1977, at 39.

probably always been the case since at least the time of the Eisenhower administration and its doctrine of massive retaliation. A fortiori this would be especially true after the Reagan administration has successfully deployed those strategic nuclear weapons systems such as the MX, Pershing 2, cruise missiles, and the Trident 2/Delta 5 that are supposedly designed for the specific purpose of "prevailing" in a "protracted" counterforce strategic nuclear war.

Indeed, it now seems to be the case that the Reagan administration is spending its time, effort and excess of new nuclear weapons systems to select as additional targets for their current version of the SIOP semi-hardened or superficially-hardened bunkers that have been constructed for the Russian equivalent of U.S. mayors for even very small towns in the Soviet Union.[76] The theory behind such "elite" targeting is that the destruction of the entirety of the Soviet political leadership will prevent a reassertion of control over the domestic population in a post-nuclear war era.[77] Of course this targeting rationale further assumes that there will exist civilian population concentrations of any significance in the Soviet Union after a nuclear holocaust, which is highly unlikely. Or to phrase this problem more concretely, in the aftermath of a nuclear holocaust what political, military or economic difference will it make if the Soviet counterpart to the mayor of Mattoon, Illinois (population 19,800) is alive or dead?

Even more problematically, however, if as the Reagan administration apparently believes, the Soviet government is on the brink of political and economic collapse,[78] it would make far more sense not to target anywhere near many Soviet civilian population centers so that in the event of a general war the various national ethnic groups could rise up in revolution to overthrow their Great Russian oppressors. This they did once before en masse during the First World War when the Tsarist Empire collapsed.[79] And during the Second World War several ethnic groups such as the Ukrainians and Volga Germans proved completely unreliable.[80] Why should the Reagan administra-

---

76. Cf. *The Use of Force* (R. Art & K. Waltz eds. 1983).

77. R. Jervis, *The Illogic of American Nuclear Strategy* 71-72 (1984).

78. See Shultz, "U.S.-Soviet Relations in the Context of U.S. Foreign Policy," *Dep't. St. Bull.*, July 1983, at 65, 66; Reagan, "Arms Control and the Future of East-West Relations," *Dep't. St. Bull.*, May 1982, at 34, 35.

79. See I. Gray, *The First Fifty Years: Soviet Russia 1917-67*, at 159-61, 175 (1967); G. von Rauch, *A History of Soviet Russia* 78-87 (1972).

80. See B. Dmytryshyn, *U.S.S.R.: A Concise History* (1978); *Soviet Nationalities Policy in Practice* 102 (R. Conquest ed. 1967) (Praeger Publications in Russian History and World Communism No. 199).

tion target near civilian population centers in these regions or in Soviet Central Asia when their respective populaces are markedly hostile to the Great Russian administration of the Soviet empire in the first place?

In the alternative, it has been reported that during the Carter administration various government officials supervised the construction of a SIOP that incorporated a philosophy of so-called "counter-ethnic targeting" with respect to the Soviet Union.[81] In other words, major population centers inhabited primarily by the Great Russian people were selected for repeated and especially severe nuclear destruction because of their constituent ethnicity alone. (Apparently Carter's national security adviser Zbigniew Brzezinski—an expatriate Pole—participated in this enterprise with a great deal of fervor.) Whatever the alleged justification for this practice, all U.S. government officials who were involved in the nuclear targeting of ethnic groups as such actually committed the international crime of conspiracy to commit genocide, as recognized by articles 1, 2, 3 and 4 of the U.N. Convention on the Prevention and Punishment of the Crime of Genocide (1948).[82] And to the extent that the Reagan administration has merely continued to incorporate the Carter administra-

---

81. W. Arkin & P. Pringle, *SIOP: The Secret U.S. Plan for Nuclear War,* 189-190 (1983).
82. Genocide Convention of 1948, 78 *U.N.T.S.* 277 (signed by U.S. on Dec. 11, 1948), *reprinted* in N. Robinson, *The Genocide Convention: A Commentary* (1960).

ARTICLE I

The Contracting Parties confirm that genocide whether committed in time of peace or in time of war, is a crime under international law which they undertake to prevent and to punish.

ARTICLE II

In the present Convention, genocide means any of the following acts committed with intent to destroy, in whole or in part, a national, ethnical, racial or religious group, as such:

(a) Killing members of the group;
(b) Causing serious bodily or mental harm to members of the group;
(c) Deliberately inflicting on the group conditions of life calculated to bring about its physical destruction in whole or in part;
(d) Imposing measures intended to prevent births within the group;
(e) Forcibly transferring children of the group to another group.

ARTICLE III

The following acts shall be punishable:

(a) Genocide;
(b) Conspiracy to commit genocide;
(c) Direct and public incitement to commit genocide;
(d) Attempt to commit genocide;
(e) Complicity in genocide.

ARTICLE IV

Persons committing genocide or any of the other acts enumerated in article III shall be punished, whether they are constitutionally responsible rulers, public officials or private individuals.

tion's counter-ethnic targeting philosophy in its version of the SIOP, all civilian and military government officials who knew or should have known about this practice and are in a position to terminate it must assume full personal responsibility under international law for actually committing the crime of conspiracy to commit genocide.[83] So much for the alleged legality of the Reagan administration's revised and improved rendition of Carter's Presidential Directive 59.

A Preemptive Nuclear Strike Upon the Soviet Union

The Reagan administration's counterargument in support of the deployment of these offensive, first-strike counterforce strategic nuclear weapons systems such as the MX, Pershing 2, and Trident 2 is that the Soviet Union currently possesses the option to launch a surprise nuclear attack upon U.S. ICBM silos, and therefore that the United States must match the Soviet capability in this regard.[84] Despite the harrangue by the Committee on the Present Danger, however, and later under its influence by the Reagan campaign and administration, there is absolutely no indication that the Soviets have or will have the capability to launch a "disarming" surprise first-strike upon U.S. ICBM silos.[85] Even if the Soviets did, U.S. SLBM's and quick-alert bombers would still remain secure for the purpose of executing a retaliatory attack.[86] The high probability of such an eventuality should be sufficient to deter any type of Soviet first-strike counterforce nuclear attack upon the United States.

83. Department of the Army Field Manual, *The Law of Land Warfare,* ¶ 501 (1956).
    501. Responsibility for Acts of Subordinates
    In some cases, military commanders may be responsible for war crimes committed by subordinate members of the armed forces, or other persons subject to their control. Thus, for instance, when troops commit massacres and atrocities against the civilian population of occupied territory or against prisoners of war, the responsibility may rest not only with the actual perpetrators but also with the commander. Such a responsibility arises directly when the acts in question have been committed in pursuance of an order of the commander concerned. The commander is also responsible if he has actual knowledge, or should have knowledge, through reports received by him or through other means, that troops or other persons subject to his control are about to commit or have committed a war crime and he fails to take the necessary and reasonable steps to insure compliance with the law of war or to punish violators thereof.
See also *Application of Yamashita,* 327 U.S. 1 (1946).
    84. *See* Reagan, "Peace and National Security," *Dep't. St. Bull.,* April 1983, at 8-9; Reagan, "U.S. Strategic Weapons Program," *Dep't. St. Bull.,* Dec. 1981, at 67-69.
    85. *See* Boyle, *supra* note 64, at 271.
    86. *See id. See also Report of the President's Commission on Strategic Forces* (Apr. 6, 1983).

But putting these technical arguments aside, it is crucial to address the legal, moral and philosophical dimensions of Reagan's argument in favor of the U.S. government reciprocating some alleged Soviet capability to launch a surprise nuclear attack upon its adversary. Just because the Soviet Union might someday decide to pursue a patently illegal policy of developing a first-strike counterforce strategic nuclear weapons capability provides absolutely no good reason why the U.S. government should automatically do the same. The United States of America has to analyze the strategic nuclear equation in light of both its own vital national interests and its own cherished national values. In particular, America cannot abandon or pervert its national values simply because its adversary might not share them. Likewise, America cannot ignore its vital national interest in upholding the international legal order just because the Soviets might not share that same interest. If America mimics the Soviets, then America gradually becomes like them and eventually becomes indistinguishable from them in the eyes of our allies, neutrals, adversaries, and, most tragically of all, ourselves. In other words, the United States government will become just as Machiavellian in its conduct of both foreign affairs and domestic policy as the Soviets allegedly are, though this author does not subscribe to such a demonical interpretation of Soviet behavior.

Therefore, even if the Soviet Union sets out to develop an offensive first-strike counterforce strategic nuclear weapons capability against U.S. ICBM silos, that does not provide either a sufficient justification or a sound reason for the United States to do the same. We must not imitate the Soviets under any circumstances. They must not become the ones who dictate our nuclear weapons policies to us. Indeed, if the SALT II Treaty had been ratified by the United States of America, as it has been by the Soviet Union,[87] there would exist no hypothetical rationale for either superpower to pursue the development of a first-strike counterforce strategic nuclear weapons capability. The main obstacle to the prevention of a first-strike nuclear arms race between the two superpowers has proven to be the Reagan administration's

---

87. *See The Current Digest of the Soviet Press*, July 18, 1979, at 13 (The Politburo of the CPSU Central Committee, the Presidium of the USSR Supreme Soviet, and the USSR Council of Ministers wholly and completely approve of the Salt II Treaty). The law adopted by the USSR Supreme Soviet on July 6, 1978, *Vedomosti SSSR* (1978), no. 28, item 439, Article 11, *reprinted in* W. Butler, *Basic Documents on the Soviet Legal System* 288 (1983) states "In accordance with the USSR Constitution, the international treaties of the USSR shall be ratified by the Presidium of the USSR Supreme Soviet."

obstinate refusal to support the ratification of the SALT II Treaty because the latter is alleged to be "fatally flawed" in some mysterious manner.[88] The time has long passed for the Reagan administration to have abandoned the anti-Carter rhetoric of the Reagan campaign.

Nuclear Deterrence of Conventional Warfare

We must set aside all the exotic theories of strategic nuclear deterrence that have been developed by the United States government to start with the basic premise that in accordance with the fundamental rules of international law, the threat to use nuclear weapons can only be justified, if at all, on the grounds of legitimate self-defense as recognized by article 51 of the United Nations Charter. But although the requirement of legitimate self-defense is a necessary precondition for the legality of any theory of nuclear deterrence, it is certainly not sufficient. For the threat to use nuclear weapons must also take into account the customary and conventional international laws of humanitarian armed conflict.

Professor Burns H. Weston at the University of Iowa College of Law has usefully reduced the essence of the international laws of humanitarian armed conflict into six basic principles:[89]

Rule 1. It is prohibited to use weapons or tactics that cause unnecessary or aggravated devastation and suffering.

Rule 2. It is prohibited to use weapons or tactics that cause indiscriminate harm as between combatants and noncombatant military and civilian personnel.

Rule 3. It is prohibited to use weapons or tactics that cause widespread, long-term and severe damage to the natural environment.

Rule 4. It is prohibited to effect reprisals that are disproportionate to their antecedent provocation or to legitimate military objectives, or disrespectful of persons, institutions and resources otherwise protected by the laws of war.

Rule 5. It is prohibited to use weapons or tactics that violate the neutral jurisdiction of nonparticipating states.

Rule 6. It is prohibited to use asphyxiating, poisonous or other

---

88. *See* Boyle, *supra* note 64, at 278.

89. Weston, "Nuclear Weapons Versus International Law: A Contextual Reassessment," 28 *McGill Law J.* 542, 554 (1983).

gases, and all analogous liquids, materials or devices, including
bacteriological methods of warfare.

At first glance it would appear that the only type of threatened nuclear
warfare now realistically contemplated by the United States government which might in a totally theoretical sense be somewhat consistent with the criteria of international humanitarian law could
possibly be a "battlefield nuclear war" in Europe. Certainly the most
important of all circumstances under which the U. S. government
forthrightly proclaims its near instantaneous readiness to use nuclear
weapons concerns the "defense" of the NATO alliance. It is longstanding American governmental policy that in the event of a Soviet
conventional attack upon Western Europe, the United States is fully
prepared to respond with nuclear weapons, proceeding, if necessary,
up the ladder of escalation from battlefield nuclear weapons, to tactical nuclear weapons, to theater nuclear forces, and finally culminating with a strategic nuclear attack by the United States upon the
Soviet Union itself. That is well-established American and NATO
policy, but is it correct, efficacious, or even sensible?

An international legal analysis would say no because the responsive
use of nuclear weapons to repel a conventional attack would be
totally disproportionate to the threat presented and therefore constitute an impermissible act of self-defense.[90] The counterargument that
the use of U.S. battlefield nuclear weapons stationed in Europe would
entail a roughly proportionate response to a Soviet conventional attack rests upon the basis of pure speculation, not established fact.
Putting aside their inherent escalatory potential into nuclear Armageddon, NATO has already determined that its battlefield nuclear
weapons are essentially useless if not suicidally dangerous, because
it has no idea about their precise yields, accuracy, survivability, or
operational reliability under battle conditions.[91] Once again, although in theory the proposition that a "battlefield nuclear war is
legal" might sound appealing, in practice it fails to live up to its
hypothetical expectations.

---

90. *See, e.g.,* A. Thomas & A. J. Thomas, Jr., *Legal Limits on the Use of Chemical and
Biological Weapons* 208 (1970); D. Bowett, *Self-Defense in International Law* 13 (1958); J.
Murphy, *The United Nations and the Control of International Violence* 17 (1982).

91. McNamara, "The Military Role of Nuclear Weapons: The Perceptions and Mispercep-
tions," 62 *Foreign Aff.* 59, 68-70 (1983); *N.Y. Times,* Mar. 15, 1983, at A3, col. 1 (Report
by NATO's North Atlantic Assembly urging U.S. to reduce stock of battlefield nuclear weapons
in Europe because of obsoleteness and unreliability).

This observation should lead the United States government to the conclusion that it is far better for NATO to phase out all of its battlefield, tactical and theater nuclear weapons systems from Europe as part of a negotiated process with the Soviet Union for doing the same, and build up, if necessary, U.S. and NATO conventional forces to a level sufficient to deter any anticipated, though unlikely, Soviet conventional invasion of Europe. A similar argument from a non-legal perspective has already been developed by such a distinguished public figure as George Ball.[92] His analysis is fully supportable by basic principles of international law.

The only minor point of contention this author might have concerning Ball's position is that it is not necessarily inevitable that the United States would have to couple a negotiated denuclearization of Europe with an enormous buildup in NATO conventional forces. Such Euro-nuclear negotiations could be tied into the Mutual and Balanced Force Reduction (MBFR) negotiations, which, admittedly, are currently stalemated in Vienna.[93] Yet in the proposals on the table so far, both sides are in basic agreement on the principle that NATO and the Warsaw Pact should each reduce to the identical level of 900,000 men, with no more than 700,000 ground troops.[94] The achievement of a rough equality in conventional forces at such lower levels between NATO and the Warsaw Pact would materially reduce any incentive for the latter to launch a conventional attack while at the same time it would obviate the need for a massive buildup in NATO's conventional forces. An effective conventional deterrent could be maintained at lower levels of potential violence on both sides of the "balance of terror" without the need for either to field a nuclear deterrent to a conventional attack.

The exact differential in the conventional force ratio between NATO and the Warsaw Pact becomes even less important when it is realized that many of the latter's component forces are completely unreliable. In the most improbable event the Soviets did decide to launch an offensive invasion of Western Europe,[95] it is highly unlikely

92. Ball, "The Cosmic Bluff," *N.Y. Rev. Books*, July 21, 1983, at 37-41.
93. Brady, "Negotiating European Security: Mutual and Balanced Force Reductions," 6 *Int'l Security Rev.* 189 (1981).
94. *See* "The Negotiations on the Mutual Reduction of Forces and Armaments and Associated Measures in Central Europe," *Arms Control Rep.*, July 1984, at 401.
95. Salt II Statement of Witnesses in Third Week of Hearings Before the Senate Foreign Relations Committee, 96th Cong., 1st Sess. 21544 (1979) (statement of Professor Richard Pipes).

that the national military forces of Poland, Hungary, Czechoslovakia, and Romania would fight by their side. It is also open to considerable doubt whether or not the forces of East Germany would be prepared to invade West Germany at the behest of the Soviet Union. Perhaps the greatest deterrent to a Soviet invasion of Western Europe is this realization by the U.S.S.R.'s Great Russian governing elite that in the event of outright military hostilities the armed forces of all these Warsaw Pact countries might very well exploit the opportunity to rise up in revolt against their respective Soviet occupying forces, thus effectively joining the struggle on NATO's side. Furthermore, nominally Soviet citizens living in the Ukraine, Byellorussia, Estonia, Latvia, Lithuania, the Caucasus and Soviet Central Asia might decide to do the exact same thing. And the Red Army itself could then very well collapse when its non-Russian soldiers refuse to fight and die for their Soviet masters.

The replication of this pattern of virulent nationalistic behavior during both the First and Second World Wars continues to serve as a sufficient deterrent to any Great Russian leadership elite giving serious contemplation to an invasion of Western Europe.[96] Indeed, this author submits that historically the primary deterrent to a Soviet invasion of Western Europe has always been its Great Russian elite's acute anxiety engendered by the highly tenuous nature of the influence they exert over their so-called Warsaw Pact allies as well as over substantial segments of their own population. Neither the U.S. strategic nuclear deterrent, nor the U.S. creation of a nuclear-trip wire for NATO by the stationing of 350,000 American troops in West Germany, nor the deployment of thousands of nuclear weapons in NATO countries has contributed more than marginally to the effectiveness of this essentially self-induced perceptual deterrent.

Therefore it is totally misleading for Reagan administration apologists to blithely assert that the peace of Europe has somehow been preserved for the past thirty years because of the presence of battlefield nuclear weapons on NATO territory.[97] Rather, the peace of Europe has somehow been miraculously maintained during this period despite the presence of thousands of nuclear weapons on both

96. *See* von Rauch, *supra* note 79; Gray, *supra* note 79; J. Clarkson, *A History of Russia* 683-85 (1969).
97. Rowny, "Nuclear Arms Control and the NATO Alliance," *Dep't. St. Bull*, Aug. 1984, at 38.

sides of the continent. Yet the United States and NATO, on the one hand, and the Soviet Union and the Warsaw Pact, on the other, must not continue to rely upon providence to protect them from the outbreak of a battlefield or theater nuclear war in Europe.

In accordance with basic principles of international law, a conventional attack by the Soviet Union and the Warsaw Pact upon Western Europe should be resisted by NATO mounting a conventional defense. Under such apocalyptic circumstances the only possible utility nuclear weapons might have is that the threat of their use could serve as a deterrent to their use by an adversary. This situation would be similar to that which prevailed during the Second World War when it came to the non-use of chemical weapons and poison gas. Pursuant to the Geneva Protocol of 1925, neither set of belligerents used such weapons in the European theater of operations, though each side maintained a stockpile in order to deter their first-use by its adversaries.[98] The Geneva Protocol worked quite effectively to prevent the use of these early weapons of mass and indiscriminate destruction during the utter desperation of the Second World War despite the fact that their potency had been amply demonstrated during the First World War. Conversely, just as the prior existence of these early weapons of mass and indiscriminate destruction proved to be politically and militarily irrelevant to the outbreak of the Second World War, so too the existence of battlefield, tactical and theater nuclear weapons systems in Europe will likewise demonstrate themselves to be immaterial to the successful or unsuccessful prevention of World War III.

Today the Soviet Union has already given a unilateral pledge of "no-first-use" of nuclear weapons that creates a binding international legal obligation on its own accord.[99] NATO and the United States must respond in kind by doing the same,[100] and then expressing their readiness to conclude a formal treaty to that effect with the members of the Warsaw Pact. Considerations of international law would fully support such a "no-first-use" treaty as a preliminary step toward the

---

98. *See* A. Thomas & A.J. Thomas, Jr., *Legal Limits on the Use of Chemical and Biological Weapons* 137-48 (1970). *See also* Daniell, "Churchill Says Britain Will Use Gas if Reich Tries It in Russia," *N.Y. Times*, May 11, 1942, at A1, col. 8.

99. *See* Weiler, "No First Use: A History," *Bull. Atomic Sci.*, Nov. 1983, at 33; Nossiter, "Soviet Forswears Using A-Arms First," *N.Y. Times*, June 16, 1982, at 1, col. 3.

100. Bundy, Kennan, McNamara & Smith, "Nuclear Weapons and the Atlantic Alliance," 60 *Foreign Aff.* 753 (1982); McNamara, *supra* note 91, at 59.

complete elimination of battlefield, tactical and theater nuclear weapons from the continent of Europe. Yet, while the Soviet Union has already agreed to conclude a no-first-use treaty, the ̃Reagan administration has rejected such a positive and worthwhile endeavor.[101]

Is it Lawful to Possess Nuclear Weapons?

The final question that needs to be addressed concerning the relevance of international law to the so-called paradox of nuclear deterrence is whether or not it is lawful for a state even to possess nuclear weapons. A great deal has been said about this subject on both sides of the dispute. The author submits, however, that the question itself is completely speculative and misdirected, if not outrightly misleading. It obfuscates the fact that today's acknowledged nuclear weapons states (viz., United States, Great Britain, France, Soviet Union, Peoples Republic of China) do not simply possess nuclear weapons. Rather, they have actively deployed nuclear weapons in enormous numbers and varieties by attaching them to delivery vehicles that are interconnected with sophisticated command, control, communication and intelligence (C^3I) networks.[102] Such nuclear weapons systems are ready for almost instantaneous launch upon immediate notice. Hence the only meaningful question concerns the legality of modern nuclear weapons *systems* as they are currently deployed and programmed for use.

If the nuclear weapons states had actually kept all their nuclear devices stored in warehouses where they were separated from their respective delivery vehicles, it might be pertinent to answer the question whether or not such mere possession of nuclear weapons was legal under international law. Yet that historically has not been the case. The nuclear weapons systems maintained by all the world's nuclear weapons states, and especially by the two superpowers, are far beyond this stage of mere possession, and have been at the point of deployment and preparation for immediate use in a thermonuclear war for quite some time. As pointed out earlier in this chapter, under

101. *Compare N.Y. Times*, Dec. 5, 1984, at 4, col. 5 (Chernenko agrees to treaty against first-use of nuclear weapons) *with Christian Science Monitor*, Dec. 5, 1984, at 2, col. 2 (Reagan spokesman rejects no first-use treaty).

102. P. Bracken, *The Command the Control of Nuclear Forces* 212 (1983).

the Nuremberg Principles, such planning, preparation and conspiracy to commit crimes against peace, crimes against humanity, war crimes, and genocide, inter alia, constitute international crimes in their own right.

The appropriate analogy from domestic law to be applied here is not the hand gun kept in the bedroom bureau drawer for the purposes of legitimate self-defense against a home intruder. But rather, a shotgun that is fully loaded and pointed at the head of another human being, with the safety catch off, the hammer cocked, the firing mechanism set on a hair-trigger, and the assailant's finger ready, willing and able to twitch at an instant's notice or even because of a mistake or an instinctual reflex. This is clearly illegal behavior under the domestic criminal legal system of any state in the world community today, and therefore under international law as well, since it violates a general principle of law recognized by all civilized nations.[103]

In any jurisdiction within the United States of America, such criminal activity purposely and knowingly engaged in by two individuals with respect to each other would render both guilty of aggravated assault, assault with a deadly weapon, and reckless endangerment of a human being, inter alia. Moreover, as would be true for dueling, Russian roulette, or playing "chicken" with automobiles, the fact that two or more individuals voluntarily participated in such a joint criminal enterprise would not excuse either from personal responsibility. In the case of modern nuclear weapons systems, the two nuclear superpowers have both committed and are continuing to commit on an everyday basis the international crime of recklessly endangering the entire human race. They cannot exonerate themselves from joint and several criminal responsibility for such illegal behavior by invoking the unlawful conduct of their co-felons.

So much then for the argument made by some international law professors that just because five states in today's world community already possess and deploy nuclear weapons systems and several more are diligently pursuing policies designed to acquire a nuclear weapons capability, their behavior somehow negates the existence of international legal rules prohibiting the possession and deployment

---

103. I.C.J. Stat. art. 38, para. 1(c): "1. The Court, whose function is to decide in accordance with international law such disputes as are submitted to it, shall apply: . . . c. the general principles of law recognized by civilized nations;" *reprinted in* S. Rosenne, *Documents on the International Court of Justice* 77 (1974).

of nuclear weapons and related delivery and C³I systems.[104] Since when have a small band of criminals been permitted to argue that their own lawless conduct destroys the validity of the very laws they have violated? The maxim *ex injuria non oritur jus* is a general principle of law recognized by all civilized nations, and therefore a rule of international law as well.[105]

The repeated commission of criminal acts by a few miscreant states cannot create a right for them to continue to do so unless, perhaps, the rest of the international community might explicitly agree to abrogate the applicable rules of law. To the contrary, as of January 1, 1986 there were 133 state parties to the 1968 Treaty on the Non-Proliferation of Nuclear Weapons (NPT), article 2 of which prohibits non-nuclear weapons state parties from acquiring a nuclear weapons capability.[106] The fact that of the five acknowledged nuclear weapons states, only three (United States, Great Britain, Soviet Union) are parties to the NPT does not mean that the non-nuclear weapons state parties have thereby implicitly consented to the legality of their possession and deployment of nuclear weapons and related delivery and C³I systems. Even if the NPT were to be abrogated by the non-nuclear weapons state parties because the nuclear weapons state parties have already committed a material breach of the treaty by failing to perform their obligations under article 6,[107] the possession and deployment of nuclear weapons and their related systems would still remain illegal because it violates the various rules of international law enumerated above.

Indeed, any international agreement purporting to legalize the possession and deployment of nuclear weapons and their related systems

104. Reisman, "Nuclear Weapons in International Law," 4 *N.Y.L. Sch. J. Int'l & Comp. L.* 339, 342 (1983).

105. Brownlie, "Some Legal Aspects of the Use of Nuclear Weapons," 14 *Int'l & Comp. L. Q.* 437, 451 (1965).

106. Treaty on the Non-Proliferation of Nuclear Weapons, July 1, 1968, 21 *U.S.T.* 483, *T.I.A.S.* No. 6839, 729 *U.N.T.S.* 161. Article 2 provides:

Each non-nuclear-weapon State Party to the Treaty undertakes not to receive the transfer from any transferor whatsoever of nuclear weapons or other nuclear explosive devices or of control over such weapons or explosive devices directly, or indirectly; not to manufacture or otherwise acquire nuclear weapons or other nuclear explosive devices; and not to seek or receive any assistance in the manufacture of nuclear weapons or other nuclear explosive devices.

107. *Id.* at art. 6:

Each of the Parties to the Treaty undertakes to pursue negotiations in good faith on effective measures relating to cessation of the nuclear arms race at an early date and to nuclear disarmament, and on a treaty on general and complete disarmament under strict and effective international control.

would violate a peremptory norm of international law and thus be void in accordance with article 53 of the 1969 Vienna Convention on the Law of Treaties.[108] If piracy, slavery, armed aggression, crimes against peace, crimes against humanity, war crimes, and genocide are universally considered to violate jus cogens, then a fortiori the threat by the two nuclear superpowers to exterminate the entire human race, coupled with their imminent capability to do so, must likewise do the same. International law professors must face up to the fact that for them to argue that the present system of nuclear deterrence as practiced by the two superpowers and their nuclear cohorts is lawful, they must in essence deny the very existence of such a phenomenon known in the international legal studies profession as a peremptory norm of international law. This author seriously doubts that such would be the intention of even those who are most fervently committed to promoting the abstract proposition that nuclear deterrence is legal.

Conclusion

From a functionalist perspective, several points become clear concerning the relevance of international law to the so-called "paradox" of nuclear deterrence. First, a surprise, preemptive nuclear strike by the United States upon the Soviet Union is absolutely prohibited for any reason whatsoever. Consequently, all first-strike counterforce strategic nuclear weapons systems such as the MX, Pershing 2, and Trident 2/Delta 5 warhead must not be deployed, and the United States should seek to obtain a mutual and negotiated ban on the deployment of their Soviet counterparts. This development would facilitate the conclusion of a formal international agreement prohibiting the adoption of a "launch-on-warning" nuclear response doc-

---

108. Vienna Convention on the Law of Treaties, May 23, 1969, U.N. Doc. A/Conf. 39/27, at 289 (1969), [1980] *Gr. Brit. T.S.* No. 58 (Cmd. 7964) (entered into force Jan. 27, 1980), *reprinted in* 8 *I.L.M.* 679 (1969); 63 *Am. J. Int'l L.* 875 (1969). Article 53 provides:

A treaty is void if, at the time of its conclusion, it conflicts with a peremptory norm of general international law. For the purposes of the present Convention, a peremptory norm of general international law is a norm accepted and recognized by the international community of states as a whole as a norm from which no derogation is permitted and which can be modified only by a subsequent norm of general international law having the same character.

trine by either the Soviet Union or the United States. Pursuant thereto, all first-strike contingency scenarios should be removed from U.S. war-plans, and Congress should pass implementing legislation making it a serious federal crime for U.S. government officials and military officers to practice first-strike scenarios during war games or otherwise.

Second, a U.S. nuclear attack upon Soviet population centers is absolutely prohibited under all circumstances, and even if undertaken in retaliation for a prior nuclear attack against U.S. population centers. Consequently, the doctrine of "mutual assured destruction" must be abandoned as the cornerstone of American strategic nuclear deterrence policy. Nevertheless, the Reagan administration's plan to substitute for it the development of a "protracted nuclear war-prevailing" capability is not the proper direction in which to move. Nor, for that matter, is Reagan's Strategic Defense Initiative (SDI), for reasons more fully explained at the end of Chapter 4. Rather, the correct approach is prescribed by article 6 of the 1968 Treaty on the Non-Proliferation of Nuclear Weapons (NPT), which both the United States and the Soviet Union are bound to obey as parties: "Each of the Parties to the Treaty undertakes to pursue negotiations in good faith on effective measures relating to cessation of the nuclear arms race at an early date and to nuclear disarmament, and on a treaty on general and complete disarmament under strict and effective international control."[109]

Hence, the United States government must in good faith negotiate genuine and effective nuclear arms control and reduction agreements with the Soviet Union that likewise prevent the modernization of both superpowers' strategic nuclear arsenals. Ultimately, the formal ratification of SALT II or of some cosmetic substitute by the United States government will prove to be the necessary precondition for any progress in negotiating nuclear arms reduction agreements with the Soviet Union. Strategic arms reduction talks (START) can only succeed within the context of a ratified SALT II. The essence of a START agreement can still be obtained if the United States govern-

---

109. Treaty on the Non-Proliferation of Nuclear Weapons, July 1, 1968, 21 *U.S.T.* 483, *T.I.A.S.* No. 6839, 729 *U.N.T.S.* 161. *See* Comment, "Reagan Changes Course on Non-Proliferation," 216 *Science* 7 (1982). For some indication of what the Reagan administration's nebulous non-proliferation policy might be, see L. Dunn, "Controlling the Bomb (1982)," *reviewed by* Boyle, 77 *Am. J. Int'l L.* 981 (1983). Dunn became Special Assistant for Nuclear Affairs at the State Department in the Reagan administration.

ment ratifies the SALT II Treaty; then both superpowers agree to lower its numerical limitations on strategic nuclear delivery vehicle launchers; and then to extend indefinitely the life of such a ratified Treaty as so amended. At that point further percentage reductions in the SALT II limitations could be negotiated on a periodic basis, while both superpowers would declare and observe a bilateral moratorium on the testing of nuclear weapons and the modernization of their strategic nuclear weapons systems.

In the meantime, while moving toward the goals set forth in NPT article 6, the United States government must announce that in the event of a nuclear or conventional attack upon the United States or the members of the NATO alliance by the Soviet Union, America would not under any circumstances actually use its nuclear weapons against Soviet population centers. The United States should seek a reciprocal statement from the Soviet Union along those lines, and offer to conclude a formal treaty specifically prohibiting both a nuclear attack upon, as well as the strategic nuclear targeting of, their respective civilian population centers. International lawyers working for the Departments of Defense, State, and Justice must be given the authority to vet the SIOP in accordance with these and all other requirements of international law.[110]

Finally, since nuclear weapons must never be used in response to a conventional attack, NATO should adopt a "no-first-use" of nuclear weapons policy for the defense of Europe and agree to conclude a treaty to that effect with the Warsaw Pact. NATO and the Warsaw Pact should commence immediate negotiations for the removal of all battlefield, tactical, and theater nuclear weapon systems from the continent of Europe. And the MBFR negotiations at Vienna should be revitalized in order to prevent a massive buildup in conventional military forces on either side of the continent.

110. *See* U.S. Dep't of Defense Instruction No. 5500.15 (Oct. 16, 1974). Paragraph 2 provides:
   All actions of the Department of Defense with respect to the acquisition and procurement of weapons, and their intended use in armed conflict, shall be consistent with the obligations assumed by the United States Government under all applicable treaties, with customary international law, and, in particular, with the laws of war.

Chapter 4.

Trial Materials on Nuclear Weapons and International Law

This chapter contains materials that you can utilize for the purpose of preparing to defend an anti-nuclear civil resistance case. All these materials have actually been used in anti-nuclear protest cases that this author has consulted on. The first document is a response to the federal government's motion in limine to exclude considerations of international law that was written by a former student of mine, Mr. Kary Love, Esq. of Moline, Illinois in the case of *United States v. Schweiters.* This is followed by expert witness testimony on nuclear weapons and international law that I actually gave in the *Schweiters* and the *Jarka* cases. Then comes Mr. Love's excellent oral argument to a federal district judge to allow my testimony to be considered by the jury after his offer of proof on this matter. This is then followed by the jury instructions which we drafted together and Mr. Love requested in the *Schweiters* case, as well as the pertinent instructions on nuclear weapons and international law from the *Jarka* case. Because there is now occurring a substantial amount of civil resistance activities to protest against the Reagan administration's Strategic Defense Initiative (SDI), this chapter concludes with a short piece written by this author on the violations of international law involved in the Star Wars program.

1. Sample for Motion in Limine.

IN THE UNITED STATES DISTRICT COURT
CENTRAL DISTRICT OF ILLINOIS
AT ROCK ISLAND

UNITED STATES OF AMERICA,	)	
Plaintiff,	)	
vs.		
SISTER NANCY SCHWEITERS,	)	Criminal Nos. 84-40025
STEPHEN P. QUILTY,	)	84-40024
RUTH ANN GALLAGER,	)	84-40024
JUDITH A. HEWITT,	)	84-40023
MARY VANDEVOORDE,	)	84-40022
Defendants.	)	

RESPONSE TO GOVERNMENT'S MOTION IN LIMINE

Come now the above named defendants, by Kary Love, of Love Thompson & Sale, their attorney, and for their Response to the Government's Motion in Limine state:

    I. THE TESTIMONY SOUGHT TO BE EXCLUDED WILL ESTAB-
    LISH EITHER AN ABSOLUTE DEFENSE UNDER TREATIES BIND-
    ING ON THE UNITED STATES UNDER ARTICLE VI OF THE
    CONSTITUTION, OR WILL BE SUFFICIENT TO NEGATE THE
    REQUISITE MENS REA OF THE OFFENSES CHARGED AND
    MUST ACCORDINGLY BE ALLOWED.

Article VI section 2 of the Constitution of the United States provides:

> This Constitution, and the laws of the United States, which shall
> be made in pursuance thereof; *and all treaties made, or which shall
> be made, under the Authority of the United States, shall be the
> supreme law of the land....*

The United States of America has become a "contracting party" to numerous international treaties governing the "laws of war." [See: Geneva Convention 1949 [No. IV] Relative to the Protection of Civilian Persons in Time of War, 12 August 1949, 6 *U.S.T.* 3516, *T.I.A.S.* 3365, 75 *U.N.T.S.* 287; Geneva Convention [No. III] Relative to the Treatment of Prisoners of War, 12 August 1949, 6 *U.S.T.* 3316, *T.I.A.S.* 3364, 75 *U.N.T.S.* 135; Geneva Convention [No. II]

for the Amelioration of the Condition of Wounded, Sick and Ship-
wrecked Members of the Armed Forces at Sea, 12 August 1949, 6
U.S.T. 3217, *T.I.A.S.* 3363, 75 *U.N.T.S.* 85; Geneva Convention
[No. I] for the Amelioration of the Condition of the Wounded and
Sick in Armed Forces in the Field, 12 August 1949, 6 *U.S.T.* 3114,
T.I.A.S. 3362, 75 *U.N.T.S.* 31: See also, the 1907 Hague Convention
Respecting the Laws and Customs of War on Land, 18 October 1907,
36 *Stat.* 2277, *T.S. No.* 539, 1 *Bevans* 631. Additionally, the United
States was instrumental in establishing, and is a party to, the 1945
Charter of the International Military Tribunal at Nuremberg. [See The
London Agreement, Aug. 8, 1945, 59 *Stat*, 1544, *E.A.S.* No. 472,
82 *U.N.T.S.*

The Nuremberg Charter was authored as a means to prosecute and
punish Nazi war criminals, and defined "crimes against peace," and
"crimes against humanity." [See: F. Boyle, "The Relevance of International Law to the So-Called Paradox of Nuclear Deterrence,"
1984, a copy of which is attached hereto, pp. 11-12] According to
Professor Boyle, "...the Nuremberg Principles have universally been
considered to constitute an authoritative statement of the rules of
customary international law dictating individual criminal responsibility for crimes against peace, crimes against humanity, and war
crimes." *Id.* at 12.

It is the defendants' position, that the United States position at
Nuremberg was that individuals who "participated" in "planning,
preparation, initiation or waging of a war of aggression, or a war in
violation of international treaties," committed a "crime against
peace." This was the argument made by Justice Jackson, Chief Prosecutor for the United States at Nuremburg:

> The case as presented by the United States will be concerned with
> the brains and authority back of all crimes... We want to reach the
> planners and designers the inciters and leaders without whose civil
> architecture the world would not have been so long scourged with
> the violence and lawlessness, and wracked with the agonies and
> convulsions of this terrible war. [II *Trial of the Major War Criminals
> Before the International Military Tribunal* 104-5 (1948).]

Defendants submit that it is a valid theory of international law, in
fact is one urged by the United States at Nuremberg, that an individual

has a duty to extricate themselves from a known violation of international law even at the expense of violating domestic law. [See F. Boyle, *supra*.]

The International Tribunal recognized this precept throughout the Nuremberg proceedings. [See, F. Boyle, *supra*, pp. 27-8] In the case of a German industrialist whose companies produced equipment used in committing crimes against humanity, the Tribunal determined there was individual responsibility under principles of international law, even though the acts committed did not violate (or in fact were in furtherance of) domestic law:

> It is urged that individuals holding no public offices and not representing the state, do not and should not come within the class of persons criminally responsible for a breach of international law. It is asserted that international law is a matter wholly outside the work, interest and knowledge of private individuals. The distinction is unsound. International law, as such, binds every citizen just as does ordinary municipal law.... The application of international law to individuals is no novelty. [*The Flick Case*, 6 *Trials of the Major War Criminals* 1192 (1952).]

The article by Professor Boyle makes clear that this principle has been incorporated into the pantheon of international law by the Nuremberg Tribunal. Furthermore, Professor Boyle makes clear that current United States nuclear policies may be regarded as violating precepts of international law that are binding on the United States, and that are binding on United States citizens under both Article VI of the Constitution and the decisions of the Nuremberg Tribunal. Consequently, defendants submit that they, under international law, have an affirmative duty to disassociate themselves from any participation or collusion in the illegal United States nuclear policies to avoid criminal responsibility under international law. Defendants submit that, under the above analysis, they have a defense to the current charges under international law. By analogy, had the defendant's prayed for peace in a German factory producing "death ovens," in 1944, they would have had a valid international law defense to a criminal trespassing charge. Additionally, they would have had no fear of liability as a war criminal before the Nuremberg Tribunal.

A. IF THE COURT REJECTS THE ABSOLUTE DEFENSE UNDER
   INTERNATIONAL LAW, THE DEFENDANTS ARE STILL EN-
   TITLED TO ADDUCE EVIDENCE OF THE FOREGOING THE-
   ORY TO NEGATE THE CRIMINAL MENS REA THE
   GOVERNMENT MUST PROVE AS A PREDICATE OF CRIMI-
   NAL LIABILITY.

Both the violation of 18 U.S.C. § 1382 charged against Defendant
Vandevoorde and the charges under Ill. Rev. Stat., ch. 38 § 21-3(a)
against the remaining defendants require proof of some "mens rea."
The information filed against Defendant Vandevoorde charges that
she "knowingly re-enter[ed]." Accordingly, the government must
prove this "mens rea."

As to the remaining trespass charges, Ill. Rev. Stat., ch. 38 § 4-1
states that: "A material element of every offense is a voluntary act...."
Section 4-3 provides that: "A person is not guilty of an offense...unless,
with respect to each element described by the statute defining the
offense, he acts while having one of the mental states described in
Sections 4-4 through 4-7." Sections 4-4 through 4-7 define the mental
states of intent, knowledge, recklessness or negligence. Accordingly,
the government is required to prove the requisite "mens rea" with
respect to the trespass charges as well.

Section 14.04 of the Devitt & Blackmar Federal Jury Practice and
Instructions contains an instruction as to the meaning of "knowingly"
which excludes conduct done because of "mistake or accident or
other innocent conduct." Defendants submit that adducing evidence
of the foregoing theory of international law will enable them to show
sufficiently that, at worst, their acts were the result of mistake or other
innocent grounds. Additionally, as to those defendants charged under
the Illinois Criminal Code, Ill. Rev. Stat., ch. 38 § 4-8, provides that:
"A person's ignorance or mistake as to a matter of either law of fact
is a defense if it negatives the existence of the mental state which the
statute prescribes with respect to an element of the offense."*

Defendants submit that the testimony of international law expert
Francis Boyle is admissible to negate the requisite *mens rea* of the
offenses charged and the Motion in Limine must therefore be denied.

   II. THE DEFENSE OF NECESSITY IS NOT FORECLOSED AS TO
       THESE DEFENDANTS BY THE SEVENTH CIRCUIT DECISION
       IN *U.S. v. QUILTY*

The defense of necessity is clearly available to those defendants who have been charged under the Assimilative Crimes Act with offenses defined by the Illinois Criminal Code. The Illinois defense of necessity does not contain the requirement that there be "no reasonable, legal alternative to violating the law," such as *U.S. v. Bailey*, 444 U.S. 394 (1980) imposed on the federal common law defense, and upon which the Seventh Circuit relied in making its statement in *U.S. v. Quilty*, 741 F.2d 1031 (1984) which is quoted by and asserted by the government in its Motion in Limine. The Illinois necessity defense, based upon the Model Penal Code § 3.02, provides:

> Conduct which would otherwise be an offense is justifiable by reason of necessity if the accused was without blame in occasioning or developing the situation and reasonably believed such conduct was necessary to avoid a public or private injury greater than the injury which might reasonably result from his own conduct. [I.R.S., ch. 38 § 7-13]

The Seventh Circuit, according to the government's theory that the decision in *Quilty, supra,* is definitively applicable to the instant case, has already established one element of this defense when it stated:

> It is of course, impossible to argue that nuclear war is not more harmful than a peaceful...anti-nuclear prayer demonstration at the Arsenal. [*Id.* at 1033]

In the event the defendants establish that they were without fault in developing the current "illegal" nuclear policies of the United States, and that their belief that nuclear war might result if they don't pray for peace is reasonable, then they will be entitled to be acquitted by reason of necessity under the Illinois statute. On the issue of resultant nuclear war in the event defendants' goal of disarmament is not reached, defendants ask the Court to take judicial notice, pursuant to Rule 201 of the Federal Rules of Evidence, of an article appearing in the *New York Times*, October 10, 1981 at A10, column 1, which reported that during an 18 month period NORAD experienced 151 false alarms, four of which were considered to be serious enough that B-52 crews and ICBM units were placed on increased alert. With missiles now deployed in Western Europe so that the Soviet Union now has a mere six minutes in which to determine the validity of a similar malfunction of its radar detection systems, the potential hazard has increased mutlifold since 1980.

Finally, even under the federal common law analysis enunciated in *Bailey, supra,* defendants submit that they can adduce evidence sufficient for a jury to find that "no reasonable legal alternative to violating the law" was available to defendants despite the Seventh Circuit's dictum in *Quilty.* Without exhaustively itemizing every item of potential evidence, and in the interest of brevity, defendants suggest that it is possible to show that the reasonable alternatives suggested by the Seventh Circuit, use of the electoral process, speech on public streets, in parks, in auditoriums, and by release of information to the news media, have been denied to the defendants, or are otherwise "unreasonable." For example, defendants may show that despite overwhelming public support for nuclear arms control talks, little significant progress, if any, has been made. That, in fact, the regimes of international law set up to ensure peace have been repudiated and rejected by the United States. For example, the attempted withdrawal from the compulsory jurisdiction of the International Court of Justice in the suit brought against the United States by Nicaragua. The United States mining of Nicaraguan harbors in violation of the 1907 Hague Convention on the Laying of Submarine Mines, to which both the United States and Nicaragua are parties. The violation of the Non-Circumvention Clause found in Article 12 of the SALT II Treaty by the deployment of Pershing II missiles in the Federal Republic of Germany. It is possible that, upon the defendants having adduced evidence of the foregoing acts of international lawlessness by the United States in violation of treaties and conventions to which it is a party, that a jury might find that it is possible to argue that defendants had no reasonable alternative but to pray for peace in the face of such an unprecedented breakdown in the United States' commitment to the rule of law.

For all the foregoing reasons, defendants suggest that the Motion In Limine must be denied.

February 7, 1985

> Respectfully submitted,
> Kary Love
> Attorney for the Defendants
> 620 17th Street

Moline, IL

*See, *People v. Grant*, 101 Ill. App. 3d. 43, 427 N.E. 2d 810, 56 Ill. Dec. 478 (1st Dist. 1981) (regarding requirement of proof of *mens rea* for conviction under Ill. Rev. Stat., ch. 38 § 21-3(a)).

2. Sample Direct Examination of an Expert Witness on Nuclear Weapons and International Law.

Qualification as an Expert

FRANCIS ANTHONY BOYLE

called as a witness on behalf of the Defendants, having been first duly sworn, was examined and testified as follows:

DIRECT EXAMINATION

By Defense Counsel (DC) [Mr. Kary Love or Ms. Janine Hoft]:

Q. Professor Boyle, could you state your full name for the record.

A. My name is Francis Anthony Boyle.

Q. And Professor Boyle, where do you live?

A. Right now I reside at 504 East Pennsylvania Avenue, Champaign, Illinois, 61820.

Q. What is your occupation?

A. I'm a Professor of International Law at the University of Illinois in Champaign.

Q. And how long have you been at the University of Illinois?

A. Seven years.

Q. What sort of subjects do you specialize in?

A. The College of Law basically hired me to teach their public international law courses; however, I've also taught criminal law for the past seven years, and courses on the philosophy of law, international human rights law, and international organizations.

Q. What is your personal educational background?

A. I received my Bachelor's Degree from the University of Chicago specializing in international relations. From there I went to Harvard University to become qualified in international law. There are two ways you could do that. I did it both ways. The first is to obtain a law degree. I have a Doctor of Law with high honors from the Harvard Law School in 1976. I also have a Master's Degree and a Ph.D. in political science specializing in international law and its relationship with international politics from Harvard University, and those were in 1978 and 1983, respectively.

Q. Professor Boyle, how many articles or books have you written concerning international law?

A. I have written, I would say, 12 or 13 major articles and a larger number of smaller articles, shorter pieces. I have one book that will be published in June by Duke University entitled *World Politics and International Law*.

Q. And these articles that you mentioned—have any of them been published?

A. Yes, all of these are published articles, basically in professional journals.

Q. Have you written articles concerning nuclear weapons policy?

A. Yes, I have written two articles, specifically major articles. I have other shorter pieces, but two major articles dealing with nuclear weapons policy.

Q. Can you tell us in the course of your experience in operating or acting as a professor in international law, have you had occasion to study, or research or investigate the issue of the legality of United States nuclear weapons policies?

A. Yes. As a matter of fact I have devoted a substantial amount of my time to the subject. I have been a member of the Coordinating Council of a group known as The Lawyers' Committee on Nuclear Policy for about the past three years now. It's in the resumé. In June of 1983 I was invited by the United States Military Academy at West Point to address their Senior Conference on the question of *Nuclear Deterrence and International Law*. The conference basically consisted of a group of about 200 high-level officials from the Department of State, Department of Defense, and other agencies of the federal government, academia and people of that nature. The paper I delivered there was entitled *Nuclear Weapons and International Law*. West Point published it in their Senior Conference proceedings, and it was later published in a law review.[1]

The second piece I have just finished is entitled *The Relevance of International Law to the Paradox of Nuclear Deterrence*.[2]

---

1. Boyle, "Nuclear Weapons and International Law: The Arms Control Dimension," 21 U.S.M.A. West Point Senior Conference Proceedings: The Nuclear Debate 147 (1983); *and in* 4 N.Y.L. Sch. J. Int'l & Comp. L. 257 (1983). *See also* 76 Am. Soc'y Int'l L. Proc. 322 (1982).

2. Boyle, "The Relevance of International Law to the Paradox of Nuclear Deterrence," forthcoming in *Northwestern Law Review*; 11 *Recht En Kritiek*, No. 3 (Dutch trans. 1985). *See* Chapter 3 *supra*.

Q. And have you written any articles specifically concerning U.S. involvement in Central America?

A. Yes. Again, I have written two major pieces on that as well as some shorter ones. One is entitled *International Lawlessness in the Caribbean Basin*, which appeared in a publication called *Crime and Social Justice*.[3] The second article was entitled *American Foreign Policy Toward International Law and Organizations: 1898 to 1917*.[4] Half of that article was devoted to the history of American intervention in Central America and the Caribbean from the Spanish-American War up through the late 1920s.

Q. Do you belong to any professional associations or committees?

A. Yes, I do. I am a member of the American Society of International Law, the American Bar Association, the American Political Science Association, the Lieber Group on the Laws of War, which is a group that specializes in armed conflict, the Geneva Conventions, and the humanitarian laws of armed conflict. I am a consultant to Amnesty International. I have served as a consultant to the American Friends Service Committee. I suspect there are others that I can't remember off the top of my head, but I have devoted a good deal of my time participating in various professional groups. Generally, I spend most of my time on problems of human rights and armed conflict, specifically how to promote human rights and stop armed conflict.

Q. You mentioned, I think, one conference. But have you participated in any other conferences or tribunals concerning international law?

A. Yes. I give approximately 15 to 20 lectures per year in this country and abroad, primarily related to three areas. I have devoted approximately one-third to nuclear weapons, one-third to U.S. foreign policy toward Central America and the Caribbean, and one-third to United States policy in the Middle East—which is not an issue in this trial. For example, last December I was invited to lecture on U.S. military intervention in Central America at the Harvard Law School. I have recently been involved in three different international

---

3. "International Lawlessness in the Caribbean Basin," 21-22 *Crime and Social Justice* 37 (1984); *and in* International Progress Organization, *The Reagan Administration's Foreign Policy* 89 (H. Kochler ed. 1985). *See also* Australia *Int'l L. News*, Sept., 1984; 78 *Am. Soc'y Int'l L. Proc.* 144 (1984); 78 *Am. J. Int'l L.* 172 (1984).

4. Boyle, "American Foreign Policy Toward International Law and Organizations: 1898-1917," 6 *Loy. L.A. Int'l & Comp. L.J.* 185 (1983). *See also* 76 *Am. Soc'y Int'l L. Proc.* 130, 135, 144 (1982).

tribunals. One was a group called the International Progress Organization, which is a non-governmental organization in consultative status with UNESCO. I chaired a panel of jurists from around the world that was inquiring into the legal aspects of the Reagan administration's foreign policy, specifically, nuclear weapons, Central America, the Middle East and South Africa.[5]

In January of 1985, I was invited to give testimony before the International Nuclear Warfare Tribunal in London convened by the International Peace Bureau headquartered in Geneva and chaired by Sean MacBride, the Nobel Peace Prize winner and founder of Amnesty International.

In October of 1984, I was asked by the organizers of a group known as "The Permanent Peoples Tribunal" to defend the position of the United States government in a case brought against the United States by Nicaragua. The United States government refused to send its own lawyer to defend itself, so in the absence of an official governmental lawyer, I was asked to defend the U.S. government.

Q. Did you defend the U.S. government to the best of your ability?

A. Yes, although I certainly did not approve of what I was defending.[6]

STATE'S ATTORNEY: Objection.

THE COURT: Objection sustained as to the last voluntary comment of the witness.

THE WITNESS: But it was my government and as a lawyer, I certainly felt an obligation to defend it if nobody else would.

BY DC:

Q. In April of 1984, did you have an opportunity to debate the Legal Adviser to the U.S. Ambassador to the United Nations?

A. Yes. I was asked in April of 1984 to debate United States foreign policy toward Central America and the Caribbean with the Legal Adviser to the United States Ambassador to the United Nations. This was before the convention of the American Society of International Law in New York City.[7]

Q. Professor Boyle, I only have one final question to ask you. Has

---

5. *See* Appendices *infra.*
6. Boyle, "Statement on Behalf of U.S.A.," in *On Trial: Reagan's War Against Nicaragua* 153 (1985).
7. *See* 78 Am. Soc'y Int'l L. Proc. 144 (1984).

anyone paid you anything or given you any form of compensation to appear here today and give your testimony?

A. No. But I have asked the defendants to pay for my out-of-pocket expenses to travel from Champaign to Chicago and back.

Q. Why then has someone as busy as you undoubtedly are taken an entire day off from your full schedule in order to appear here and testify today for no fee?

A. Simply in order to express my unbiased and objective scholarly opinion as to the requirements of international law.

DC: At this point, we would ask that Professor Boyle be qualified as an expert. If the State's Attorney would like to cross examine him, we would open him up to that.

STATE'S ATTORNEY: No objection.

THE COURT: Very well.

The Nature of International Law

Q. Could you describe for us this, what may be to the members of the jury, rather nebulous concept of international law? What is it?

A. I think it is important to keep in mind that international law is not some foreign alien substance that has been established by an outside body or group of states. Rather the current international legal system that we see today was set up essentially by the United States of America at the end of the Second World War. Not all of it, but most of it—the great body of legal rules that I will be discussing here today. The reason why the United States government set up these institutions and these rules and bodies of law such as the United Nations Charter, the Nuremberg Principles, the O.A.S. —

Q. Have you told us what the O.A.S. is?

A. I'm sorry. The Organization of American States—the United Nations Charter, the Geneva Conventions, the Nuremberg Principles, etc. was the belief that in the post-World War II era, if the United States of America ever wanted to avoid the scourge of a Third World War, it would be necessary to have a rule of law that would be established for the purpose of: number one, maintaining international peace and security; number two, adjudicating disputes between states; and then number three, promoting and advancing international human rights. So it is what we see today—the contemporary international legal order. At least historically until the Reagan administration, the United States government has always taken the leading role in trying to develop rules of international law and international organizations for the peaceful settlements of disputes, and the protection of fundamental human rights.

International Law Is Part of U.S. Domestic Law

Q. You talked about the United States' role in initiating this international body of law. How is the United States bound by international law?

A. We're bound both internationally and domestically. The basic principle of customary international law is that treaties must be obeyed. When the United States government enters into a treaty with another state, that treaty is submitted to the Senate to receive its advice and consent as required by the United States Constitution. Once that treaty has received the Senate's advice and consent, the treaty is then a binding obligation on the United States both in its relations with other states and also in internal law. That is, in our internal relations, in U.S. courts. The United States government, and, indeed, sometimes even United States citizens are then bound to act in a manner as required by that treaty.

Q. Does the United States Constitution tell us anything about the authority that international law should play?

A. Yes. Article 6 of the United States Constitution contains what is called the "Supremacy Clause," and that is quite explicit. It says that all treaties are entitled to be treated as the supreme law of the land. That is the exact language—the supreme law of the land.

Also, the United States Supreme Court has held in the *Belmont* and *Pink* cases that that protection, that right to be treated as the supreme law of the land, also applies to executive agreements. An executive agreement is an international agreement that also binds the United States government but has not received the formal advice and consent of the Senate for procedural reasons. But it is still binding on the U.S. government, and it is entitled to be treated as the supreme law of the land. What that means then is that if there exists a prior inconsistent federal or state law, the treaty or agreement should prevail.

With respect to customary international law, that, too, is part of U.S. domestic law. And, of course, the precedent for that is the decision by the United States Supreme Court in the famous case of the *Paquete Habana*, decided in roughly 1899, I believe, and holding that international law is a part of U.S. domestic law.

The Hague Regulations

Q. Professor Boyle, turning your attention specifically now to nuclear weapons policy and international law: What principles of this general body of international law are relevant to the use and the threat of use of nuclear weapons?

A. You have to go back and look a bit at the history of the development of these principles. Basically, the main source of these rules goes back to the First and Second Hague Peace Conferences of 1899 and 1907. The rules of the 1899 conference have been incorporated into those of the 1907 conference. It's called "Hague Convention No. 4"—on the conduct of land warfare.[8] And if you read through this convention to which the United States government is bound as a party, you'll see several principles that are articulated therein. First —

Q. Excuse me. When you say "United States is a party," what does that mean?

A. That means we are bound by the terms of that convention, bound to obey internationally and domestically.

Q. Specifically, Professor Boyle, do international law and the Hague Regulations prohibit the use of weapons in any way?

STATE'S ATTORNEY: Objection, Judge.

THE COURT: Overruled.

Your answer?

THE WITNESS: Yes.

Q. And in what way do they do that?

A. According to Hague Convention 4, there are various types of either weapons or ways for conducting warfare that are absolutely prohibited under all circumstances. Hence there are a variety of

---

8. *See* Hague Conventions on Land Warfare, *reprinted in The Laws of Armed Conflict* 57-92 (D. Schindler & J. Toman eds. 1981) [hereinafter cited as Hague Conventions].

principles that can be derived from the Hague Regulations that are applicable to the use of nuclear weapons.

First, for example, you cannot use weapons that cause unnecessary suffering on human beings.[9] A typical example of this was the early convention dealing with dum-dum bullets, bullets that would enter the body and expand and rip apart your insides.[10] That was prohibited. And the whole body of this law started with the St. Petersburg Declaration of 1868 that prohibited bullets of a very small size, beneath which there would be serious problems in finding them in your body and pulling them out.[11] Any weapon that is considered to cause unnecessary suffering is clearly prohibited. This would clearly be the case with nuclear weapons.

Second, poison. It's quite clear, and indeed, on this I speak not simply about the Hague Regulations,[12] but you can even find this in the Department of Army's Field Manual[13] on the conduct of land warfare produced by our own government: Poison or the use of poison weapons is clearly prohibited by the Hague Regulations and likewise by the Geneva Protocol of 1925.[14] The United States government is a party to the Geneva Protocol. We joined in 1975,[15] and that Protocol specifically prohibits the use of poison gas, chemical weapons, poison, biological weapons or any form of analogous substance or liquid. This would apply to weapons involving radiation, since it is determined that radiation is toxic, poisonous to man. So, any use of nuclear weapons would violate these prohibitions of the Hague Regulations and the Geneva Protocol of 1925.

A third basic principle of international law is that you cannot adopt methods or tactics of warfare or weapons that fail to distinguish between combatants and non-combatants; that is, between soldiers and civilians.[16] Indeed, the whole basis, the whole premise of the laws of war, which the United States government fully supports by

---

9. *See* Hague Conventions, *supra* note 8, at 77.

10. *Id.*

11. *See* Declaration of St. Petersburg of 1886, *reprinted in The Laws of Armed Conflict* 95-97 (D. Schindler & J. Toman eds. 1981).

12. The term "Hague Regulations" refers to the rules of warfare set forth in Annexes to these Hague Conventions of 1899 and of 1907.

13. Dep't. of the Army Field Manual 27-10: *The Law of Land Warfare* (1956) [hereinafter cited as Field Manual 27-10].

14. *See* Geneva Protocol for the Prohibition of Gases, *reprinted in The Laws of Armed Conflict* 109-19 (D. Schindler & J. Toman eds. 1981) [hereinafter cited as Geneva Protocol].

15. *Id.* at 114.

16. *See* Hague Conventions, *supra* note 8, at 77-78.

the way, is this distinction between combatants and non-combatants; that soldiers are in the business of fighting and dying, but civilians aren't. So, therefore, it is only permitted for a government to conduct its hostilities against armed combatants, not innocent civilians.

Nuclear weapons fail to make the distinction between combatants and non-combatants. We have nearly 10,000 nuclear warheads in the United States targeted on the Soviet Union and a substantial portion of these are directly targeted on civilian population centers.

STATE'S ATTORNEY: I have to object to the last portion. There seems to be no foundation on that last statement. He was called as an expert on international law.

THE COURT: I'm going to sustain the objection as to the last comment concerning targeted weapons. It wasn't really responsive to your question. I think your question was answered; would you ask another question.

The Nuremberg Principles

Q. Upon what other sources do you base your statement that nuclear weapons violate principles of international law?

A. The clearest body of rules that would relate to nuclear weapons and the illegality of the use or even the threat to use nuclear weapons are the Nuremberg Principles.[17] Again, the United States government was a party to the international agreement that established the Nuremberg Tribunal in 1945.[18] I should also point out that the Hague Regulations were affirmed by the Nuremberg Tribunal.

I suspect all of you have heard of the Nuremberg Tribunal that was established after the Second World War, and it was established at the direct request of the United States government. This was our tribunal. Stalin and Churchill wanted to take out the Nazi leaders and shoot them, but Roosevelt insisted there be a trial and that these men be judged in accordance with due process of law and in accordance with the rule of law.

Building on the Hague Conventions, the Nuremberg Tribunal ap-

17. *See* Principles of the Nuremberg Tribunal, *reprinted in The Laws of Armed Conflict* 833-36 (D. Schindler & J. Toman eds. 1981) [hereinafter cited as Nuremberg Principles.
18. *See* The London Agreement, Aug. 8, 1945, 59 *stat.* 1544, *E.A.S.* no. 472, 82 *U.N.T.S.*, 279, *reprinted in The Laws of Armed Conflict* 823-31 (D. Schindler & J. Toman eds. 1981).

plied the principles of the Hague Conventions and in addition other principles to the trial of the major Nazi war criminals in Europe. This Tribunal resulted in a Judgment and also eventually in a set of principles that, in turn, were approved by unanimous vote of the United Nations General Assembly and is considered binding upon every government in the world today. And again, I think almost any international lawyer would agree with my assessment that these are binding as matters of customary international law on both the United States and any government in the world today: they are crimes against peace, crimes against humanity and war crimes.

You have in the documents there the formal definitions, and I would not want to contradict the language—I take it you will introduce them into evidence—what is a crime against peace, a crime against humanity and a war crime. But to give you a basic description of these ideas:

A crime against peace is waging a war of aggression; or even if you were not conducting a war of aggression, even assuming you might be conducting a war of legitimate self-defense, a war in violation of other international treaties or agreements.

So, for example, if the United States government were to claim, "Well, we were attacked first by the Soviet Union and, therefore, we were entitled to resort to nuclear weapons because it is legitimate self-defense," then that statement is not necessarily correct. You are entitled to defend yourself but only in accordance with the types of international agreements and treaties that the United States government has already agreed to, and using the weapons and tactics that we have already agreed to.

The second category of crime recognized by the Nuremberg Tribunal is what is known as a crime against humanity. The concept of crime against humanity was developed by the parties to the Nuremberg Charter to deal with Hitler's extermination of the Jewish people, and to make it very clear that this was an international crime even though the Jewish people were German citizens. Until the time of the Nuremberg Tribunal, it was not a violation of international law for a state to exterminate its own citizens—only if it killed aliens or foreigners. Nuremberg sought to close that loophole by developing this concept of crimes against humanity. And if you read, certainly the definition of crimes against humanity, you'll see one salient point for nuclear warfare, dealing with the destruction of cities. Wanton destruction of cities is a crime against humanity.[19]

The third principle set forth in the Nuremberg Tribunal, the third substantive crime was war crimes; that is, violations of the laws and customs of warfare. These are the traditional war crimes that I suspect most people are familiar with. At the time of Nuremberg, they were essentially found in the Hague Regulations of 1907. And again, I don't wish to go through the Hague Regulations any more. They are quite long and quite extensive. And I take it you will offer them to the Court as a matter of evidence. If you don't have them here, they can be found in a book I have over there.

Moreover, the Nuremberg Principles, the Judgment, and the Charter, also established inchoate crimes with respect to these substantive offenses; that is, crimes that did not approach the point of actually committing the substantive offense itself.

Q. Professor Boyle, could you give us some examples of what you mean by these inchoate crimes?

A. Attempt to commit a crime against peace, crime against humanity, or war crime is a crime itself; or planning or preparation to commit a crime against peace, crime against humanity, or war crime is a crime itself. Incitement to commit these crimes is a crime itself, or conspiracy to commit a crime against peace, a crime against humanity, or a war crime is a crime itself. Clearly, the United States government today is planning, preparing, and conspiring to commit at a minimum crimes against humanity and war crimes.

STATE'S ATTORNEY: Objection, Judge.

THE COURT: Objection sustained to the last statement.

STATE'S ATTORNEY: I ask the jury be asked —

THE COURT: The jury will disregard it. There has been no foundation for such an opinion.

Q. Can you tell me whether or not the Nuremberg Principles apply in times of peace as well as times of war?

A. Yes, in time of peace and in time of war. If you look at the Nuremberg Principles you will see that not only do they prohibit the actual commission of crimes against peace, crimes against humanity and war crimes, but they also prohibit conspiracy to commit crimes

---

19. Nuremberg Principle VI states that the definition of war crimes includes "wanton destruction of cities, towns, or villages, or devastation not justified by military necessity." *See* Nuremberg Principles, *supra* note 17, at 836.

against peace, crimes against humanity, war crimes; and attempts to commit such crimes. All those crimes are what criminal law professors call the "inchoate crimes." If you go back and read the arguments offered by the prosecutors at Nuremberg, you will see that the reason they recognized these inchoate crimes was to prevent or forestall the heinous offenses in the first place.

The Genocide Convention

Q. What, if any, application does the Genocide Convention of 1948[20] have to the general sources of international law and the use of nuclear weapons?

A. Yes. If you remember, I was discussing the Nuremberg Principles and, particularly, the one crime that was established therein called crime against humanity. That was intended to deal, as I mentioned, with Hitler's policy of exterminating German Jews. The practice of a crime against humanity that was committed by Hitler and the Nazi war criminals against the Jewish people in the Second World War was considered so abhorrent that the United States government and other members of the international community decided that a special treaty had to be adopted that would prohibit this type of activity specifically by name both in war and in peace. And it was on the basis of that sentiment that the Genocide Convention was drafted and approved by the United Nations General Assembly in 1948. It built upon the principle of a crime against humanity.

The Genocide Convention, then, specifically prohibits any government official, whether military or civilian, from pursuing policies that would be designed to kill or inflict deleterious harm upon even one individual because of his racial, ethnic, religious, or national characteristics.[21] And for purposes of nuclear warfare, the Convention makes it clear that conspiracy, incitement or complicity in commission of genocide, whether in war or peace, constitutes an international crime. So the Genocide Convention is likewise relevant to this question of waging and planning nuclear warfare.

---

20. *See* Genocide Convention of 1948, 78 *U.N.T.S.* 277 (signed by the U.S. on Dec. 11, 1948), *reprinted in The Laws of Armed Conflict* 171-86 (D. Schindler & J. Toman eds. 1981) [hereinafter cited as Genocide Convention].

21. *Id.* at 172.

Now, I should point out that the United States government has not technically ratified the Genocide Convention for a variety of reasons. If you would like me to go into some of them, I will. But I think most international law professors would agree that the Genocide Convention is an expression of customary international law and the terms are binding upon the United States government, also military officials.

I should also point out that this body of law that I have just discussed—the Hague Regulations, the Nuremberg Principles, the Genocide Convention—are binding not only on civilian government officials and military officers but also upon civilians, also upon —

Q. Civilians who are not affiliated with the government?

A. That's correct.

The U.S. Army Field Manual

Q. Turning back now to the sources of the international laws of war, what, if anything, has the United States Army done to incorporate the laws of war into its own policies?

A. Well, you have before you a document entitled *The Law of Land Warfare*, Department of the Army Field Manual 27-10, dated 1956.[22] That Field Manual is still a valid manual within the United States Army for the conduct of warfare by the United States Army around the world.

Q. Can you tell me, if you know, the binding effect of the Army's Law of Land Warfare Manual on its own personnel?

A. Yes, all of its personnel are bound by *The Law of Land Warfare*. They are ordered to conduct hostilities in accordance with *The Law of Land Warfare* and, indeed, that manual is intended to be an expression, a complete encapsulization of the requirements of international law as applicable to the United States Army in the conduct of its hostilities.[23] And this, by the way, also includes nuclear weapons. Nuclear weapons are specifically dealt with in the manual.[24]

Q. Can you tell me, if you know, what the Department of the Army Field Manual states with respect to the laws of war and warfare?

A. Yes, the Department of the Army Field Manual is quite clear.

22. *See Field Manual* 27-10, *supra* note 13.
23. *Id.*, ¶1, at 3.
24. *Id.*, ¶35, at 18.

And I guess I know this because my teacher at the Harvard Law School wrote the Department of Army Field Manual for the Army. I studied the manual with him at great length when I took a course with him on the laws of armed conflict at Harvard Law School.

This manual expressly incorporates the Nuremberg Principles[25] and states quite clearly that the Nuremberg Principles are binding upon all U.S. military personnel, all government officials and all U.S. civilians.[26] And, hence, any of them can be guilty of crimes against peace, crimes against humanity, war crimes and conspiracy to commit these offenses, incitement to commit them, attempts to commit them or complicity in their commission. In addition, the U.S. Army Field Manual does also expressly incorporate the Hague Regulations of 1907.[27]

Finally, the U.S. Army Field Manual does have several sections that refer to the Geneva Conventions of 1949.[28] The United States government is a party to the Geneva Conventions of 1949. And there are a variety of provisions in the Geneva Conventions of 1949 that would be violated in the event nuclear weapons were used. Again, the United States government and the Army itself expressly accept all these principles on the laws of war. And there are equivalent documents put together by both the Navy and the Air Force. I do not have them here with me, but they have similar publications.

Q. Could you tell me what, if anything, the Department of Army Field Manual says about civilian responsibility for violation of the Nuremberg Principles?

A. Civilians are equally responsible. If a civilian is responsible for or involved in one way or another with the commission of crimes against peace, crimes against humanity and war crimes, they are responsible for committing crimes under international law and are subject to prosecution and punishment for those crimes.[29] Again the Field Manual makes that very clear.

---

25. *Field Manual* 27-10 incorporates both treaties and conventions and the body of unwritten or customary international law. *Id.*, ¶14, at 4. On December 11, 1946, a unanimous vote of the United Nations General Assembly affirmed the international law principles recognized by the Nuremberg Charter. These principles were subsequently codified and adopted by the International Law Commission of the United Nations in 1950. *See* Nuremberg Principles, *supra* note 17, at 833, 835.

26. *See Field Manual* 27-10, *supra* note 13, ¶7, at 4-7.

27. *Id.*, ¶5. at 4.

28. *Id.*, ¶5. at 5.

29. *Id.*, ¶498, at 178.

Q. As a point of interest, would it be a defense to the commission of a war crime, the violation of the Nuremberg Principles, that those violations were not made illegal under domestic law?

A. No. But as a matter of fact, the body of international law I have explained to you is part of U.S. domestic law.

Q. How is that so?

A. Well, first of course, the treaties are the supreme law of the land under article 6 of the Supremacy Clause, and that would include the Hague Regulations of 1907. Later on the United Nations Charter will be discussed. That would also include the Geneva Conventions of 1949. Those are the supreme law of the land. And *Paquete Habana* incorporates customary international law into U.S. domestic law.

And so the rules set forth in the U.S. Army Field Manual refer not simply to international law but U.S. domestic law. And even if there was a U.S. law to the contrary—and I don't believe there is—nevertheless it could not authorize a violation of international law. You cannot plead domestic law to excuse yourself from the commission of a violation of international law.[30]

Superior Orders

Q. Is it true that following superior orders can be used in justification of any crimes?

A. No! The Nuremberg Tribunal rejected the defense of superior orders. The Nazi leaders made the argument at Nuremberg that they were basically following orders of the fellow higher up, the highest fellow on the ladder: "I was just told to do this by Hitler." Nuremberg said: When it comes to the commission of crimes against peace, crimes against humanity and war crimes, the defense of superior orders will not be allowed so long as there exists a moral choice on your part not to obey those orders.[31] However, it can be introduced in mitigation of punishment. The Department of Army Field Manual is quite clear on this—that in the event U.S. government officials, military officers, or even civilians were to commit crimes against

---

30. For example, Nuremberg Principle II expressly recognizes that if an act is prohibited by international law, the person committing the act is not relieved of responsibility simply because an internal or domestic law does not impose a penalty for the act. *See* Nuremberg Principles, *supra* note 17, at 835.

31. *Id.* at 863.

peace, crimes against humanity and war crimes, they would not be entitled to a defense of superior orders.[32]

Additional Qualification on the Targeting of U.S. Nuclear Weapons

Q. Now, in the course of your research and your study, have you attempted to investigate the United States military policy regarding targeting and conditions under which nuclear weapons are permitted to be used by the United States?

A. That is correct. Right now I have just finished writing a monograph entitled *The Relevance of International Law to the Paradox of Nuclear Deterrence*. [*See* Chapter 3.] The monograph itself is complete and I believe you did submit it to the Judge in the motion in limine.

I am also a member of a group known as the Lawyers' Committee on Nuclear Policy, and I am part of their Council. I am also a member of a group known as the Lawyers Alliance for Nuclear Arms Control. Both groups deal with questions of nuclear weapons and, in particular, giving advice, writing, lecturing and conducting litigation in court with respect to nuclear weapons and international law. In order to give advice or formulate opinions on nuclear weapons as they relate to international law, I have had to do an enormous amount of research on the effects of nuclear weapons, how they are deployed, how they would be used, and matters of that nature. In particular, with respect to the monograph I just wrote, I have a couple of shelf-loads of books sitting on my desk that deal specifically with questions of the effects, uses, targeting and strategy of nuclear weapons. It's up to me, then, to try to relate that body of literature which is produced by military people, scientists, strategic thinkers or government officials to questions of international law.

Q. In the course of conducting your research and investigation into U.S. nuclear weapons targeting and U.S. policies, what types of materials did you rely on in ascertaining what the official U.S. government military strategies in those areas are?

A. The research problem is that much of this material is classi-

---

32. *See Field Manual* 27-10, *supra* note 13, ¶ 509, at 182-83.

fied—highly classified—so you cannot get a precise idea of what is happening on a day-to-day basis. Indeed, people who deal with the question of targeting nuclear weapons have to sign special security agreements; and they are not authorized to talk about it to anyone.

Nevertheless, it is possible, on the basis of the literature in the field, to derive some information. Actually, a good deal of information can be found in the secondary literature and official reports by the government, and most academics who write in this field rely upon these sources. The government does reveal an enormous amount of material itself in order to formulate their own judgments. In particular, I am on the Pentagon's mailing list. Every day I receive from them a packet of materials this thick dealing with questions of defense, national security and nuclear weapons policy. The Freedom of Information Act[33] has also enabled researchers to get a good deal of information. In addition, perhaps against the oaths they have taken, many former and current government officials have leaked documents and materials to the press where it has subsequently been published.

I make an attempt in my own research to read almost anything I can get my hands on that provides information on precisely how the United States nuclear weapons establishment is set up and will operate in the event of war. But I can't guarantee I have it all.

Q. Is the information that you relied on in ascertaining the official United States government targeting and U.S. policies regarding nuclear weapons the type that experts in your field would use in ascertaining these strategies?

A. Yes. As a matter of fact, the only people who would have better information than I are those who are in the government who would be under an injunction of secrecy not to reveal it.

Q. Have you been able to ascertain in the course of your research and study what the United States government nuclear targeting and U.S. policies are?

A. Yes I have, to the best of my ability, on the basis of the literature in the public record.

Q. Can you give me an idea of some of the sources that you relied upon in the course of that research?

A. Sure. As I said, official government reports and documents put

---

33. 5 *U.S.C.* § 552(a) (1982).

out by the Army and Air Force; scholarly studies that were based on the Freedom of Information Act and investigative reporting; a very large number of books. There is an enormous amount of literature that has been done in this field. So it is quite a compendium of material.

The Targeting of Nuclear Weapons

Q. Professor Boyle, how do nuclear weapons violate the principles of crimes against humanity and other principles of international law that you have enunciated?

STATE'S ATTORNEY: Objection.

Q. How do they violate those laws?

STATE'S ATTORNEY: Objection, Judge.

THE COURT: Overruled. You may answer.

THE WITNESS: Well, you have to look at how the United States government realistically contemplates using its nuclear weapons forces. And from all that I have studied, that appears in the public records, I don't see how, among the various scenarios that the United States government has developed for the use of nuclear weapons, that can be done consistent with the requirements of international law. The plans for targeting of U.S. nuclear weapons are found in what is known as the Single Integrated Operational Plan, or the SIOP. This consists of a list of targets that are going to be destroyed in the Soviet Union in the event of a nuclear war. Right now, we have approximately 10,000 strategic nuclear warheads targeted for delivery on all major population centers, military command centers, and nuclear weapons sites in the Soviet Union. If those weapons, as they are currently planned to do, are dropped on Soviet cities, this would clearly violate the Nuremberg Principles. This concept of crime against humanity specifically prohibits the wanton destruction of cities. It would clearly violate the Hague Regulations. It would clearly violate the Genocide Convention. And I am just talking about the major violations here.

Presidential Directive 59

Q. Are you familiar with Presidential Directive 59?

A. I am.

Q. Can you tell me what that is?

A. Presidential Directive 59 was promulgated by President Carter in August of 1980, and it calls for, at least in theory, the waging of a limited nuclear war against the Soviet Union.[34] Presidential Directive 59 was picked up by the Reagan administration.[35] It was explicitly endorsed by the Reagan administration, and expanded and elaborated upon in Secretary of Defense Caspar Weinberger's 5-year Defense Guidance Program calling for the Department of Defense not simply to fight a limited nuclear war but, in addition, to prevail in a protracted nuclear war.[36]

Q. To the best of your knowledge, is that current U.S. policy?

A. That is current United States policy to the best of my knowledge. Indeed, several officials in the Reagan administration have admitted that, essentially, they adhere to Presidential Directive 59.

Q. What, if anything, about Presidential Directive 59 and the policy enunciated thereunder is, in your view, violative of the principles of international law that we have talked about?

A. Within Presidential Directive 59—you have to understand that the Air Force and SAC headquarters take this policy and attempt to turn it into an actual targeting policy. They developed a list of targets known as the Single Integrated Operational Plan. That is the list of targets that will be destroyed by the United States government in the event of a nuclear war. These targets are set forth in an order of priority and certain systems are allocated to certain targets and the plan is drawn up to do this.

By the way, if you could get someone from SAC here, I am sure he would give you much better testimony as to what it says than I do. The appropriate people to talk to are the Joint Strategic Target Planning Staff at SAC. They are the ones who draw these targets up.

The problem is you are never quite sure—and there has been a history of problems—if SAC is actually going to do what the government has decided. But to the best of my knowledge, there are several problems with the list of targets in the priorities that SAC currently has.

---

34. President Carter's Remarks at the Annual Convention of the American Legion, 16 Weekly Comp. Pres. Doc. 1549, 1553 (Aug. 21, 1980).

35. *See* R. Scheer, *With Enough Shovels: Reagan, Bush & Nuclear War* 11-12 (1982).

36. For a discussion of the Five-Year Guidance Plan, *see* R. Scheer, *supra* note 35, at 8, 32. *See also*, Bethe, Gottfried & Currey, "The Five-Year War Plan," *N.Y. Times*, May 30, 1982, at A1, col. 1; *id.*, June 10, 1982, at A31, col. 1.

First-Strike

Q. When you say "problems," do you mean problems with international law?

A. Problems of international law. First, it does appear that there are first-strike scenarios.

Q. Could you describe what a "first-strike scenario" is?

A. There are several possibilities. One is, in the event of a serious geopolitical crisis between the United States and the Soviet Union, for example, there is supposed to be a scenario for the United States government to be the first to use nuclear weapons against the Soviet Union.

There has been advice given by members of the military that we be the first to use nuclear weapons in the Korean War, in Vietnam, and many other times. But so far our officials have been wise enough not to listen to that advice.

In the event that the United States government would be the first to resort to the use of nuclear weapons, it would be a clear-cut violation of the terms of the United Nations Charter and the various principles I have set forth here as well as another Hague Convention of 1907 dealing with the opening of hostilities that requires a formal declaration of war. So a surprise attack is clearly illegal and certainly planning a surprise attack is clearly illegal. But again to the best of my knowledge, we do have scenarios that would enable the president to launch a surprise attack on the Soviet Union.

NATO's First-Use Policy: Battlefield Nuclear War

Second, and this is public knowledge, in the event that the Soviet Union decides to launch a conventional invasion of Western Europe, the United States government and NATO have stated that our acknowledged policy will be to use nuclear weapons first in order to defeat that invasion. This is our first-use policy against a Soviet conventional invasion.

Indeed, as I understand it, the Rock Island Arsenal here does produce components of nuclear devices and weapons that are currently in Europe, including the Pershing missile. These weapons—artillery shells, missiles—will be used first to blunt a Soviet conventional attack. The problem with that is this: although the United States government and NATO had and would have a right to defend themselves against the Soviet attack, again as Nuremberg made clear, as the Hague Regulations made clear, you are not entitled to do whatever you want to defend yourself, but rather you have to use the measures that are necessary and proportionate, and discriminative to stop the Soviet conventional attack. And so far the United States government and NATO have not been willing, I think, to live up to that international obligation.

Q. You say that they would be entitled or privileged to use a necessary, proportionate, and discriminative response to that attack. What about the use of nuclear weapons—would that be violative of those principles?

A. First of all, of course, nuclear weapons, in response to the conventional attack, would not be proportionate. It would be completely disproportionate. Second, as is the very nature of nuclear weapons, they are not discriminating. They are not like an artillery shell, or rifle or machine gun; nor are they even like a bomber that would pick a target and bomb it. Nuclear weapons are inherently indiscriminate—especially if you are talking about nuclear weapons in Europe which has one of the highest population densities in the entire world. We are talking about killing millions of people.

Again, the Nuremberg Principles made it quite clear that you have no right to kill millions of people whatever your objectives are.

Counter-Ethnic Targeting

Q. How does it appear that the United States is preparing to violate the Genocide Convention?

STATE'S ATTORNEY: Objection, Judge.

THE COURT: Overruled. Go ahead.

THE WITNESS: As I said before, there is what is known as Presidential Directive 59, developed during the Carter administration, which I am sure some of you have read about in the newspapers. This Directive dealt with a revision of the plan for the targeting of nuclear weapons on the Soviet Union. Within this Presidential Directive 59, according to what I have read and what has been recorded, there is a plan for what is known as counter-ethnic targeting.

Counter-ethnic targeting goes along the following lines. The Soviet Union is being ruled by the ethnic group known as the Great Russians. These are the people who were originally out of Moscow historically, and are still the predominant ethnic group in the Soviet Union. They still run the country; therefore, the theory goes that if you really want to hurt them, the best thing to do would be to target cities inhabited primarily by the Great Russians and target them for severe and repeated nuclear destruction. That was an innovation again apparently put in during the Carter administration and, to the best of my knowledge, at the insistence or certainly the participation of Zbigniew Brzezinski, former national security adviser to the president. He was an expatriate Pole, and has certain opinions about Russians.

This targeting doctrine called for their destruction not because they were enemies but simply because they were Great Russians. And under the Genocide Convention, that is specifically prohibited. Counter-ethnic targeting is clearly a conspiracy to commit genocide. These people have been targeted to be killed by nuclear weapons only on the basis of their ethnicity and not for any other reason at all. It is precisely analogous to Hitler exterminating Jews simply because they were Jews. Here the United States government would be exterminating Great Russians simply because they are Great Russians and no other reason at all.

You cannot kill these people for that reason, just as Hitler could not kill people because they were Jews. U.S. government officials can't kill people because they are Great Russians, and yet that apparently is what our government is planning to do. In the event of a war, the cities that are inhabited by the Great Russians, particularly Moscow, Leningrad, will be devastated several times over so that there is no realistic possibility anyone could survive. That type of activity or planning or preparation to commit that type of activity is clearly prohibited by the terms of the Genocide Convention. But it is still carried on to the best of my knowledge by the United States government today.

Q. Would it be correct to say, then, that the existence of that policy, even in times of peace that we are enjoying right now, would in your view constitute a violation of the Genocide Convention?

A. In my opinion, yes. It is an ongoing criminal activity. It is one thing to decide that you are going to destroy your enemy and your enemy is engaged in one way or another in undertaking actual hostilities against you. But it is quite another thing to decide to exterminate millions of people simply on the basis of their ethnicity. That is precisely what the Genocide Convention meant to deal with; and the Nuremberg concept of crimes against humanity dealt with that issue.

Q. In your view, based on your knowledge and experience, is there any justification in the laws of war and international law for this counter-ethnic targeting referred to?

A. Not that I can think of. As I said, the justification that had been presented by the members of the Carter administration was simply political: "Well, they are the ones who are really running the government over there and, therefore, we should kill them and the government will collapse. And in the event the war is over, there will be no one to run the Soviet Union and the whole country, the whole empire would collapse."

The problem I have with that argument is that I think the Soviet people are even less responsible for their rulers than we are. We at least get to elect them. They don't. So I have hard problems with understanding what is our right to kill millions of people who have very little choice to say who their leaders are.

Personal Criminal Responsibility

Q. Professor Boyle, what duties or liabilities are imposed under international law on nations that threaten or use nuclear weapons?

A. The best principle here is a United States Supreme Court case—*Application of Yamashita*, which built upon the Far Eastern equivalent of the Nuremberg Tribunal. After the war in the Pacific, there was an international military tribunal established to try Japanese war criminals. And one of the war criminals tried there was General Yamashita. He was a military commander of an island that had on it U.S. prisoners of war. And while the island was being attacked, apparently some of the soldiers, subject to his command, though without his knowledge, proceeded to commit atrocities on U.S. prisoners of war.

After the war, he was tried for war crimes, and he himself was held responsible for the atrocities perpetrated by his soldiers, even though he did not order that they commit these atrocities.

And the military tribunal of the Far East held that all military officers or government officials who knew or should have known that troops or other individuals subject to their control were about to commit or have committed war crimes and did nothing to stop them or punish them are fully responsible themselves for those crimes and can be punished as war criminals.

That principle then was upheld by the United States Supreme Court. Yamashita was sentenced to death and, in order to avoid the death penalty, he petitioned to the United States Supreme Court on a writ of habeas corpus. The United States Supreme Court denied that and upheld the principle of law which I just enunciated to you; namely, all civilian officials or military officers who knew or should have known that troops or other individuals subject to their control have committed or are about to commit war crimes, and they either failed to stop it or else failed to punish violators of the laws and customs of war, are likewise responsible for those war crimes themselves.

Now, that's official U.S. law, and you can find that rule enunciated in the United States Army Field Manual of 1956. That's a standard black letter rule for both international law and U.S. domestic law, and our soldiers and sailors are trained in accordance with that.

So, applying that to the question of nuclear weapons, one would have to say that those United States government officials who know or should know that nuclear targeting is being done in a manner to devastate Soviet cities simply for the purpose of killing large numbers of people as opposed to legitimate military targets or for the purpose of killing Great Russians simply because they are Great Russians and not anything else, are responsible for those crimes.

This, then, gets into some of the justifications for the defendants' activities. Certainly a reading of the *Yamashita* case would raise questions as to what your obligation is in light of something like *Yamashita* to prevent what you believe to be the crime of conspiracy to commit genocide, crimes against peace, crimes against humanity and war crimes, grave breaches of the Geneva Conventions, and violations of the Hague Regulations.

Ongoing Criminal Activity by the Government

Q. Have you a view as to what, if any, privilege would exist under the principles that you have just discussed with respect to taking action to stop or oppose the commission of war crimes?

A. Well, certainly you have to understand it, I think, within the confines of defenses available under domestic law. And here I take it we are operating under Illinois law. We have the defenses of necessity, choice of evils—another word for it—and compulsion. Certainly under the defense of necessity or choice of evils I would think anyone would be entitled to look at the ongoing criminal activity; namely, conspiracy or complicity in the commission of these heinous crimes: as I said, genocide, crimes against peace, crimes against humanity, and war crimes. It is a breach of the Geneva Conventions and the United Nations Charter, and the Hague Regulations.

THE COURT: Excuse me. Would you go over that again.

A. I pointed out that this is not simply an activity or crimes that might occur in the future but rather these are so-called inchoate crimes. They are going on now. That is, planning, preparation, plotting and conspiracy to commit these crimes are ongoing crimes themselves. So what you have on the one hand is the ongoing crimes and, on the other, the defendants' judgment that in an effort to impede, impair, prevent or whatever these ongoing crimes, that it was necessary to prevent them, to appear and pray, to take whatever action they did. In my opinion, that would certainly be a reasonable response to the heinousness of the crimes that are actually being perpetrated.

Q. So then your testimony is that there is a public injury occurring right now, in that there is conspiracy or at least complicity to commit genocide going on?

A. As well as the rest of these crimes.

The Right to Prevent the Commission of International Crimes

Q. Within that principle of international law, where does any responsibility on the part of the U.S. citizens come?

THE WITNESS: There would be two sources of international law applicable, I think, to our situation. The first would be, again, the Judgment of the Nuremberg Tribunal itself,[37] once again for the purpose of prosecuting Nazi war criminals. And in the Nuremberg Judgments, if you read them, there is language to the effect—and here they were talking about the crimes perpetrated by Hitler against German Jews, against Russians, Slavs, and Gypsies, and many others—indicating that citizens did have an obligation to take whatever steps they could to try to prevent these types of heinous crimes.

The second source, in my opinion, would be the Statute of the International Court of Justice, article 38.[38] That article sets forth what are known as the sources of international law. One of the sources of international law is what is known as General Principles Of Law Recognized By Civilized Nations. General Principles Of Law Recognized By—

STATE'S ATTORNEY: Objection, Judge. I'd ask that the witness not repeat a statement.

THE COURT: Objection overruled. Go ahead.

THE WITNESS: Recognized By Civilized Nations. One of these general principles of law recognized by all civilized nations is the duty to act to prevent the commission of a crime. And so in my opinion, I would certainly say under international law, as a general principle of law, there is certainly a duty to act to prevent the commission of threatened war crimes, crimes against peace, crimes against humanity and genocide. But I would also certainly argue that as a matter of common law, there should be recognized a common law right to take steps necessary to inhibit this type of activity. It is very clear under international law that there would be no problem with this. It is also very clear under the *Paquete Habana* case that international law is a part of the United States law.

The Illegality of Nuclear Deterrence

Q. Professor Boyle, based on your research and your expertise in international law, do you have an opinion as to the overall illegality of the nuclear weapons policy of the U.S. government?

---

37. *See Trial of the Major War Criminals Before the International Military Tribunal* 171 (1947).

38. *See Documents on the International Court of Justice* 79 (S. Rosenne ed. 1979).

THE WITNESS: I do.

STATE'S ATTORNEY: Objection, Judge.

THE COURT: Overruled.

Q. And what is that opinion?

THE WITNESS: In my opinion, and I have stated this in articles and have delivered it in conferences, all United States government officials and also officials of the Soviet Union who launch or wage their nuclear war either on the Soviet Union or on the United States, respectively, would be guilty of crimes against peace, crimes against humanity, war crimes, grave breaches of the Geneva Conventions, and acts of genocide at a minimum. And, most probably, they would all be subject to prosecution and conviction as war criminals just as happened at Nuremberg and as happened in the Far East after the Second World War. Hence, today, they are all guilty of the international crimes of planning, preparing, and conspiring to commit crimes against peace, crimes against humanity, war crimes and genocide, at a minimum.

The Imminence of the Danger

Q. Professor Boyle, in the course of your research, have you had occasion to investigate situations, if any, under which the United States satellite and radar systems have either operated or malfunctioned?

A. Yes, I have.

Q. Can you tell me what you know about that?

A. Again, a lot of it is highly classified, but there have been some congressional investigations launched due to a leaky door at the Pentagon indicating that U.S. nuclear forces were put on a false nuclear alert and there were mistaken indications that we were under nuclear attack. I believe you have there with you one of these reports. I read it quite some time ago, so I can't say that I'm up on all of it right now.

But, for example, during a certain period referred to in there, I think NORAD experienced something like 150 malfunctions and failures. A few of these were quite serious. The most serious—oh, I think about two years ago now, was during what was supposed to be a routine test of the operation of the system. A computer programmer took a computer tape that was to simulate an all-out nuclear attack on the United States of America. And instead of putting it into the computer channel that would indicate it was a test, he fed the tape into a live channel, so that the people at NORAD actually believed we were under an attack. And this took them at least ten minutes to figure out, if I remember correctly—again I haven't read that report in a while. I think it took approximately—approximately ten minutes for them to figure out that this just wasn't true. The problem is that these weapons systems have to be fired within half an hour.

Q. Why is that?

A. Within half an hour—that is basically the time it would take an ICBM to leave the territory of the Soviet Union and strike an ICBM silo here in the United States of America.

So you are talking about a half hour and already ten minutes have been used up. And at that level they had not even gotten to the president to decide this matter. As I understand it, they had gotten to the level of the joint chiefs of staff and were just about either—or just had informed the secretary of defense. So it took ten minutes to do that. This is important, I think, to the defense of the defendants in terms of imminence, how immediate the danger there is that we are dealing with when it comes to nuclear weapons.

It could be the case, for example, that in a crisis between the United States and the Soviet Union—along the lines of the Cuban missile crisis, or the Yom Kippur War in 1973 when President Nixon put our forces on nuclear alert—that a similar mistake could be made and someone might actually believe we are being attacked and order retaliation by the use of nuclear weapons. That is eminently feasible. Indeed, there are many people, distinguished public officials, who believe that something of this nature could very well happen.

The Effects of Nuclear War and Nuclear Winter

Q. I'm going to show you what I have marked as defendants' exhibit No. 9 for identification purposes and ask if you can identify that exhibit for me and tell the Court whether or not you are familiar with it.

A. Yes, this is defendants' exhibit no. 9, *The Effects of Nuclear*

War, published by the Office of Technology Assessment. It is a branch of the Congress of the United States of America to investigate into so-called technical issues. And, indeed, this material, this report here has now been superseded by the recent research that has been conducted on so-called "nuclear winter." Superseded not in the sense that this is invalidated but in the sense that the situation is far worse than anything described in this report. Under the "nuclear winter" report, it appears that even if there was a limited nuclear exchange between the United States and the Soviet Union, there would develop the sort of nuclear winter that would lead to dramatic temperature decreases on the planet, to the destruction of human beings as a species, and most forms of life.

I should point out that in the *New York Times* in either last Saturday's or Sunday's edition, there was a headline indicating that the Pentagon has just published a 13-page pamphlet, stating that it now accepts the conclusions of the nuclear winter research. I have not been able to get a copy of that pamphlet yet and read it, but the *New York Times* did have excerpts from the report and its conclusions. Apparently the Pentagon itself does not dispute the fact that in the event of a nuclear exchange at even a limited level between the two superpowers, nuclear winter would occur and would probably extinguish life as we know it today. Again, that deals, I think, with the defendants' defense here that they were acting in the face of imminent threat to themselves and to the entire human race.

The Geneva Protocol of 1925

Q. The effects of nuclear war, as outlined in the Office of Technology Assessment report, those effects would constitute violations of international law?

A. Clearly, clearly. There is also another treaty involved here: the Geneva Protocol of 1925. The United States government became a party to the Geneva Protocol in 1975 and the Geneva Protocol prohibits the use in warfare of poison gas, chemical weapons, bacteriological weapons and all analogous substances and liquids. Many international scholars believe that the radiation coming from a nuclear attack is the equivalent to poison toxin, and, therefore, prohibited by the Geneva Protocol of 1925 which, as I stated, the United

States government today is a party to. And that again if you read these types of studies, you will see that so many die from the blast but then large numbers after that die from radiation poisoning. And the use of poison weapons or weapons that involve poison or rely upon poison or analogous substances, under the language of that treaty, are prohibited.

Q. Thank you Professor Boyle. I have no further questions.

3. Oral Argument to Admit an Offer of Proof.

THE COURT: Do you have any additional comments generally on the offer of proof?

MR. LOVE: You mean any argument at all?

THE COURT: Yes.

MR. LOVE: I certainly do and I'd like the opportunity to make it.

Your Honor, with respect to Professor Boyle's testimony, we were attempting there to make out a defense of privilege which in my view has its foundation in the common law defense which allows an individual who was aware of the fact that crimes were ongoing to take reasonable action to stop that crime or to bring it to the attention of the appropriate authorities.

THE COURT: You are saying that this is the only way that that can be done?

MR. LOVE: I am.

THE COURT: The way it was done was the only reason for it to be done?

MR. LOVE: I'm saying the reasonableness of these particular acts is a question that ought to go to the jury under the defense of privilege and that is something the jury ought to be determining. It would be our contention that based on the *Paquete Habana*, international law and the principles that Professor Boyle has testified to have become incorporated in and a part of the general common law that this Court has to apply. One of those common law principles is the privilege to take action if it is reasonably proportionate to stop ongoing crimes, and that is exactly what the defense is in this case.

We feel that under the decisions that I have cited earlier of the Seventh Circuit that we have made out a case that is supported by the law and has some foundation in the evidence. And for the Court not to allow this evidence to go to the jury is interfering with my clients' fundamental rights to be presumed innocent and also inter-feres with their right to due process and put on a case in their favor.

Secondly, I think the evidence adduced in the offer of proof also establishes a jury question with respect to the necessity defense. And I think that this question—this evidence ought to be admitted, it ought to be considered by the jury in order to have my clients' rights to the presumption of innocence adequately protected.

THE COURT: What are the elements of the necessity defense?

MR. LOVE: Well, we really have two necessity defenses. The de-fense that —

THE COURT: I realize your argument that the unlawful re-entry would come under the federal rule and in criminal trespass of land it would come under the state rule because of the Assimilative Crimes Act; is that correct?

MR. LOVE: That is correct.

THE COURT: I guess my question to you is this: the Court has spent some time reading the state court decisions dealing with ne-cessity and my understanding is that basically they constitute—as a parole matter they involve the application of the same rules; that there is no substantive difference between the application of the federal rule and the application of state rule. If that is not true, I'd appreciate if you could cite me to a state case that would indicate that distinction.

MR. LOVE: Well, if I could direct the Court's attention to my Instruction No. 12, which is drawn from the Illinois Pattern Instruc-tions, the one distinction that I see is that there is no immediacy requirement. And I think the absence of the immediacy requirement is a significant distinction between the elements of the federal and the elements of the state necessity defense.

THE COURT: What about the aspect dealing with no other rea-sonable alternative?

MR. LOVE: I don't think there is any question that the Illinois courts have imposed that requirement as a matter of interpretation.

THE COURT: Do you have any other arguments?

MR. LOVE: The only thing I would say, Judge, is that in my view under the international law defense and the question of privilege, we are in the following situation here: Hypothetically, if I may, I would submit that it is implicit in our defense that if people had gone to Dachau prior to the time that the Nazis started using it for their criminal purposes and while they were aspiring to do so, that they'd be charged under German domestic law with trespass and they would have been privileged to commit that trespass. To uphold the principles of the law of mankind, and that is exactly what we have here, it is enough that it should go to the jury and the jury should be able to decide the question. I have nothing further.

THE COURT: Thank you.

4. Sample Jury Instructions.

A. From *United States v. Schweiters*

1. Defense of Privilege Under International Law

The Genocide Convention of 1948, adopted by the United Nations General Assembly, is binding upon the government of the United States, its civilian and military officials, and its citizens, as a matter of customary international law.

International law makes any of the following acts punishable as a crime against international law:

(a) Genocide;

(b) Conspiracy to commit genocide;

(c) Complicity in genocide.

The foregoing acts are crimes against international law whether committed in times of war or peace.

Genocide means any of the following acts committed with intent to destroy, in whole or in part, a national, ethnical, racial or religious group, as such:

(a) Killing members of the group;

(b) Causing serious bodily or mental harm to members of the group;

(c) Deliberately inflicting on the group conditions of life calculated to bring about its physical destruction in whole or in part.

If you find from a consideration of all the evidence that the defendant reasonably believed that conspiracy to commit genocide, or complicity therein, was being committed by civilian or military officials of the United States and that these defendants acted out of an honest belief that they were privileged under international law to take reasonable steps to uphold international law, and the acts committed by defendants in this case were such reasonable steps, you must find the defendants not guilty.

Genocide Convention of 1948

> *Paquete Habana*, 175 U.S. 677
> (1899)
> *U.S. v. Grimes*, 413 F.2d 1376
> (7th Cir. 1969)
> *U.S. v. Walsh*, 627 F.2d 88 (7th
> Cir. 1980)

2. Second Defense Under International Law

The Charter of the International Military Tribunal, commonly known as the Nuremberg Tribunal, was an executive agreement signed by the government of the United States in 1945, and is binding upon the government of the United States, its civilian and military officials, and its citizens, as a matter of customary international law.

Any person, whether a member of the armed forces or a civilian, who commits any of the following acts during peace or war commits a crime against international law:

(a) Crimes against peace: namely, planning, preparation, initiation or waging of a war of aggression, or a war in violation of international treaties, agreements or assurances, or participation in a common plan or conspiracy for accomplishment of any of the foregoing;

(b) War crimes: namely, violations of the laws or customs of war. Such violations shall include, but not be limited to, murder, wanton destruction of cities, towns or villages, or devastation not justified by military necessity.

(c) Crimes against humanity: namely, murder, extermination and other inhumane acts committed against any civilian population, before or during the war.

Conspiracy, direct incitement, and attempts to commit, as well as complicity in the commission of crimes against peace, crimes against humanity and war crimes are all violations of international law.

The fact that domestic law does not impose a penalty for an act which constitutes a crime under international law is not a defense to a crime against international law.

If you find from a consideration of all the evidence that the defendant reasonably believed that conspiracy to commit crimes against peace, war crimes or crimes against humanity, or complicity therein, was being committed by civilian or military officials of the United States, and that the defendant acted out of an honest belief that they were privileged under international law to take reasonable steps to uphold international law, and the acts committed by the defendant in this case were such reasonable steps, you must find the defendant not guilty.

> Department of the Army, *The Law of Land Warfare, Department of the Army Field Manual* FM 27-10 §§ 498, 500 and 511
>
> Charter of the International Military Tribunal, Art. VI, U.S. Statutes at Large, Vol. 59, pp. 1544-1589
>
> *Paquete Habana*, 175 U.S. 677 (1899)
>
> *U.S. v. Grimes*, 413 F.2d 1376 (7th Cir. 1969)

3. Rights Protected by the First Amendment

The First Amendment to the Constitution guarantees citizens the rights of freedom of speech, freedom of assembly, freedom to petition the government for redress of grievances and freedom to exercise their religion.

Pointed expression of anguish about current domestic and foreign affairs of the government is expression protected by the First Amendment and cannot be criminally punished except in the most compelling circumstances.

If you find from all the evidence of this case that the governmental act defining the offense is being applied to the defendants in a way that restricts the defendants' rights of conscience, expression, assembly or exercise of religion, then there arises a presumption against the constitutionality of the governmental act and the government bears the burden of proving that the application of this legislative act to the defendants is justified.

In order to meet this burden of proof, the government must establish the following propositions:

First: That application of the legislative act to the defendants in this case is reasonably necessary to maintain the order, security and discipline necessary to military operations at Rock Island Arsenal; and

Second: That the portion of Rock Island Arsenal where defendants committed the acts charged was not open to the general public and that visitors were not encouraged to visit that portion of the installation.

If you find from all the evidence of this case that the government has failed to prove each one of these propositions, and that First Amendment rights are involved, then you must find the defendants not guilty.

If you find from all the evidence of this case that First Amendment rights of the defendants are not involved, and all other elements of the offense have been proven beyond a reasonable doubt, then you must find the defendants guilty.

> *U.S. v. Gourley*, 502 F.2d 785
> (10th Cir. 1974)
> *Kiskilla v. Nichols*, 433 F.2d 745
> (7th Cir. 1970)
> *Cline v. Rockingham Sup. Ct.*,
> 502 F.2d 789 (1st Cir. 1974)
> *Flowers v. U.S.*, 407 U.S. 197
> (1972)

4. Ignorance or Mistake

A person's ignorance or mistake as to a matter of either fact or law is a defense to the charge if it negates the existence of the mental state, here "knowingly," which the issued instruction requires be proven as an element of the offense charged.

A person's reasonable belief that his conduct does not constitute an offense is a defense if:

(1) He acts in reliance on decisions of the United States Supreme Court or Appellate Courts of the United States; or

(2) He acts in reliance on treaties or, where there is no controlling treaty, the customs and usages of civilized nations as evidenced by the ordinances of foreign states, the opinions of eminent statesmen and the writings of distinguished jurists and commentators who by years of research and experience have made themselves peculiarly well acquainted with international law.

A defense based on ignorance or mistake is an affirmative defense.

> Ill. Rev. Stat. ch. 38 § 4-8

Paquete Habana, 175 U.S. 677
(1899)

5. Necessity

Conduct which would otherwise be an offense is justifiable by reason of necessity if the defendant was without blame in occasioning or developing the situation and reasonably believed that such conduct was necessary to avoid a public or private injury greater than the injury which might reasonably result from his own conduct.

> I.P.I. 24-25.22, p. 570
> *People v. Jarka,* Chicago Daily Law Bulletin, February 26, 1985, 19th Judicial Cir. No. 002170
> *Commonwealth v. Berrigan,* 472 A.2d 1099 (Penn. 1984)

B. From *People v. Jarka*

1. International law is binding on the United States of America and on the State of Illinois.
2. The use or threat of use of nuclear weapons is a war crime or an attempted war crime because such use would violate international law by causing unnecessary suffering, failing to distinguish between combatants and noncombatants and poisoning its targets by radiation.
3. An individual citizen has an obligation and duty under international law to prevent war crimes, crimes against peace and crimes against humanity.

5. Boyle, "Star Wars vs. International Law: The Force Will Be Against Us," *updated from* American Branch, International Law Association, *International Practitioner's Notebook,* October 1985 (No. 32).

When President Reagan first announced his so-called Strategic Defense Initiative (SDI) on March 23, 1983, that act represented nothing less than a formal statement by the U.S. government of its intention to pursue a policy that will eventually result in the commission of numerous material breaches of the 1972 U.S.-U.S.S.R. Anti-Ballistic Missile System (ABM) Treaty. In other words, the SDI program actually constitutes an anticipatory breach of the ABM Treaty itself. The evidence seems to indicate that the Soviet Union has interpreted the SDI in this fashion. Undoubtedly, therefore, the Soviets will respond in kind, and the monumental ABM Treaty will gradually fall into desuetude even if not specifically denounced or abrogated by either superpower.

As originally proclaimed, this Star Wars program was to involve the research, development, and testing of a variety of advanced space-based ABM technologies. However, two former high-level U.S. diplomats involved in the ABM Treaty negotiations (i.e., Gerard Smith, Head of the SALT I delegation, and John Rhinelander, its Legal Adviser) pointed out that only "research" on spaced-based ABM systems or components was permitted by article 5 of the ABM Treaty, whereas their development, testing, and deployment were specifically prohibited. Hence, the Reagan administration quickly changed its public rhetoric to claim that the SDI program will currently involve only research on, and not development and testing of, space-based ABM technologies. Nevertheless, the record clearly indicates that the Star Wars program involves all three elements and therefore would specifically violate this provision of the ABM Treaty, among others.

Such deleterious events place into proper perspective what is really happening in the current round of negotiations over strategic and theater nuclear forces and space weapons with the Soviet Union at Geneva. The Reagan administration has instructed the U.S. delegation only to discuss, not to negotiate, the Star Wars program with the Soviets, and to obtain their acquiescence in the SDI if possible. Essentially this means that the United States delegation is attempting to procure Soviet agreement to either the formal or informal abrogation of the ABM Treaty.

If that should occur, however, then negotiated restrictions on strategic nuclear weapons systems by the two superpowers will prove to be impossible to obtain at Geneva. If the ABM Treaty is formally or informally abrogated, then the 1972 SALT I Interim Accord that freezes the number of ICBM and SLBM launchers will become a nullity because of the mutual interdependence of these two seminal agreements. The establishment of this interconnection was at the suggestion of the United States over the initial opposition of the Soviet

Union. Similarly, the SALT I Interim Accord ballistic missile freeze was continued by the 1974 Vladivostok Agreement concluded between President Ford and General Secretary Brezhnev, which also incorporated other important elements of SALT I. The Vladivostok Agreement then served as the basis for the subsequent negotiation of the SALT II Treaty, which placed limits on the number of warheads per ballistic missile.

Thus the SDI program will require the formal or informal termination of the ABM Treaty, the SALT I Interim Accord, the Vladivostok Agreement and the SALT II Treaty. Yet, the theoretical success of SDI as a defensive or non-first-strike weapon ultimately depends upon a continuation of the SALT I and SALT II numerical limitations on ballistic missile launchers and warheads, which in turn ultimately depend upon a continuation of the ABM Treaty, which in turn must be formally or informally abrogated to pursue SDI. Undaunted by the illogic of this conundrum, in May of 1986 President Reagan announced his intention no longer to observe the SALT I and SALT II numerical limitations. Nothing could provide a better indication of the duplicity behind the Reagan administration's fatuous claim that SDI is intended to be a purely defensive weapon.

In addition, SDI would probably violate the 1967 Outer Space Treaty, which prohibits the deployment of some of SDI's envisioned weapons of mass destruction in outer space. It appears from a public description of some of these SDI weapons that they are clearly intended to be given an offensive capability. In particular, SDI weapons would serve a most useful purpose as part of a U.S. first-strike strategy for the instantaneous destruction of those elements of the Soviet command, control and communications system that are dependent upon satellites.

Furthermore, testing some of the SDI's proposed technologies would violate the pathbreaking 1963 Limited Test Ban Treaty, which specifically prohibits any type of nuclear explosion in outer space. One of the most favored SDI technologies at this time is the so-called x-ray laser, which depends upon a nuclear explosion to generate it. Clearly, the testing and deployment of an x-ray laser in outer space would constitute a material breach of the Limited Test Ban Treaty and the Outer Space Treaty. Even more immediately, it was the Reagan administration's supposed need to test the x-ray laser that served as a pretext for its rejection of the Soviet invitation to duplicate their imposition of a unilateral moratorium on the underground testing of nuclear weapons on August 6, 1985 that will continue until January 1, 1987.

As for the Reagan administration's so-called "reinterpretation" of the ABM Treaty, this concoction was cooked up in the office of Richard Perle, who had always opposed the conclusion of meaningful arms control agreements between our two countries going all the way back to the SALT I negotiations from which the ABM Treaty emerged. The Reagan administration's perversion of the meaning of the ABM Treaty has yet to receive the endorsement of any respectable international law professor or lawyer who is not on the government's payroll. Indeed, it has been explicitly repudiated by the conservative international lawyers who negotiated the ABM Treaty on behalf of the Nixon administration. In opposition to these facts, we are expected to accept the disingenuous assurance by Legal Adviser Abraham Sofaer that the classified negotiating history of the ABM treaty really supports the Reagan administration's reinterpretation of it out of existence. Although this specious argument might be successful at deceiving certain segments of the American people into supporting SDI, it will not convince the Soviet government, whose interpretation of the ABM Treaty is what really counts.

Quite obviously, SDI is not a blueprint for the elimination of nuclear weapons, but rather will serve as a catalyst for an unrestricted buildup in both offensive and defensive nuclear weapons systems by the two superpowers and their allies. Indeed, with the explicit approval and active support of the Reagan administration, the Pentagon has proceeded apace with the design, testing, and deployment of three separate, independent, and potentially offensive first-strike counterforce strategic nuclear weapons systems: the Air Force's MX, the Navy's Trident 2, and the Army's Pershing 2. To this formidable arsenal should also be added the MK12A warhead for the MIRVed (3 RVs) Minuteman 3 ICBM system that can also exercise a substantial countersilo capability. That is an astounding and truly disturbing situation.

This author is confident the Soviet leadership could not even begin to comprehend why the United States government, professing a genuine commitment to nuclear arms control and reductions, would want to field four offensive first-strike counterforce strategic nuclear weapons systems at the same time. Based upon all the evidence so far available, the most likely and logical conclusion for the Politburo to have drawn is that the Reagan administration has exploited the American public's paranoid fear over the so-called "window of vulnerability" in order to generate the requisite high degree of popular support for the expenditure of funds exorbitant enough to deploy such new nuclear weapons systems that would for the first time provide the U.S. president with the theoretical capability to wage a "successful" offensive limited nuclear war against Soviet ICBM silos. From the Soviet perspective, therefore, an essential precondition for the Reagan administration's pursuit of a first-strike strategic nuclear weapons capability becomes the construction of seemingly effective anti-ballistic missile system defense in order to defeat any anticipated retaliatory attack by the residue of Soviet nuclear forces.

For these reasons, the Reagan administration's proposals to defend a multibillion dollar land-based MX system with a trillion dollar land-based and space-based anti-ballistic missile system compound one folly with another to create strategic and economic insanity. It must be made emphatically clear to the Soviet Union that the United States will not terminate the life of the ABM Treaty when it comes up for review in 1987, or beyond. That objective would require the formal termination of the Star Wars program, though genuinely basic research could still be conducted as a hedge against some technological development that might encourage either side to "break out" of the ABM Treaty on six-months notice as permitted by its terms. But unless the Reagan administration disavows the Star Wars program immediately, the accelerating force of the nuclear arms race between the two superpowers and their allies will completely overwhelm what limited capability mankind still possesses to stop and then reverse its awesome momentum. The force of the universe will truly be against us all.

Chapter 5.

Trial Materials on Central America and International Law

This chapter contains trial materials that you can utilize to prepare a civil resistance case involving U.S. military intervention in Central America and the Caribbean Basin. All of these materials have actually been used in real cases that this author has consulted on. The first document is the defendants' response to the government's motion in limine in the *Jarka* case. This is followed by the expert witness testimony I actually gave with respect to Central America and international law in *Jarka*. Next come jury instructions from that case. This chapter concludes with several short pieces that I have authored dealing with various aspects of U.S. foreign policy toward Central American and the Caribbean Basin, which have been used to prepare a variety of civil resistance cases involving this region of the world. These comments are collected here for the sake of your convenience and ease of reference and citation.

1. Sample for Motion in Limine.

IN THE CIRCUIT COURT OF LAKE COUNTY, ILLINOIS
NINETEENTH JUDICIAL CIRCUIT

PEOPLE OF THE STATE OF
ILLINOIS,   )
Plaintiff,   )

v.   )
)
ANN JARKA, ELIZABETH LEWIS, STE-   )   Nos. 002170,
PHEN HARDIN,   )
SONNY LOPEZ, CHARLIE BRON-   )   002196-002212,
SON, CLARA MIRFIELD,   )
BRETTE MARGOLIS, DANIEL KUHN,   )   00214, 002236-00238.
LAWRENCE HILDES,   )
ROBERT RUDNER, DANIEL ROCH-   )
MAN, BRADLEY STEIN,   )
SUSAN CHESSMORE, ANTHONY   )
HINTZE, BRENDA McCARTHY,   )
DOROTHY GARTLAND, SAMAN-   )
THA McEVILLY, JANET HORMAN,   )
JODY HOWARD, and MARY   )
PATTEN.   )

DEFENDANTS' MEMORANDUM IN RESPONSE TO
STATE'S MOTION IN LIMINE TO BAR NECESSITY DEFENSE

> There are higher values than the value of literal compliance with
> the law. As soon as we acknowledge this fact, we recognize that
> the justification defense is essential to the rationality and justice of
> all penal provisions. *Com. v. Berrigan*, 472 A.2d 1009, 1114 (Penn.
> 1984). Justice J. Spaeth, concurring (citations omitted).

Defendants seek to assert the defense of necessity during their trial
for the offenses of mob action and resisting arrest, allegedly committed on November 13, 1984. Necessity is defined by statute as
follows:

> Conduct which would otherwise be an offense is justifiable by
> reason of necessity if the accused was without blame in occasioning
> or developing the situation and reasonably believed such conduct
> was necessary to avoid a public or private injury greater than the
> injury which might reasonably result from his own conduct. Ill.
> Rev. Stat. Ch. 38, § 7-13.

The statute contains two parts, 1) lack of blame on the part of the
defendant, and 2) that the defendant reasonably believed the conduct

was necessary. *People v. Parker*, 113 Ill. App. 3d 321, 328 (4th Dist. 1983). The defendants are entitled to present evidence of the defense of necessity as they meet these two requirements.

Defendants will offer evidence—through their own testimony and that of expert witnesses—that the greater public injury they sought to avoid was the increasing U.S. nuclear arms build-up and U.S. intervention in Central America.

As to the first element of the defense, these defendants have never participated in official U.S. decision-making or military action; they are not members of any branch of government. Therefore, they are without blame in occasioning the situation whereby, for example, the U.S. has mined Nicaraguan harbors, has sent military arms and advisors to help the contras overthrow the elected government of Nicaragua, has stationed nuclear submarines in the Caribbean, and has supplied nuclear capable artillery to certain Central American factions, thereby greatly increasing the probability and imminence of nuclear war in our hemisphere.

The second element of the defense of necessity is that the defendants must have reasonably believed that their actions were necessary to avoid a public or private injury greater than the injury that might result from his or her own conduct. The defendants believe that the prosecution will present evidence that the defendants linked arms or sat in the middle of Sheridan Road, in a non-violent manner, blocking the traffic into Gate 4 of Great Lakes Naval Training Base. The greatest injury that reasonably might have resulted from defendants' actions was that traffic might have been stopped or delayed for a short period. The greater injuries which defendants sought to avoid or avert are the ongoing slaughter and torture of innocent people in Central America through direct and covert actions of the United States, the imminent danger of a major military conflict in Central America involving the United States, the frightening build-up of nuclear weapons by the United States, and the increasing possibility that Central America could become a flashpoint for nuclear war.

The defendants, who represent a variety of ages and religious and lay concerns, will show through their own testimony their histories of involvement in political and social concerns; they will show through the testimony of other witnesses that they had reasonable grounds to believe that their actions were necessary as part of a broader public movement to reverse U.S. military policy in Central

America and stop the nuclear arms race. They hoped by their actions to educate the general public and the trainees at the Naval Base about these issues. It was not necessary for defendants to believe that their actions alone would accomplish the goals of stopping war in Central America or ending the arms race. As Pennsylvania Superior Court Justice J. Spaeth stated in his concurring opinion in *Com. v. Berrigan*, 472 A.2d 1099 (Penn. 1984):

> Appellants do not assert that their action would avoid nuclear war (what a grandiose and unlikely idea!). Instead, at least so far as I can tell from the record, their belief was that their action, in combination with the actions of others, might accelerate a political process ultimately leading to the abandonment of nuclear missiles. And that belief, I submit, should not be dismissed as "unreasonable as a matter of law." A jury might or might not find it unreasonable as a matter of fact. But that is for a jury to say, not for a court. At 1114-5.

In its Motion in Limine, the prosecution cites *People v. Kirzka*, 92 Ill. App.3d 288, 416 N.E.2d 36 (1st Dist. 1980) for the proposition that the "offenses charged were not committed with the intention of preventing any legally recognized injury." In *Kirzka*, the defendants sought to interpose themselves between females seeking abortions and employees of an abortion clinic. The injury that the defendants were claiming [that] was greater than their conduct was the "killing of any unborn fetus," at 36. The court held, however, that this alleged "injury" was a legally protected right according to *Roe v. Wade*, 410 U.S. 113 (1973) and *Planned Parenthood v. Danforth*, 428 U.S. 52 (1976).

In contrast, the injury sought to be prevented here is *not* a legally protected right of the U.S. government. To the contrary, various U.S. policies in Central America violate international law, international treaties, the U.S. Constitution and the will of the Congress of the United States. Examples of such violations are the U.S. mining of Nicaraguan harbors, covert U.S. aid to anti-government factions in Nicaragua, continued U.S. violations of Nicaraguan air and water space, the infamous CIA manual instructing military personnel on successful methods of assassinating political opponents, the secret development and deployment of nuclear weapons, as well as the continuing secrecy and misinformation given to the American public and elected lawmaking bodies regarding these actions. The defendants will produce expert witnesses in support of these claims.

International law consistently prohibits nuclear proliferation and condemns U.S. policies and practices in Central America. Principles of international law certainly may be considered by this court. As the U.S. Supreme Court has said,

> International law is part of our law and must be ascertained and administered by the courts of justice of appropriate jurisdiction, as often as questions of right depending upon it are duly presented for their determination. *The Paquete Habana*, 175 U.S. 677, 700 (1900).

The United Nations Charter is a treaty to which the U.S. is party and therefore, under the U.S. Constitution, part of the Supreme Law of the land.

> This country has a continuing obligation to observe with entire good faith and scrupulous care all of its undertakings under this (United Nations) treaty, including support of resolutions adopted by the Security Council. 74 Am. Jur. 2d *Treaties*, Sec. 14 (1974). 22 U.S.C.S. Sec. 287(c); *U.S. v. Steinberg*, 478 F. Supp. 29, 33 (1979).

Furthermore, under Article IV, Section 2 of the U.S. Constitution, these defendants, as Illinois citizens, are entitled to the privileges and immunities of U.S. citizens and therefore, also have the right to rely on international law.

On May 10, 1984, the International Court of Justice, which is the principal judicial organ of the United Nations, condemned the U.S.'s activities in Nicaragua and ordered as provisional measures, that:

> The United States of America should immediately cease and refrain from any action restricting, blocking or endangering access to or from Nicaraguan ports, and in particular, the laying of mines.
> The right to sovereignty and to political independence possessed by the Republic of Nicaragua...should be fully respected and should not in any way be jeopardized by any military or paramilitary activities which are prohibited by the principles of international law, in particular the principle that States should refrain in their international relations from the threat or use of force against the territorial

> integrity or the political independence of any State, and the prin-
> ciple concerning the duty not to intervene in matters within the
> domestic jurisdiction of a State.
> *Military and Paramilitary Activities in and against Nicaragua* (Nic-
> aragua v. United States of America) Provisional Measures, *I.C.J.
> Reports*, p. 169 (1984).

The fact that the Reagan administration walked out of the International
Court hearings on Nicaragua underscores the urgency of the situation
and the need for alternative action.

The U.S. invasion of Grenada on October 25, 1983, in which
1900 U.S. marines fought for a week, is another example of illegal
U.S. intervention. It was deplored as a gross violation of international
law by eleven members of the United Nations Security Council and
108 members of the U.N. General Assembly. (83 *Dep't St. Bull.* 89
(Dec. 1983) and 84 *Dep't St. Bull.* 92 (Jan. 1984).)

Moreover, a lawsuit filed in federal court in November 1983 by
eleven members of Congress against President Reagan claims that
the invasion of Grenada violated the War Power Clause of the U.S.
Constitution, Article I, Sec. 8. The district court refused jurisdiction;
that refusal is currently being appealed. *Conyers v. Reagan*, F. Supp.
(D.D.C. 1984).

Nuclear weapons contravene international law because their use
makes no distinction between civilian and military targets. The atomic
bombs dropped on Japan are history's glaring proof. The use of nuclear weapons directly violates Protocol I of the Geneva Conventions:

> In order to ensure respect for and protection of the civilian popu-
> lation and civilian objects, the Parties to the conflict shall at all
> times distinguish between the civilian objects and military objec-
> tives and accordingly shall direct their operations only against mil-
> itary objectives. Article 48, Part IV of the Protocol Additional to the
> Geneva Conventions of 12 August 1949, and Relating to the Pro-
> tection of Victims of International Armed Conflicts (Protocol I).

A nation's inviolable right to sovereignty is another principle of
international law being violated by the U.S. in Nicaragua. This right
of sovereignty prohibits direct and indirect military intervention as
well as coercion of either a political or economic nature. (Articles
18, 19, and 20 of the Charter of the Organization of American States;

Bogota, April 30, 1948. Entered into force for the U.S., December 13, 1951.)

The defense in this case will present evidence of the interventionist and coercive policies and practices of the U.S. throughout Central America. The defendants will testify that their conduct was the culmination of a week–long effort to make their concerns known to the recruits at the Great Lakes Naval Training Base in the aftermath of the re-election of the U.S. president who was responsible for the U.S. foreign policy which repeatedly violated international law.

The State here argues that the defendants should be prohibited from asserting the necessity defense in that there were other alternatives to their acts which were not unlawful, citing *People v. White*, 78 Ill. App. 3d 979, 397 N.E.2d 1246 (4th Dist., 1979). In *White*, the defendant escaped while on leave from a community corrections center when he learned that his wife had been raped and his daughter beaten. The defendant had been informed about rules and procedures concerning emergency leave; he did not follow those rules, which provided that he should contact his counselor to request emergency leave. The court found that defendant had a legal option available to him which he did not follow. "When there is yet another alternative—besides the two evil choices—and such alternative, if carried out, will cause less harm, then a person is not justified in breaking the law," at 1247. The court held that defendant was properly barred from testifying as to his reason for escaping because the "evil" he sought to prevent had already occurred.

White followed *People v. Unger*, 66 Ill.2d 333, 362 N.E.2d 319 (1977), which is also a case where the defendant escaped from prison and sought to use a necessity defense. As our Supreme Court noted, traditionally courts have been reluctant to permit the necessity defense to be relied upon by escapees, because of public policy considerations. 66 Ill.2d at 338. Defendants in the case before the bar suggest that the public policy considerations of prison escape cases make those cases of limited value to this court.

The court in *Unger* found that certain considerations would go to the weight and credibility of the defendant's testimony, but would not be necessary as a matter of law to establish a meritorious necessity defense. Those considerations were (among others) that there is not time for complaint to authorities, and there is not time to resort to the courts. The presence or absence of these alternatives to escape would go to the defendant's credibility, not his ability to use the necessity defense. The court found that defendant was entitled to submit his defense of necessity to the jury even though there was some question as to defendant's reasons for escaping.

Similarly, in the instant case, the fact that there may be other alternatives to defendant's actions does not make the defense of necessity totally unavailable as a matter of law. The question of the reasonableness of defendant's actions is one for the jury to decide.

The state of Pennsylvania has a justification defense which is similar to Illinois' necessity statute. The court in *Commonwealth v. Capitolo*, 471 A.2d 462 (Pa. Sup. Ct. 1984), noted that the statute does not by its language require that a defendant prove exhaustion of other alternatives. Similarly, the Illinois statute does not require exhaustion of alternatives. The Pennsylvania court observed that whether or not all other legal alternatives are ineffective, unavailable or already exhausted depends in part on how soon the threatened harm will become manifest. 471 A.2d at 469. The daily slaughter of people in Central America, and the imminent threat of nuclear holocaust, are proof of the immediacy of the threat, as defendants' witnesses will show.

In *City of Chicago v. Mayer*, 56 Ill.2d 366 (1974), the defendant was a medical student who was a first-aid assistant at a demonstration in 1969 in Chicago. During the demonstration, a man was injured and lay in the middle of the street. Because the defendant feared that if the injured man were moved it could result in permanent spinal injury, he interfered with the police when they tried to move the injured man. The trial court ruled that the necessity defense was not available to defendant because "he is not an ordinary reasonable man, he is a third-year medical student." The Supreme Court disagreed, finding that "the necessity defense must be viewed in light of the factual situation of the particular case, which might include a defendant in a particular position to reasonably believe or anticipate an injury not apparent to someone who lacks similar knowledge, information or training." 56 Ill.2d at 370-371.

The reasonableness and necessity of defendants' conduct must be judged within the context of international law. It is reasonable that defendants exercise their rights and it is necessary that defendants carry out their duties. The principles of international law can only be effective through the serious adherence to them by peoples of all countries.

International law imposes duties and corresponding liabilities upon individuals as well as nations. This has been recognized since the late 1940s when the Nuremberg Tribunal judged Nazi leaders.

> That international law imposed duties and liabilities upon individuals as well as upon States has long been recognized...Crimes against international law are committed by men, not by abstract entities, and only by punishing individuals who commit such crimes can the provisions of international law be enforced...The true test, which is found in varying degrees in the criminal law of most nations...is whether moral choice was in fact possible. (Judgment of the Nuremberg International Military Tribunal, 41 *American Journal of International Law* 172, at 175 (1947).)

Individuals can be punished for violations of international law and therefore logically have a duty to uphold and adhere to international law.

Furthermore, if the U.S. government is committing violations of international law in Central America, as the evidence will show, each U.S. citizen's complicity in these violations is an international crime in and of itself. The International Law Commission of the U.N. had adopted the following principle of international law:

> Complicity in the commission of a crime against peace, a war crime, or a crime against humanity...is a crime under international law. Principle VII, *Principles of International Law Recognized in the Charter of the Nuremberg Tribunal and in the Judgment of the Tribunal.* Adopted by the International Law Commission of the United Nations, 1950.

The defendants here ask the Court to consider the facts and circumstances of their case; the jury might find that these defendants by their training and beliefs, were in a special position whereby they reasonably perceived an injury not apparent to most people. Questions of reasonableness and credibility, as discussed earlier are for the jury to decide.

As stated in defendants' affidavits which are appended to this Memorandum, they have considered and tried other means of affecting

U.S. policies and practices. They have voted, lobbied, marched and leafletted; they have written to newspapers, they have prayed. They come from a perspective which traces its roots to Mahatma Gandhi, the Suffragettes, civil rights protesters, and those few who opposed Adolph Hitler.

Defendants believed that no other course of conduct was reasonably available to allow them the same opportunity to communicate their beliefs to the trainees at Great Lakes, to the people and the government of this country. They believed that their actions, in combination with actions of others, might accelerate a political process ultimately leading to the abandonment of present U.S. military policies.

The issue now before this Court is not whether the necessity defense should prevail; rather, it is whether the defendants may have the opportunity to present this defense to the jury. Defendants have shown that they meet the threshold elements specifically provided by the statute. Therefore, defendants respectfully request that this Court deny the State's Motion in Limine.

Respectfully submitted,

SHELLEY A. BANNISTER	JANINE L. HOFT
MARGARET BYRNE	343 S. Dearborn, Suite 1607
BANNISTER & BYRNE	Chicago, IL 60604
4669 North Manor	
Chicago, IL 60625	

2. Sample Direct Examination of an Expert Witness on Central America and International Law.

There are several sections from Chapter 4.2 *Sample Direct Examination of an Expert Witness on Nuclear Weapons and International Law* that will be incorporated here by reference for the sake of convenience:

Qualification As an Expert
The Nature of International Law
International Law Is Part of U.S. Domestic Law
The Nuremberg Principles
The U.S. Army Field Manual
Personal Criminal Responsibility
Ongoing Criminal Activity by the Government

The Right to Prevent the Commission of International Crimes
You should be sure to insert these sections into your direct examination of an expert witness on Central America and International Law
at the appropriate points in the dialogue.

FRANCIS ANTHONY BOYLE,

called as a witness, having been previously sworn under oath, was
examined and testified as follows:

DIRECT EXAMINATION (Cont.)

DEFENSE COUNSEL (Ms. Janine Hoft): Q. Switching now, Professor Boyle, to the concept of international law and U.S. intervention
in Central America—are you familiar with the United States government's policies toward those countries?

THE WITNESS: Yes, I am.

Q. And how have you familiarized yourself with those policies?

A. Well, I have studied this matter at great length and have done
extensive research and writing—just as I have done with nuclear
weapons. I have lectured and debated on these subjects and have
also traveled in the Caribbean area.

Q. And are the sources that you have mentioned generally relied
upon by other experts in the international law field?

A. Yes, they are.

Grenada

Q. Are you familiar with the recent intervention in November of
last year in Grenada?

A. Yes, I am.

Q. And do you have an opinion as to the legality of the United
States' invasion of that island?

A. Yes. I was the —

STATE'S ATTORNEY: Objection, Judge.

THE COURT: Overruled. Go ahead.

THE WITNESS: I was the organizer of a group of nine international
law professors here in the United States of America, and drafted our
statement [*infra*] condemning the invasion of Grenada as a violation
of international law; particularly, the Charter of the United Nations[1]

---

1. *See* U.N. Charter, *reprinted in* 1A *International Organization and Integration* I.A.2.a.
(1981).

and the Charter of the Organization of American States.[2] Those were the two basic principles of law that, in my opinion, were violated with respect to Grenada.

Q. What does the United Nations Charter require in order for one country to perpetrate any kind of intervention in another country?

THE WITNESS: Well, the general principle of the United Nations Charter is found in article 2(4). That prohibits the threat or use of force—and it's important to make clear, threat or use of force—in international relations directed against the territorial integrity or political independence of any state or in any other manner inconsistent with the terms of the United Nations Charter. Now, that principle, as I said, and the whole Charter itself was the idea of the United States Government. This was our principle, our idea.

There is one major exception, and that can be found in article 51 of the United Nations Charter. That exception provides that in the event of an armed attack upon your state or a neighboring state, you have a right to defend yourself or to defend that neighboring state from the armed attack.

The problem was that with respect to Grenada, there is absolutely no evidence at all that Grenada was about to attack anyone. And so the invasion of Grenada would not fit within the terms of this exception to article 2(4).

O.A.S. Charter

Q. What does the Organization of American States Charter provide as to when a state can intervene in the internal or external affairs of member states?

A. The Organization of American States again was founded by the United States of America. This was our idea, we set it up. It, too, incorporates the principle of article 2(4) of the United Nations Charter and, in addition, has this article 51 exception for self-defense. However, it is even more explicit than the United Nations Charter about various forms of intervention, and it states quite clearly that intervention by one American state into the affairs of another American

---

2. *See* Treaty of the Organization of American States, *opened for signature* Apr. 30, 1948, 2 *U.S.T.* 2394, *T.I.A.S.* No. 2361. *U.N.T.S.* 1609.

state is absolutely prohibited for any reason whatsoever. It's quite clear. You can read it.

This was formulated at the direct request of the Latin American States, who had objections to the policy that had been pursued by the United States government during the first three decades of this century, whereby we were repeatedly sending marines down into various countries in Central America and the Caribbean and interfering in their domestic affairs. We wanted the Latin American countries to join up in the O.A.S. And one of the conditions for their doing this was our agreement to this principle that intervention into the domestic affairs of Latin American states would be prohibited for any reason whatsoever.

Central American Defense Council Pact (CONDECA)

Q. Do you have an opinion as to what the effect of the Grenada invasion is with respect to understanding the policies of the current administration toward other countries in Central America?

STATE'S ATTORNEY: Objection.

THE COURT: I will overrule it. Go ahead.

THE WITNESS: There is a direct connection in my opinion. It's a bit technical, so please bear with me. I don't mean to sound too much like a lawyer.

The Reagan administration, as I am sure you read from the newspapers, attempted to claim it had a right to invade Grenada by this grouping of little islands in the Eastern Caribbean called the Organization of Eastern Caribbean States. Certainly, in my opinion, that is just an incorrect legal argument. It is made very clear in the terms of both the O.A.S. Charter and the U.N. Charter that the obligations of both of those Charters prevail over any other type of international commitment or arrangement that the United States government might be a party to.

So this little group of states could not authorize an invasion of Grenada. But shortly after Grenada was invaded, the Reagan administration then attempted to set up a similar type of grouping in Central America, which is known as the Central American Defense Council Pact. And the reason being, that since apparently they were successful in convincing the American people that this little grouping of Caribbean states could authorize the invasion of Grenada, this other group, which is known by the Spanish acronym CONDECA, could likewise authorize military action against Nicaragua. But, again, as a matter of law, I think it's incorrect. It is made quite clear in the terms of the O.A.S. Charter and the United Nations Charter that the obligations of both those Charters must prevail over any other obligations or arrangements or pacts or groups of states.

And, by the way, I should point out that the CONDECA Pact was set up aboard a United States battleship, which sort of gives an indication of its illegality.

Nicaragua

Q. Turning specifically to Nicaragua. Are you familiar with the U.S. government's policy toward that country?

A. Yes, I am.

Q. And is that familiarity based upon the same sources as your other knowledge?

A. Yes—extensive reading and writing in this area, government documents, articles, etc. Almost anything I can read on the subject that is out there in print, I do attempt to read, yes.

Q. And what have you found in your research is the United States doing in Nicaragua?

STATE'S ATTORNEY: Objection.

THE COURT: Overruled. Go ahead.

THE WITNESS: Well, as the president of the United States of America said the other night, his objective in Nicaragua is to make the government down there say "uncle." Clearly, that is prohibited by the terms of the O.A.S. Charter. The Charter would permit the following: In the event that there was evidence, for example, that there were attacks from Nicaragua through Honduras against El Salvador, certainly the United States government would have a right to stop those attacks. And at the start of the Reagan administration, they said that that was the policy, that the sole policy was to stop Nicaragua from attacking El Salvador through Honduras. But as time went on, it became clear that that was not the policy or that the policy had changed, depending on your perspective, and that now the policy is, as the president said the other night, basically to change the structure of the government in Nicaragua or to overthrow it. Or, as he put it, to make them say "uncle."

That objective, again, is clearly prohibited by this article of the O.A.S. Charter that I had mentioned to you. Although the United States government has a right to stop any attacks by Nicaragua against its neighbors, it has no right to go down there and change the form of government. That's for the Nicaraguan people to determine for themselves under the terms of the O.A.S. Charter and the United Nations Charter.

The Contras

Q. Who, Professor Boyle, are the contras?

A. The contras—that is a Spanish abbreviation for the counterrevolutionaries—is a military force now consisting of, oh, estimates run from ten to fifteen thousand men on the border between Nicaragua and Honduras, which is to the north, and on the south, five thousand men between Nicaragua and Costa Rica. This force was established by the United States government—particularly the Central Intelligence Agency—and as it appears now, primarily for the purpose of overthrowing the government in Nicaragua. And, again, as I said, that is prohibited under the terms of the O.A.S. Charter and the U.N. Charter.

Q. What kinds of specific activities are the contras engaged in?

STATE'S ATTORNEY: Judge, objection.

THE COURT: Foundation?

DEFENSE COUNSEL: Q. Are you familiar with the specific activities of the contra forces in Nicaragua?

THE WITNESS: Yes. I have read extensively on this. In addition, I have attended several international conferences where documentary evidence has been produced from individuals in Nicaragua who have been subjected to attacks by the contra forces.

Q. What specific activities are the contras engaged in?

STATE'S ATTORNEY: Objection.

THE COURT: Overruled.

THE WITNESS: It appears that the contras are doing two types of things. One—they are attacking specific military objectives. Two—they are engaging in a policy designed to terrorize the civilian population living in these regions in both the north of Nicaragua and in the south in order to get them not to cooperate with the government. This includes robberies, rapes, mutilations, torture, killing of non-combatants. As I said, under the laws of war, it is perfectly acceptable to kill soldiers, but not civilians.

From the best that I can see, what we have here is that the contras are engaging in what we lawyers call a gross and consistent pattern of violations of fundamental human rights and particularly, the Geneva Conventions of 1949.[2]

U.S. Responsibility

Q. Under international law, how are the atrocities committed by the contras attributable to the United States?

A. This is under the Geneva Conventions of 1949 that I had mentioned before and also the *Yamashita* case. The Geneva Conventions of 1949—again, the United States government was very supportive of this. They were designed in order to make clear that the atrocities perpetrated by Hitler during the Second World War should not be repeated. Or, if they were repeated, that it would be made very clear that these were war crimes under international law. So we had the four Geneva Conventions.

The appropriate one of the four conventions is the Fourth Convention that protects civilians. And article 29 of the Fourth Convention makes it quite clear that if a government in an international armed conflict sets up a band or a group—a mercenary group of soldiers—and that group operates as its agent—that's the key word that is used in Article 29—as its agent—then the government that set this group up is fully responsible for any violations of the Geneva Conventions committed by the group. And it is clear from everything I have read, and indeed even our own government officials have admitted this, that the contras have engaged in violations of the Geneva Conventions.

Article 147 of the Geneva Convention describes what's called a grave breach. These are very serious breaches. Any violation is a war crime. But these are the most serious of all. And, again, murder, mutilation, torture, rape, things of that nature, are grave breaches of the Geneva Conventions. And article 146 of the Fourth Convention says that any individual who commits grave breaches must be prosecuted by a government that gets hold of him, no matter where they are located, no matter what government it is, or no matter what the nationality of the person who is alleged to have committed the war crime.

Q. So how does this article fit into the responsibility of the U.S. government in that regard, under that article?

A. Well, if you read that article in light of the *Yamashita* case, which I mentioned to you before, all U.S. civilian government officials or military officers who knew or should have known that the contras are committing war crimes in Nicaragua, and they have failed to take steps to stop the war crimes or to punish those who have committed those war crimes, are guilty of those crimes. They are responsible for those crimes.

Again, this is true under the Geneva Conventions and under this case decided by our own United States Supreme Court, and indeed even in accordance with the Army Field Manual that I have mentioned to you before. These principles are set out quite clearly in the terms of the Field Manual.

El Salvador

Q. Are you familiar with the United States government's relationship to El Salvador?

A. I am.

Q. Is that familiarity based on these sources that are generally relied upon by other experts in your field?

A. Yes, it is.

Q. And what is the United States government's relationship to the government of El Salvador?

STATE'S ATTORNEY: Objection, Judge.

THE COURT: Overruled.

THE WITNESS: Well, not to describe it in general, but under international law, we lawyers would characterize what is going on in El Salvador as a civil war. Again, you can determine that for yourselves just by reading the newspapers. And, again, under international law, customary international law, under the terms of the O.A.S. Charter, under the terms of the United Nations Charter, that is a matter to be decided by those people themselves. This is an internal affair. It is not one for outside intervention by the United States government.

The source where this principle came from in international relations, why you are not supposed to intervene in civil wars, is because the United States was the one who promoted that principle. During our own Civil War, we argued that the British had no right to choose up sides between the North and the South, and we so informed them. When the war was over, we almost went to war with England unless they agreed to pay damages for support that they had given to Confederate raiders. And, eventually, the principle was established in the famous pathbreaking Treaty of Washington that states will remain out of civil wars in other countries.[3] And it was that principle, then, that the United States government got the entire international community to agree upon and was eventually enshrined in those other treaties and documents I have told you about.

It is clear to me that we have chosen sides in this civil war in favor of the military dictatorship that currently governs the state of El Salvador and in my opinion, that is prohibited by the terms of the O.A.S. Charter, the United Nations Charter, and customary international law.

Puerto Rico

Q. Are you familiar with the relationship of the United States government to Puerto Rico?

A. I am.

Q. And what is that relationship?

A. Well, to put it frankly, the United States government stole Puerto Rico from Spain in 1898. And, again, the official U.S. government documents establish this. At that time, Spain was the colonial power in Puerto Rico and also in Cuba. There was a revolution in Cuba, and the Spanish conducted a very harsh policy directed against the Cuban people, including the establishment of concentration camps, torture, and a wide variety of other terrible practices.

There was an imperialist sentiment in this country that we should

---

3. *See* Treaty of Washington, May 8, 1871, United States-United Kingdom, 17 *Stat.* 863, *T.S.* No. 33.

just go in and take over Cuba, Puerto Rico, and the other islands in the Caribbean from the Spanish. Nevertheless, we sent an ultimatum to the Spanish Queen that she either improve her policy in Cuba, or we would declare war. The Spanish Queen sent a message back saying that she would improve the policy toward Cuba and particularly cut out the human rights violations. And yet a few days later, Congress declared war anyway even though Spain had capitulated to the ultimatum, and we then invaded Cuba, Puerto Rico. We also took Guam and the Philippines. We eventually gave independence to Cuba. Cuba attained independence in 1906. The Philippines obtained independence in 1946. But we still hold on to Guam, and we have what is known as a commonwealth relationship with Puerto Rico. Puerto Rico has not been given independence.

Ongoing Criminal Activity

Q. In your opinion, do the United States government's policies in Central America and the Caribbean constitute ongoing criminal activity?

A. Clearly, we are violating the Geneva Conventions of 1949, and committing grave breaches of the Geneva Conventions. Perhaps the most recent glaring example in my mind of that was, as you probably read, this so-called manual that was produced by the Central Intelligence Agency that called upon members of the contra group to commit murder and assassination of innocent civilians in Nicaragua. That type of activity is specifically prohibited not only by the Geneva Conventions, but even by the United States Army's own Field Manual that says assassination is absolutely prohibited under all circumstances.[4] Yet, our C.I.A. was producing a manual calling for the assassination of individuals.

Privilege to Act

Q. In your opinion, what is the reasonableness under international law of the actions of these defendants in taking responsibility for changing U.S. policies?

4. *See* Dep't of the Army Field Manual 27-10: *The Law of Land Warfare* 17 (1956).

STATE'S ATTORNEY: Objection.

THE COURT: Objection sustained.

DC: Q. Do you have an opinion as to the reasonableness of U.S. citizens who attempt to change policies that you described as illegal?

STATE'S ATTORNEY: Objection, Judge.

THE COURT: Objection sustained.

DC: Q. You have laid out to us the responsibilities of individual citizens under international law. What is your opinion as to how individual citizens should reasonably act?

STATE'S ATTORNEY: Objection.

THE COURT: Sustained.

DC: Q. Under international law, what are the responsibilities of individual citizens toward the U.S. government's policies in Central America?

THE WITNESS: Well, as I mentioned with respect to nuclear weapons, the principle is just about the same. If you read the Judgment of the Nuremberg Tribunal,[5] it does appear that there is an obligation of individuals to the extent they can to prevent these heinous violations of international law; particularly war crimes, crimes against peace and crimes against humanity. Likewise, as I argued under article 38 of the International Court of Justice Statute, to which we are a party, those general principles of law recognized by all civilized states are a source of international law. And certainly one of these general principles of law recognized by all civilized states is the right to prevent the ongoing commission of crime.

DC: No further question.

THE COURT: Thank you. Cross examination.

STATE'S ATTORNEY: Thank you, Judge.

CROSS EXAMINATION

BY STATE'S ATTORNEY

Q. Professor Boyle, you were discussing with defense counsel some violations of international law by the United States. Is international law violated often by other countries also?

DC: Objection.

THE COURT: Overruled.

THE WITNESS: It depends on how you look at it. The United States government historically has not violated international law all that

5. *See Trial of the Major War Criminals Before the International Military Tribunal* 171 (1947).

much no matter what other states have done. Now we see a shift in the position of the United States government saying that since some other states might violate international law, we're going to do it too.

STATE'S ATTORNEY: Q. Professor, that's not quite my question. My question is: Do other states, other countries, violate international law?

THE WITNESS: Yes, other countries do.

Q. Does this happen, through your research, do you know if this happens often?

A. Well, you are asking a very general question. If you could ask me specific states, I could be more specific about it. But in my opinion, if you look at the amount of activity that goes on in the world today, it's fairly remarkable that we do have substantial compliance with many rules of international law; in particular, the United Nations Charter. What creates problems are those instances of glaring examples of egregious violations—like the Soviets have done in Afghanistan, like the United States government did in Grenada, or like the U.S. government is currently doing in Nicaragua. So it's the exceptions that really stand out.

Q. Could you say through your research that United States policy is generally in compliance with international law?

A. Well, under the Reagan administration, in my research, I can say that in the particular areas I am familiar with—nuclear weapons policy, Central America, and also the Middle East, which is not at issue here—my answer to that question would have to be no. It is not in compliance with the basic rules of international law. I regret to have to say no because I don't believe that historically that has been the case of the United States government and should not be the case.

Q. In the past, have there been sanctions on countries for violation of international law?

A. Yes, there have.

DC: Objection.

THE COURT: Overruled. Go ahead.

THE WITNESS: Yes, there have, such as the Nuremberg Tribunal, which I have discussed here, that the United States government did participate in and that led to the execution of several Nazi war criminals. And, likewise, in the Far East, there was the execution of several Japanese war criminals, including General Yamashita.

STATE'S ATTORNEY: Thank you, Professor.

DC: Just a few questions.

REDIRECT EXAMINATION
BY DEFENSE COUNSEL

Q. What is the effect, Professor Boyle, on the United State's responsibilities under international law of the violations by other countries of international law?

STATE'S ATTORNEY: Objection, Judge.

THE COURT: Overruled. I think he may answer.

THE WITNESS: Well, this is a point I had made in my debate with the United States Legal Adviser to our United Nations Ambassador. The Reagan administration takes the position that, well, since some other governments might violate international law, thereby we have a right to violate international law. But it doesn't work that way. You do have a right to defend yourself. You do have a right to take certain steps to rectify that violation. But just because there are murders, muggings and rapes down the street, say here in Waukegan, doesn't give you a right to go out and do it too.

It's the same way in the international system. There are mechanisms and procedures set up to deal with lawbreakers. For example, in Central America: If, as the Reagan administration believes, the Nicaraguan government is actually providing weapons and equipment and supplies to rebels, it can go to the Organization of American States.

Q. Professor Boyle, has the U.S. in fact been sanctioned for its activities in Nicaragua?

A. Already, the International Court of Justice has issued an opinion in May of last year, what is known as an Interim Order of Protection ordering the United States government to terminate all forms of military action, paramilitary action, or threats or use of force against the government in Nicaragua; and the United States has refused to comply with that order issued by the International Court of Justice.

Q. Who set up the International Court of Justice?

A. Once again, the United States of America set up the International Court of Justice. This idea went back to President Theodore Roosevelt's Secretary of State, Elihu Root, who was a great international lawyer. He sent the American delegation to the Second Hague Peace Conference in 1907 with the idea of establishing an International Court of Justice that would be identical to our Supreme Court of the

United States, but would hear disputes between states. That program was interrupted by the First World War, but eventually came into effect in 1921. Then that Court was continued after the Second World War. So the World Court is literally the United States of America's great gift to mankind, and indeed we then went out and tried to convince everyone else in the world to join the World Court.

And yet here today, tragically, not only has the Reagan administration refused to obey the decision of the World Court, but now just recently, as you probably read in the newspapers, they have walked out of the World Court and have stated that they will not even appear to argue their case and will not pay any further attention to what this Court tells the United States of America to do.

DC: Nothing further.

THE COURT: Recross?

STATE'S ATTORNEY: No recross.

THE COURT: Thank you. You may step down. Call your next witness.

3. Sample Jury Instructions from *People v. Jarka*.

You should also consult Chapters 4 and 6 for other sample jury instructions on relevant principles of international law.

1. To sustain the charge of mob action, the state must prove the following propositions:

First: That the defendant assembled with one or more persons without lawful authority;

Second: That he knew or intended that the purpose of the assembly was to block the roadway;

Third: That the defendant did not act out of necessity.

If you find from your consideration of all the evidence that each one of these propositions has been proved beyond a reasonable doubt, you should find the defendant guilty.

If you find from your consideration of all the evidence that any one of these propositions has not been proved beyond a reasonable doubt, you should find the defendant not guilty.

2. Conduct which would otherwise be an offense is justifiable by reason of necessity if the defendant was without blame in occasioning or developing the situation and reasonably believed that such conduct

was necessary to avoid a public or private injury greater than the injury which might reasonably result from his own conduct.

3. The gross and consistent pattern of human rights violations committed by the contras in Nicaragua are attributable to the United States in that the United States established and supports the contras as an agent of the United States.

4. It is also a principle of international law, binding on the United States and the State of Illinois, that no state or group of states has the right to intervene, directly or indirectly, for any reason whatsoever, in the internal or external affairs of any other states.

5. International law is binding on the United States of America and on the State of Illinois.

6. An individual citizen has an obligation and duty under international law to prevent war crimes, crimes against peace and crimes against humanity.

4. Boyle et al., "International Lawlessness in Grenada," *78 American Journal of International Law* 172 (1984).

The Reagan administration's arguments purporting to justify the invasion of Grenada under international law must not be allowed to inveigle the American people into supporting this violent intervention into the domestic affairs of another independent state. Throughout the twentieth century, the U.S. government has routinely concocted evanescent threats to the lives and property of U.S. nationals as pretexts to justify armed interventions into sister American states. The transparency of these pretexts was just as obvious then as it is now. The Reagan administration has not established by means of clear and convincing evidence that there did in fact exist an immediate threat to the safety of U.S. citizens in Grenada. Even then, such a threat could have justified only a limited military operation along the lines of the Israeli raid at Entebbe for the sole purpose of evacuating the major concentration of U.S. nationals at the medical college.

Nor can the Reagan administration's backup rationale of terminating the "chaotic conditions" allegedly then present in Grenada be properly invoked to justify the military invasion. Even when it actually exists, chronic disorder in a country does not permit neighboring states to intervene for the purpose of re-establishing minimum public security, let alone imposing a democratic form of government.

Neighboring states do possess a right of individual or collective self-defense under article 51 of the United Nations Charter to preserve the integrity of their own borders from external attack originating from some unstable neighbor. But any other type of violent response on their part requires explicit authorization by the U.N. Security Council, or at a minimum, by the appropriate regional organization.

In this case the Organization of American States (OAS) was the only collective agency mandated by the regional community of states to maintain international peace and security for the Western Hemisphere in accordance with the purposes and principles of the United Nations Charter. Article 18 of the OAS Charter provides that no state or group of states has the right to intervene, directly or indirectly, for any reason whatever, in the internal or external affairs of any other state. Article 20 declares that the territory of a member state is inviolable and therefore may not be the object, even temporarily, of military occupation or of other measures of force taken by another state, directly or indirectly, on any grounds whatever. Finally, article 21 reiterates the solemn obligation of article 2(4) of the United Nations Charter that American states will not have recourse to force except in cases of self-defense pursuant to existing treaties. In direct violation of these international obligations the Reagan administration has forthrightly admitted that it invaded Grenada for the illegitimate purpose of deposing the leftist military junta that had seized power after the coup against Prime Minister Maurice Bishop, and then installing a government more favorably disposed to the United States.

The members of the Organization of Eastern Caribbean States (OECS) could not lawfully authorize the U.S. invasion of Grenada. Article 8 of its Charter restricts OECS competence in such matters to situations amounting to an "external aggression" and then only in accordance with the right of individual or collective self-defense recognized by U.N. Charter article 51 and in accordance with the OAS Charter. Furthermore, OECS article 8 requires unanimous agreement among member states before action can be taken, and that condition was never fulfilled here. There is no evidence that Grenada was either about to attack, or engaged in the infiltration of terrorists into, another Caribbean state. If such evidence had existed, the U.S. could have responded immediately under U.N. Charter article 51 with measures necessary and proportionate to protect the victim.

If the OECS truly believed the new regime in Grenada created a serious threat to the future peace and stability of the region, the appropriate remedy would have been to bring the matter to the attention of the OAS. As the designated regional organization under Chapter 8 of the U.N. Charter, the OAS possesses sufficient competence to act under circumstances not tantamount to an "external aggression" or "armed attack" upon a member state. For example, during the 1962 Cuban missile crisis the U.S. resorted to the OAS when the Kennedy administration realized it was not able to justify the "quarantine" of Cuba under U.N. Charter article 51 because there existed no immediate threat of attack or aggression by Cuba. Unanimous OAS approval for the quarantine exercised a profound impact upon Khrushchev's decision to remove the missiles. By comparison, following Teddy Roosevelt's antiquated "big stick" policy, the Reagan administration prefers the imposition of unilateral military solutions as a panacea for curing the endemic instability throughout the Caribbean and Central America. Historically any U.S. foreign policy founded upon blatant violations of international law has proven to be counterproductive and ultimately self-defeating over the long haul.

Both the OAS and U.N. Charters unequivocally condemn the U.S. invasion of Grenada as a gross violation of the most fundamental principles of international law. Just recently 11 members of the U.N. Security Council and 108 members of the U.N. General Assembly, among them several staunch U.S. allies, have deplored this invasion for precisely these reasons. The U.S. government has suffered the most serious setback to its traditional role in upholding the integrity of the international legal order since President Johnson's strikingly similar invasion of the Dominican Republic in 1965. Even though Johnson subsequently obtained OAS approval for a military occupation, this invasion was followed in short order by Leonid Brezhnev's promulgation of a reincarnated version of the Johnson Doctrine to justify the Soviet invasions of Czechoslovakia in 1968 and of Afghanistan in 1979. In stark contrast to the Johnson administration, President Reagan has not even bothered to request the OAS to intervene in this matter for the limited purpose of organizing and supervising elections leading to the creation of a democratic government in Grenada. The total lack of such an OAS imprimatur will raise serious doubts concerning the international legitimacy of any successor government.

U.S. military action in egregious violation of international law sends a strong message to the entire international community that in the opinion of the U.S. government the traditional rules restricting the use of force no longer apply in settling the myriad of contemporary international disputes. When even the U.S. flouts international law, the only consequence can be an increasing degree of international violence, chaos and anarchy. U.S. military forces are not up to the task of policing the entire globe. And as the War Powers Act proves, the American people would not permit them to do so anyway despite the inclinations of the Reagan administration to the contrary.

International lawlessness in Grenada will return to haunt the future of American foreign policy around the world. Yet right now the Reagan administration seems to be planning an identical fate for the Sandinista government in Nicaragua under the subterfuge of reviving the moribund Central American Defense Council Pact, which is functionally similar to the OECS Charter. In order to forestall this immediate present danger, Congress must enact a Central American equivalent to the Clark Amendment for Angola, which would expressly prohibit the expenditure of any governmental funds in support of overt or covert military or paramilitary operations in the Western Hemisphere without explicit congressional authorization. Otherwise the Reagan administration will continue to provoke a broader war throughout Central America that can serve as a pretext for another round of illegal U.S. military intervention in the region.

Francis A. Boyle
Professor of Law
University of Illinois in Champaign

Abram Chayes
Frankfurter Professor of Law
Harvard Law School

Isaak Dore
Associate Professor of Law
St. Louis University

Richard Falk
Milbank Professor of International Law
Princeton University

Martin Feinrider
Associate Professor of Law
Nova Law Center

C. Clyde Ferguson, Jr.
Stimson Professor of Law
Harvard Law School

J. David Fine
Associate Professor of Law
Loyola University in New Orleans

Keith Nunes
Visiting Professor of Law
Loyola University in New Orleans

Burns Weston
Murray Professor of Law
University of Iowa

5. Boyle, "U.S. Intervention in Grenada: Further Responses," American Branch, International Law Association, *International Practitioner's Notebook*, July 1984 (No. 17).

In regard to Luke Finlay's correspondence in the last issue of the *Notebook* (April 1984), there is no point in fruitlessly debating whether or not the deposed Governor-General of Grenada, Sir Paul Scoon, might have possessed some residuum of constitutional powers to request foreign military intervention under the circumstances prevalent in Grenada after the Austin-Coard coup. The fact of the matter was that President Reagan gave the "green light" for the Grenadian invasion to the Pentagon on Saturday, October 22, 1983. According to Sir Paul's own account of his role, it was not until late Sunday evening that he even considered external assistance to be necessary, and then what he asked for was not an invasion but help from outside. Since Sir Paul's request for assistance came well after Reagan's order to invade, the former becomes completely immaterial to analyzing the legality or illegality of the U.S. invasion. As the distinguished and generally pro-American *Economist* concluded in a special report of March 10, 1984: "The Scoon request was almost certainly a fabrication concocted between the OECS and Washington to calm the post-invasion diplomatic storm. As concoctions go, it was flimsy." Those international lawyers and Reagan administration apologists who purport to attribute any semblance of legal validity to this bogus request must [rape] the truth in order to do so.

As for Cecil Olmstead's objection, the Reagan administration's invasion of Grenada was a clearcut violation of U.N. Charter Articles 2(3), 2(4), and 33 as well as of Articles 18, 20 and 21 of the Revised OAS Charter for which there was no valid excuse or justification under international law. As such, it constituted a "crime against peace" as defined by the 1945 Charter of the Nuremberg Tribunal. The question of whether or not U.S. foreign policy is currently being conducted by a coterie of "war criminals" is definitely not a "political" matter.

. . . .

When we were admitted to the practice of law, we all took solemn oaths to uphold the Constitution and Laws of the United States of America. Despite whatever the members of the Reagan administration might say or do in public, the conventional and customary rules of international law have always constituted an integral part of the municipal legal system of the United States of America as proclaimed, respectively, by article VI, clause 2 of the U.S. Constitution, and the seminal case decided by the United States Supreme Court in 1900, *Paquete Habana*, 175 U.S. 677. It is our solemn oaths as lawyers which have compelled me and many other international law professors to publicly criticize the Reagan administration's invasion of Grenada. And I believe I speak for all of us when I personally commend the Editors of this *Notebook* for allowing us to express our considered viewpoints on these legal matters.

6. Boyle, *USOCA Memorandum to the Senate on the World Court*, May 1, 1984.

USOCA

U.S. Out of Central America
National Office . 2940 16th Street Suite 7
San Francisco, CA 94103 . (415) 550-8006

April 30, 1984
Dear Senator:

We are writing to request your urgent and immediate action to put a halt to the dangerous lawlessness of President Reagan. Specifically, we propose that you and some of your colleagues immediately file suit against the president for his unconstitutional infringement upon the recognized right of the Senate to give its advice and consent to all international treaties concluded on behalf of the U.S. government. We firmly believe that President Reagan has violated this right in his efforts to defeat the jurisdiction of the International Court of Justice in the case brought by the government of Nicaragua.

In the recent period of time, the Reagan administration has increasingly exempted itself from the rule of international law and as a result has aggravated the ostracism of the United States in the world community. We are gravely concerned that President Reagan is unilaterally leading the American people into an escalating conventional war as well as the real danger of a nuclear confrontation with the Soviet Union.

This dangerous escalation is exemplified by the mining of Nicaragua's harbors and damage to commercial vessels; by the continued financing of the El Salvador regime; by the deployment of some 30,000 military personnel in "war games" in the Caribbean; and by the growing prominence of the CIA and the military in the planning and execution of U.S. foreign policy.

We are especially concerned that President Reagan is taking these actions without the consent of the American people. Furthermore, regarding the president's decision to evade the jurisdiction of the International Court of Justice in the case brought by Nicaragua, we believe that this action is not only politically dangerous but also a constitutional infringement upon the established right of the Senate.

We urge you to file suit against the President. If this suit is successful, it would prevent the U.S. from evading the jurisdiction of the International Court of Justice. This in turn would enable the Court to render a decision on the merits of the case and thus facilitate a peaceful and diplomatic mediation of a very dangerous situation in Central America.

We are enclosing for your information a legal commentary from Professor Francis A. Boyle of the University of Illinois College of Law and a copy of President Truman's 1946 declaration by which the U.S. recognized the jurisdiction of the International Court of Justice.

If you or any member of your staff would like further information or wish to discuss this matter, please do not hesitate to call Tony Platt or Bob Barber at USOCA's national office (415-550-8006).

Sincerely yours,

Francis Boyle
Professor of Law
University of Illinois

Arthur S. Miller
Professor Emeritus
George Washington University
National Law Center

Saul Mendlovitz
Professor of Law
Rutgers Law School - Newark

John Quigley
Professor of Law
Ohio State University

Duncan Kennedy
Harvard Law School

Steve Dycus
Professor, Vermont Law School

Martin Feinrider
Associate Professor of Law
Nova Law Center

Samson B. Knoll
Professor Emeritus, Monterey
Institute of International Studies

George Wald
Nobel Laureate
Harvard University

Marlene Dixon
Center for the Study of
American Militarism
San Francisco

Tony Platt
U.S. Out of Central America
(USOCA)

Jerry Sanders
Director, Security Project
World Policy Institute

Arthur Kinoy
Professor of Law
Rutgers Law School - Newark

Bertram Gross
Professor Emeritus
City University, New York

Noam Chomsky
Institute Professor
Massachusetts Institute of Technology

Linus Pauling
Professor of Chemistry
Linus Pauling Institute of Science and Medicine

Benjamin Spock, M.D.

Richard Criley
Vice Chairperson
Northern California ACLU

John George
Chair
Alameda County Board of Supervisors
Oakland, California

Charles Garry
Attorney

Barry Winograd
Adjunct Professor

Marvin Stender
Attorney

University of San Francisco Law
School

Jeffrey Segal   Richard Falk
National Lawyers Guild   Professor of International Law
Regional Vice-President   Princeton University
Southern Region

* * * *

STATEMENT TO MEMBERS OF THE UNITED STATES SENATE

As a professor of international law, I am opposed to President
Reagan's attempt to defeat the jurisdiction of the International Court
of Justice (ICJ) in the Nicaragua case. However, I would like to suggest
that something more tangible be done: Namely, that you and some
of your colleagues bring suit against the president for what is an
unconstitutional infringement upon the recognized right of the U.S.
Senate to give its advice and consent to all international treaties
concluded on behalf of the United States government. Despite the
fact that the U.S. acceptance of the compulsory jurisdiction of the
ICJ is called a "Declaration," it is nevertheless a "Treaty" that has
received the advice and consent of two-thirds of the Senate, and the
various Declarations of Acceptance by other states establish a separate "Treaty" regime within the framework of the ICJ Statute. What
President Reagan is attempting to do here is to alter, amend, and
change a formal U.S. treaty commitment without receiving the further
advice and consent of the Senate. Offhand I cannot recall any instance where a president has asserted a right to amend a formal U.S.
treaty obligation without obtaining further advice and consent from
the Senate. Under the terms of the declaration itself, it would seem
that the only options left open to him would be either to denounce
the entire declaration, subject to the six month notification period,
or else to obtain the further advice and consent of the Senate to his
purported amendment of the treaty. If the Senate fails to challenge
President Reagan on this point, it could establish a very unhealthy
precedent for future presidents to engage in similar unilateral amendments of U.S. treaty commitments acting on their own accord, and
thus undermine the Senate's constitutional right to give or withhold
its advice and consent to U.S. treaties.

Indeed, for the Senate to fail to challenge the president on this point now would undo a precedent established over seventy-five years ago by the Senate in its treatment of the Hay and Root arbitration treaties. During the McKinley administration, Secretary of State John Hay negotiated a series of arbitration treaties with several other states for the submission of disputes to the Permanent Court of Arbitration, which was the first forerunner to the ICJ. Hay drafted these treaties to provide that a future dispute could be submitted by the president alone, without the need for any further advice and consent by the Senate. The Senate refused to accept the treaties as drafted because it believed that the formal submission of any dispute required its further advice and consent, and amended these treaties to so provide. President Theodore Roosevelt refused to ratify the Hay arbitration conventions as so amended. Nevertheless, his Secretary of State Elihu Root ultimately convinced the president that such treaties even with the Senate amendment were in the national security interest of the United States. Root proceeded to negotiate a series of 22 arbitration treaties with other states for the submission of disputes to the Permanent Court of Arbitration, all of which contained the requirement that the formal submission itself (known by the French word *compromis*) would require the further advice and consent of the Senate. The Senate eventually gave its advice and consent to the Root arbitration treaties, and Roosevelt ratified them, thus conceding the Senate's prerogative. This experience firmly established the principle that any international agreement for the submission of a dispute to international arbitration or adjudication required the advice and consent of the Senate, and that the president had absolutely no independent power under the Constitution to act in such matters without the explicit advice and consent of the Senate. For today's Senate to acquiesce in what President Reagan is trying to do in the Nicaragua case would in essence countermand the principle which your Senate predecessors in the McKinley and Roosevelt administrations fought so hard to establish.

Concerning the relevance of *Goldwater v. Carter*, 444 U.S. 996 (1979), to this suggestion, in that case only Justices Rehnquist, Burger, Stevens and Stewart found a political question to be present, and the last is no longer on the Court. Justices Powell and Brennan argued that a political question was not present, though the former felt the dispute was not yet ripe. Justices Blackmun and White maintained that a plenary hearing was required on the issues of political question, ripeness and standing. Justice Marshall simply concurred in the result of the decision. So under *Goldwater v. Carter* the issue of whether or not a political question would be presented by such a suit is still unresolved.

If you or any member of your staff would like to speak with me further about this issue, please feel free to get in touch.

Respectfully submitted,

Francis A. Boyle

7. Boyle, "C.I.A.'s Contra Manual Incited War Crimes," *New York Times*, Nov. 24, 1984.

With respect to the apparent whitewash of high-level C.I.A. officials by the agency inspector general's report on the "contra" manual affair (Nov. 15), *U.S. Army Field Manual 27-10: The Law of Land Warfare* (1956), prescribes the appropriate standards of law applicable to such situations and long recognized as valid by the United States government.

According to paragraph 498, any person, whether a member of the armed forces or a civilian, who commits an act that constitutes a crime under international law is responsible for it and liable to punishment. Such offenses in connection with warfare include what are commonly known as "war crimes." Paragraph 499 defines "war crimes" as the technical expression for a violation of the law of war by any person or persons, military or civilian. Every violation of the law of war is a war crime.

According to paragraph 31, political assassination is a violation of the law of war. And pursuant to paragraph 500, conspiracy, direct incitement and attempts to commit, as well as complicity in the commission of, war crimes are similarly punishable as war crimes.

Finally, according to paragraph 501, any U.S. government official who had actual knowledge, or should have had knowledge, through reports received by him or through other means that persons subject to his control were about to commit or had committed war crimes and who failed to take the necessary and reasonable steps to insure compliance with the law of war or to punish violators of it is similarly guilty of a war crime.

Thus, all civilian officials in the Central Intelligence Agency who either knew or should have known of the existence of this manual and of its provision to the contras are "war criminals," according to the government's own definition of that term. Congress must insist that President Reagan dismiss all high-level C.I.A. officials guilty of such war crimes.

The American people cannot permit any aspect of our foreign affairs and defense policy to be conducted by acknowledged war criminals.

8. Boyle, "A Legal Analysis of the Resolution Declaring Oak Park, Illinois a Sanctuary Village," Oak Park Village Hall, Jan 31, 1987. *See also* Boyle, "The Sanctuary Movement and International Law," American Branch, International Law Association, *International Practitioner's Notebook*, April 1985 (No. 30).

Good day. My name is Francis A. Boyle, and I am professor of international law and criminal law at the University of Illinois College of Law in Champaign. I will not take the time to detail my scholarly credentials in these fields now, but I do have a copy of my resum that I would like to submit for your further consideration at a later time. I should also point out that I do not appear here today as a representative of the University of Illinois or of the Sanctuary Movement, but solely in my personal capacity as a recognized expert in the fields of international law and criminal law.

In direct violation of the basic requirement of international law mandating the peaceful settlement of international disputes, the Reagan administration has purposefully implemented a foreign policy toward Central America that creates a great danger of escalation in military hostilities to the point of precipitating armed intervention by U.S. troops into combat against both the guerillas in El Salvador and the legitimate government of Nicaragua. The Reagan administration has illegally intervened into the civil war in El Salvador by providing enormous amounts of military and economic assistance to a brutal military dictatorship that has used it to perpetrate a gross and consistent pattern of violations of the most basic human rights of the people of that country. Fundamental principles of international law and politics dictate non-intervention into a civil war by foreign governments because the determination of one state's form of government is universally considered to fall essentially within its domestic jurisdiction. The Reagan administration's illegal intervention into El Salvador's civil war contravenes the international legal right of self-determination for the people of that country as recognized by article 1, paragraph 2 of the United Nations Charter.

This horrendous civil war in El Salvador, and the illegal U.S. military intervention which has only exacerbated it, have created a substantial number of refugees fleeing the conflict in dire fear for their lives. The 1951 U.N. Convention Relating to the Status of Refugees and its 1967 Protocol, to which the United States is a party, define a "refugee" as: "any person who owing to well-founded fear of being persecuted for reasons of race, religion, nationality, membership of a particular social group or political opinion, is outside the country of his nationality and is unable, or owing to such fear, is unwilling to avail himself of the protection of that country; or who, not having a nationality and being outside the country of his former habitual residence is unable or, owing to such fear, is unwilling to return to it." Congress enacted the U.S. Refugee Act of 1980 in part for the purpose of bringing United States immigration law up to the higher standards enunciated in the U.N. Protocol. The Refugee Act created a statutory definition of "refugee" which corresponds in substance to the definition found in the U.N. Protocol.

One who qualifies as a "refugee" within the meaning of that definition is entitled to apply to the government of the country where he is present for asylum. According to the Refugee Act of 1980, an alien physically present in the United States or at a land border or port of entry may apply for asylum, irrespective of such alien's status, and the alien may be granted asylum in the discretion of the attorney general if the attorney general determines that such alien is a refugee within the meaning of the Act. This right to apply for asylum applies even to those aliens illegally present in the United States so long as they qualify as refugees.

Nevertheless, the Reagan administration has taken the position that those illegal aliens who have fled from the conflicts in Central America are not entitled to qualify as refugees and thus for political asylum because they are alleged to be present in this country primarily for economic reasons. On its face, this claim is at odds with the obvious facts of a prolonged civil war in El Salvador and the brutal genocide practiced against the indigenous people of Guatemala by their own government. The Reagan administration's disingenuous position on this matter constitutes a clear-cut violation of its obligations under both the U.S. Refugee Act of 1980 and the 1967 U.N. Protocol to the Refugees Convention.

The reason why the Reagan administration has denied reality in these cases is that for it to act otherwise by determining that such refugees are entitled to asylum would constitute a tacit recognition by the U.S. government of the heinous nature of the violations of fundamental human rights being perpetrated on an everyday basis by the military dictatorships that are actually ruling El Salvador and Guatemala. This in turn would undercut the pseudo-legitimacy of the democratic facades surrounding the Duarte government in El Salvador and the Cerezo government in Guatemala in the perceptions of both U.S. public opinion and the international community. Furthermore, in the event foreign governments such as those in El Salvador and Guatemala are found to be engaging in a gross and consistent pattern of violations of the fundamental human rights of their own citizens, a number of U.S. statutes should be triggered that would mandate the cut-off of various forms of U.S. military and economic assistance to the offending governments. The Reagan administration seeks to forestall that inevitable day of reckoning by denying these legitimate refugees their recognized right to asylum under both U.S. domestic law and international law.

As if that were not enough, there is a second and independent principle of both international law and U.S. domestic law that is being violated by the Reagan administration here. In the event the Immigration and Naturalization Service (INS) apprehends an illegal alien, in addition to asylum, he is entitled to apply for a form of statutory relief known as Withholding of Deportation. The U.N. Refugees Convention and Protocol expressly incorporated this basic right of customary international law known by its French name as *nonrefoulement*. The U.N. Refugees Convention article 33, section 1, states unequivocally: "No contracting state shall expel or return a refugee in any manner whatsoever to the frontiers of territories where his life or freedom would be threatened on account of his race, religion, nationality, membership of a particular social group or political opinion." The Refugee Act of 1980 amended U.S. immigration law to bring it into conformity with this requirement. The attorney general cannot deport or return any alien to a country if the attorney general determines that such alien's life or freedom would be threatened in such country on account of race, religion, nationality, membership in a particular social group, or political opinion. The attorney general must withhold deportation of that alien even if he is in this country illegally.

By contrast, the Reagan administration has continued to deport refugees back to Central America even in the face of mounting evidence that many suffer the fate of certain persecution, torture and death upon their return. This fact has now been documented by the American Civil Liberties Union and Amnesty International. Furthermore, the Catholic Archbishop of San Salvador has publicly stated that Salvadoran refugees who are returned home by the Reagan administration are currently being persecuted by their own government.

In other words, the Reagan administration is sacrificing the lives of these innocent human beings in the name of its own perverted determination of what the U.S. national security interest requires despite the rules of international law and U.S. domestic law to the contrary. That is the stark dilemma which inspired the creation of the Sanctuary Movement in the United States. Nevertheless undaunted, the Reagan administration decided to target its founders for prosecution because of their assistance to innocent human beings illegally deprived of refuge in this country. And most tragically of all, the judge in the Sanctuary Case ruled that the above matters could not even be raised by defense counsel in the presence of the jury despite the fact that these considerations were clearly relevant to determining the defendants' guilt or innocence.

The judge's granting of the government's motions in limine to exclude such testimony unconstitutionally deprived the Sanctuary defendants of all the defenses they might have been able to establish under international law and the First Amendment. In my professional opinion, this was the gravest of all the injustices that have so far been inflicted by the United States government during the course of its persecution of the Sanctuary Movement. Perhaps the only point of consolation we might derive from this unsavory incident is that in their ruthless endeavor to destroy the Sanctuary Movement by making martyrs of its founders, the Reagan administration has heedlessly overlooked that famous aphorism by the early Christian apologist Tertullian: "The blood of martyrs is the seed of the Church."

It is that same terrible and tragic predicament which has led to the submission of the Resolution that is before you now. I would respectfully suggest that the Village of Oak Park owes an obligation to its employees to ensure that they do not become accomplices in any way, shape or form to the commission of such gross violations of international law, of U.S. domestic law, and of the fundamental human rights of these completely innocent people, that are undeniably being carried out by the Immigration and Naturalization Service on a daily basis. Even more seriously, by its policy of deporting innocent civilian refugees back to El Salvador and Guatemala, the INS has rendered the United States government an accomplice to the commission of international crimes. Hence you *must* act to completely disassociate the Village of Oak Park from any degree of complicity in the commission of such international criminal activity by means of adopting this Resolution.

To be specific, both the United States government and the government of El Salvador are parties to the Four Geneva Conventions of 1949. Under common article 1 thereof, the United States government is under an obligation not only to respect the terms of the Conventions itself, but also to ensure respect for the terms of the Conventions by other parties such as El Salvador "in all circumstances." Nevertheless, the military dictatorship that effectively rules El Salvador has perpetrated numerous breaches of common article 3 to the Four Geneva Conventions of 1949 as well as of their 1977 Additional Protocol II—to which El Salvador is a party and the United States has signed and intends to ratify—against the innocent civilian population of that country.

These violations constitute what are popularly known as "war crimes." These international crimes that have been committed by the military dictatorship in El Salvador include but are not limited to: violence to life and person, in particular murder of all kinds, mutilation, cruel treatment and torture; taking of hostages; outrages upon personal dignity, in particular humiliating and degrading treatment, rape and any form of indecent assault; summary executions; collective punishments; acts of terrorism; pillage, etc. For the Immigration and Naturalization Service knowingly to return innocent civilian refugees back to El Salvador where it is highly probable that such heinous war crimes will be perpetrated upon them by the Salvadoran military forces renders the United States government an accomplice to the commission of such war crimes under the Geneva Conventions and Protocol II, as well as under the rules of customary international law including the well-established Nuremberg Principle VII on complicity.

With respect to the deplorable human rights situation in Guatemala, it has been abundantly documented that the military dictatorship which effectively rules that country has for a considerable period of time engaged in a policy of genocide against its own indigenous people. On Februry 9, 1986 the United States Senate gave its advice and consent to the ratification of the 1948 Genocide Convention. According to article 1 thereof, the contracting parties confirmed that genocide, whether committed in time of peace or in time of war, is a crime under international law which they undertake to prevent and to punish. Article 2 defines the crime of genocide to mean any of the following acts committed with intent to destroy in whole or in part a national, ethnical, racial, or religious group as such: (a) killing members of the group; (b) causing serious bodily or mental harm to members of the group; (c) deliberately inflicting on the group conditions of life calculated to bring about its physical destruction in whole or in part, etc. Moreover, article 3 provides that genocide, conspiracy to commit genocide, direct and public incitement to commit genocide, attempt to commit genocide, and *complicity* in genocide are all international crimes in their own right. Hence, for the Immigration and Naturalization Service to return innocent civilian refugees back to Guatemala in full knowledge that there is a very high probability that genocide might be perpetrated upon them renders the United States government guilty of the international crime of complicity in the commission of genocide.

In light of the above analysis, I see no problem under United States domestic law or international law with the Village of Oak Park deciding to designate itself as a Sanctuary Village in accordance with the terms of this Resolution. As you already know, the Director of Congressional and Public Affairs for the Immigration and Naturalization Service's Western Region has admitted that a city's decision not to assist the INS in the enforcement of federal immigration laws does not violate federal law. This is because article 1, section 8, clause 4 of the United States Constitution grants Congress the power to "establish an uniform rule of naturalization." The United States Supreme Court has historically interpreted this provision of the Constitution to mean that Congress has the exclusive and plenary power to determine all regulations that are to be applied to aliens per se in the United States, whether they are here legally or illegally.

In other words, state and local governments have absolutely no role to play in the regulation of aliens per se except, perhaps, with respect to their right to own land and in the case of illegal aliens, to receive certain types of social welfare benefits. Consequently, I see no reason why the Village of Oak Park should expend any of its scarce economic resources by assisting the Immigration and Naturalization Service to carry out its statutorily delegated tasks in a manner that clearly violates both the letter and the spirit of these exclusive and plenary powers that have been granted to Congress by the terms of the Constitution. It would be far better for the Village of Oak Park to conserve its resources in order to implement the beneficient intention of Resolution Section 8 to the effect that the provision of Oak Park Village benefits, opportunities and services shall not be conditioned upon matters relating to citizenship or residency status.

Finally, the adoption of this Resolution designating Oak Park a Sanctuary Village and prohibiting Village employees from providing assistance to the Immigration and Naturalization Service would be fully consistent with the obligation you and your employees have to uphold the Constitution and laws of the United States of America. According to article VI of the United States Constitution, treaties and statutes are deemed to be the "supreme law of the land." Under the terms of this proposed Resolution, Oak Park employees would simply be required to respect the provisions of the 1967 Protocol to the U.N. Refugees Convention, the 1980 U.S. Refugee Act, the 1948 Genocide Convention, as well as the Geneva Conventions of 1949 and their 1977 Additional Protocol II.

With respect to the Reagan administration's intimations that it will terminate federal revenue sharing funds for any community that designates itself to be a City, Village, or Township of Refuge or Sanctuary, I will circulate to you copies of a formal Memorandum of Law prepared by the law firm of McGrath & McGrath in Champaign, Illinois with respect to the 1986 Urbana City of Refuge Resolution. As you will see, this Memorandum explains exactly why the Reagan administration has absolutely no substantive legal authority or power whatsoever to carry out such a malicious threat in the event you were to designate Oak Park to be a Sanctuary Village. These intimidating statements uttered by federal officials in Washington are simply meant to frighten state and local government officials such as yourselves from discharging your recognized responsibilities to respect the rules of international law, the principles of the United States Constitution, the treaties and statutes of the United States of America, and the fundamental rights of these innocent human beings.

For all these reasons, then, I would strongly urge you to adopt this Resolution designating Oak Park to be a Sanctuary Village. Thank you.

Appendix
McGrath & McGrath
44 E. Main
508 Lincoln Building
Champaign, IL 61820-3603
February 10, 1986

To The Members of the Urbana City Council:

The City of Urbana receives monies under a federal revenue sharing program through enactment of legislation by the United States Congress. Under this law, Congress has authority to condition the receipt of monies by cities. These conditions are specified by Title 31 United States Code, Sections 6701 et seq. and by regulations promulgated in 31 Code of Federal Regulations, Sections 51 et seq.

Congress has authority to suspend or terminate revenue sharing funds only when those funds themselves are being spent for impermissible purposes. If the City of Urbana, for instance, used federal revenue sharing funds for discriminatory purposes, the United States Congress could investigate and suspend or terminate those monies allocated under federal revenue sharing laws. Congress does not have any oversight, however, into any area of city business which does not involve the expenditures of federal monies. Should the City of Urbana designate itself as a "City of Refuge," Congress would have no authority to intervene by terminating the federal revenue sharing allotment to the City of Urbana.

A related issue involves the executive functions of the president of the United States. The president, acting through his executive offices, is not empowered to suspend, terminate, or impound monies appropriated by an act of Congress. The Impoundment Act, Title 2 United States Code, Section 681 et seq. requires an act of Congress to approve any requested presidential impoundment of congressional appropriations. Therefore, the executive branch, acting through the Immigration and Naturalization Service, is not independently empowered to suspend federal appropriations to the City of Urbana.

Separation of powers between the legislative and executive branches, as well as between federal and local governments, are the underpinnings of our federalist system. The federal branches of government have only those powers which are specifically authorized by statute. The City of Urbana would not face any loss of revenue by enacting the proposed "City of Refuge" legislation.

Sincerely,

Susan W. McGrath
Attorney at Law
William D. McGrath
Attorney at Law

9. Boyle, "Nicaragua Must Survive," University of Illinois Program in Arms Control, Disarmament and International Security, 6 *ACDIS Bulletin*, Winter 1985/1986 (No. 3).

Despite the terrible circumstances of a war inflicted by the Reagan administration, I accepted the kind and gracious invitation of the Nicaraguan government to visit their country for the week of November 16-23, 1985. During this time I was able to investigate and experience on a first-hand and very personal basis the dire and tragic consequences of U.S. military aggression that has been perpetrated upon the people of Nicaragua by the Reagan administration. What I discovered in Nicaragua has profoundly shocked my conscience and moral sensibility as a citizen of the United States and a member of the human community.

The Reagan administration's campaign of military aggression against the Nicaraguan people by air, land, and sea has demonstrated its blatant disregard and gross disrespect for the fundamental principles of international law, for the maintenance of international peace and security among nations, and for the right of self-determination for the Nicaraguan people. These policies have violated the most sacred principles of the United Nations Charter, the Charter of the Organization of American States, the Geneva Conventions of 1949, and the Interim Order of Protection issued on Nicaragua's behalf by the International Court of Justice in May of 1984. There is no justification in international law, religious morality, or humanitarian philosophy for the Reagan administration's vicious and brutal attack upon the Nicaraguan people.

Contrary to press reports in the United States, I found that the counterrevolutionary army created by the U.S. Central Intelligence Agency in Honduras constitutes nothing more than a mercenary band of cowards, terrorists and criminals who attack innocent Nicaraguan civilians—old men, women, children, invalids and religious people. They do not have the courage to fight against the valiant members of the Nicaraguan army, but instead concentrate their military attacks upon clinics, churches, farms, cooperatives, schools and other sources for the provision of basic social and humanitarian services to the Nicaraguan people. The contras wage a war of terror and aggression against the common people of Nicaragua in violation of the laws and customs of warfare, the Geneva Conventions of 1949, and every known principle of international humanitarian law.

Under the Fourth Geneva Convention of 1949, the United States government is fully responsible for the gross violations of international humanitarian law perpetrated against the Nicaraguan people by these CIA contra mercenary bands. This juridical fact renders those Reagan administration officials responsible for conducting the contra war guilty of "grave breaches" of the Geneva Conventions that create personal criminal responsibility on their part for the commission of war crimes. Under both international law and American domestic law these officials deserve to be severely punished as war criminals.

In light of the 40th anniversary of the Judgment of the Nuremberg Tribunal, the American people must realize that the Reagan administration's policies against Nicaragua constitute Crimes against Peace, Crimes against Humanity, and War Crimes as defined by the Nuremberg Principles. Forty years ago representatives of the United States government participated in the indictment, prosecution and punishment of Nazi government leaders for committing some of the same heinous international crimes that members of the Reagan administration are today inflicting upon the innocent people of Nicaragua. The American people must remember and reaffirm the Nuremberg Principles by holding their government officials fully accountable under international and U.S. domestic law for the commission of these detestable international crimes.

It is obvious from my visit to Nicaragua that the Reagan administration has refused to submit to the jurisdiction of the International Court of Justice for the express purpose of avoiding a peaceful end to this unjust war. The Reagan administration's adamant refusal to appear before the World Court to defend itself against the legitimate complaints of the Nicaraguan government clearly demonstrates that its policies are premised upon illegal intervention and terrorist violence that could never be justified before the court of world public opinion and in the eyes of the international community. The American people must insist that the Reagan administration fully comply with the World Court's Interim Order of Protection already issued on behalf of Nicaragua as well as with its forthcoming final decision on the merits. Hopefully, the latter judgment will fully support the just claims of the Nicaraguan government to relief, protection and compensation under basic principles of international law.

Recently, the American people have heard a great deal of criticism by the Reagan administration of the Nicaraguan government's decision to decree a state of emergency. Most regretfully, a sustained and concerted attack upon its borders and an attempted campaign of massive destabilization and terror has forced the government of Nicaragua to enact these minimal measures designed to ensure the safety and security of its people. While some civil liberties have been temporarily suspended as part of a program to deal with the enormity of the threat created by the current aggressive policies of the Reagan administration, it is clear from their content and execution that these measures have not been motivated by any desire to protect the government from a dissatisfied people, but rather to protect the citizens of Nicaragua from the depredations of Reagan's counterrevolutionary forces.

Despite these externally fomented pressures, I found a remarkable sense of comraderie that pervades Nicaraguan society as a whole. There was no evidence of tension or diminished support by the Nicaraguan people against the Sandinista government. On the contrary, the undoubted weariness of the people is directly attributable to the terror and devastation wreaked by the contras. Proof that the emergency measures were essentially designed to deal with the military threat may be found in the facts that daily life goes on in the major urban areas much as before. There is no curfew; no presence of excessive military personnel; no evidence of a "police state." Overall, the Nicaraguan people trust and support their government and the government protects and respects its people.

I witnessed firsthand the freedom of religion in Nicaragua. I attended religious services and talked to religious people. This is a religious country where the vast majority of people are devoutly Catholic. The Nicaraguan government recognizes and respects this fact and has done nothing to restrict the basic right of all people in Nicaragua to practice their religious beliefs. Despite reports in the American press to the contrary, I found an enormous degree of support by the Catholic religious peoples of Nicaragua for the Sandinista government.

I was surprised to discover more freedom in an embattled and invaded Nicaragua than exists in many other Latin American and Caribbean countries that are the victims of brutal repression and gross violations of fundamental human rights perpetrated by military dictatorships with the full support of the United States government. Before the American people criticize the state of emergency in Nicaragua, they should first examine the Reagan administration's reprehensible role in denying the basic human rights and fundamental freedoms of the people in El Salvador, Honduras, Guatemala, Chile, Haiti, the Philippines, South Africa, Namibia, Lebanon and of course the Palestinian people. In its declaration of the state of emergency, the Nicaraguan government has fully complied with its obligations under the U.N. Covenant on Civil and Political Rights, the U.N. Covenant on Economic and Social Rights, and the Inter-American Human Rights Convention. By contrast, the United States government has signed these basic international human rights treaties, but the Reagan administration has refused to ratify any one of them. The American people should understand that the U.S. government must first ratify these international human rights treaties before it can obtain any standing under international law to complain about the state of emergency in Nicaragua.

During my time in Nicaragua, I paid special attention to the condition of the Mosquito Indians and the other indigenous peoples of the Atlantic Coast. Members of the Nicaraguan government were quite frank in admitting that serious mistakes have been made in dealing with the indigenous peoples of the Atlantic Coast. Some of those responsible for these excesses have been punished, and the Nicaraguan government has undertaken a conscientious effort to reevaluate and improve its policies toward them in order to take into account their different historical, cultural, religious and political experiences. I met with a Mosquito representative on the newly created Autonomy Commission and she has stated her opinion that despite the mistakes of the past she now believes the government in Managua is seriously trying to reach a solution to the outstanding problems of the indigenous peoples of the Atlantic Coast with their active participation and in a manner fully acceptable to them.

Despite the allegations of the Reagan administration, I found no evidence that the indigenous peoples of the Atlantic Coast have been the victims of the international crime of genocide. At this time their major problems—as for the rest of the people of Nicaragua—have been created by the mercenary war being conducted by the Reagan administration from its sanctuaries in Honduras. If the war would stop, I feel confident that the government in Managua could readily obtain an agreement acceptable to the indigenous peoples of the Atlantic Coast that would allow them to fulfill their cultural, economic, religious and political aspirations within the context of an autonomous relationship with the rest of the country.

The American people must realize that before the Reagan administration has any standing under international law to accuse the Nicaraguan government of genocide against the Mosquitos, the U.S. government must finally ratify the 1948 Genocide Convention, and then examine its own treatment of Blacks, Indians, Eskimos and the other indigenous peoples of North America in light of the requirements of the Genocide Convention. I am confident that there exists absolutely no comparison between the policies of the Nicaraguan government toward the Mosquitos and the manner in which the U.S. government has historically treated the indigenous peoples of North America by means of extermination, slavery, genocide and continued bantustanization.

I wish to conclude by calling upon all the peoples of America and people of good will around the world to do all that is in their power to resist and oppose the Reagan administration's illegal policies against Nicaragua. I ask other American citizens to join in this endeavor by actively participating in the work of U.S. Out of Central America, the Pledge of Resistance, the Sanctuary Movement, and the Nicaragua Must Survive Campaign, among others. In particular, the most useful thing that American citizens can do at this critical moment in the war is to sign the Pledge of Resistance. If a million American citizens were to indicate that they are fully prepared to engage in a massive campaign of nonviolent civil resistance in the event of direct U.S. military intervention against Nicaragua, this public show of support and solidarity could serve as a significant deterrent to the implementation of such a criminal act by the Reagan administration.

Make no mistake about it, Nicaragua will not be another Grenada, and it could be far worse than Vietnam. The Nicaraguan people are fully prepared to die for their freedom and independence. They will not succumb to another round of U.S. intervention and imperialist domination without a fight to the death by their entire society. Such a war would create tens of thousands of American casualties, and hundreds of thousands of Nicaraguan casualties. It will be the common people of both America and Nicaragua that will pay the price with their blood for the pursuit of such a criminal course of conduct by the members of the Reagan administration.

Such a war would fundamentally alter the nature of American society with its constitutional system of government and its commitment to the rule of law. The civil rights and civil liberties of all American citizens would have to be drastically curtailed by the Reagan administration in order to prosecute such an unjust war against Nicaragua. If the Reagan administration is allowed to escalate this war with Nicaragua any further, the American people will forfeit any right to claim political or moral leadership for the democratic peoples in Europe, the Western Hemisphere and the Pacific. We will turn ourselves into the common enemies of mankind. And in the process, we will destroy the nature of our own being. For all these reasons, then, Nicaragua must survive.

10. Boyle, "Determining U.S. Responsibility for Contra Operations Under International Law," 81 *American Journal of International Law* —- (Jan. 1987).

The only significant point of disagreement this author might have with the 27 June 1986 decision on the merits by the International Court of Justice in the case of *Nicaragua v. United States of America* concerns its failure to hold the United States government fully responsible for the violations of the laws and customs of warfare committed by the contra forces in Nicaragua. The Court carefully premised this result on the finding that it had insufficient evidence to reach a definitive conclusion on such a delicate matter. Nevertheless, the Court held it established that the United States government largely financed, trained, equipped, armed, and organized the contras (paragraph 108). Somewhat questionably, in the Court's estimation, it remained to be proven that the Reagan administration actually exercised operational control over the contra forces.

The Court realized full well that its ruling in favor of Nicaragua would be subjected to an enormous amount of hostile criticism from the one source that has traditionally served as its foremost proponent—the U.S. government. Therefore, in an effort to minimize that criticism, the Court apparently decided to avoid adjudicating the politically charged issue of whether U.S. government officials are personally responsible for any degree of complicity in the commission of international crimes by contra forces against the civilian population of Nicaragua. But just because the Court failed to answer this question out of an excess of caution for the perfectly sound reason of better preserving its institutional integrity from unjustified attack provides absolutely no good reason why American international lawyers should not examine the responsibility of U.S. government officials for violations of the laws and customs of warfare committed by our surrogate contra forces in Nicaragua. This Comment will enter upon an area where the Court has feared to tread in the hope that various members of the Court might reconsider their position on this matter at least sub silentio when it comes to the determination of Nicaragua's damages.

The Reagan administration has disavowed responsibility for some of these contra surrogates in order to cling to the pretense that it has obeyed congressionally mandated restrictions on the conduct of its covert war against Nicaragua. Nevertheless, however the Reagan administration wishes to characterize this war for domestic political purposes, it cannot alter the relevant standards of international law that apply to determine U.S. responsibility for contra activities in Nicaragua. These standards do not depend upon whether the contra war is characterized as covert or overt, or whether it is conducted by the CIA, surrogate Nicaraguans and Americans, or even by U.S. military forces. Furthermore, it is irrelevant to their applicability whether the Reagan administration's attempt to overthrow the Sandinista government is legal or illegal under international law. Rather, as the Court correctly observed, responsibility turns on the question of whether the U.S. government actually exercises operational control over the activities of the contras.

In his dissenting opinion, Judge Schwebel relied quite extensively on Christopher Dickey's critically acclaimed *With the Contras* (1985) to establish several of his factual assertions. Some of Dickey's other findings can likewise be usefully employed here for the purpose of establishing the precise degree of the Reagan administration's responsibility for its contra proxy war against Nicaragua. Shortly after taking office, on March 9, 1981 President Reagan issued a formal "presidential finding" that called for a stepped-up covert action campaign in Central America (p. 104). On November 16, 1981, President Reagan approved National Security Decision Directive 17, that called for the expenditure of $19 million to build a 500-man force to carry out a ten-point covert action program outlined and approved therein (p. 112). And in December of 1981, the Reagan administration informed the House and Senate Intelligence Oversight Committees that a major covert action program was warranted in Central America and indeed was already underway (pp. l01, 112).

Within the U.S. governmental bureaucracy, overall supervision and control for the contra war was vested in the so-called Core Group, presided over by Thomas O. Enders, assistant secretary of state for inter-American affairs, and consisting of Nestor Sanchez, deputy assistant secretary of defense, Dewey Clarridge, Latin American division chief of the CIA's Directorate for Operations, and Lt. Col. Oliver North, from the staff of the National Security Council (pp. 102, 289). From there the chain of command for the contra war descended directly to the CIA station chief in Tegucigalpa Honduras and the U.S. Ambassador to that country, John Negroponte. The former exercised "control" over the contra's civilian Directorate (p. 171), which had been created by the CIA (pp. 156-58).

The actual conduct of contra hostilities in Nicaragua was under the command of a "unified general staff," which was headed up by the same Tegucigalpa CIA station chief and an unnamed U.S. military officer who was in charge of special U.S. training and paramilitary activities in the area (p. 153). From Dickey's account it is also quite clear that these officials *knew* that the contras were perpetrating large-scale atrocities against the civilian population of Nicaragua, but did little to rectify the situation for quite some time. Eventually, the counterproductive nature of these atrocities forced the CIA to set up a new command and control system for the contra forces, including the appointment of a new contra field commander in the Fall of 1983 (pp. 244-46). But the atrocities did not stop then. Indeed, it was evident from a trip this author took to Nicaragua as recently as November 16-23, 1985 that the deliberate infliction of barbarous outrages upon the civilian population of Nicaragua still remained the operational rationale behind the contra's terror war.

Obviously, in the brief format prescribed here it would be impossible to summarize all the indicia of U.S. operational control exercised over the contra forces that have so far emerged into the public record, especially in the aftermath of the Hasenfus affair and the Iran-contra scandal, which have confirmed many of these particulars. But even in light of the minimal evidence adduced above, it would only be fair to determine the Reagan administration's degree of responsibility for violations of the laws and customs of war committed by the contra forces in Nicaragua in accordance with the U.S. government's own official interpretation of the rules of customary international law in such matters. These rules can be found in *Department of the Army Field Manual* 27-10: *The Law of Land Warfare* (1956). This Manual was drafted anonymously by the late Richard R. Baxter, then professor at the Harvard Law School, later to become editor-in-chief of the *American Journal of International Law*, and finally judge of the International Court of Justice. Until his untimely death in 1980, Professor Baxter was internationally recognized as this country's foremost expert on the laws of war.

Paragraph 498 of the Manual makes it clear that any person, whether a member of the armed forces or a civilian, who commits an act which constitutes a crime under international law is responsible therefore and liable to punishment. Such offenses in connection with war comprise crimes against peace, crimes against humanity, and war crimes. Here Professor Baxter basically incorporated the triumvirate of international crimes recognized by the Nuremberg Charter, Judgment, and Principles into the Manual.

According to paragraph 499, the term "war crime" is the technical expression for a violation of the law of war by any person or persons, whether military or civilian. Every violation of the law of war is a war crime. Paragraph 500 explicitly recognizes the existence of inchoate crimes with respect to such grievous international crimes. It provides that conspiracy, direct incitement, and attempts to commit, as well as complicity in the commission of crimes against peace, crimes against humanity, and war crimes are punishable. Thus Judge Schwebel erred in his conclusion that customary international law does not recognize the inchoate crime of "incitement" to commit war crimes when he tried to absolve the Reagan administration from responsibility for its advocation of war crimes (i.e., assassinations) to the contras by means of its infamous "psychological operations" manual (Schwebel Appendix paragraph 219).

Paragraph 501 of the Manual recognizes the existence of and standard for vicarious responsibility on the part of commanders for acts of subordinates. Any military commander or civilian official is responsible for the commission of international crimes "if he has actual knowledge, *or should have knowledge*, through reports received by him or through other means, that troops *or other persons subject to his control* are about to commit or have committed a war crime and he fails to take the necessary and reasonable steps to insure compliance with the law of war or to punish violators thereof." (Emphasis added.) Here Professor Baxter essentially incorporated the test of vicarious responsibility enunciated by the United States Supreme Court in its seminal decision *Application of Yamashita*, 327 U.S. 1 (1946).

Field Manual paragraph 509 denies an alleged war criminal the defense of superior orders, whether military or civil, unless the individual did not know and could not reasonably have been expected to know that the act ordered was unlawful, though superior orders may be considered in mitigation of punishment. Paragraph 510 provides that the fact that a person who committed an act which constitutes an international crime acted as head of state or as a responsible government official does not relieve him from responsibility for his act. On these as in other matters, Professor Baxter once again generally incorporated the terms of the Nuremberg Principles.

Hence, according to the U.S. Army Field Manual itself, all U.S. government officials and military officers who exercised any degree of "control" over the contra forces and knew or should have known that the latter were engaging in war crimes and failed to do anything about it are themselves responsible for such violations of the laws and customs of warfare. This latter category of officialdom who at least *should have known* that their surrogate contra forces were perpetrating atrocities upon the civilian population of Nicaragua and failed to do anything about it would include the immediate superiors to all of the aforementioned government officials who actually *knew* about the situation: Namely, Secretaries of State Haig and Shultz, Secretary of Defense Weinberger, Director of Central Intelligence Casey, National Security Advisers Allen, Clark, McFarlane and Poindexter, and presumably the President and Vice-President.

In addition to the rules of the U.S. Army Field Manual and the Nuremberg Principles, the Four Geneva Conventions of 1949 also apply to the Reagan administration's undeclared war against Nicaragua by means of surrogate contra forces. According to common article 1 of the Fourth Geneva Convention for the protection of civilians in time of war, the U.S. government has an obligation not only to respect but also to ensure respect for the terms of the Convention "in all circumstances." Article 2 thereof makes it clear that the Convention shall apply to all cases of declared war "or of any other armed conflict which may arise between two or more of the High Contracting Parties, even if the state of war is not recognized by one of them." And under article 29, the U.S. government is responsible for the treatment accorded to Nicaraguan civilians by its "agents," which in this case would include the contra forces.

According to article 147 of the Fourth Geneva Convention, the contra forces have committed the following "grave breaches" against the civilian population of Nicaragua: "wilful killing, torture or inhuman treatment, ... wilfully causing great suffering or serious injury to body or health, unlawful deportation or transfer or unlawful confinement of a protected person, compelling a protected person to serve in the forces of a hostile Power, or wilfully depriving a protected person of the rights of fair and regular trial prescribed in the present Convention, . . . and extensive destruction and appropriation of property, not justified by military necessity and carried out unlawfully and wantonly." Pursuant to article 146, the U.S. government "shall be under the obligation to search for persons alleged to have committed, or to have ordered to be committed, such grave breaches, and shall bring such persons, regardless of their nationality, before its own courts." Instead, the Reagan administration has refused to discharge even its most elementary obligation under the Geneva Conventions to suppress those "grave breaches" already committed by its surrogate contra forces in Nicaragua.

In a similar vein, the Reagan administration has indicated that it will pay absolutely no attention to the World Court's 1986 decision on the merits in favor of Nicaragua, just as it violated the Court's 1984 Indication of Provisional Measures on behalf of Nicaragua, repudiated the Court's 1984 ruling that it did indeed have jurisdiction to entertain Nicaragua's complaint against the United States, and then in a fit of vindictive pique, terminated the U.S. government's acceptance of the compulsory jurisdiction of the Court in 1985. Nevertheless, the major significance of the World Court's three rulings in favor of Nicaragua will become evident in the pitched battle for U.S. public opinion over the termination or escalation of the Reagan administration's undeclared war against that country. In direct reaction to the Reagan administration's overall foreign policies, large numbers of American citizens have engaged in various forms of nonviolent civil resistance to protest against what they believe to be ongoing criminal activity under well-recognized principles of international law and U.S. domestic law. The Reagan administration's illegal military intervention into Central America has probably been responsible for the greatest number and degree of nonviolent civil resistance activities in America today.

The most prominent of these groups is the self-styled Pledge of Resistance Movement, whose 75,000 adherents have taken a pledge that in the event the Reagan administration decides to invade Nicaragua by means of U.S. military forces, its membership will launch a nationwide campaign of nonviolent civil resistance activities. The Pledge of Resistance Movement has already called out its members on several occasions to demonstrate against the repeated votes by Congress to provide military and so-called "humanitarian" assistance to the U.S.-controlled contras. These activities consisted of sit-ins and other forms of nonviolent protest conducted at federal military installations and the offices of U.S. congressional representatives and senators who voted in favor of such aid. In significant part these courageous individuals have been motivated to protest by the firm conviction that the Reagan administration's covert war against Nicaragua violates fundamental principles of international law, U.S. domestic law, and the terms of the United States Constitution.

. . . .

To this list of transgressed prohibitions will now be added the World Court's unequivocal 1986 decision on the merits in favor of

Nicaragua. The Court's judgment will play a critical role in our defense of Pledge of Resistance protesters as well as in the vitally important expansion of their Movement. Despite conventional wisdom to the contrary, there currently exists a distinct possibility of direct U.S. military intervention into Nicaragua. This is because of the abject military ineffectiveness of the contra forces due to the vicious and brutal nature of their terror war. The contras' potential sources for indigenous support have long ago evaporated (except on the Atlantic Coast) because of the inhumane cruelty they have perpetrated upon the civilian population of Nicaragua. As evident to anyone who has recently visited that country, there is no way the contras can ever depose the Sandinista government by themselves, and the Reagan administration must be painfully well aware of this fact.

Hence, the $100 million military assistance package that Congress recently voted to provide the contras was probably nothing more than a holding operation designed by the Reagan administration to keep a surrogate military force in the field until after the November elections. Direct U.S. military intervention before then could have jeopardized Republican control of the Senate; yet afterwards there will remain little external restraint upon the belligerent preferences of the Reagan administration. Either it will have to negotiate in good faith with the Nicaraguan government, or else launch a U.S. invasion of that country. A third option would be to keep the contras alive until 1989 when the Reagan administration could conveniently turn the entire problem over to its successor, but only at the horrendous cost of inflicting thousands of more innocent Nicaraguan civilian casualties during the interim.

Whatever the Reagan administration eventually decides to do about its surrogate covert war against Nicaragua, at a minimum the American people must insist that the Reagan administration ensure that the contras conduct their hostilities in accordance with the laws and customs of war and the Four Geneva Conventions of 1949. In the unfortunate event that the Reagan administration is allowed to escalate its war against Nicaragua any further, the American people will forfeit any right to claim political or moral leadership for the democratic peoples in Europe, the Western Hemisphere and the Pacific. We will turn ourselves into the common enemies of mankind, and in the process, we will destroy the nature of our own being. As international lawyers, it is incumbent upon us to devise constructive

strategies for using the World Court's resounding condemnation of
the Reagan administration's undeclared war against Nicaragua in
order to head off the further development of such a monumental
tragedy.

Chapter 6.

Trial Materials on South Africa and International Law

This chapter begins with a short piece written by the author that was actually used in the *Streeter* case and, subsequently thereto, in numerous anti-apartheid and student divestment protest cases around the country. It is followed by a slightly edited version of the Trial Brief in *Chicago v. Streeter*, which was drafted by Mr. Timothy Wright, Esq. of Chicago, Illinois with the assistance of this author. Since the *Streeter* brief has been used as a model to prepare motions in limine in anti-apartheid and student divestment protest cases all over the country, it is reprinted here in extenso. Next comes oral argument by a former student of mine, Mr. Bryan Savage, Esq., of Urbana, Illinois to admit my testimony into evidence at the criminal trial in the University of Illinois Student Divestment Protest Case. You will then find an edited version of the actual testimony I gave in that case that is taken from the criminal proceedings and the disciplinary proceedings therein. This is followed by an oral argument made by Mr. Harvey Welch, Esq. of Urbana to admit our expert witness testimony in the criminal proceedings for that case. The chapter concludes with some of the jury instructions that were requested in the *Streeter* case.

1. Boyle, "Destructive Engagement in Southern Africa," American Branch, International Law Association, *International Practitioners' Notebook*, January 1985 (No. 29).

From the very moment of its inception, the primary objective of the Reagan administration's foreign policy toward Southern Africa was to secure the withdrawal of Cuban troops from Angola in the expectation of claiming a victory against Castro and "world communism." It had little to do with promoting self-determination and human rights for the non-white majority in South Africa, or obtaining independence for Namibia, or even terminating aggression by the South African apartheid regime against its immediate neighbors. The Reagan administration's evisceral hatred for Castro led it to adopt policies toward Southern Africa that contravened the principles of international law and the pertinent resolutions of international organizations mandating both the independence of Namibia and the destruction of apartheid. The Reagan administration's myopic concentration on the Cuban presence in Angola has only led the United States farther into the deadly embrace of the aggressive South African apartheid regime.

The Reagan administration's policy of so-called "constructive engagement" violates the international legal right of the people of South Africa to self-determination as recognized by United Nations Charter article 1(2). This specious policy simply encourages the further practice of oppression and discrimination against the non-white majority of that country. It has also facilitated aggressive conduct by the South African apartheid regime—either directly or indirectly by means of surrogates— against neighboring governments in Angola, Mozambique, Lesotho, Zimbabwe and the Seychelles, in violation of article 2(4) of the United Nations Charter.

In the collective viewpoint shared by most Black African states, the Reagan administration's policy of "constructive engagement" has only rendered the United States government an accomplice to the commission of the international crimes of apartheid and genocide as recognized by the universally accepted International Convention on the Suppression and Punishment of the Crime of Apartheid (1973) and the Convention on the Prevention and Punishment of the Crime of Genocide (1948), respectively. It is a shocking disgrace that the United States of America has not yet become a party to either one of these two seminal conventions providing for the international protection of the fundamental human rights of members of ethnic groups threatened with extermination.

Nevertheless, under the Anglo-American common law doctrine of accomplice liability—which is one of those "general principles of law" referred to by article 38(1) of the Statute of the International Court of Justice—the Reagan administration's "constructive engagement" with the South African apartheid regime has aided and abetted the latter's commission of the underlying substantive offenses of apartheid and genocide, and thus subjects the former to responsibility as a principal in the first degree to the commission of these heinous international crimes. Under general principles of law long recognized by all civilized nations, "constructive engagement" with criminals has always created accomplice liability, even if the motive for such complicitous behavior is allegedly beneficent. According to the jurisprudence of Anglo-American criminal law, legal responsibility is created by the mere intention to purposefully or knowingly engage in "constructive" behavior with a criminal enterprise, irrespective of the supposed motive for being "constructive." Intention, not motive, is all that is required to produce criminal responsibility.

Integrally related to the Reagan administration's policy of "constructive engagement" in the commission of apartheid, genocide and aggression is its support for the illegal South African occupation of Namibia. The Reagan administration's failure to actively support the independence of Namibia has undercut the good political relations with Black African states that were successfully promoted during the Carter administration. The right of the Namibian people to self-determination had been firmly established under international law long before the South African and American governments decided to intervene into the Angolan civil war. Consequently, the Reagan administration had no right to obstruct the achievement of Namibian independence by conditioning it upon or "linking" it to the withdrawal of Cuban troops from Angola in any way.

Cuban troops are in Angola at the express request of the legitimate government of that country in order to protect it from overt and covert aggression mounted by the South African apartheid regime from Namibia. There is absolutely no international legal justification for South African aggression against, and continued military occupation of, Angola in order to maintain and consolidate its reprehensibly illegal occupation of Namibia. The Angolan government has repeatedly stated that when South Africa leaves Namibia it will request the withdrawal of Cuban troops, and Cuba has agreed to withdraw its troops whenever so requested by Angola. According to the relevant rules of international law, that is the proper sequence of events to be followed. With South Africa finally dislodged from Namibia, there would be no need for the presence of Cuban troops in Angola. By contrast, the Reagan administration's "linkage" of Cuban troops in Angola with the independence of Namibia encourages South African aggression against Angola, and thus perpetuates the presence of Cuban troops in the region.

The Reagan administration has willfully refused to carry out its obligations under U.N. Security Council Resolution 435 (1978) providing for the independence of Namibia, as required by article 25 of the U.N. Charter. Both the U.N. General Assembly and the Organization of African Unity have determined that the Southwest African Peoples' Organization (SWAPO) is the "sole and authentic" representative of the Namibian people. Yet the Reagan administration has attempted to circumvent both the Security Council and SWAPO by sponsoring the conclusion of a separate deal on Namibia between South Africa, on the one hand, and the so-called "front-line" states and Angola, on the other, even though none of them possess any legal authorization to negotiate on behalf of the Namibian people. As part of this duplicitous process, the Reagan administration has stationed U.S. diplomats in Namibia in explicit violation of the U.N. mandated embargo against granting any form of international diplomatic recognition to the illegal South African occupation of Namibia.

It is obvious that the South African apartheid regime, with the "constructive engagement" of the Reagan administration, has substituted force for the rule of international law in its conduct of foreign policy in Southern Africa, and has engaged in a gross and consistent pattern of violations of the most fundamental human rights of its own people. It has thus created a serious threat to the maintenance of international peace and security under article 39 of the United Nations Charter that calls for the imposition of additional enforcement measures by the Security Council under Chapter VII. Since the U.N.–mandated arms embargo of 1977 has proven insufficient to induce South African compliance with the most rudimentary requirements of international law, the Security Council must now invoke its enforcement powers under U.N. Charter articles 25, 39 and 41 to require that all other members of the United Nations impose the sanctions of "complete or partial interruption of economic relations and of rail, sea, air, postal, telegraphic, radio and other means of communications, and the severance of diplomatic relations'' upon the South African apartheid regime.

To be sure, under article 27 the Reagan administration could veto the adoption of any enforcement measures by the Security Council under Chapter 7 of the U.N. Charter. Nevertheless, that would not be the end of the matter. In the event of such a veto by the Reagan administration, the matter could then be turned over for action to the U.N. General Assembly in accordance with the procedures set forth in the Uniting for Peace Resolution of 1950. Under the powers granted to it by this pathbreaking resolution, the General Assembly could recommend, but not require, that all U.N. members impose on their own accord the specific set of sanctions described in article 41 against the South African apartheid regime. Of course the recommendation of such sanctions would have to be approved by a two-thirds vote of the United Nations General Assembly. But it is no longer the case that the United States can successfully force its will upon that body.

Admittedly, if the General Assembly were to adopt such sanctions, they would not be binding upon the member states of the international community, but only recommendatory. Nevertheless the General Assembly's adoption of such sanctions would provide the legal basis for any state that has the will to carry them out to do so without being held legally responsible for violating any rules of customary international law to the contrary or any terms of the United Nations Charter. In this way the South African apartheid regime's gross international lawlessness could be effectively opposed by all members of the world community in a manner consistent with the requirements of international law.

Moreover, since the United States government originally proposed and sponsored the passage of the Uniting for Peace Resolution in the General Assembly for the express purpose of circumventing the abusive exercise of the veto power by the Soviet Union in the Security Council during the Korean War, the Reagan administration would be estopped to deny that such collective measures against the South African apartheid regime by the membership of the General Assembly were lawful. In the *Certain Expenses Advisory Opinion* of 1962, the International Court of Justice gave its stamp of approval to the Uniting for Peace procedure when it was used to create the United Nations

Emergency Force (UNEF) for the purpose of facilitating the termination of the 1956 Middle Eastern War. Since the United States government took the lead role in arguing the *Certain Expenses* case before the International Court of Justice, it would be extremely difficult for the Reagan administration to repudiate the World Court's express approval of the Uniting for Peace procedure without running the substantial risk of being accused of rank hypocrisy by the entire world community. Most regrettably, so far the Reagan administration has not been deterred by that prospect during the first four years of its tenure. But if the United States of America will not act to extirpate the aggressive fruits of apartheid in southern Africa, then other members of the international community must lead the way.

2. Trial Brief in *Chicago v. Streeter*.

IN THE CIRCUIT COURT OF COOK COUNTY, ILLINOIS
MUNICIPAL DEPARTMENT, LAW DIVISION

CITY OF CHICAGO,	)	
Plaintiff,	)	
	)	Nos. 85-108644, 85-108645,
-v-	)	85-120326, 85-108644,
	)	85-108645, 85-108648,
ALLEN STREETER, et al.,	)	85-108649, 85-108651,
	)	and 85-108652
Defendants.	)	

TABLE OF CONTENTS

Introduction ....
  I. Criminal Statute ....
 II. The Circumstances Justifying The Conduct ....
III. The Cloak Of Legal Authority ....
     A. International Law ....
        1. Sources Of International Law ....
           a. Generally ....
           b. In The United States ....
        2. International Law Considerations In The Present
           Case ....

     a. Violations Of International Law By South Africa ....
     b. U. S. Complicity ....
    3. Individuals Have An Affirmative Duty Under International Law To Take Steps That Are Reasonably Calculated To Stop Breaches Of International Law ....
    4. Alternatively, Individuals Have A Privilege To Take Steps That Are Reasonably Calculated To Stop Breaches Of International Law ....
IV. Defendants' Actions Were Justified By Necessity ....
  A. Illinois Necessity Statute ....
  B. Common Law Necessity ....
  C. Elements Of The Necessity Defense ....
    1. Defendants Were Without Blame In Occasioning The Situation In South Africa ....
    2. Defendants Reasonably Believed That Their Conduct Was Necessary To Avoid A Greater Public Injury Than That Which Might Have Resulted From Their Conduct ....
     a. Defendants Were Faced With A Clear And Imminent Danger ....
     b. The Immediate Stimulus ....
    3. Defendants Could Reasonably Expect That Their Action Would Be Effective In Abating The Danger ....
    4. Defendants Had No Legal Alternative Which Would Have Been Effective In Abating The Danger ......
    5. There Is No Existing Law That Precludes The Use Of The Necessity Defense In This Case ....
V. Expert Testimony ....
VI. Burden Of Proof ....

Introduction

Defendants,[1] who fairly represent all walks of life in Chicago such

1. Allan Streeter, City of Chicago Alderman, 17th Ward; Robert Lucas, Director of KOCO; Jane Ramsey, Executive Director of the Jewish Council on Urban Affairs; Ralph Henley, Pastor; Stephen Culen, Director of AFSCME; Orlando Redekopp, Pastor; Thomas Savage, Metropolitan Sanitary District; Heather Booth, Organizational Consultant to Citizen Action; and, Edward Palmer, President, Black Press Institute.

as: clergy, organized labor, elected officials, community organizers, college students and almost all ethnic and religious persuasions, were arrested and charged with criminal trespass in the present case. At trial, proof will be offered to justify the defendants' decision to remain in front of the door of the South African Consulate until Consulate General Willie P.N. Lotz relented on his long-standing refusal to participate in a discussion on the detentions, killings and deprivation of human rights occurring in South Africa that would lead to meaningful change in South Africa. Defendants are here, facing criminal charges, because of this stand.

At trial, defendants will prove:

1. The white minority government of South Africa is guilty of perpetrating acts of horror against Blacks in South Africa.
2. These acts of horror constitute a breach of international laws, and crimes against humanity, as defined by the Nuremberg Principles.
3. The executive branch of the United States federal government is guilty of complicity in said acts of horror.
4. The United States government, while aiding and abetting the horrendous crimes of the South African government through "constructive engagement," has breached national and international law and the United States Constitution.

The intent of this memorandum will be to: (1) review the criminal statute under which defendants are charged; (2) establish what the horrendous South African crimes and international law have to do with this criminal trial; (3) discuss the defendants' rights, and their obligation, to do what they did; and (4) show why the situation made their action necessary.

I. The Criminal Statute

The City of Chicago Municipal Code Section 193-1.4, entitled "Unlawful Trespass," provides:

A person commits trespass when he knowingly:
(a) Enters the property, or any part thereof, of another when, immediately prior to such entry, he receives notice, either oral or written, from the owner or occupant that such entry is forbidden; or
(b) *Remains upon the property, or any part thereof, of another after*

> receiving notice, either oral or written, from the owner or oc-
> cupant to depart; or
> (c) Enters upon property open to the public, or any part thereof,
> and remains thereon with a malicious and mischievous intent
> after receiving notice, either oral or written, from the owner or
> occupant to depart;
> (d) Wilfully defaces, mars, injures or destroys any building or part
> of any building or any property of another with paint, tar, acid,
> grease, oil or other such substance which would detrimentally
> alter the outer face of . . . property . . . of another, or any
> fence, tree, shrub or plant appurtenant thereto.
> Any person convicted of trespass shall be fined not less than
> one hundred dollars ($100.00) nor more than five hundred dol-
> lars ($500.00). (Passed Coun. J. 3/26/68, p. 2562; amended.
> 10/16/72, p. 3876.) (emphasis added)

In all likelihood, the prosecution will attempt to prove defendants
committed the acts proscribed by § 193-1.4(b) and (c). With respect
to both subsections, defendants believe that the City of Chicago will
be unable to prove the requirement of proper notice.

Assuming proper notice was given, defendants will prove they
were lawfully present at the South African Consulate because the
circumstances cloaked them in "legal authority." Even if all the elements of the crime charged are proven, the defense of necessity
justifies defendants' presence at the South African Consulate.

In proving all elements of subsection (c), the City of Chicago must
prove specific intent on the part of defendants: namely, that defendants remained "thereon with a *malicious and mischievous intent* after
receiving notice."

According to the U.S. Supreme Court's holding in *Mullaney v.
Wilbur*, 421 U.S. 684 (1975), the City of Chicago has the burden of
proof with respect to establishing the existence of all elements of the
crime beyond a reasonable doubt.[2] In the case of a specific intent
crime, this would include the need to prove beyond a reasonable
doubt not only general mens rea but also the specific intent element
necessary to constitute the crime. For example, in the instant case
the prosecution must prove beyond a reasonable doubt not only that
defendants knowingly remained on the property after receiving notice

2. 421 U.S. at 705.

from the owner or occupant, but also that defendants did so for a "malicious and mischievous" purpose.

Since defendants generally believed the Nuremberg Principles, the United Nations Charter and various other international conventions and treaties prohibit the crimes of apartheid in South Africa as well as U.S. complicity in said crimes, defendants therefore were acting in accordance with the requirements of international law and U.S. common law and, thus, under the cloak of legal authority.

II. The Circumstances Justifying the Conduct

The multitudes of deaths, the horrendous crimes against humanity and violations of international law occurring in South Africa, in addition to U.S. complicity in those acts should be a part of this trial because they were the stimulus to which defendants responded. The appropriateness of defendants' response (i.e., the alleged trespass) can only be gauged if the enormity of the stimulus is in full view. Defendants will prove their belief and the existence of the following facts:

1. South Africa operates under a system called apartheid. Because of circumstances of birth, 73 percent of South Africa's citizens who are Black are excluded by law from participation in their country's political system; they cannot vote, regardless of their education or achievements.

2. The State has consistently sanctioned a high level of violence in repressing opposition to apartheid. Over the years hundreds of demonstrators have been murdered by the government. In Sharpeville in 1960, 69 demonstrators were killed by police. In the Soweto uprisings of 1976, at least 575 people died during and after the demonstrations. In February of 1985, at least 20 people were killed in what has been termed the Crossroads Massacre, and most recently, on the 25th anniversary of the Sharpeville massacre in Langa Township, near Uitenhage, at least 19 Blacks were killed and 35 were hospitalized. However, some reports indicate that over 40 people were killed and the majority of those were shot in the back.

3. Similar to the system used against Jews in Nazi Germany, every Black person must at all times carry a "pass" that indicates official permission to live or travel in the place he or she happens to be. Passbook laws have resulted in the detainment, conviction and imprisonment of one-third to one-half of the Black popu-

lation. In 1983 alone, over 300,000 Blacks were arrested under the pass laws, a violation that whites by definition cannot commit.

4. The police can arrest and detain persons indefinitely without charging any crime; detainees are known to have been tortured. Consistent, detailed and credible allegations of torture and maltreatment have been made in sworn affidavits by detainees, defendants, and even state witnesses.

5. The United States executive policy of constructive engagement and the substantial corporate investments in South Africa makes the United States one of South Africa's leading partners. The more than $14 billion in U.S. investments in South Africa result in financial resources to maintain apartheid, and create a vehicle for technological transfers that benefit the repressive minority regime. For example, U.S. computers monitor the pass book system; U.S. companies supply weapons and trucks to the military; U.S. banks supply badly needed foreign exchange and capital. In sum, U.S. investments help provide the economic muscle and political stability necessary to continue apartheid.

6. The actions of the South African government and the assistance afforded by the United States executive branch clearly violate international law and the U.S. Constitution and present an imminent and compelling threat to the lives and freedom of South African Blacks.

III. The Cloak of Legal Authority

The aforementioned facts, which will be proved at trial and were reasonably believed by defendants, cloak their conduct with "legal authority," making their presence at the South African Consulate entirely lawful. The sources of this cloak are: (a) international law; (b) the United States Constitution; (c) the Illinois necessity statute; and, (d) the common law privilege accorded citizens to prevent the commission of a crime.

A. International Law

This section of the brief shall address the points of international law applicable in the present case, and identify the sources from which they are drawn. Defendants submit that the South African government is engaged in flagrant violations of international law such as to constitute crimes against humanity as defined by the Nuremberg Principles, and torture as proscribed by international conventions, among other violations of international law; that the United States government is aiding in the commission of those crimes by "constructively engaging" the South African government; and that under international law, defendants had a privilege, if not an affirmative duty to undertake such actions as were necessary to prevent the commission of further violations.

1. Sources of international law
   a. Generally

The Statute of the International Court of Justice, which establishes the Court as the principal judicial organ of the United Nations, provides in Article 38(1) that the following shall be sources of international law:

   a) international conventions . . .
   b) international custom, as evidence of a general practice accepted as law;
   c) the general principles of law recognized by civilized nations;
   d) . . . judicial decisions and the teachings of the most highly qualified publicists of the various nations . . .

The Statute of the International Court of Justice is an integral part of the United Nations Charter, and therefore both the Charter and the Statute have received the advice and consent of the United States Senate as a treaty. Hence, the Statute of the International Court of Justice is entitled to the full benefits and protection of the Supremacy Clause found in Article VI of the United States Constitution.

   b. In the United States

Article III, Section 2 of the United States Constitution provides that the judicial power shall extend to all "Cases, in Law and Equity, arising under the Constitution, the Laws of the United States, and Treaties made, or which shall be made, under their authority." Treaties and other sources of international law are, in fact, part of U.S. law and may be considered by this court. The treaties and international agreements to be discussed are entitled to the benefits of the Supremacy Clause. *See U.S. v. Belmont*, 301 U.S. 325 (1973); *U.S. v. Pink*, 315 U.S. 203 (1942).

As the U.S. Supreme Court said in *The Paquete Habana*, 175 U.S. 677 (1900):

International law is part of our law and must be ascertained and administered by the courts of justice of appropriate jurisdiction, as often as questions of right depending upon it are duly presented for their determination. (*Id.* at 700.)

It has long been established, however, that treaties are not the only source of international law falling under the judicial power of United States courts. The American approach to the sources of international law was enunciated by the U.S. Supreme Court in *The Paquete Habana*:

> [W]here there is no treaty, and no controlling executive or legislative act or judicial decision, resort must be had to the customs and usages of civilized nations; and, as evidence of these, to the works of jurists and commentators, who by years of labor, research and experience, have made themselves particularly well-acquainted with the subjects of which they treat. Such works are resorted to by judicial tribunals, not for the speculations of their authors concerning what the law ought to be, but for trustworthy evidence of what the law really is. (*Id.* at 700.)

In recent years, U.S. courts have looked beyond the writings of publicists for evidence of customary international law. In *Filartiga v. Pena-Irala*, 630 F.2d 876 (2nd Cir. 1980), the court found a binding international prohibition of torture evidenced by the United Nations Declaration of Human Rights (General Assembly Resolution 217 (1948)), the Declaration on the Protection of All Persons From Being Subjected to Torture (General Assembly Resolution 3452 (1975)), the European Convention for the Protection of Human Rights and Fundamental Freedoms (213 *U.N.T.S.* 221 (1950)), the International Covenant on Civil and Political Rights (Annex to General Assembly Resolution 2200 (1966)), the American Covenant on Human Rights (*O.A.S. Official Records*, O.E.A./Ser. K/XVI/1.1, Doc. 65, Rev. 1, Corr. 1, 1970) and the United Nations Charter itself. Despite the fact that, at the time the Universal Declaration of Human Rights was signed, the United States had denied that the instrument possessed any legal status, the court stated that such an instrument "creates an expectation of adherence," and "insofar as the expectation is gradually justified by State practice, a declaration may by custom become recognized as laying down rules binding upon the States." (630 F.2d at 883). The court further referred to reports by human rights organizations and writings of legal scholars as evidence of an "international consensus" against torture. (*Id.* at 884).

In *Fernandez v. Wilkinson*, 505 F. Supp. 787 (D. Kan. 1980), *aff'd on other grounds*, 654 F.2d 1382 (10th Cir. 1981), a Kansas district court found that the principles of customary international law could be drawn from "an overview of express international conventions" (*id.* at 798), and thus found, *without reference to international practice*, that the Universal Declaration of Human Rights (*supra*), the European Convention (*supra*), and the International Covenant (*supra*) were, on their face, indicative of the customs and usages of international law.

Similarly, in *Lareau v. Manson*, 507 F. Supp. 1177 (D. Conn. 1980), *aff'd in part*, 651 F.2d 96 (2d Cir. 1981), a district court in Connecticut found that the United Nations Standard Minimum Rules for the Treatment of Prisoners (E.S.C. Res. 663C (1957) and E.S.C. Rules 2076 (1977)) were part of the "body of international law, (including customary international law), concerning human rights which has been built upon the foundation of the United Nations Charter." (507 F. Supp. at 1183). It further found that the Charter itself is evidence of principles of international law recognized as part of U.S. law. (*Id.*)

In other cases, U.S. courts have referred to United Nations resolutions as evidence of "the general principles of law recognized by civilized nations," again in the absence of any consistent pattern of conformity in state practice. Thus, in *Rodriguez-Fernandez v. Wilkinson*, 654 F.2d 1382 (10th Cir. 1981), the court cited the Universal Declaration of Human Rights and the American Covenant on Human Rights as being "international law principles for notions of fairness." Similarly, in earlier cases, individual judges resorted to the United Nations Charter and to U.N. resolutions as evidence of "standards of decency" (see the separate concurrences of Black, J. and Murphy, J. in *Oyama v. California*, 332 U.S. 613 (1948); dissent of Goldberg, J. in *Rudolph v. Alabama*, 379 U.S. 899 (1963); majority opinion in *Estelle v. Gamble*, 429 U.S. 97 (1976)).

Under Article IV, Section 2 of the U.S. Constitution, it is clear that defendants, as Illinois citizens, are entitled to the privileges and immunities of United States citizens and therefore also have the right to rely on international law.

Accordingly, defendants submit the following:

1. That Professor Francis A. Boyle is a "jurist and commentator" who, by "years of labor, research and experience," is qualified to give "trustworthy evidence of what [international] law really is."

2. That international treaties and conventions, as well as the Charter and resolutions of the United Nations and other international organizations are sources of international law and may be referred to as such, whether or not there is evidence of state practice in conformity therewith.

2. International Law Considerations In The Present Case

Defendants' reliance on international law seeks to establish two alternative defenses: first, that under international law defendants had an affirmative duty, or at least a privilege, to act to prevent the commission of crimes against humanity and other breaches of international law, and second, that even if no such affirmative duty or privilege existed, prevention of crimes against humanity and violations of international law is a "greater value" within the sense of the necessity defense put forward in this case.

Clearly then, before the question of defendants' affirmative duty or privilege to prevent breaches of international law can be analyzed, it is necessary to detail those provisions of international law which defendants submit are being violated.

a. Violations Of International Law By South Africa

The minority government of South Africa has and is engaging in a gross and consistent pattern of violations of the most basic fundamental human rights accorded all human beings in addition to various other violations of international law respecting its own citizens and neighboring countries.

First, the South African government has committed acts of genocide against its own citizens as defined and prohibited by the United Nations Convention Against Genocide. Prevention and Punishment of the Crime of Genocide, General Assembly Resolution 260(A)(III).

Second, the South African government has committed the internationally recognized crime of apartheid as affirmed by the U.N. Convention Against Apartheid. International Convention on the Suppression and Punishment of the Crime of Apartheid, General Assembly Resolution 3068(XXVIII) (1973).

Third, the South African government has engaged in a gross and consistent pattern of violations of the fundamental human rights of its own people as recognized by the Universal Declaration of Human Rights, General Assembly Resolution 217(A)(III) (1948) and the International Covenant on Civil and Political Rights, (Annex to General Assembly Resolution 2200 (1966)).

Fourth, the South African government has consistently engaged in torture, which is a crime recognized by international law. Declarations on the Protection of All Persons from Being Subjected to Torture and Other Cruel, Inhumane or Degrading Treatment or Punishment, General Assembly Resolution 3452(XXX) (1975).

Fifth, the South African government is engaging in crimes against humanity as proscribed by the Nuremberg Principles. Charter of the International Military Tribunal, August 8, 1945, 59 *Stat.* 1544, *E.A.S.* 472.

Sixth, the South African government has illegally occupied Namibia despite authoritative determinations by the United Nations General Assembly, the United Nations Security Council, and the International Court of Justice, that it must withdraw from Namibia and set Namibia free as an independent and sovereign state. United Nations Security Council Resolution 435 (1978).

Finally, the South African government has launched and waged a war of aggression against the legitimate government of Angola in order to consolidate its illegal occupation of Namibia and also for the illegal purpose of installing a puppet government in Angola. During the course of this endeavor, the South African government has committed acts of aggression against neighboring governments in violation of Article 2(4) of the United Nations Charter, and in numerous other violations of the Fourth Geneva Convention of 1949 and thus is responsible for war crimes. Inasmuch as the aforementioned principles are treaties signed by the South African government or adopted by them, or have become part of customary international law, they too are binding on the South African and U.S. governments. The provisions of these various instruments and their applicability to the South African and U.S. governments will be discussed successively.

(1) Prevention and Punishment Of The Crime of Genocide (1948)

The South African government is guilty of perpetrating criminal acts of horror against Blacks in South Africa. The acts constitute a breach of international law, to wit: the Convention on the Prevention and Punishment of the Crime of Genocide, General Assembly Resolution 260A(III) (1948).

The Genocide Convention provides in pertinent part:

Article I

The Contracting Parties confirm that genocide, whether committed in time of peace or in time of war, is a crime under international law which they undertake to prevent and to punish.

Article II

In the present Convention, genocide means any of the following acts committed with intent to destroy, in whole or in part, a national, ethnical, racial or religious group, as such:

(a) Killing members of the group;

(b) Causing serious bodily or mental harm to members of the group;

(c) Deliberately inflicting on the group conditions of life calculated to bring about is physical destruction in whole or in part;

(d) Imposing measures intended to prevent births within the group;

(e) Forcibly transferring children of the group to another group.

Article III

The following acts shall be punishable:

(a) Genocide;

(b) Conspiracy to commit genocide;

(c) Direct and public incitement to commit genocide;

(d) Attempt to commit genocide;

(e) Complicity in genocide.

Defendants, at trial, will show that the South African government has committed, and is committing, acts of genocide against its own citizens as defined and prohibited by the Genocide Convention. The evidence offered will show that the South African government was and is guilty of: killing Blacks; causing serious bodily and mental harm to Blacks; deliberately inflicting on Blacks conditions of life calculated to bring about its physical destruction in whole or in part; and a host of other illegal acts committed against the Black people in South Africa.

(2) The Crime of Apartheid

By installing and operating a governmental policy of ''separateness," the South African government is guilty of committing the international crime of apartheid.

The system of apartheid has been made criminal by the International Convention on the Suppression and Punishment of the Crime of Apartheid, General Assembly Resolution 3068(XXVIII) (1973).

The Convention on Apartheid provides in pertinent part:

Article I

1. The States Parties to the present Convention declare that apartheid is a crime against humanity and that inhuman acts resulting from the policies and practices of apartheid and similar policies and practices of racial segregation and discrimination, as defined in article II of the Convention, are crimes violating the principles of international law, in particular the purposes and principles of the Charter of the United Nations, and constituting a serious threat to international peace and security.

2. The States Parties to the present Convention declare criminal those organizations, institutions and individuals committing the crime of apartheid.

Article II

For the purposes of the present Convention, the term "the crime of apartheid," which shall include similar policies and practices of racial segregation and discrimination as practised in southern Africa, shall apply to the following inhuman acts committed for the purpose of establishing and maintaining domination by one racial group of persons over any other racial group of persons and systematically oppressing them:

(a) Denial to a member or members of a racial group or groups of the right to life and liberty of person:

(i) By murder of members of a racial group or groups;

(ii) By the infliction upon the members of a racial group or groups of serious bodily or mental harm, by the infringement of their freedom or dignity, or by subjecting them to torture or to cruel, inhuman or degrading treatment or punishment;

(iii) By arbitrary arrest and illegal imprisonment of the members of a racial group or groups.

(b) Deliberate imposition on a racial group or groups of living conditions calculated to cause its or their physical destruction in whole or in part;

(c) Any legislative measures and other measures calculated to prevent a racial group or groups from participation in the political, social, economic and cultural life of the country and the deliberate creation of conditions preventing the full development of such a group or groups, in particular by denying to members of a racial group or groups basic human rights and freedoms, including the right to work, the right to form recognized trade unions, the right to education, the right to leave and to return to their country, the right to a nationality, the right to freedom of movement and residence, the right to freedom of opinion and expression, and the right to freedom of peaceful assembly and association;

(d) Any measures, including legislative measures, designed to divide the population along racial lines by the creation of separate reserves and ghettos for the members of a racial group or groups, the prohibition of mixed marriages among members of various racial groups, the expropriation of landed property belonging to a racial group or groups or to members thereof;

(e) Exploitation of the labour of the members of a racial group or groups, in particular by submitting them to forced labour;

(f) Persecution of organizations and persons, by depriving them of fundamental rights and freedoms, because they oppose apartheid.

Thus, it is clear that the South African governmental policy of apartheid contravenes international law and the South African government is guilty of ongoing criminal activity under this convention of international law.

Defendants, at trial, will show that the South African government practices the crime of apartheid in all of its pernicious forms, and will provide evidence of its practice.

3. Human Rights Violations

The South African government has engaged in a gross and consistent pattern of violations of the fundamental human rights of its own people as proscribed by the Universal Declaration of Human Rights, General Assembly Resolution 217A(III) (1948). The Declaration provides in pertinent part:

Article I
All human beings are born free and equal in dignity and rights.

They are endowed with reason and conscience and should act towards one another in a spirit of brotherhood.

Article 2

Everyone is entitled to all the rights and freedoms set forth in this Declaration, without distinction of any kind, such as race, colour, sex, language, religion, political or other opinion, national or social origin, property, birth or other status . . .

Article 7

All are equal before the law and are entitled without any discrimination to equal protection of the law. All are entitled to equal protection against any discrimination in violation of this Declaration and against any incitement to such discrimination.

Article 12

No one shall be subjected to arbitrary interference with his privacy, family, home or correspondence, nor to attacks upon his honour and reputation. Everyone has the right to the protection of the law against such interference or attacks.

Article 13

1. Everyone has the right to freedom of movement and residence within the borders of each State.

2. Everyone has the right to leave any country, including his own, and to return to his country.

See also the International Covenant on Civil and Political Rights, Annex to General Assembly Resolution 2200 (1966).

Defendants, at trial, will provide evidence on the denial of the most basic human rights to Blacks in South Africa by the South African government. Defendants will show that Blacks are treated unequally under the law and that treatment is based solely on race; that Blacks are not allowed to freely move about in South Africa.

In sum, defendants will show the systematic deprivations of human rights by the South African government.

(4) Torture

The South African government has consistently engaged in torture which is a crime recognized by international law. Declaration on the Protection of All Persons from Being Subjected to Torture and Other Cruel, Inhuman or Degrading Treatment or Punishment, General Assembly Resolution 3452(XXX) (1975).

The Declaration makes torture a criminal act by the responsible party. The defendants will prove that the South African government has systematically used torture against Blacks in South Africa.

(5) Nuremberg Principles

The South African government is guilty of crimes against humanity as described in the Nuremberg Principles.

The Nuremberg Principles are contained in the Charter of the International Military Tribunal, August 8, 1945, 59 *Stat.* 1544, E.A.S. 472 ("London Agreement"), which states:

> Article 6: The following acts, or any of them, are crimes coming within the jurisdiction of the Tribunal for which there shall be *individual responsibility*:
> (c) CRIMES AGAINST HUMANITY: namely, *murder, extermination, enslavement,* deportation, *and other inhumane acts committed against any civilian population,* before or during the war, or *persecutions on* political, *racial* or religious *grounds in execution of or in connection with any crime within the jurisdiction of the Tribunal,* whether or not in violation of the domestic law of the country where perpetrated.
> *Leaders, organizers, instigators and accomplices participating in the formulation or execution of a common plan or conspiracy to commit any of the foregoing crimes are responsible for all acts performed by any persons in execution of such a plan.*
> Article 7: The official position of defendants, whether as Heads of State or responsible officials in government Departments, shall not be considered as freeing them from responsibility or mitigating punishment.
> Article 8: The fact that the Defendant acted pursuant to order of his Government or of a superior shall not free him from responsibility, but may be considered in mitigation of punishment if the Tribunal determines that justice so requires.
> (Emphasis added.)

As defendants' expert, Prof. Francis A. Boyle, will testify, and their Memorandum shows, these principles bind the South African government.

(6) Illegal Occupation of Namibia

The South African government has illegally occupied Namibia despite authoritative determinations by the United Nations General Assembly, the United Nations Security Council, and the International Court of Justice that it must withdraw from Namibia.

Resolution 435 (1978) reads, in pertinent part:

> The Security Council,
>
> Recalling its resolutions 385 (1976) of 30 January 1976 and 431 (1978) and 432 (1978) of 27 July 1978,
>
> Having considered the report of the Secretary-General submitted pursuant to paragraph 2 of resolution 431 (1978) and his explanatory statement made in the Security Council on 29 September 1978 (S/12869),
>
> Taking note of the relevant communications from the Government of South Africa to the Secretary-General,
>
> Taking note also of the letter dated 8 September 1978 from the President of the South West Africa People's Organization to the Secretary-General,
>
> Reaffirming the legal responsibility of the United Nations over Namibia,
>
>> 1. Approves the report of the Secretary-General on the implementation of the proposal for a settlement of the Namibian situation and his explanatory statement;
>>
>> 2. Reiterates that its objective is the withdrawal of South Africa's illegal administration from Namibia and the transfer of power to the people of Namibia with the assistance of the United Nations in accordance with Security Council Resolution 385 (1976);
>>
>> 3. Decides to establish under its authority a United Nations Transition Assistance Group in accordance with the above-mentioned report of the Secretary-General for a period of up to 12 months in order to assist his Special Representative to carry out the mandate conferred upon him by the Security Council in paragraph 1 of its resolution 431 (1978), namely, to ensure the early independence of Namibia through free elections under the supervision and control of the United Nations.

(7) Acts of Aggression

The South African government is engaged in acts of aggression against the legitimate government of Angola in addition to the legitimate government of Namibia (discussed above). All this is in violation of the United Nations Charter, Article 2(4). Article 2(4) reads:

Article 2
The Organization and its Members, in pursuit of the Purposes stated in Article 1, shall act in accordance with the following Principles. . . .

4. All Members shall refrain in their international relations from the threat or use of force against the   territorial integrity of political independence of any state, or in any other manner inconsistent with the Purposes of the United Nations.

It is clear that the South African government has breached this convention of international law. Defendants, at trial, will show that the South African government has invaded the borders of Angola committing acts of aggression therein. During the course of their illegal invasion, the South African government has committed numerous violations of the Fourth Geneva Convention of 1949. Defendants will produce evidence to show those specific criminal violations by the South African government.

b. U.S. Complicity

The U.S. government's collaboration with the South African government (by U.S. foreign policy, and by U.S. corporate and financial institutions) violates international law and the specific resolutions of the United Nations General Assembly. The continued collaboration of Western powers, principally the United States, with apartheid, has been condemned by the United Nations General Assembly as the "main obstacle to the liquidation of the racist regime and the abolition of the criminal and inhuman apartheid system." General Assembly Resolutions 34/93 A, E, Q of December 12, 1979.

As Prof. Boyle has stated in an article entitled "Destructive Engagement In Southern Africa":

The Reagan administration's policy of so-called "constructive engagement" violates the international legal right of the people of South Africa to self-determination as recognized by the United Nations Charter, Article 1(2). This specious policy simply encourages the further practice of oppression and discrimination against the non-white majority of that country. It has also facilitated aggressive conduct by the South African apartheid regime—either directly or indirectly by means of surrogates—against neighboring governments in Angola, Mozambique, Lesotho, Zimbabwe and the Seychelles, in violation of Article 2(4) of the United Nations Charter.

In the collective viewpoint shared by most Black African States, the Reagan administration's policy of "constructive engagement" has only rendered the United States government an accomplice to the commission of the international crimes of apartheid and genocide as recognized, respectively, by the universally accepted International Convention on the Suppression and Punishment of the Crime of Apartheid (1973) and the Convention on the Prevention and Punishment of the Crime of Genocide (1948) . . .

Nevertheless, under the Anglo-American common law doctrine of accomplice liability—which is one of those "general principles of law" referred to by Article 38(1) of the Statute of the International Court of Justice—the Reagan administration's "constructive engagement" with the South African apartheid regime has aided and abetted the latter's commission of the underlying substantive offenses of apartheid and genocide, and thus subjects the former to responsibility as a principal in the first degree to the commission of these heinous international crimes. Under general principles of law long recognized by all civilized nations, "constructive engagement" with criminals has always created accomplice liability, even if the motive for such complicitous behavior is allegedly beneficent. According to the jurisprudence of Anglo-American criminal law, legal responsibility is created by the mere intention to purposefully or knowingly engage in "constructive" behavior with a criminal enterprise, irrespective of the supposed motive for being "constructive." Intentional behavior is all that is required to produce criminal responsibility.

International Practitioner's Notebook No. 29, January, 1985.

At trial, defendants will show that the U.S. government is aiding and abetting the commission of those crimes by "constructively engaging" with the South African government.

In August, 1946, the governments of France, Britain, United States and the Soviet Union signed an Agreement for the Establishment of an International Military Tribunal (5 *U.N.T.S.* 251) to try persons charged with crimes under a Charter annexed to the Agreement.

Article 6 enunciated the acts which would thenceforth constitute crimes against peace, war crimes and crimes against humanity and for which there would be individual responsibility (See discussion of "Nuremberg Principles," *infra*).

In 1946, the General Assembly of the United Nations resolved that it "affirms the principles of international law recognized by the Charter of the Nuremberg Tribunal and the Judgment of the Tribunal" (General Assembly Resolution 95(I)). The Nuremberg Principles, which essentially restate the provisions of the Charter, were later formulated by the International Law Commission on the instruction of the General Assembly (See *Yearbook of the International Law Commission* 1950, II, p. 195). In 1954, the International Law Commission expanded the Nuremberg Principles into a Draft Code of Offenses Against the Peace and Security of Mankind (G.A.O.R. IX, Supp. 9, p. 11).

Like the Nuremberg Principles, the Draft Code contains, in its Article 3, a provision that heads of state or government officials shall not, by reason of their official capacities, be relieved from responsibility.

As an original signatory to the Charter of the Nuremberg Tribunal, upon which the Principles and Draft Code are based, the United States cannot now assert that these instruments of customary international law do not constitute binding international obligations. By virtue of its "constructive" support for the illegalities being committed by the government of South Africa, which illegalities themselves constitute crimes, the administration of the United States is itself indirectly guilty of the commission of crimes in contravention of U.N. resolutions, crimes against humanity, offenses against the peace and security of mankind and various other violations of international law. Defendants accordingly submit that:

1. Insofar as the United States government aids and abets the government of South Africa in its violations of the instruments recited above, it is complicit in crimes against humanity, offenses against the peace and security of mankind and various other violations of international law as discussed above.

2. The Government of the United States is obliged by both treaty and customary international law to refrain from "constructively engaging" with the criminal South African government. Failure to do so constitutes a crime against humanity within the meaning of the

Nuremberg Principles, an offense against the peace and security of mankind within the meaning of the Draft Code, and various other violations of international law.

3. Individuals Have An Affirmative Duty Under International Law To Take Steps That Are Reasonably Calculated To Stop Ongoing Criminal Activity

Defendants contend that they had not only a right, but a positive duty under international law to take such steps as were possible to prevent the commission of the crimes outlined above. This duty derives from Article 8 of the Charter of the International Military Tribunal and Article 4 of the Draft Code which state, respectively:

"The fact that the Defendant acted pursuant to order of his Government or of a superior shall not free him from responsibility, but may be considered in mitigation of punishment."

"The fact that a person charged with an offense defined in this code acted pursuant to an order of his Government or of a superior does not relieve him of responsibility in international law if, in the circumstances at the time, it was possible for him not to comply with that order."

The International Military Tribunal at Nuremberg, faced with the contention that international law provides no punishment for individuals, held as follows:

"That international law imposed duties and liabilities upon individuals as well as upon States has long been recognized . . . Crimes against international law are committed by men, not by abstract entities, and only by punishing individuals who commit such crimes can the provisions of international law be enforced . . . The true test, which is found in varying degrees in the criminal law of most nations . . . is whether moral choice was in fact possible." (Judgment of the Nuremberg International Military Tribunal, 41 *American Journal of International Law* 172, at 175 (1947)).

Similarly, in the trial of German industrialists for war crimes committed during World War II, the Tribunal stated, with respect to private individuals:

"International law, as such, binds every citizen just as does ordinary municipal law. Acts adjudged criminal when done by an officer of the government are criminal when done by a private individual. The guilt differs only in magnitude, not in quality. The offender in either case is charged with personal wrong and punishment falls on the offender in *propria persona.* The application of international law to individuals is no novelty." (*"The Flick Case"*, VI *Trials of War Criminals* (1952) *reprinted in part in* II Friedmann, *The Law of War: A Documentary History* 1281, New York, Random House, 1980.)

Defendants submit that inasmuch as these cases are based on an agreement of the United States of America to establish a tribunal for the prosecution of war crimes, the cases, and the terms of the Charter itself, are tantamount to an interpretation of a treaty. Since, by the terms of Article 6 of the Constitution of the United States, treaties made under the authority of the United States are to be the Supreme Law of the land, their individual obligations arising as a result of such treaties override any obligations under state law. They further contend that if international law punishes individuals for complicity in the commission of war crimes, crimes against peace, crimes against humanity and offenses against the peace and security of mankind, by inference, international law must authorize acts taken to prevent those crimes.

Justice Robert K. Jackson of the U.S., chief prosecutor in the 1945 Nuremberg War Crimes Trials, clearly establishes that the Nuremberg Principles bind private citizens:

[T]he very essence of the [Nuremberg] *Charter* is that *individuals have intentional duties* which transcend the national obligations of obedience imposed by the individual state." 6 F.R.D. 69, 110 (1946); 22 *Trials, supra,* 411, 466 (1948).

The Tokyo war crimes tribunal went so far as to declare:

[A]nyone with knowledge of illegal activity and an opportunity to do something about it is a potential criminal under international law unless the person takes *affirmative measures to prevent* the commission of the crimes." Tokyo War Crimes Trial Decision, *reprinted in* L. Friedman, II *The Law of War: A Documentary History* 1283 (1972).

Defendants thus had a duty to take affirmative action under international law, the reasonable exercise of which made their presence at the front door of the South African Consulate lawful.

Accordingly, defendants contend:

1. Under international law, individuals have a positive duty to take such steps as are necessary to prevent the commission of war crimes, crimes against peace, crimes against humanity, offenses against the peace and security of mankind, and various other violations of international laws.

2. The duty imposed by international law is supreme vis-a-vis the domestic law of any state.

4. Alternatively, Individuals Have A Privilege Under International Law To Take Steps That Are Reasonably Calculated To Stop Ongoing Criminal Activity

If the principle of individual responsibility for offenses against international law or complicity in those offenses, as outlined in the preceding section, does not infer a positive duty to act to prevent them, it must at least imply a right to take such steps as are reasonably calculated to bring about that end.

In *Spicer v. The People*, 11 Ill. App. 294 (1882), defendant was convicted of committing an assault and battery when the defendant attempted to break up a fight.

In overruling the conviction, the court stated: "a man may lay his hands upon another to prevent his fighting or otherwise committing a breach of the peace." *Wharton's Cr. Law*, Sec. 1260. Thus, in Illinois, the courts have recognized a common law privilege to prevent the commission of crimes.

Accordingly, defendants will show that they believed that the government of the United States was wilfully and knowingly violating international law, and that their actions were the only ones open to them to bring about a cessation of those violations.

IV. Defendants' Actions Were Justified By Necessity

Defendants, in remaining at the South African Consulate, were justified by the necessity of arousing national and international concern and thereby preventing the loss of life and liberty, the commission of torture and crimes against humanity as perpetrated against the Black population of South Africa. The South African government has perpetrated genocide, apartheid, grave breaches of the Fourth Geneva Convention of 1949, violations of the United Nations Charter, and of the Universal Declarations of Human Rights; and the United States government has become an accomplice to the commission of those heinous violations of international law by its policy of "constructive engagement." Hence, these defendants acted to the extent that they could to prevent ongoing criminal activity by the South African government which has been aided and abetted by the United States government. Thus, the evil which they sought to prevent (i.e., the aforementioned international crimes) is much greater than the evil they allegedly perpetrated (i.e., the trespass) and therefore, the defendants should be entitled to the defense of necessity.

Common law has long recognized that a criminal defendant may exonerate his action by use of the "necessity defense." The necessity defense has been accepted by American courts from the founding of this country. In *The William Gray*, 29 F. Cas. 1300 (No. 17694) (C.C.D. N.Y. 1610), the court ruled that "inevitable necessity" justified a violation of the embargo act when storms compelled a ship's crew to drive the vessel into a forbidden foreign port in order to save lives and property. The court stated:

> Ancient principles ingrafted into the common law of the country from which our jurisprudence is borrowed [as well as] . . . common sense and the feelings of mankind justified the defendants' 'criminal' conduct. (*Id.* at 1302.)

See also *United States v. Ashton*, 24 F. Cas. 873 (No. 14470) (C.C.D. Mass. P034) (ship's crew acquitted of mutiny where they reasonably believed the ship was unseaworthy and their lives imperiled).

In these early federal cases, the availability of a necessity defense in American law was solidly confirmed. Several states, including Illinois, have enacted legislation defining a necessity defense into their criminal codes. *See, e.g., Colo. Rev. Stat.*, § 18-1-1702 (1973); *N.H. Rev. Stat. Ann.*, § 627.3 (1974); *N.Y. Penal Law*, § 35.05 (McKinney 1975); *Ore. Rev. Stat.*, § 161.200 (1977), 18 Pa. C.S. 6503.

A. Illinois Necessity Statute

The Illinois necessity defense statute is Ill. Ann. Stat., Ch. 38 § 7-13 (Smith-Hurd 1972), which provides:

> Conduct which would otherwise be an offense is justifiable by reason of necessity if the accused was without blame in occasioning or developing the situation and reasonably believed such conduct was necessary to avoid a public or private injury greater than the injury which might reasonably result from his own conduct.

There are two elements to the statute: (1) lack of blame on the part of defendant, and (2) defendant reasonably believed the conduct was necessary. *People v. Perez.* 97 Ill. App. 3d 278, 422 N.E.2d 945, 947 (1st Dist. 1981). *See also People v. Krizka*, 92 Ill. App. 3d 298, 416 N.E.2d 36 (1981); *City of Chicago v. Mayer*, 56 Ill. 2d 366, 308 N.E.2d 601 (1974). The courts have also discussed a third requirement, i.e., that defendant have no other legal option available. *People v. White*, 78 Ill. App. 3d 979, 397 N.E.2d 1246 (4th Dist. 1979).

As to the second element, the Illinois cases have been discussed in two parts: 1) that defendant is faced with an immediate danger, and 2) that defendant can expect his or her action will be effective in abating the danger. In *People v. Krizka, supra*, defendants stopped scheduled abortions at a clinic and tried to raise the necessity defense. The court said: "necessity is viewed as involving the choice between two admitted evils . . . where other optional courses of action are unavailable." *Id.* at 37. In *Krizka*, the necessity defense was not allowed. Defendants claimed their acts of trespass were necessary to save the lives of unborn fetuses. The court, however, reasoned that since *Roe v. Wade*, 410 U.S. 113 (1973) made abortion legal in the first trimester, defendants were not preventing a legally recognized injury; thus, the trespass was not justified. *Id.* The logic of this case suggests, however, that if abortion were *not* legal, then defendants would have been justified in trespassing to prevent abortions because: (1) the danger to the fetuses was immediate and would constitute a greater injury than the trespass; and (2) the act of trespass prevented abortions scheduled at that time - a direct effect in abating the harm. The case at bar is clearly distinguishable from the *Krizka* case. Here, both the South African government and the United States government are actively engaging in generally recognized criminal activity, whereas in the *Krizka* case, abortion was not illegal.

In *City of Chicago v. Mayer, supra,* the defendant prevented police from moving an injured man and was charged with obstruction. The Illinois Supreme Court remanded to allow the defendant to raise the necessity defense. Defendant tried to show that a man was injured and that the danger of a greater injury would have been imminent if police had been allowed to move him.

Illinois' necessity defense requires that the defendant have no legal alternative. For instance, in *People v. White, supra,* the defendant, a prisoner, escaped while out on a job interview. The prisoner had heard that his wife had been raped and his child beaten, and escaped to see them. The prison offered an emergency leave procedure, that defendant failed to follow. Further, the illegal act (the rape and beating) had already been performed. Since there was a legal alternative to escape and the harm had ended, his conduct was not justifiable by reason of necessity. *Id.* at 1247. Thus, under Illinois law defendant must first show that he/she did not create the situation. Second, defendant must show that it was reasonable to believe the illegal act (trespass in the case at bar) was necessary. The reasonableness of the belief may be proved by giving evidence that the danger was imminent and that defendant's act could effectively avert the danger. The next section will discuss the common law version of the necessity defense and the similarity between the common law and the Illinois version of the defense.

B. Common Law Necessity

In some states the necessity defense developed through court decisions. *See Commonwealth v. Brugmann,* 13 Mass. App. 373, 433 N.E.2d 457 (1982); *Commonwealth v. Hood,* 389 Mass. 581 (Ma. 1983); *State v. Kee,* 398 A.2d 384 (Me. 1979); *People v. Hubbard,* 115 Mich. App. 73, 320 N.W.2d 294 (Mich. App. 1982); *People v. Chachere,* 104 Misc. 2d 521, 428 N.Y.S.2d 781 (Suffolk 1980); *Commonwealth v. Berrigan,* 472 A.2d 1099 (Pa. Super. 1984); *Commonwealth v. Capitolo,* 471 A.2d 462 (Pa. Super. 1984); *State v. Warshow,* 410 A.2d 1000 (Vt. 1980).

The versions of the common law necessity defense formulated by the different states and the federal courts have varied as to specific requirements. Nonetheless, through the varying versions runs a common thread: an individual may justifiably break the letter of the law when he acts reasonably to prevent a serious harm and the injury he seeks to avoid is greater than the injury produced by his criminal conduct.

In *Commonwealth v. Brugmann, supra,* defendants were convicted of trespassing at the site of a nuclear power plant. In reviewing the necessity defense, the appellate court said that the defense "exonerates one who commits a crime under the 'pressure of circumstances' if the harm that would have resulted from compliance with the law significantly exceeds the harm actually resulting from the defendant's violation of the law." *Id.* at 460. The court also set out the familiar elements of the common law necessity defense:

> It is apparent that the application of the [necessity] defense is limited
> to the following circumstances: (1) the defendant is faced with a
> clear and imminent danger, not one which is debatable or spec-
> ulative; (2) the defendant can reasonably expect that his action
> will be effective as the direct cause of abating the danger; (3) there
> is no legal alternative which will be effective in abating the danger;
> and (4) the legislature has not acted to preclude the defense by a
> clear issue. 433 N.E.2d at 461. *See also Commonwealth v. Hood,*
> 389 Mass. 58 (1983).

The Illinois statute and the common law defense are quite similar. For example, the first two elements of the common law version shown above are equivalent to the second element of the Illinois statutory defense. In other words, for a defendant to show that he reasonably believed illegal conduct was necessary to avoid a greater harm, defendant is required to show both the imminent danger he was attempting to avoid, and that the conduct in question might reasonably be expected to have an effect in avoiding the harm.

The Illinois courts have also required that there should not be a legal alternative that would be effective. *See* discussion of *People v. White, supra.* That requirement is identical to the third common law element. Another example of the similarity between the Illinois statute and the common law defense is that under the fourth and last common law element, the legislature must not have precluded the defense by making a clear choice as to the values at issue. Although Illinois law has not specifically made that an element, the concept was used and expanded beyond legislative choice in *People v. Krizka,* 416 N.E.2d at 36. As discussed in Section A above, the court in *Krizka* refused to allow the necessity defense where the "harm" defendants tried to prevent was an activity legalized by the U.S. Supreme Court. Whereas, in the case at bar, defendants acted for the purpose of preventing ongoing criminal activity. Where neither the courts nor the legislature has made an activity illegal, the defense may be raised.

The facts of this case will be discussed using a combination of Illinois and common law elements of the necessity defense, to wit: (1) defendants were without blame in occasioning the situation in South Africa; (2) defendants reasonably believed their conduct was necessary; and (3) defendants could reasonably expect that their conduct would be effective; (4) defendants had no legal alternative that would have been effective; and (5) there is no existing law that precludes the use of the necessity defense.

C. Elements of the Necessity Defense

It is clear that under common law and the Illinois necessity statute, the elements are effectively identical. Each of the elements of necessity will be discussed in the context of the facts defendants will prove at trial.

1. Defendants Were Without Blame In Occasioning The Situation In South Africa

Defendants did not participate in formulating any of the South African policies pertaining to apartheid. Nor have defendants been responsible for any United States government or corporate policies which encourage or acquiesce in the existence of apartheid. Defendants are therefore without blame in occasioning the situation that now exists in South Africa.

Experts will testify to the extent of and the effects of the executive branch policy of constructive engagement, and to the extent and effects of U.S. corporate investments and activities in South Africa in perpetrating the South African apartheid system and the South African government plans and efforts to enact a new constitution, further entrenching the system of apartheid—clearly a situation not occasioned or developed by defendants, but rather constituting the background against which defendants acted. Finally, defendants will prove themselves without fault by introducing evidence of their elected officials and their own fruitless and persistent efforts to avert these harms by every available means.

Defendants contend that the City of Chicago will be unable to disprove beyond a reasonable doubt that defendants were without blame in occasioning the situation which caused them to remain at the South African Consulate.

2. Defendants Reasonably Believed That Their Conduct Was Necessary To Avoid A Greater Public Injury Than That Which Might Have Resulted From Their Conduct

Defendants will show that they had reasonable grounds to believe that their actions were necessary as part of a broader movement to alter U.S. policy in South Africa and bring about an end to the murder, torture, political imprisonment, and the deprivation of the right to participate in the body politic which Blacks have been forced to endure.

Defendants must prove the reasonableness of their belief that the harms they were averting were greater than the harms created by trespassing. To that end, defendants will show that they reasonably believed that the executive branch policy of constructive engagement and the South African government's acts of killings, torture, and base deprivation of human rights pose a greater public or private injury than the act of trespass.

Defendants will prove that international law crimes, a system of torture and domestic policies pre-existed their actions, have continued since, and, if the system of apartheid and the U.S. executive branch policy of constructive engagement is not terminated, will continue. Defendants' right to act on behalf of themselves and their fellow citizens in appropriate circumstances is beyond dispute. *See, e.g.*, Committee Comments - 1961, revised by Charles H. Bowman, S.H.A. ch. 38, § 7-13.

a. Defendants Were Faced With A Clear And Imminent Danger

The horrors of South Africa's system of apartheid are well known and require no detailed specification here. Apartheid, which translates literally to "separateness," is a system in which one's place in society is based on racial classification. As a recent United Nations study stated:

A person's racial classification is of the utmost importance to him, for it decides, *inter alia*, where he may live, how he may live, what work he may do, what sort of education he will receive, what political rights he will have, if any, whom he may marry, the extent of the social, cultural and recreational facilities open to him, and generally, the extent of his freedom of action and movement.[3]

The apartheid system enables a small white minority to maintain political, social and economic control of the Black majority and, in so doing, to maintain its own wealth, power and prestige. The system has been denounced in numerous U.N. resolutions and decisions,[4] in Congress,[5] and in many state legislatures and city councils.

The principal components of the apartheid system include:

(1) The Bantustan policy. Under this policy the fiction has been created that all South African Blacks are citizens, not of South Africa, but one of ten homelands or "bantustans," despite the fact that most South African Blacks have never even visited their "homeland." For some Blacks the policy has meant forced relocations;[6] for others it has simply served as a transparent means by which the white regime attempts to "legitimize" their denial of South African citizenship. Under the bantustan policy, Blacks, who account for 73% of South Africa's population, are allotted only 13% of the country's land, which is barren, rural and undeveloped.[7] This policy is carried out against the wishes of the affected Blacks, in clear violation of international norms of self-determination and freedom from racial discrimination. In essence, this policy attempts to denationalize South African Blacks. The United Nations and the United States government refuse to recognize the Bantustan policy and both entities have explicitly condemned it.

---

3. United Nations, *Apartheid and Racial Discrimination in Southern Africa*, OPI11335 (1968), at 6.
4. *See, e.g.*, U.N. Centre Against Apartheid, *Resolutions and Decisions Adopted by the United Nations Security Council on the Question of Apartheid 1960-1982* (2 Notes and Documents, Jan. 1983). In 1977 the United Nations went so far as to impose a mandatory arms embargo on South Africa. S.C. Res. 418, 32 U.N. SCOR (2046th mtg.) 5, U.N. Doc. S/INF/33 (1977), 32 U.N. SCOR (2046th mtg.) 5, U.N. Doc. S/INF/33 (1977), *reprinted in* U.N. Centre Against Apartheid, *supra*, at 7-8.
5. *See, e.g.*, Title VIII, Sec. 804(b), P.L. 98-181 (H.R. 1959).
6. Since 1964 the South African government has forcibly relocated 3.5 million blacks to the bantustans; and it has plans to relocate another two million in the future. *Time*, Sept. 24, 1984, at 34.
7. Davis, Cason & Hovey, "Economic Disengagement and South Africa: The Effectiveness and Feasibility of Implementing Sanctions and Divestment," 15 *Law and Policy in International Business*, 529, 533-34 (1983).

(2) Influx Control. Freedom of movement of Blacks in urban or "white" areas is highly restricted by "influx control" laws such as Blacks (Abolition of Passes and Coordination of Documents) Act, No. 67 of 1952, which requires all Blacks over 16 years of age to carry "pass books" which document their legitimate presence in white areas. In 1982, the government made 206,000 pass law arrests, with most of the violators deported to the bantustans.

(3) Removal of "Black Spots". "Black spots" are land areas lawfully owned and usually well developed by Blacks, and which the government now wants for white ownership. Between 1970 and 1979, the South African government forcibly relocated over 300,000 "black spot" residents to the bantustans.

(4) Indefinite Detention Without Charge or Trial. Section 28 of South Africa's Internal Security Act, No. 74 of 1982, permits indefinite detention of any person likely to commit an act endangering the maintenance of law and order. Section 29 of the Internal Security Act allows for indefinite incommunicado detention without charge or trial for purposes of interrogation. Section 31 authorizes detention of potential state witnesses in political trials. Detentions under Sections 29 and 31 are not reviewable in any court, and the detainees have no guaranteed access to counsel. In 1983, 453 South Africans, the vast majority of them Black, were placed in detention without trial. By September the figure for 1984 was 572.[8]

(5) The Banning of Individuals Organizations, Gatherings, and Publications. By executive fiat, authorized by the Internal Security Act, the Minister of Law and Order can ban individuals, organizations, gatherings and publications. Banned individuals are prohibited from speaking with more than one person at a time (including family members) and being quoted. Such individuals must also remain in proscribed areas and may be excluded from other areas. Outdoor political gatherings have been banned and restrictions have been placed even on funerals. From July, 1982 to June, 1983, over 900 publications and films were banned because they were "possibly prejudicial to the security of the state." In 1983, 130 South Africans were "listed" under the Internal Security Act, which means that they could not be quoted in the press, and a dozen South Africans were banned and restricted to their homes or other specified places and

---

8. *Time*, Sept. 24, 1984 at 34.

since 1961, more than 1,400 individuals and numerous organizations have been banned.[9]

(6) The Illegal Occupation of Namibia. Despite numerous United Nations General Assembly and Security Council resolutions, South Africa continues its illegal occupation of Namibia.[10] South Africa's exploitation of Namibia's natural and human resources and its aggression against the Namibian people constitute flagrant defiance of international law.

b. The Immediate Stimulus

The events that led to the defendants' actions were triggered by the new South African Constitution. It provides for three separate parliaments: one for whites, one for Indians and one for "Coloured," or South Africans of mixed race. Each house is to vote separately on its "own affairs" such as housing, which affects only its group. "General affairs," such as economic policy, are to be voted on by all three chambers. But whites will retain control of all major parliamentary committees, and all general legislation must be approved by all three parliaments. Moreover, the new Constitution offers neither the franchise nor any political rights to Blacks. Consequently, as the U.N. General Assembly declared in a resolution, the effect of the new Constitution is to deprive the indigenous Black majority of all fundamental rights, including the right of citizenship, and to transform South Africa into a country for "whites only" in keeping with apartheid policy.[11]

The South African government scheduled elections under the new Constitution for "Coloureds" on August 22, 1984 and for Indians on August 28, 1984. In an effort to oppose the new Constitution, in the summer of 1984 a nationwide campaign developed, urging "Coloureds" and Indians to boycott the elections.

The organizations campaigning for a boycott operated fairly openly in the period leading up to the elections. However, on August 21, 1984, leaders of the United Democratic Front (UDF)—the principal organization opposing the new Constitution—were arrested in early

9. Davis, Carson & Hovey, *supra* note 7, at 543.

10. *See Advisory Opinion on Legal Consequences for States of the Continued Presence of South Africa in Namibia (South West Africa) Notwithstanding Security Council Resolution 276 (1970)*, [1971] I.C.J. 16, 57-58.

11. *U.N. Chronicle*, January 1984, at 15.

morning security police raids carried out in Johannesburg, Durban and other areas. There were further arrests the next day, resulting in the detention of leaders of the Azanian Peoples Organization—another active opposition group—and the UDF. Many supporters of an election boycott were also arrested and on election day more than 100 people were arrested, amidst scenes of considerable police brutality, when they attempted to gather at or near polling places.[12]

The leaders who were arrested were held under Section 50 of the Internal Security Act of 1982, which permits 48 hours' detention incommunicado. Thereafter, they were served with detention orders based on unspecified acts and utterances that "attempted to create a revolutionary climate."

Despite these repressive measures, the movement against the new Constitution and against the apartheid system itself continued within South Africa. By September, 1984 there were widespread protests against various government policies. It was the largest showing of anti-apartheid forces within South Africa since the Soweto uprisings in 1976. On November 5, a two-day work stoppage occurred involving over 800,000 workers in the Johannesburg area.

As discussed above, in the Illinois case of *People v. Krizka, supra,* defendants were found not to be justified in their actions because the "harm" they were trying to prevent was abortion—a lawful activity. In contrast, the injury sought to be prevented here is not a legally protected right. The apartheid system and the new South African Constitution violate well settled international legal principles. Under international law acts or threats of violence against civilian populations, the forced movement of civilians, torture, and cruel, inhuman or degrading treatment or punishment are unlawful. (See earlier discussion of international law.) By supporting the South African government, the U.S. government is violating international law and citizens are justified in taking action to bring the situation to the attention of the public and attempting to stop U.S. support of the apartheid system in South Africa as a means to prevent the acts of killings, torture and deprivation of basic human rights occurring in South Africa.

---

12. Amnesty International, *South Africa: Detentions Related to the 'Coloured' and Indian Elections* 4 (October 30, 1984).

3. Defendants Could Reasonably Expect That Their Action Would Be Effective In Abating The Danger

At the time that defendants acted, demonstrations in opposition to the system of apartheid and in support of the opposition movement within South Africa were occurring throughout the world. Defendants reasonably believed that in acting as they did, they would be contributing to the effort to end the apartheid system. The reasonableness of the defendants' beliefs is demonstrated by the fact that in the past anti-apartheid efforts have led to changes in government and corporate policies.[13] Yet probably the best evidence of the reasonableness of the defendants' belief is a brief examination of the accomplishments vis-à-vis national concern over the crimes of apartheid. In the space of a few months focused attention on apartheid has:

—Called into open debate an issue which had been treated with intentional silence by the Reagan administration, and prompted in December 1985 the first public condemnation of South Africa from President Reagan.
—Led several senators to announce their intention to introduce legislation which would impose sanctions against South Africa and increase the chances for passage of such legislation.
—Led 35 members of Congress, who describe themselves as conservatives, to write to the South African ambassador, stating their intention to support divestment legislation if fundamental change does not occur within South Africa.
—Caused South Africa's honorary consul in Boston to resign his post.
—Led Pittsburgh's Mayor Caliguiri to call upon Pittsburgh merchants to stop selling krugerrands, the gold coin which supports apartheid, and led several krugerrands dealers to promise publicly that they would discontinue the sale of krugerrands.
—Convinced the First Bank of St. Paul to end the sale of krugerrands.
—Prompted Seattle's Mayor Royer to call for the closure of the

---

13. For example, in 1982 General Electric pulled out of a major mining project in South Africa, in large part because of such anti-apartheid efforts. Company officials in Johannesburg conceded that General Electric's decision to sell its stake in a joint venture with a major South African mining company, estimated to cost $138.6 million, was influenced by anti-apartheid pressure in Connecticut, where G.E. has its headquarters. In the first half of 1983, a number of companies withdrew from South Africa, in part because of international opposition to investment there. David, Carson & Hovey, *supra* note 7, at 561.

South African consulate on the grounds that it constitutes "an embarrassment," and led both State Senator George Flemming and City Councilman Norman Rice to announce that they would sponsor divestment acts.

—Contributed toward a much broader public understanding of the issues surrounding apartheid and U.S. policy toward South Africa, and proved that there is an American constituency concerned about this issue.

—20 pieces of legislation concerning apartheid have been recently introduced·in Congress.

—Ford Motor Company has decided to stop doing business in South Africa.

—First National Bank of Boston, Massachusetts, has stopped all lending to the South African government and South African businesses.

—Los Angeles Mayor Tom Bradley recently announced the city's plan to divest $1 billion in pension funds from companies doing business in South Africa and to set up a public corporation to fight apartheid.

Thus, it was perfectly reasonable for defendants to believe that their actions would be effective in helping to end the system of apartheid.[14]

While the point might be made that defendants' action was far removed from its alleged target—South Africa's system of apartheid—it would be unduly narrow for the Court to rule that defendants' actions in this country were illegal because this country is not the focus of the harm, knowing full well that neither defendants nor others can protest in South Africa without incurring the repressive sanctions of the South African government. It is clear that, as U.S. citizens, defendants were demonstrating at precisely the right place—the South African consulate. Thus if the system of apartheid is to be changed, international pressure is essential. As the prestigious Study Commission on U.S. Policy Toward South Africa has stated, ". . . none of

---

14. See *Commonwealth v. Berrigan*, 472 A.2d at 1115, ("their belief was that their action, *in combination with* the actions of others, *might accelerate a political process* ultimately leading to the abandonment of nuclear missiles. And *that* belief, I submit, should not be dismissed as 'unreasonable as a matter of law.'") (Spaeth J., concurring). Cf. *State v. Kee*, 398 A.2d 384, 386 ("*If*, here, defendant confronted circumstances which *in fact* threatened 'imminent physical harm to himself or another,' defendant's contention would be   correct that his subjective belief as to particular course of conduct 'necessary' to prevent the occurrence of that physical harm would not be open to further question on grounds of whether it met ordinary standards of reasonableness.")

this means that outside forces are without influence, and the United States must be counted among the most important of these."

Moreover, the General Assembly has declared that "any collaboration with the racist regime and apartheid institutions is a hostile act against the purposes and principles of the United Nations and constitutes a threat to international peace and security." Gen. Assembly Resolution 34/93 A of Dec. 12, 1979; Resolution 34/44 of Dec. 23, 1970; Resolution 33/23 of Nov. 29, 1978.

Further, in many ways U.S. policy has given support to South Africa. The United States has become the largest trading partner and second-largest foreign investor in South Africa. *New York Times*, Jan. 23, 1985, at A23. And as Representative John Conyers, Jr., recently stated in an article in the *New York Times*:

> Despite increased repression in South Africa since 1981, the Administration has lifted export restrictions on military and police equipment as well as on nuclear technology, allowing sales to South Africa of hundreds of millions of dollars' worth of previously prohibited items, including technology useful in the manufacture of nuclear and conventional arms, turbojet aircraft with intelligence-gathering capabilities and sophisticated computer equipment used by the regime's security forces. Under the auspices of constructive engagement, the Administration has permitted the South African police to be trained in this country, defended South Africa in the face of United Nations condemnation and nourished South Africa economically by supporting a $1.1 billion International Monetary Fund loan in 1982—a year in which the South African military budget grew about the same amount." *Id.*

Thus, it becomes clear that at the time defendants were demonstrating against apartheid they believed and, in fact, did contribute to the effort to end the apartheid system as evidenced by the aforementioned events.

4. Defendants Had No Legal Alternative Which Would Have Been Effective In Abating The Danger

For many years groups opposed to apartheid have sought to increase public awareness and to lobby Congress in support of legislation which would impose sanctions against South Africa. Yet their efforts have not been sufficiently effective.

Perhaps the best example of this involves the efforts to get the 98th Congress to enact legislation in 1984, imposing sanctions against South Africa.[15]

Defendants contend that this past record of legislative inability, when coupled with the increasing repressive measures by the South African government, made it necessary for them to take dramatic action. While it might be argued that defendants could have demonstrated peaceably without trespassing, the stark truth is that such action would not have had nearly as much impact in arousing public opinion or in alerting elected officials to the need for prompt action as the actions which defendants took.

5. There Is No Existing Law That Precludes The Use Of The Necessity Defense In This Case

Neither the legislature nor the courts have precluded use of the necessity defense in this case. In fact, unlike cases involving nuclear power plants, where Congress has expressly indicated its commitment to the development of nuclear power, cases involving weapons production, where Congress has endorsed the production of armaments and cases involving abortion clinics, where the Supreme Court has enunciated a constitutional principle permitting abortion, neither Congress, the Supreme Court, nor the legislature of this state has ever endorsed apartheid or the repressive policies of the South African government. On the contrary, the legislature of the State of Illinois is now considering a bill condemning apartheid. Also, the City of Chicago has recently introduced legislation calling for pension fund divestment, a prohibition on the purchase of South African goods and goods from companies doing business in South Africa. Thus, defendants are not contravening an established policy.

---

15. The account of these developments contained herein is drawn from a January 9, 1985 Congressional Research Service Memorandum to the House Committee on Foreign Affairs, Subcommittee on Africa (Attention: Steve Weissman). In 1983 legislation (H.R. 1693) was introduced that would have required U.S. companies doing business in South Africa to comply with fair employment principles, prohibited any new U.S. bank loans to the South African government or its parastatals, and prohibited the sale of krugerrands in the United States. The House of Representatives passed the bill as amended in March 1984. While accepting a version of the House bill, the Senate failed to accept the requirement that U.S. companies doing business in South Africa comply with fair employment practices, the prohibition on new bank loans, and the prohibition on the sale of South African krugerrands. However, because the House and Senate were unable to agree on the inclusion of a bank loan provision, no legislation was ultimately enacted.

V. Expert Testimony

To establish the affirmative defense of necessity, defendants must present evidence sufficient to raise a reasonable doubt as to defendants' guilt or innocence. *People v. White*, 78 Ill. App. 3d 979, 397 N.E.2d 1246, 1247 (1979), Ill. Rev. Stat., ch. 38, § 3-2. "[U]nless the state's evidence raises the defense for him, the defendant must present 'some evidence' in support thereof in order for the defense to be properly raised." *People v. Perez*, 97 Ill. App. 3d 278, 422 N.E.2d 945, 947 (1st Dist. 1981). Expert testimony will be required for defendants to present evidence that proves the reasonableness of their belief that the harms they were attempting to avert were greater than the harms they created by trespassing. The need for expert testimony in such cases has been recognized elsewhere:

> By limiting appellants' evidence to their own testimony of their reasons for committing the trespass, the trial court . . . effectively denied appellants the opportunity to prove justification. For as already discussed, it was not enough for appellants to prove that they *believed* the 'harm or evil sought to be avoided [by their conduct was] greater than that sought to be prevented by the law defining [their conduct as criminal trespass]. Pa. C.S.A. § 503(a)(1). They had to prove that they *reasonably* so believed. And they could not prove their reasonableness without proving what in fact "the harm or evil sought to be avoided" was . . . . By rejecting appellants' offer of the expert testimony and documentary evidence summarized in their offer of proof, the trial court precluded appellants from proving that their beliefs were reasonable. *Commonwealth v. Berrigan*, 472 A.2d 1099, 1105 (Pa. Super. 1984), *quoting Commonwealth v. Capitolo*, 471 A.2d 462, 467-68 (Pa. Super. 1984).

An Illinois court has recently upheld the use of the necessity defense in a similar case and has allowed defendants to show reasonableness with the use of expert testimony. *See People v. Jarka, et al.*, Circuit Court, Lake County, Nos. 002170, 002196-00212, 00214, 002236-00238. *See also City of Chicago v. Mayer*, 308 N.E.2d 601 (1982) where the Court said, "the necessity defense must be viewed in light of the factual situation of the particular case, which might include a defendant in a peculiar position to reasonably believe or anticipate an injury not apparent to someone who lacks similar knowledge, information, or training."

Similarly, defendants here must be allowed to present expert testimony on the situation in South Africa or they will be precluded from proving the reasonableness of their beliefs.

VI. Burden of Proof

Once the defendant has presented some evidence in support of the necessity defense, the state then has "the burden of proving the accused's guilt beyond a reasonable doubt as to that issue as well as all other elements of the offense." *People v. Perez*, 422 N.E.2d 945, 947 (Ill. App. 1981).

Dated: May 13, 1985

> Respectfully submitted,
> Timothy W. Wright, III
> David Neely
> Nancy Gaitskill
> Tom Royce
> Keith Davis
> Clarence Burch
> Lewis Meyers
> Julie Aimen
> Attorneys for Defendants
> 109 North Dearborn Street
> Suite 1300
> Chicago, IL 60602
> (312) 641-5570

3. Sample Direct Examination of an Expert Witness on South Africa and International Law.

MR. SAVAGE: Your Honor, this motion in limine is, in substance, a request to make an offer of proof with respect to an affirmative defense of necessity, which the defendants wish to assert at trial. We anticipate, on the basis of remarks made by the state, that they would object to the introduction of evidence material and relevant to the defense during the trial. We are asking the Court to rule that the necessity defense is available to the defendants and that the evidence contained in this offer is material and relevant to it. See *People v. Unger*, 66 Ill.2d 333, 362 N.E.2d 319 (1977).

Section 3-2 of Chapter 38 of the Illinois Revised Statutes describes the defendants' burden of proof: "An affirmative defense means that unless the state's evidence raises the issue involving the alleged offense, the defendant has to raise the issue, must present some evidence thereon in order to do so." The phrase, "some evidence," is described by the court in *People v. Brown*, 132 Ill. App. 2d 875, 271 N.E.2d 395 (2d Dist. 1971) as slight evidence. That holding is consistent with the Committee Comments following Section 3-2 in Chapter 38. The court in *People v. Espenscheid*, 109 Ill. App. 2d 107, 249 N.E.2d 866 (3d Dist. 1969), described "slight evidence" as "evidence, which could, if believed by the jury, raise a reasonable doubt."

I would note that it's not up to you today, your Honor, to determine whether the evidence would be believable to a jury; that's the question for the jury. Your question is to determine whether there's been offered today such evidence as could raise a reasonable doubt in a jury's mind. And, if such evidence has been offered, it would be reversible error under *Unger* to refuse to allow defendants to present such evidence.

Section 7-13 of Chapter 38 is the statutory statement of the defense of necessity. The necessity defense also exists at common law in Illinois. According to the statute, there are two elements to the defense. The first is that the accused must be without blame in occasioning or developing the situation. And, secondly, the accused must have reasonably believed that his conduct was necessary to avoid a public or private injury greater than the injury which might reasonably result from his own conduct. I would suggest that the Court read the phrase, "the situation," in the first element of the defense, to mean "public or private injury" in the second element.

Through the testimony of Professor Boyle, we intend to offer proof today of four distinct public injuries which the defendants reasonably believed existed. Three of them depend for their existence on the fourth. The fourth public injury that I'm referring to here is violations of international law by the South African government, which violations amount to war crimes under the Nuremberg Principles and other atrocities under international law.

The other three evils which the defendants reasonably believed existed and which describe the situation are: the complicity by the United States government through U.S. foreign policy in the crimes of the South African government; complicity by U.S. corporations doing business in South Africa, by aiding and abetting the South African government and benefitting from the criminal enterprise of the South African government; and complicity by the University of Illinois Trustees by investing in such corporations.

All the Court must conclude in order to grant the prayer and the motion is that there is competent evidence that the defendants' beliefs as to one of the four evils, the public injuries, were reasonable. And, then also, it must conclude that there is competent evidence that the defendants reasonably believed that their actions were necessary to avoid that particular public injury.

The second element, that the defendants reasonably believed the action taken was necessary, is analyzed in the case law. In order to make a prima facie case for the second element, defendants must show they reasonably believed three other things.

First, there can't be any reasonable alternative to what they did. On this point I would cite you *People v. Perez*, 97 Ill. App. 3d 278, 422 N.E.2d 945 (1st Dist. 1981). I don't think that means that all alternatives open to them had to be exhausted, although I think we can show that here they were. That again would be *People v. Unger*. And, in that case certainly all of the options open to the defendants were not exhausted. And, also I would cite you to a Pennsylvania case, *Commonwealth v. Capitolo*, 324 Pa. Super. 61, 471 A. 2d 462 (1984). The Pennsylvania Statute is similar to Illinois', and that court noted in a case involving civil resistance that the statute did not, by its language, provide for an exhaustion of alternative remedies or means. The court said that one of the considerations that should be entertained with respect to concluding whether the defendants reasonably believed there were no alternatives would be the immediacy of the evil to be avoided. Here I would have the Court note that the atrocities in South Africa are manifest daily in a most brutal way.

Secondly, the defendants must also show that they reasonably believed that their actions were calculated to effect a change. I don't think this means that they have to show they believed their actions alone would have changed any of the evils that they might reasonably have believed existed. Their belief is that their actions, in concert with others across the nation and across the world, would be effective. For authority in this regard I would cite you to another Pennsylvania case, *Commonwealth v. Berrigan*, 325 Pa. Super. 242, 472 A. 2d 1099 (1984), holding that such a belief is reasonable.

Lastly, the defendants have to show evidence that the harm which resulted from their actions was less than the harm they sought to combat.

As to the issue of whether defendants may present the testimony of experts to show the reasonableness of their beliefs, I would quote from *Commonwealth v. Berrigan*, which is a Pennsylvania case, as follows, ''By limiting appellants' evidence to their own testimony of their reasons for committing the trespass, the trial court effectively denied appellants the opportunity to prove justification. For as already discussed, it was not enough for appellants to prove that they believed the harm or evil sought to be avoided by their conduct was greater than that sought to be prevented by the law defining their conduct as criminal trespass. They had to prove that they reasonably so believed. And, they could not prove their reasonableness without proving what, in fact, 'the harm or evil sought to be avoided' was. By rejecting appellants' offer of expert testimony and documentary evidence summarized in their offer of proof, the trial court precluded appellants from proving that their beliefs were reasonable.''

There are two cases which will be described by Professor Boyle involving this type of international law necessity defense. One case was cited in the motion, and that's *People v. Jarka*, where I believe the court actually instructed the jury that for the United States to threaten the use of nuclear war would be a breach of international law. And, another case in Chicago, involving demonstrators who were arrested on a city trespass charge at the South African Consulate, protesting apartheid policies, *Chicago v. Streeter*. The motion was allowed and the evidence was introduced in that case, after the court considered the issue.

So, with that said, what I would like to do is offer the evidence which I have in support of the elements of the defense and have the Court conclude whether or not that meets the requirements under the statute and under the case law, and whether we can do this at trial.

THE COURT: You may proceed.

FRANCIS ANTHONY BOYLE

called as a witness on behalf of the defendants, being first duly sworn, was examined and testified as follows.

257

DIRECT EXAMINATION BY MR. SAVAGE

At this point you should consult the following headings from Chapter 4.2, which are incorporated here by reference:

Qualification as an Expert
The Nature of International Law
International Law Is Part of U.S. Domestic Law
The Nuremberg Principles [*See also* Chapter 4.2]

Q. Criminal responsibility under the Nuremberg Principles, I assume, attaches to individuals and not the state, is that correct?

A. Well, both. I mean, it can attach to a state as well as an individual. And, indeed, at Nuremberg the Nazi war criminals argued that the Nazi state itself was responsible for these crimes, but not they as individuals because the crimes must be imputed to the state under the Act of State Doctrine. The Nuremberg Tribunal rejected that and said that there is personal criminal responsibility on their part for the commission of these crimes, and they simply cannot attribute that to the state itself.

Q. I take it that as a result of your various studies and particularly your studies as a Professor at the University of Illinois Center for African Studies, that you are familiar with the facts surrounding the system of apartheid, the internal and foreign policies of the government of South Africa?

A. Yes, I am.

Q. And, in your opinion now, would you say that the South African government is guilty of violations of the Nuremberg Principles?

A. Certainly, without a doubt. In particular, crimes against peace, as evident by a continuing pattern of aggressive actions that are being undertaken against surrounding states, as we saw just last week in the newspapers—constant attacks upon Angola, upon Botswana, Lesotho, Mozambique, Zimbabwe, that have been repeatedly condemned by both the United Nations Security Council and also by the United States government itself.

Crimes against Humanity, the second Nuremberg Principle. And, let me repeat this definition: "murder, extermination, enslavement, deportation and other inhumane acts committed against any civilian population." Again, very similar, analogous to what Hitler was doing to German Jews—the archetypal case. Clearly, right now, there are approximately two to three Black people in South Africa, per day, who are being killed. And certainly they are being kept in conditions that approach enslavement, and inhumane acts are going on against them all the time.

The Genocide Convention [*See also* Chapter 4.2]

Q. Let me show you now a document marked for identification purposes as defendants' group exhibit 1. Do you recognize that document?

A. Yes. This is the International Convention on the Prevention and Punishment of the Crime of Genocide. And, as you know from probably reading the newspaper, the United States Senate recently gave its advice and consent to the Genocide Convention. The Genocide Convention originated out of this Nuremberg Principle of crime against humanity. The theory was that what Hitler had done to the Jews was such an horrendous crime that the entire international community had to adopt a treaty that would specifically prohibit this type of activity and make it very clear that any government official who had participated in genocide or any of the inchoate offenses with respect to genocide, was guilty of an international crime and in addition, must either be prosecuted by his own government or extradited to another government that would have jurisdiction to try him.

And, so what happened with the Genocide Convention is that the U. N. General Assembly attempted somewhat to elaborate upon the Nuremberg Principle of crime against humanity. And, so in Article 2 of the Genocide Convention, you will note, genocide means any of the following acts committed with intent to destroy in whole or in part, a national, ethnical, racial or religious group, as such. And, so when the South African government undertakes the measures it has against South African Blacks, simply because they are Blacks, this is genocide. Just as when Hitler undertook the steps that he did against German Jews, simply because they were Jews, that was a crime against humanity and genocide itself.

And, what is discussed here in Article 2, killing members of the group, that is clearly going on every day in South Africa. Causing serious bodily or mental harm to members of the group, that is going on every day in South Africa. Deliberately inflicting on the group conditions calculated to bring about its destruction, in whole or in part, that is going on every day. Certainly under Articles 2(a), (b) and (c), the South African government is engaging in the crime of genocide. So with respect to the situation in South Africa, which is almost identical to the policies that were pursued by the Nazi government against the German Jews, one would certainly have to conclude that the governing officials in South Africa are today committing genocide against Blacks simply because of their racial, ethnic and national characteristics. They are Black and they are being killed because they are Black. And that is genocide.

As I pointed out, Article 3 then, building on the Nuremberg Principles, deals with the inchoate offenses, and makes it a crime to commit conspiracy, incitement, attempt, or complicity, in genocide. All of these are international crimes as recognized by the entire international community. And, I should point out, as recognized by the United States government itself.

Q. What is the status of the Genocide Convention under United States law?

A. Right now it is a treaty that has received the advice and consent of two-thirds of the United States Senate. In addition, even if it had not, most publicists, international law professors, I think, would agree that the Genocide Convention is a reflection of customary international law, simply because all states agree that genocide is a crime.

Q. Again, is criminal responsibility attributable to an individual as well as a government entity?

A. That is correct, yes. And, again, building upon the precedent of the Nazi war criminal trials.

Q. And, the crime of genocide, as stated in the Convention, is a restatement about really what was the crime against humanity in the Nuremberg Charter?

A. It was an attempt to codify, further expand and explain that notion, yes. But, again the archetypal case, to keep in mind, for both a crime against humanity and genocide, was Hitler's extermination of the Jews, Slavs, Gypsies and other ethnic groups he considered to be "inferior" to Aryans. That is what is going on in South Africa today against Blacks.

Apartheid

Q. Let me show you a document marked for purposes of identification as defendants' group exhibit number 2. Would you tell me whether you recognize this document.

A. Yes. This is the International Convention on Suppression and Punishment of the Crime of Apartheid.

Q. I imagine it would go without saying that in your opinion the government of South Africa is acting in contravention of that Convention?

A. Yes. The concept of apartheid, again being an international crime, built upon the Nuremburg Principle of crime against humanity, as well as building upon the Genocide Convention. The theory here was that Blacks in South Africa were being discriminated against and treated in a condition almost equivalent to slavery and having such a whole series of heinous acts being perpetrated upon them, that the practice of apartheid should be made an international crime itself. Hence, the racial practices of the South African government against Blacks in its own country, its own citizens, are an international crime. And, this would create personal criminal responsibility on the part of individuals who engage in or practice apartheid.

There is also what is known as a peremptory norm of international law. Or what we lawyers call by the Latin term jus cogens. And apartheid violates a peremptory norm of international law.

Now the United States government has not yet signed the Apartheid Convention. However, I should point out that I do not know of a reputable professor of international law who disagrees with the proposition that apartheid is an international crime. And it creates personal, criminal responsibility on the part of those government officials who are in charge of supervising the system of apartheid as practiced in South Africa today.

The United Nations Charter

Q. Does the United States participate in the General Assembly of the United Nations and its Security Council through a treaty or an executive agreement?

A. Yes. The United States was one of the founding members of the United Nations, this was our idea. I think if you read the press today, you sort of get the idea that the United Nations was some concoction that was foisted upon us by the Third World. That is not correct. It was basically the idea of President Franklin Roosevelt. He founded it and promoted it to the rest of the world. And right now, we are a full, active participant in the U.N. General Assembly and we are also a permanent member of the United Nations Security Council.

Q. Are the resolutions of the General Assembly and the Security Council binding upon the United States as international law?

A. The resolutions of the Security Council are clearly binding on the United States government as a matter of international law. This is for two reasons. First, the United Nations Charter clearly states that all member states are under an obligation to carry out the terms of Security Council decisions. Second, that requirement of the United Nations Charter has been incorporated into U.S. domestic law, specifically by an act of Congress, known as the United Nations Participation Act. And that act gives domestic force to United Nations Security Council decisions within the United States, especially U.S. courts.

With respect to General Assembly resolutions, it depends on the type of resolution. Some types of General Assembly resolutions, those that are unanimously accepted or those that receive general acceptance from all members of the international community, are considered binding as customary international law. For example, the Nuremberg Principles were subscribed to by the United Nations General Assembly in a unanimous vote. And to that extent, that vote, that resolution constitutes customary international law that would be binding on the United States government and United States courts.

Q. Are you familiar with U. N. Charter, Articles 55 and 56?

A. Yes, I am.

Q. Can you tell me what they are?

A. Basically those two provisions of the United Nations Charter contain the statement of what are the fundamental requirements when it comes to the international protection of human rights. And, certainly one of the most important provisions in Articles 55 and 56, is the prohibition against discrimination on the grounds of race.

Q. And, as a part of the U. N. Charter, they have the status of a treaty under the U.S. Constitution?

A. That is correct.

The Universal Declaration of Human Rights

Q. Okay. Are you familiar with a document entitled the Universal Declaration of Human Rights?

A. I am. The Universal Declaration of Human Rights has to be read in conjunction with Articles 55 and 56 of the United Nations Charter. At the time when the Charter was drafted, the thought was held that there should be attached to the U. N. Charter, a Bill of Rights that would be very similar to the relationship between the United States Constitution and the first ten amendments to the United States Constitution, which are properly called the U.S. Bill of Rights.

This then led to the formulation of the Universal Declaration of Human Rights, which was adopted by a consensus resolution of the United Nations General Assembly. That Universal Declaration of Human Rights today is considered to be binding on all states in the world community as a matter of customary international law. And, indeed, it is the case today that the United States government, the Department of State, routinely treats the Universal Declaration of Human Rights as binding as a matter of customary international law.

The Declaration was then followed by two treaties that were eventually adopted in 1966 by the United Nations General Assembly in order to implement, that is carry out, the terms of the Declaration. And, here, of course, the most important treaty, for our purposes, is the U. N. Convention on Civil and Political Rights. This was intended to further elaborate, expand upon, the terms of the Universal Declaration of Human Rights establishing what is the basic minimum standard that all individuals in the world community should be entitled to. So there is a direct line from the U.N. Charter requirements of articles 55 and 56, attempted to be further specified by the Universal Declaration, which were then further specified and codified in the International Covenant on Civil and Political Rights.

Q. Now, I believe that the Universal Declaration of Human Rights is in group exhibit 3 before you. Would you turn your attention to articles 4, 5, 7 and 9, and tell me if, in your opinion, the South African government is in violation of those articles?

A. Well, those and others; but certainly article 3, everyone has a right to life, liberty and security of person. Article 4, no one shall be held in slavery or servitude; slavery and the slave trade prohibited in all forms. Five, no one shall be subjected to torture or to cruel, inhuman or degrading treatment or punishment. Six, everyone has a right to recognition everywhere as a person before the law. That is not the case with respect to Blacks in South Africa. Seven, all are equal before the law and are entitled, without any discrimination, to equal protection of the law. That is not true for Blacks in South Africa. All are entitled to equal protection against any discrimination in violation of this Declaration and against any incitement to such discrimination. Again, not true for Blacks in South Africa. Eight, everyone has a right to an effective remedy by competent national tribunal for acts violating fundamental rights granted by the constitution or law. Again, not true for Blacks in South Africa. And, nine, no one shall be subjected to arbitrary arrest, detention or exile. Again, not true for Blacks in South Africa.

Q. And, you have stated, have you not, that the Universal Declaration of Human Rights has status as customary international law?

A. Yes, and as I said, that is the official position of the United States government.

Q. And, the two U.N. Conventions that you mentioned, do they have status as customary international law?

A. It depends. The Reagan administration takes the position that the convention on economic, social and cultural rights, does not. But, the other convention, on civil and political rights, which is the one that we are primarily concerned with, is considered to enunciate basic rules of international law. And, to the extent that it enunciates these basic rules, it contains or represents customary international law. I should point out that the U.S. government has signed both conventions.

Torture

Q. In your opinion has the South African government engaged in acts of torture that are in contravention of the Universal Declaration of Human Rights and customary international law?

A. Yes.

Q. Are you familiar with a case entitled *Filartiga v. Pena-Irala*, 630 F.2d 876 (2d Cir. 1980)?

A. Yes. This was a pathbreaking case decided by Judge Kaufman in the United States Court of Appeals for the Second Circuit. The case was brought under the Federal Alien Tort Statute by relatives of a national of Paraguay, who had been tortured by members of the Paraguayan government. They managed to track down one of the fellows who did the torturing when he came to the United States.

And, they sued him under this Federal Alien Tort Statute, that gives U.S. federal courts jurisdiction to entertain a complaint by aliens for violations of what are called the laws of nations, which is essentially international law. The Alien Tort Statute was passed by Congress back in the Eighteenth Century. The term "international law" was not developed until a bit later by Jeremy Bentham. So, it used to be called the law of nations. But, they're the same type of concept.

The reason why Judge Kaufman's decision is so significant is that he found that torture was a violation of the laws of nations, of customary international law, and hence that aliens could sue in the United States courts for torture, under the circumstances that I gave to you. And, in doing this, Judge Kaufman acted very much as an international court or the United States Supreme Court would do, to determine what is customary international law with respect to torture. He looked at a variety of international conventions. There is also a very famous footnote in Judge Kaufman's decision, where he lists the names of several different international law professors, all expressing their opinion that torture was a violation of the laws of nations.

And recently last December, the United Nations General Assembly adopted an international convention prohibiting torture. And this prohibition on torture is a general principle of law that is recognized by all civilized nations, including the United States government itself. So again, we, our government, our courts, are officially on record that torture clearly violates international law and U.S. domestic law.

And to the extent that the South African government engages in torture, which it clearly does, it is not only committing an international crime, but those government officials who engage in, consent to, connive or otherwise are involved in torture, are guilty of an international crime. And indeed, I think you will note from reading some of the recent newspapers, it has been reported by even white South African doctors that the South African police routinely torture Black children. This gets us back to the international crimes of genocide, apartheid, and crimes against humanity.

Namibia

Q. And, are you familiar with the policies of the South African government with respect to the nation of Namibia, and in particular,

United Nations Security Council Resolution 435 passed in 1978, which forbade the illegal occupation of Namibia by the South African government?

· A. Yes, I am. In Resolution 435 of 1978 the United Nations Security Council held that South Africa must withdraw from Namibia. Namibia is what had been known as South West Africa. South West Africa was territory that had been given to the South African government at the end of the First World War by the League of Nations, to be administered as a sacred trust, as it was called, a sacred trust for all mankind on behalf of the people living in South West Africa, to some day prepare them for independence.

The South African government completely failed to do anything to prepare Namibia and the people living there for independence. The United Nations General Assembly made repeated calls that South Africa leave Namibia. All these calls were ignored. Eventually, the General Assembly then decided to revoke the mandate that had been given to the South African government to administer Namibia on behalf of the international community. And that revocation of the mandate was upheld by the International Court of Justice in its advisory opinion on Namibia. That then set the legal basis for Resolution 435 of 1978 which demanded that South Africa finally leave Namibia.

And I should point out that it was the United States government that promoted Resolution 435 in the United Nations Security Council. And I should also point out that in the Fall of 1980, the South African government agreed to accept and carry out the decision of the Security Council in Resolution 435. But then with the change of governments in this country, from the Carter administration to the Reagan administration, the South African government reneged, specifically reneged on its commitment to accept Resolution 435.

However, whether or not South Africa agreed or did not agree to accept Resolution 435, it would still be bound by the terms of Resolution 435 according to the U.N. Charter. But again, it's interesting that they even agreed themselves and then they reneged on that agreement. And the reason they did so was an indication from the incoming Reagan administration that the U.S. government was no longer going to insist upon Resolution 435 or independence for Namibia. This became part of the Reagan administration's policy toward South Africa known as "constructive engagement."

Q. And, are those Namibian occupation policies, in your opinion, in violation of the various rules and precepts of international law?

A. Nothing could be clearer than that the South African occupation of Namibia is completely illegal. Right now, as a result of the illegal nature of what South Africa has done in Namibia, the United Nations General Assembly withdrew its right to occupy Namibia and asserted sovereign control over Namibia. And, today it is the case that Namibia, the former South West Africa, is the only place on earth for which legal sovereignty is formally vested in the United Nations—not in South Africa. And, once again, this was officially recognized by the United States government—at least until the Reagan administration came along.

The refusal of the South African government to leave Namibia, and in addition, the practice of apartheid by the South African government were eventually considered to constitute a serious threat to the maintenance of international peace and security, and this then led the United Nations Security Council to adopt a complete and total arms embargo against South Africa in 1977. And today, South Africa is the only country in the world that is subject to formal United Nations sanctions.

And once again, the lead role in the imposition of the arms embargo in South Africa came from the United States government, and this too was in turn incorporated into United States law by the United Nations Participation Act. And it is a crime for an American citizen to sell weapons, equipment, supplies, for military purposes to the government in South Africa, because of the heinous nature of the violations of international law that that government has committed.

Crimes Against Peace

Q. Did the government of South Africa propagate acts of war against the legitimate government of Angola in order to consolidate its illegal occupation of Namibia?

A. Yes. This has been repeatedly condemned again by the United Nations Security Council. In order to hold onto Namibia, the South African government has repeatedly invaded Angola, and indeed today continues illegally to occupy territory in Angola, in violation of United Nations Security Council resolutions. In order to hold up its apartheid system internally, it has also attacked and made military aggression in violation of international law against the surrounding states: Angola, Lesotho, Botswana, Mozambique, the Seychelles, Zimbabwe.

So clearly yes, the South African government has been condemned on all accounts for this aggression. And again, that has led the Security Council to take the type of action that it did in its 1977 arms embargo. All of this constitutes crimes against peace as defined by the Nuremberg Principles. A crime against peace is waging aggressive war against other states or a war in violation of international treaties and agreements. That is what South Africa has repeatedly done against its neighbors. And this creates personal criminal responsibility for its leaders, just as was the case with the Nazi war criminals of the Hitler regime.

"Constructive Engagement"

Q. Now, you've stated in your testimony today that the various conventions we have discussed prohibit inchoate crimes such as complicity in the international law violations, by aiding and abetting, by making the crime your own and so on. Are you familiar with the various cases brought before international criminal courts after the Second World War, regarding German industrialists?

A. Yes.

Q. Can you explain to the Court what concepts of complicity were used by the courts in these cases?

A. Well, again, generally recognized principles of complicity. As I said, complicity is a doctrine, one of those general principles of law recognized by all civilized states. And, here you had German industrialists who were knowingly using slave labor or manufacturing poison gas for the extermination of Jews and others. And, it was found that because of this knowledge, they themselves could be appropriately found guilty of war crimes. And, in addition, after the war, some of these German industries paid compensation to the victims. Even today, there was a recent case just coming up this year, where a German corporation has paid compensation to survivors of the slave labor that had been perpetrated.

Q. In your opinion, under international common law principles of complicity, is the United States government, through its policy of constructive engagement, aiding and abetting the South African government in its violations of international law?

A. Well, that depends on the knowledge and purpose of officials of the United States government. Complicity would depend on whether or not U. S. government officials intended to facilitate, encourage, make their own, profit from the policies of the South African government. And, certainly the doctrine that had been pursued by the Reagan administration, known as constructive engagement, I think, creates very serious problems of complicity under well recognized principles of international law.

Under the Carter administration, the U. S. position had been quite clear, that what was going on in South Africa, internally and externally, was essentially organized criminal activity and that the United States government had to oppose it in whatever manner possible. Under the Reagan administration, under the influence of Chester Crocker, who is Assistant Secretary of State for African Affairs, that policy changed to one known as "constructive engagement." One of the other areas I teach at the University of Illinois is criminal law. And, I guess if you're talking about an individual constructively engaging in an organized criminal enterprise, that would certainly make you complicit as an aider and abetter, in that organized criminal enterprise. And, certainly, in my opinion, the South African government itself is an organized criminal enterprise, very similar to the Nazi government and its organs, as was determined by the Nuremberg Tribunal.

Corporate Complicity

Q. In your opinion, would corporations such as GM, Ford, Caterpillar, and other labor–intensive industries, which profit by their businesses in South Africa, be complicit in the violations you have described, under both common law rules of complicity and the concepts of complicity discussed by the international tribunals after the Second World War?

A. Well, what I would say is this: To the extent they have knowledge of the South African international criminal law violations that are going on, and to the extent that they knowingly participate in this system and derive profit from it, it could certainly be the case that complicity would be established. Or, from another perspective, it would certainly be reasonable for the defendants to believe that there might be complicity present.

University Complicity

Q. In your opinion now, under principles of complicity as developed in international law and in common law, and depending on the same factors, that is knowledge, could the Trustees of the University of Illinois be complicit in those violations by continuing to invest funds in corporations doing business in South Africa, thus aiding and abetting the South African government in its violations of international law?

A. Well, again, as I said, that would depend on the extent of their knowledge and their intentions. If they intended, by actively participating in an investment program for the purpose of facilitating, furthering, promoting, benefitting from or profiting from apartheid, or any of the other international crimes that I mentioned to you, again the answer would be, yes—as aiders and abetters. I do not express any opinion at all on the knowledge, intention or purpose of various members of the Board of Trustees of the University. But, simply, that it could be reasonable for the defendants to believe, certainly, that complicity is a possibility.

The equivalent here would be to the University of Illinois investing in I.G. Farben knowing full well that it was using slave labor or manufacturing poison gas for the purpose of killing and exterminating German Jews and other individuals. And that would turn on the question of intent, as is the case with respect to any charge on aiding and abetting. Namely, does the University know or should it know that conduct that it is engaging in will be further facilitating, assisting, helping, or profiting from the commission of international crimes. That is the relevant test. And I take it the students involved here concluded that the answer to that question was yes. And hence, this motivated their conduct.

Q. In your opinion then, if the defendants in this case had believed, when they were arrested, that the government of South Africa was engaged in gross violations of human rights law, would their belief be reasonable?

A. I would certainly say that, yes, their belief would be reasonable, as an international law professor. Of course, that would be an issue to be determined by the jury, not by me. But, clearly, there would be reasonable grounds for that belief and the reasonable grounds would be what I have been testifying here for the past hour now. Certainly on the basis of the facts presented, it seems that a good faith belief can be developed.

Q. And, is it your testimony that reasonable grounds could also be found for a belief that the United States government is complicit, depending upon these factors?

A. Under the doctrine of constructive engagement, yes, there are reasonable grounds for that belief. It could be a mistaken belief, but it would be a good faith belief, which is all that is required. Indeed, other governments have pointed this out to the United States government, that the doctrine of constructive engagement creates serious legal complicity problems. And, indeed, as best as I can tell, in the past six months or so, in absolute disgust at some of the practices of the South African government, even now the Reagan administration has not explicitly but certainly implicitly, disavowed the doctrine of constructive engagement.

Q. With the same kinds of limitations and qualifications, do you think there are reasonable grounds for a belief that U. S. corporations doing business in South Africa, especially the corporations which are labor intensive, are complicit under the doctrines we have been talking about?

A. Certainly if you look at the definition of aiding and abetting, that is facilitating, furthering, promoting, making it your own, investing in and making a profit from an organized criminal enterprise, this is certainly enough to make you a criminal yourself, under an aiding and abetting theory.

Q. And, with the same limitations and understanding that you cannot testify as to someone's intent, could there be reasonable grounds, on the part of the defendants, to believe that the Trustees were complicit by continuing their policy of investment in corporations doing business in South Africa?

A. Well, once again, it would be subject to the same types of qualifications. It would depend upon their knowledge, their intention, their purpose, their action. But, if any of these Trustees believed that by pursuing these particular policies they were furthering, promoting, making their own, making a profit from, the organized criminal activities going on in South Africa, that very well could create accomplice liability. And of course I take it the reason these stocks were purchased by the University was to make a profit.

Civil Resistance

Q. In your studies, especially in your studies of political science, did you have occasion to study social movements, such as the civil rights movement, in the United States?

A. Yes.

Q. And, the tactics used by civil rights advocates, such as Martin Luther King?

A. Yes. What was then popularly called civil disobedience, which I think is different from what we have in this case.

Q. Now, in your opinion, was that an effective tactic to effect changes in the civil rights laws in the United States?

A. I believe it was. Just as a matter of fact, yes.

Q. Do you have personal knowledge of the tactics used by the defendants in this case?

A. Well, as I understand it, they did engage in what is popularly called civil resistance, which is different from civil disobedience in that these defendants were attempting to prevent what they believed to be ongoing criminal activity under international law.

Q. And, you understand it was not violent civil resistance?

A. As I understand it, yes.

Q. In your opinion, could they have a reasonable belief that that was an effective tactic to effect a change either in the policies of the South African government, the complicity of the United States, complicity of the corporations or complicity of the Trustees?

A. Certainly. In my opinion, as someone who has written on this subject and has taught about it, the one thing I think that will bring the South African government along to a change is economic sanctions. And, pursued as part of a policy of getting the United States government to adopt economic sanctions against South Africa, this type of activity could clearly be very effective.

Indeed, this type of activity that has gone on, not simply here but in other places, eventually did result in the Reagan administration adopting limited economic sanctions against the South African government. And, as I see it, the ultimate objective of all of these activities, is to get the United States government to exercise its authority at the United Nations Security Council, to impose a mandatory economic embargo against South Africa. This would be very similar to what happened in 1977, when the Carter administration went to the United Nations Security Council and imposed a mandatory arms embargo against the South African government because of the policies it was pursuing internally against its Black population, because of the aggressive policies it was pursuing against its neighboring states and also because of its illegal occupation of Namibia.

Necessity

Q. In your opinion, were any of the defendants with blame in occasioning or developing the violations of international law we have discussed?

A. Not that I know of. I don't believe any of the students have been responsible for any of the policies that have been undertaken by the South African government or the United States government. Indeed, as I understand it, they have attempted to change these policies in a peaceful, not violent, manner.

Q. Are you familiar with Chapter 38, Section 7-13 of the Illinois Revised Statutes, dealing with the necessity defense?

A. Yes. I am quite extensively familiar with that statute. I was involved in both the *Jarka* and *Streeter* cases that you mentioned as their expert on international law.

Q. And under that section of the statute, would a student's actions which otherwise might constitute, for example, a violation of a criminal trespass statute, be justified, by reason of necessity, if that student was without blame in occasioning or developing the breaches of international law by the South African government, or the complicity of the United States government or the University of Illinois in said violations; and that student's actions were reasonably calculated and necessary to effect a change in the policies of the South African government, the United States and the University of Illinois; and the harm caused by that student was less than the harm caused by the South African government, the United States government and the University of Illinois; and there was no other reasonable alternative open to that student in order to effect those changes?

A. The answer is yes, certainly. When you have trespass on the one hand, and on the other hand you have crimes against peace, crimes against humanity, war crimes, genocide, apartheid, and torture, at a minimum, certainly. We could be here for the next five hours discussing the violations of international law committed by South Africa. If you look at the statute, it talks about avoiding a greater public or private harm or injury. And, clearly, these crimes that the South African government is committing are certainly a greater public and private injury than a simple trespass. And this defense has been made successfully by other students in similar criminal cases. For example, on two separate occasions the Evanston city attorney has dismissed criminal charges against students at Northwestern University protesting in favor of divestment after we have filed international law necessity motions on their behalf.

MR. SAVAGE: Your Honor, I'm done with my examination. We'll tender the witness.

CROSS EXAMINATION BY STATES ATTORNEY

Q. Professor Boyle, I just have very few questions with respect to this notion of accomplice liability under various provisions of international law which you have discussed. It was your testimony, was it not, that these are pretty much similar to currently prevailing and accepted notions of accountability or conspiratorial-accessorial liability, things of that nature?

A. Yes. As I said, the doctrine of accomplice liability is similar, it's one of these general principles of law recognized by all civilized nations.

Q. Okay. And, to what, if any, extent would the principles which you have discussed today diverge from those, say embodied in article 5 of the Illinois Criminal Code?

A. I just took a look yesterday at that provision of the Criminal Code. I would say it doesn't diverge all that much. It might be perhaps a little bit different, and it really would depend on what case you're talking about. As I said, there is no principle of stare decisis in international law, so it's hard to say that there is a black letter rule on complicity other than that it exists. But, the doctrine of complicity itself is well recognized. I think there's scope for reasonable people to disagree as to precisely what that definition is.

Q. Could you state to a reasonable degree of professional, scholarly certainty, if you will, that these notions would embody what is commonly known as a specific intent?

A. Well, that is not quite clear. The reason is this: that customary international law involves an amalgam of both the Anglo/American approach to criminal law notions, and the European Continental approach. And, here it is the case in the United States, that because of our requirements of due process of law recognized in our Constitution, we seem to have a much higher standard of proof when it comes to establishing intent as an element of a crime, than might be the case as recognized by other states of the world community, or perhaps by international law.

As I said, there is no one case that deals with this particular issue. So, what I'm doing here is basically relying upon my readings of writers who have discussed this doctrine of complicity, their particular approach to the problem. But, as pointed out earlier, writers, publicists, are considered a subsidiary means for the determination of rules of law. So, I think the U. S. standard might be a little bit higher than would be recognized by other states of the international community.

Q. All right. And, if, in a given situation, the American rule, so to speak, were to come in conflict with any one or more of the principles of international law which you enumerated, what would happen?

A. Well, let's suppose that an individual is being tried for the crime of genocide in an American court, because it will be a crime as soon as Congress passes implementing legislation. If he were being tried in an American court, he would be held to American standards of law and proof beyond a reasonable doubt. If Congress decides to put a specific intent element in there, then certainly that would be binding on a United States court. However, foreign courts could look at that issue quite differently. And, if, for example, the individual was being tried in a court of another nation or an international court set up to deal with that issue, they would not necessarily be bound by the

U. S. approach to the subject of specific intent. And, as I said, due to the stringency of our requirements, I think our standard on specific intent is a little bit higher than what would be recognized by other courts, other states. So, our practice does not necessarily bind anyone else.

Q. Now, you're familiar with the rule prevailing in Illinois, and as I understand it probably the majority of most states, that passive acquiescence, even given antecedent knowledge of a criminal venture, would not render one subject to accomplice liability, is that correct?

A. Well, that depends. For example, passive acquiescence, when you have an obligation to do something about it, does render you guilty as an accomplice. And, that's a black letter rule of criminal law. Moreover, willful ignorance is equivalent to knowledge. So if you just close your eyes to something you know is going on, that does not relieve you from criminal responsibility. And knowingly profitting from an organized criminal activity is not passive acquiescence.

Q. But, there again, you would have, would you not, a clear scienter element, either a specific intent or knowledge, however it might be imputed, is that correct?

A. Well, in those cases here in the United States, yes.

Q. Okay. Thank you. Now, just a few final things. Now, with respect to these various provisions of international law which you have discussed, how are these means enforced? What type of legal structure is there for enforcing these provisions?

A. Well, the most important means for enforcement of these norms is internally. That is, by the United States government itself, domestically, with respect to its own citizens. Our courts apply these norms of law in both civil and criminal suits, as these issues are presented. And, other states do the same thing. So, the basic and most effective means for enforcing norms of international law come internally by the state itself, and then also by a state acting in its relations with other states. Thus, by the United States in its conduct of foreign affairs.

And, here, we have made it repeatedly clear, and even various officials in the Reagan administration have made it repeatedly clear, to the South African government, that apartheid violates international law, that aggression against these surrounding states violates international law. So, that is the most effective way that this is carried out. And, I should point out that when the United States government stands for a proposition in the international arena, that has probably the most persuasive significance of all. And, indeed, it was the United States government that led the way at the U. N. Security Council in 1977 to adopt what you call enforcement measures against the South African government, prohibiting any state of the world community to sell arms, munitions or supplies of war, to the South African government.

And, it is the hope of many people then, that the United States government will return to the Security Council and this time impose economic sanctions binding on all members of the world community, against the South African government, because of what it is doing to its own Black people and the aggressive policies it is pursuing against surrounding states. So, there are international enforcement mechanisms at the Security Council. There is an external enforcement mechanism by means of the United States government dealing with the South African government.

Q. Now, what means of recourse would a citizen of this or another country have if that person saw or felt that he or she saw a violation of any of these provisions of international law that you have testified to today? Are there any institutions, government agencies to which one could petition for redress?

A. Well, the way the system is set up, it is extremely difficult, if not impossible, for an individual himself or herself, to obtain redress for violations of international law. This is because in general, international law is considered to bind states. And, so in the event there is violation, it is supposed to be up to the concerned state to do the petitioning and the redressing.

I am not saying that this is clear across the board. There are notable exceptions. For example, in Europe, there's the European Convention on Human Rights. The same system applies here in the Western Hemisphere with the Inter-American Convention on Human Rights. But, unfortunately, South Africa is not a party to a similar type of system where any individual could petition to a court or a body or the Security Council or whatever, to get sanctions or redress of grievances.

Q. Okay. So, to summarize your testimony, albeit that the process is perhaps frustrating, there would be means whereby, say an American citizen, could bring actual or perceived violations of international law to the attention of American or international legal and governmental authorities?

A. Well, no, I'm sorry if you misunderstood my testimony. There really is no way that a United States citizen himself could prosecute a claim against the South African government before an international tribunal or forum or things of that nature.

Q. Okay, perhaps you misunderstood me. I'm not speaking in terms of stating a cause of action or receiving personal or any type of redress, I'm speaking in terms of seeing to it or requesting or encouraging that some sort of enforcement action take place, some sort of remedial action on the part of whatever international tribunal.

A. No. Individuals generally do not have standing to appear before international tribunals. So, that option would be effectively precluded for U. S. citizens.

Q. Okay. To whom would an American citizen make his desires known, to what entities could an American citizen apply, which entity itself could begat an audience before an international tribunal?

A. Well, I think that what an American citizen has to do is try to change the policy of the United States government or to convince the executive branch of the United States government to bring a complaint to an international body, tribunal, forum, call it what you want. So, it's a question of getting our government to understand the right policy and then to get our government to act upon that particular policy. But, they, themselves, cannot do this. They have to really change governmental policy one way or another. As I understand it, that's what these defendants were trying to do when they protested.

Q. Thank you. No further questions.

4. Oral Argument to Admit an Offer of Proof.

MR. WELCH: If it please the Court, counsel, your Honor. First regarding the complicity argument, we're not here to prove any complicity. We're here to prove reasonable belief that possible complicity could have existed. I think there was adequate evidence adduced to certainly sustain a reasonable belief. And, I would reject the People's characterization that the the United States government, under "constructive engagement," as well as United States corporations and the

University of Illinois, in their investments, are merely acquiescent in South African crimes under international law.

There has been testimony, which has not been rebutted, that in regard to the decisions of the United States corporations, they are made in the sense of any business decision, after careful and reasonable analysis and study of a problem or a situation, evaluating its position and its profitability to the corporation.

Regarding the United State government and its policies, again, I think a reasonable inference can be made that the policies and the practices of the departments of the executive branch of the government, particularly the Department of State, are not arrived at by mere acquiescence, but are again, the result of counsel and deliberation between the various component actors in the system.

And, I would again submit to you that the investment policies of the University of Illinois, in corporations doing business in South Africa, is again a decision that is not arrived at lightly but is one that is a result of reason and deliberate study of the facts and circumstances underlying the investment decisions to be taken.

But getting to the heart of the matter, the argument being made by the People was one more of fact than of law, regarding the availability of the necessity defense. What weight to give to the reasonableness of the defendants' beliefs and the believability of the witnesses? Those types of issues of credibility are ones that raise questions of fact and not of law for the jury. And the authority for that is *Unger*. Your Honor, I again would call your attention to the Committee Comments after the necessity defense in Chapter 38, Section 7-13. The Committee said it was putting no limitations on the use or availability of the necessity defense, because is it was impossible, as they saw it, to foresee all of the possible applications that such a defense would entail.

Your Honor, I would disagree with the authority cited to you by the People. I think that necessity must be looked at in the circumstances in which it arose. We are urging the Court to pay particular attention to the situations that involve nonviolent political protest. We believe the cases cited by the People focus on completely different issues such as escape situations. We think that necessity must be considered in the facts and circumstances under which it arose. And, that in these facts and circumstances, we want you to consider it in light of nonviolent political protest and some of the other authority that we have cited to you specifically on those points, your Honor. We think they are more persuasive and controlling in the situation that this Court is faced with and in the facts and circumstances that this trial will entail.

We think that public policy considerations are different in some of the cases cited by the People, especially the escape and abortion cases, than in situations involving nonviolent political protest. And, we believe that the issues of reasonability and defendants' beliefs are also different. Again, your Honor, we believe that if this is at all a question of fact, then it must be put before a jury, for a jury to decide what weight to give to the evidence. We believe that due process requires that if we can meet the standards that are applicable for admissibility, that we should be allowed to at least attempt to persuade the jury of the reasonableness of our clients' beliefs by our expert witness testimony and international law evidence.

We would further state that we don't believe that it changes in any way the People's attempt to prosecute and to effectuate the prosecution of this case. But, that a denial of the use of the evidence would severely constrain and restrict the defendants from presenting exculpatory evidence and facts that are vital and needed in their defense and create a denial of due process of law. Thank you.

5. Sample Jury Instructions from *Chicago v. Streeter.*

You should also consult Chapters 4 and 5 for other relevant jury instructions with respect to international law.

1. Each defendant is presumed to be innocent of the charge placed against him or her. This presumption remains with him or her throughout every stage of the trial and during your deliberations on the verdict, and is not overcome unless from all the evidence in the case you are convinced by a preponderance of the evidence that the defendant(s) are guilty.

The City of Chicago has the burden of proving the guilt of the defendant(s) by a preponderance of the evidence and the burden remains on the City throughout the case. The defendant(s) are not required to prove their innocence.

2. The City of Chicago has the burden of proof by a preponderance of the evidence.

A preponderance of the evidence means that considering all of the evidence in the case that the proposition on which the City of Chicago has based its case is more probably true than not true.

3. The jury is instructed that there was in force in the City of Chicago at the time of the alleged occurrences in question a certain ordinance known as Trespass under Chapter 193, Section 1.4B of the Municipal Code of Chicago, which provides in part as follows: "A person commits trespass when he knowingly: remains upon the property, or any part thereof, of another after receiving notice, either oral or written, from the owner or occupant to depart."

4. To sustain the charge of trespass to land, the City must prove the following proposition:

That after each defendant received notice from the owner or the occupant to depart, he or she remained upon the land of another.

If you find from your consideration of all the evidence that this proposition has been proved by a clear preponderance of the evidence as to a defendant then you should find that defendant guilty.

If, on the other hand, you find from your consideration of all the evidence that this proposition has not been proved by a clear preponderance of the evidence as to a defendant then you should find that defendant not guilty.

5. The defendant(s) have raised the affirmative defense of necessity. Under the law, the City of Chicago must prove by a preponderance of the evidence that the defendant(s) did not act out of necessity.

6. Conduct which would otherwise be an offense is justifiable by reason of necessity if the defendant(s) was without blame in occasioning or developing the situation and reasonably believed that such conduct was necessary to avoid a public or private injury greater than the injury which might reasonably result from his own conduct.

7. An act is not done out of necessity where there is an alternative action to the defendant that is not illegal.

8. The phrases "reasonable belief" or "reasonably believes" means that the person concerned, acting as a reasonable person, believes that the described facts exist.

Chapter 7.

The Hypocrisy and Racism Behind the Formulation of U.S. Human Rights Foreign Policy

I shall always consider it to be one of the great honors of my life that I was asked by The Lawyers' Committee on Nuclear Policy (LCNP) to lecture on their behalf in the Soviet Union on the general subject of *Nuclear Weapons and International Law* as a guest of the Association of Soviet Lawyers (ASL) from September 11-20, 1986. During this trip, I lectured or spoke to professionals at the Institute for Canadian and United States Studies; the Faculty of Law at Leningrad University; the Association for Peace and Friendship (APF) in Leningrad; the Leningrad ASL Chapter; the ASL and APF Chapters in Kiev; the ASL and APF Chapters in Moscow; to the Department of International Law at Patrice Lumumba University, and others too numerous to mention here. These lectures were delivered to audiences usually consisting of professors, institute researchers, lawyers, and peace activists. I also gave extensive interviews to the local news media in all three cities concerning the activities of LCNP, and my opinions on U.S. nuclear weapons policies.

Throughout these lectures I made it quite clear that I was only speaking on my personal behalf as a professor of international law at the University of Illinois in Champaign. But that I knew many LCNP members would be in basic agreement with most of the substantive positions I was taking. That being said, I would like to set forth here the general thrust of my lectures and the responses and questions I received from the members of the audiences I addressed.

This series of four lectures was broken down into the following topics: (1) *The Collapse of Nuclear Arms Control Agreements and Negotiations Between the United States and the Soviet Union*, which was based upon Chapters 15 and 18 from my preceding book *World Politics and International Law* (Duke: 1985); (2) *Star Wars vs. the ABM Treaty*, based upon a forthcoming article, a precis for which can be found at the end of Chapter 4 in this book; (3) *The Lawlessness of Nuclear Deterrence*, based upon Chapter 3 of this book; and (4) *Defending Anti-Nuclear Civil Resistance Protesters Under International Law*, derived from Chapters 1, 2 and 4 of this book. Each audience was free to choose beforehand which topic it wanted me to address. A few sessions piggy-backed topic 2 with topic 4 since these were the subjects of most interest to my audiences.

Whatever the formal subject for discussion, however, I made it quite clear that after my lecture I was open to answer all questions they might have about any of these four topics; or about the Reagan administration's nuclear weapons policies; or about American foreign policy in general. As a result, some of these sessions were quite lengthy and broad-ranging, so there was a thorough airing of viewpoints on both sides. Nevertheless, my analyses and comments were always treated with a great deal of respect and courtesy, although not complete agreement at all times.

Over all, one of the primary goals I set for myself before giving these lectures was to be as honest, forthright, and frank as I could in analyzing the issue of nuclear weapons from an international law perspective. In particular, I personally thought it would be extremely important to convey the very strong impression to all Soviet citizens I met that not everyone in the United States of America has taken leave of his or her senses during the tenure of the Reagan administration. For that reason, I vigorously criticized the Reagan administration's position on Star Wars; its refusal to replicate the Soviet imposition of a moratorium on the testing of nuclear weapons; its repudiation of the SALT I and SALT II Treaties; its attempts to undermine the ABM Treaty; its support for the deployment of Pershing 2 rockets in the Federal Republic of Germany in violation of the SALT II non-circumvention clause; its absence of good faith in the SDI/START/INF negotiations at Geneva; and its refusal to join the Soviet pledge on the no-first-use of nuclear weapons. I also emphasized the LCNP position that the use of nuclear weapons would be illegal, and expressed my personal opinion that the system of strategic nuclear deterrence as currently practiced *by both superpowers* violates fundamental norms of international law. No one in my audiences dissented from these latter two propositions, and we seemed to have been in basic agreement on most of the other points.

While in the Soviet Union, a good deal of my time was also spent explaining the differences between LCNP and The Lawyers Alliance for Nuclear Arms Control (LANAC), some of whose more prominent members had already visited that country. All of my Soviet hosts agreed that there were many more important issues related to the overall dilemma created by nuclear weapons than just arms control. They were quite happy to learn that there did indeed exist an organization of U.S. lawyers dedicated to working on all aspects of nuclear weapons. Consequently, they stated their opinion that it would be important for ASL to work with LCNP as well as LANAC. I think all of my Soviet hosts were very impressed with the fact that LCNP members spend so much of their time in the defense of anti-nuclear protesters and in the bringing of civil lawsuits designed to prevent or impede various aspects of the Reagan administration's offensive and defensive nuclear weapons buildup. With all due respect and admiration for my many friends in LANAC, they have not placed these activities on their busy agenda.

On the final night of my visit, I had dinner in Moscow with Professor Vadim Sobakin and Mr. Konstantin Shakhmuradov to negotiate the terms of LCNP's proposed international conference on the question of *Nuclear Weapons and International Law*, to be jointly sponsored by LCNP and ASL in the Fall of 1987. As the Vice President and General Secretary of ASL, respectively, they stated their opinion that their organization would very much like to establish a formal and active working relationship with LCNP on all questions concerning nuclear weapons. This would include exchanges of professors, lawyers, written materials; joint publications, lectures, conferences; an international organization of lawyers devoted to confronting the nuclear dilemma, etc. I was certain to obtain an explicit promise from ASL members in all three cities that they would give serious consideration to any proposals LCNP might have with respect to the establishment of this formal working relationship.

The Boards of both ASL and LCNP will be considering these matters at greater length between now and the Fall conference. At that time both Boards will meet to specify and formalize this relationship. In light of the Reagan administration's tragic blunder at Reykjavic, the establishment of a close working relationship between ASL and LCNP becomes even more important than ever. The further development of this relationship will determine whether or not my trip to the Soviet Union was a success.

Of all the substantive issues that I dealt with throughout my many lectures and discussions in the Soviet Union, the two that seemed to be of most interest to my Soviet hosts were (1) my analysis of the Star Wars program as an anticipatory repudiation of the ABM Treaty and (2) the various cases in which I and other LCNP members have participated in the defense of anti-nuclear civil resistance protesters using principles of international law. Since my extended analysis of the first issue will be published elsewhere, and a succinct recapitulation of the arguments can be found at the end of Chapter 4, I will not bother to repeat the major substantive points here. But I would like to conclude this book with some personal reflections derived from the Soviet reactions to our defense of anti-nuclear protesters by using principles of international law.

There was a very strong and positive Soviet response to LCNP activities on behalf of anti-nuclear protesters. Such protests have received far more coverage in the Soviet news media than here in the United States. All the Soviet lawyers, professors, researchers and lay-people demonstrated a great deal of interest in my explaining precisely how we use principles of international law to defend those engaged in nonviolent civil resistance protests against nuclear weapons, U.S. intervention in Central America, and South African apartheid. Hence these discussions ventured into quite technical analyses of U.S. constitutional law, substantive and procedural criminal law, and of course international law.

All the Soviet lawyers I met expressed a genuine fascination with the idea that we could actually obtain the acquittal of some civil resistance protesters in this country by using principles of international law. At their specific request, I left a complete set of the materials that I have developed for the defense of anti-nuclear, anti-apartheid, and Central America civil resistance protesters in this country—which can be found in this book—with the ASL Chapter in each city for further study, research, and dissemination. I received the distinct impression that my ASL colleagues will be giving serious consideration to the problem of developing international law defenses on behalf of their own civil resistance clients.

In this regard, I also had the opportunity to speak with Soviet lawyers and officials about their government's treatment of political dissidents, human rights advocates, Jews seeking to emigrate, etc. I was assured by my interlocutors that these individuals have not been prosecuted for their political beliefs or religious activities, but rather have been properly tried and punished for the violation of positive technical laws appearing in the respective criminal codes of the constituent Soviet Republics. Needless to say, I was struck by the fact that this Soviet rationale is precisely what the Reagan administration has employed in order to justify its persecution of my numerous civil resistance clients during the past five years.

According to the Reagan administration and its philosophical cohorts at the state and local levels, my clients have not at all been prosecuted for their political viewpoints or religious activities, but rather only because they have violated positive technical laws that are already on the statute books. Hence, supposedly, it is not the case here in the United States of America that anyone is persecuted for their political viewpoints or religious activities. Unfortunately, the Soviet Union says the exact same thing to justify its persecution of political and religious dissidents. Is there a meaningful difference?

It might be the case that in the Soviet Union perhaps 100% of their political/religious dissidents have been ultimately convicted and punished. To be sure, however, I will have to wait until my return to the Soviet Union in order to discover whether any of my ASL colleagues have been successful at developing international law defenses for their civil resistance clients. At the time, my general impression was that Soviet lawyers were genuinely interested in searching for a fulcrum to produce some real leverage on these cases, had never considered the utility of international law, and might be willing to give it a try.

By contrast, based upon five years of extensive experience with such civil resistance cases here in the United States, my best estimate is that our government's conviction rate is approximately in the area of 90%, though it is decreasing every day due to the herculean efforts put forth by outstanding and dedicated lawyers all around the country. Quite frankly, I do not believe that this 10% differential in the way we treat our political/religious dissidents and the way the Soviet

Union treats its political/religious dissidents is anything at all to be proud of or brag about. Indeed, even that 10% has usually had to suffer through a nightmare of personal criticism, harassment, threats, intimidation, monumental expense, mental anguish, and physical illness before they are finally let off the hook.

Is this what America is supposed to be all about? Can we not recognize that just like the Soviet Union, we too have our own political/religious dissidents, our own prisoners of conscience, our own persecuted human rights campaigners, etc? As loyal and patriotic Americans we must directly come to grips with the undeniable fact that our system for the administration of criminal justice is abused by the political and economic power-elite of this country in order to silence its own internal critics.

It is not at all convincing to respond to this critique by saying that the Soviet Union operates on a grand scale of persecution, whereas America's is relatively insignificant by comparison. Since when have we in the United States compared ourselves to the Soviet Union by setting it up as the appropriate standard of behavior by which to gauge our own internal practices? We must measure our behavior in accordance with our own standards for the rule of law, the Constitution, a democratic form of government, and the system of moral values to which we openly subscribe. We must never be satisfied with such self-serving comparisons to the Soviet Union that are typically made by American lawyers, law professors, jurists, political scientists, educators, government officials, the news media, public pundits, etc.

This same type of self-exculpatory claim has also been continually made with respect to the conduct of American foreign policy: Well it might be true that the United States government occasionally violates the rules of international law; but the Soviets do so all the time, and therefore America must act in order to protect and defend ourselves, our interests, and our allies even, when necessary, in violation of specific rules of international law to the contrary. Indeed, the Reagan administration has refined this argument one step further to claim that since the adversaries of the United States, and especially the Soviet Union, oftentimes engage in behavior that is completely lawless, thoroughly reprehensible, and frequently barbaric, the U.S. government has both the right and the duty to do the exact same thing. But as previously argued in Chapter 3 with respect to the mutual lawlessness of nuclear deterrence as practiced by both superpowers, just because some of our adversaries might pursue patently illegal policies in their conduct of foreign affairs provides absolutely no good reason why our government should automatically do the exact same thing. The United States has to analyze the equation of international relations in light of both its own vital national security interests and its own cherished national values.

In particular, America cannot abandon or pervert its national values simply because its adversaries might not share them. Likewise, America cannot ignore its vital national security interest in preserving the rules of international law and upholding the integrity of the international legal order simply because some of our adversaries might not share that exact same interest. If America mimics our adversaries, then America gradually becomes like them and eventually becomes indistinguishable from them in the eyes of our allies, friends, neutrals, and, most tragically of all, ourselves. In other words, the United States government will become just as Machiavellian, terroristic, and totalitarian in its conduct of both foreign affairs and domestic policies as some of our adversaries undoubtedly are.

To be sure, however, this author has never subscribed to the Reagan administration's demonic interpretation of Soviet behavior as being the source of all evil in the modern world. Undoubtedly this is because I was fortunate enough to have spent seven years of my life studying Kievan, Russian and Soviet history, politics and law at the University of Chicago and Harvard University with such outstanding teachers and scholars as Richard Hellie, Richard Wortman, Jeremy Azrael, Edward L. Keenan, Jr., Adam Ulam, and Harold Berman, among others. Most regretfully, however, the Reagan administration and, under its influence a substantial segment of the American people, seem to have swallowed hook, line and sinker the primitive and distorted critique of the Soviet Union that has been propagated by another Harvard teacher of mine, Professor Richard Pipes, an ex-patriate Pole who seems to be possessed by an almost irrational hatred for the Russians. In a nutshell, the Pipes' critique reduces itself to the bald-faced proposition that the Soviet Union is not much more than a barbarian horde that is bent upon world domination by using techniques similar to those of Genghis Khan's steppe warriors.[1]

1. *See, e.g., The SALT II Treaty: Hearings on EX. Y, Before the Senate Foreign Relations*

While on the faculty at Harvard, Pipes served as the resident expert on Soviet intentions for the Committee on President Danger, then as a consultant to the Reagan campaign, and from there joined the staff of the White House National Security Council where he was the Reagan administration's top specialist on the Soviet Union. As a former student of his, I was not at all surprised by the interview Pipes gave to a West German magazine while on the staff of the National Security Council to the effect that if the Soviet Union did not change its internal system, then war between it and the United States would be inevitable,[2] much to the consternation of our allies in Europe. Fortunately for all of us, Pipes returned to Harvard after two years, but his pernicious theses about the Soviet Union continue to predominate among many of the leading foreign affairs and defense establishment officials of the Reagan administration.

As a people the Russians attribute overwhelming importance to their historical background and cultural heritage—and rightly so. We here in the United States cannot even begin to comprehend how to properly conduct our relations with the Soviet Union on nuclear weapons, human rights, geopolitical affairs, international trade—or anything else for that matter—unless we first realize that we are dealing with a civilization that is over one thousand years old. Contrary to Pipes' folklore, the Russians have produced one of the great civilizations of our contemporary world. Yet, except for a few professional diplomats at the State Department whose advice has been frequently ignored, very few of the Reagan administration's top foreign affairs and defense specialists know much about them.

To be sure, the Soviet Union has its defects, its flaws, its problems and incongruities as is true for any other political representative of a world civilization. Nevertheless, it must be understood on its own terms, not our's. And it must be evaluated in accordance with its own standards, not our's. Of course, it goes without saying that these

---

Comm., 96th Cong., 1st Sess., Part 3, 53-54 (1979) (testimony of Richard Pipes) (emphasis added):

Russia is an inherently poor country . . . Such power as the Soviet Union enjoys in the world today is due almost exclusively to its military might.

In a world from which all weapons would be banned, the Soviet Union would at once become a second-rate power, *since it possesses neither the civilization* nor the material wealth that would qualify it as a superpower.

2. According to Pipes, "Soviet leaders would have to choose between peacefully changing their Communist system in the direction followed by the West or going to war." *N.Y. Times*, Mar. 19, 1981, at A8, col. 3. *See also N.Y. Times*, Mar. 20, 1981, at A2, col. 3.

appropriate criteria for judging Soviet internal and external behavior would include the rules of international law as well.

For example, in the field of human rights, the Soviet Union has ratified the following major multilateral instruments for the protection of human rights: the International Covenant on Economic, Social and Cultural Rights (1966);[3] the International Covenant on Civil and Political Rights (1966);[4] the International Convention on the Suppression and Punishment of the Crime of Apartheid (1973);[5] the International Convention on the Elimination of All Forms of Racial Discrimination (1965);[6] the Convention on the Elimination of All Forms of Discrimination Against Women (1979);[7] the Convention on the Prevention and Punishment of the Crime of Genocide (1948);[8] and the Convention on the Political Rights of Women (1953),[9] among others. Hence it would only be fair to evaluate Soviet internal behavior in accordance with the rules of international human rights law to which they have already fully and voluntarily subscribed.[10]

Nevertheless, there is one major and so far insurmountable procedural obstacle confronting the United States government whenever it attempts to raise internal human rights violations with the Soviet Union. Namely, in contrast to the aforementioned Soviet record, the United States government has absolutely one of the very worst records among all of the self-styled Western liberal democracies when it comes to the ratification of these major multilateral human rights instruments. The United States government has failed to ratify the International Covenant on Economic, Social and Cultural Rights; the

3. International Covenant on Economic, Social and Cultural Rights, *adopted* Dec. 16, 1966, *entered into force* Jan. 3, 1976, G.A. Res. 2200 (XXI), 21 U.N. GAOR, Supp. (No. 16) at 49, U.N. Doc. A/6316.
4. International Covenant on Civil and Political Rights, *adopted* Dec. 16, 1966, *entered into force* Mar. 23, 1976, G.A. Res. 2200 (XXI), 21 U.N. GAOR, Supp. (No. 16) at 52, U.N. Doc. A/6316.
5. International Convention on the Suppression and Punishment of the Crime of Apartheid, *adopted* Nov. 30, 1973, *entered into force* July 18, 1976, G.A. Res. 3068 (XXVIII), 28 U.N. GAOR Supp. (No. 30) at 166, U.N. Doc. A/9030.
6. International Convention on the Elimination of All Forms of Racial Discrimination, *adopted* Dec. 21, 1965, *entered into force* Jan. 4, 1969, 660 *U.N.T.S.* 195.
7. Convention on the Elimination of All Forms of Discrimination Against Women, *adopted* Dec. 18, 1979, *entered into force* Sept. 13, 1981, G.A. Res. 34/180, U.N. Doc. A/RES/34/180.
8. Convention on the Prevention and Punishment of the Crime of Genocide, *opened for signature* Dec. 9, 1948, *entered into force* Jan. 12, 1951, 78 *U.N.T.S.* 277.
9. Convention on the Political Rights of Women, *opened for signature* Mar. 31, 1953, *entered into force* July 7, 1954, 27 *U.S.T.* 8289, *T.I.A.S.* No. 8289, 193 *U.N.T.S.* 135.
10. *See, e.g.,* Anderson and Verr, *Draft Brief on Behalf of Washington Rabbis* (1986), *reprinted in* Appendices *infra*.

International Covenant on Civil and Political Rights; the International Convention on the Suppression and Punishment of the Crime of Apartheid; the International Convention on the Elimination of All Forms of Racial Discrimination; the Convention on the Elimination of All Forms of Discrimination Against Women; the Convention on the Prevention and Punishment of the Crime of Genocide; and the American Convention on Human Rights (1965),[11] among others.

The refusal of the United States government to ratify these major international human rights treaties simply demonstrates the rank hypocrisy that historically has determined the formulation of U.S. human rights foreign policy since the termination of the Second World War. At the very least, that is the way governments and peoples in other states, and especially in the Soviet Union, view U.S. human rights foreign policy: What right does America have to preach human rights to other states, governments, and peoples when we have adamantly refused to ratify *any* of these major multilateral international human rights treaties?

As long as the United States of America refuses to ratify these treaties, it will prove to be impossible for any government in this country to develop a coherent, consistent, and effective human rights foreign policy that will be credible abroad and supported at home. Unless and until the United States government ratifies these treaties, American human rights foreign policy will continue to be treated as a political football to be tossed around by whatever new administration comes into power in Washington according to its own ideological preferences. And my criticism on this point concerns both Democrats and Republicans.

For example, during the Carter administration, the goal of promoting human rights was occasionally used as an element of overall U.S. foreign policy to oppose or undercut so-called authoritarian regimes of the right. By contrast, during the Reagan administration, the goal of protecting human rights has been used almost exclusively to attack so-called totalitarian regimes of the left.[12] During both administrations, the cause of human rights was invoked as a justifi-

---

11. American Convention on Human Rights, *signed* Nov. 22, 1969, *entered into force* July 18, 1978, *O.A.S.T.S.* No. 36, at 1, O.A.S. Off. Rec. OEA/Sev.L/V/II.23, doc.21, rev.6 (English 1979) (U.S. signed but has not ratified).

12. *See* Kirkpatrick, "Dictatorships and Double Standards," 68 *Commentary*, November, 1979, at 34.

cation for the purpose of promoting a definite political agenda; the protection of human rights was not simply viewed as a desirable objective in its own right. To be sure, however, on this account the abuses of the Reagan administration have been far in excess of and magnitudinally different from those comparatively minor transgressions committed by the Carter administration.

So long as the United States government refuses to ratify these major treaties, the cause of human rights will be used and abused by whatever administration is in power in Washington to oppose, attack, condemn, destabilize, etc. those governments and regimes abroad with which it disagrees for primarily political reasons. The cause of human rights will continue to be exploited as a means to another end and not treated as an end in itself during the formulation and conduct of American foreign policy. This politicization of the cause of human rights by whatever government is in power in Washington will continue to detract from, if not undermine and destroy, the credibility of U.S. human rights foreign policy both at home and abroad.

If the United States government is genuinely committed to the promotion of human rights at all times, in all places, for all peoples and with respect to all governments around the world, its human rights foreign policy must be depoliticized. The primary manner in which to depoliticize a problem is to legalize it. What this means is that U.S. human rights foreign policy must be taken out of the domain of international and domestic politics, rhetoric, propaganda, emotionalism, and cynical manipulation by turning it into a straight-out legal question of treaty interpretation, application, adjudication, enforcement, and compliance. The only way this objective can be accomplished would be for the United States government to become a formal party to all the major multilateral international human rights instruments mentioned above.

If the United States becomes a party to these human rights instruments, the matter of ensuring compliance with international human rights treaties both at home and abroad can be dealt with by the standard legal techniques of negotiation, mediation, conciliation, arbitration and adjudication. There would then exist a recognized set of fixed standards set forth in numerous treaties that had already been agreed upon by the other state party to the controversy. It would no longer be possible for a state party to a human rights treaty such as the Soviet Union to argue that an alleged human rights violation thereunder is simply an internal affair vis-à-vis the U.S. government because the latter has no right or standing to complain under the terms of a treaty to which it is not a party.[13] U.S. ratification of the relevant treaty would have solved this vexing problem, among others.

The United States government cannot have it both ways. We cannot criticize other states for failing to live up to the goal of protecting international human rights, while at the same time we refuse to open up the United States of America to similar criticism by means of ratifying these treaties. America's rank hypocrisy in this matter fools no one but itself. This is not to deny that in the meantime the United States government should pursue the goal of promoting human rights around the world. But rather, to point out that this goal cannot be accomplished in an effective manner until we first ratify these treaties, open ourselves up to similar criticism, and thus remove the hypocrisy that has so far permeated our international position on human rights.

In response to this criticism, some opponents to the ratification of these treaties have argued that the United States government's internal legal system for the protection and promotion of human rights is so far superior to that found in most other states of the world that no point would be served by allowing our human rights record to be attacked by totalitarian or authoritarian states in the Second or Third World.[14] The proper response to that criticism is quite simple and forthright: If our internal system for the protection of human rights is so perfect, then we have absolutely nothing to fear from foreign criticism, especially if it emanates from totalitarian or authoritarian regimes whose internal defects are so patently obvious to all members of the international community as well as to the American people.

The international promotion of human rights is not a zero-sum game.[15] If there are deficiencies in our internal system for the pro-

---

13. *See, e.g.*, Berman, "American and Soviet Perspectives on Human Rights," 22 *Worldview*, November, 1979, at 15. The Soviet press has effectively focused on the U.S. refusal to ratify these various human rights treaties. 132 *Cong. Rec.* S1254-57 (daily ed. Febr. 18, 1986) (excerpts from the Soviet press); *Vrai et Faux Intérêt Pour les Droits de L'Homme* 9-13 (Novosti: 1986). *See also* Institute of State and Law, U.S.S.R. Academy of Sciences, *International Covenants on Human Rights and Soviet Legislation* (Novosti: 1986) (Soviet ratification of human rights agreements and Soviet enactment of domestic legislation on human rights).

14. *See, e.g., The Genocide Convention: Hearing on EX.O, 81-1 Before the Senate Comm. on Foreign Relations*, 97th Cong., 1st Sess. 8 (1981) [hereinafter *The Genocide Convention*] (statement of Senator Strom Thurmond).

15. In a zero-sum game, any player's gains are exactly balanced by the losses of others. 6 *International Encyclopedia of the Social Sciences* 62-69 (1968).

.tection of human rights, then consistent with American values, we should certainly be willing to correct them. And that axiom should hold true no matter which state is offering the criticism. Just because the Soviet Union might be deaf to the criticisms of the international community when it comes to perpetrating violations of basic human rights upon its own citizens provides absolutely no good reason why the United States should react to foreign criticism in the same obtuse manner. After all, America purports to be different from and certainly better than the Soviet Union. We should be willing to listen to international criticism of our internal behavior; and if that criticism is justified, to act upon it in order to rectify the situation. That is what America is supposed to be all about!

For example, as a professor of international and criminal law as well as a consultant on many civil resistance cases during the past several years, I can assure you that our system for the administration of criminal justice here in the United States of America is far from perfect. We could certainly improve that system in light of the standards of due process of law, whether substantive or procedural, found in some of these international human rights conventions. The U.S. government's ratification of these conventions could then serve as the constitutional basis for the enactment of domestic implementing legislation by Congress that would bring the standards of internal United States law up to the internationally recognized minimum standards articulated in these treaties. Certainly, all Americans would gain, and none would lose, from this process of internal improvement.

At this point the reader is probably asking himself, why has the United States government so far failed to ratify these major international human rights treaties? Surely this must be an anomaly produced by some sort of oversight on the part of both the executive branch of the federal government and the U.S. Senate, which must give its advice and consent to the ratification of such treaties. Technically, of course, it is the Senate which must approve any treaty by a two-thirds vote; whereas the President must ultimately ratify the treaty before it can come into force and thus bind the United States government, whether internationally or domestically. But when it comes to the non-ratification of these international human rights treaties, both of these branches of the federal government have been at fault.

And I regret to report that the failure of the United States government to ratify these covenants is purposeful, not an oversight.

Historically, the persistent refusal by the United States government to ratify these major human rights instruments is primarily attributable to considerations of racism. In particular, the opposition to the ratification of these treaties has stemmed essentially from those same political sources that have generated opposition to the final abolition of all forms of racial discrimination against Black Americans in the United States. It is these same bastions of racism today which are continuing to fight a rear-guard operation against the attainment of complete and effective equality for all segments of American society by means of opposing the ratification of these basic international human rights treaties.

We have all heard the argument advanced before, and we continue to hear the argument propounded today, by conservative southern Senators such as the late Sam Ervin, Jr. or Jesse Helms, inter alia, that the ratification of these human rights treaties would somehow violate "states' rights" and therefore would be unconstitutional under the Tenth Amendment to the United States Constitution.[16] The latter provides that all powers not delegated to the United States by the Constitution, nor prohibited by it to the states, are reserved to the states respectively, or to the people. The gist of these opponents'

---

16. Statements of this position have occurred in recent years in the context of the Senate hearings on the Genocide Convention. Senator Strom Thurmond continued to assert the "states' rights" position in its clear, traditional form:

> Matters concerning fundamental criminal conduct involving murder or conspiracy to commit murder should be primarily a matter of State domestic jurisdiction—I repeat, State domestic jurisdiction. The use of the treatymaking power in this area is inappropriate. In effect, the Convention would continue the policy made possible by the Supreme Court in its decision in *Missouri v. Holland,* . . . in which the Court held that State powers could be transferred to the Federal Government through the treatymaking process as a *de facto* method of amending the Constitution.

The Genocide Convention, *supra* note 14, at 9.

In addition, Senators Helms and Ervin have attempted to argue that the crime of genocide is solely a matter of "domestic jurisdiction," as contrasted with properly "international" matters. This argument essentially constitutes another variant of the "states' rights" doctrine, since in the context of the Genocide Convention these Senators view appropriate domestic jurisdiction as falling within the states' reserved domain under the Constitution. *See, e.g., Constitutional Issues Relating to the Proposed Genocide Convention, Hearing Before the Subcomm. on the Constitution of the Senate Comm. on the Judiciary,* 99th Cong., 1st Sess. 659 (1985) (statement of Sen. Helms). In response to this point, it is important to remember that the South African government long ago failed to convince the international community that the reprehensible manner in which it has consistently treated its own Black population—summarized by the dreaded word apartheid—was an internal matter that fell essentially within its domestic jurisdiction and for that reason could not be acted upon by the United Nations Organization in accordance with the prohibition to that effect established by article 2(7) of the United Nations Charter. *See* Sohn & Buergenthal, *International Protection of Human Rights* 634-735 (1973).

argument was and still is that the ratification of these international human rights instruments would infringe upon the states' supposedly traditional right to regulate the normal day-to-day affairs of their own citizens. By implication, presumably, this would include the right of state governments to permit public or private discrimination against Black Americans.

The legal vacuousness of such "states' rights" objections to the constitutional validity of these human rights treaties is perhaps best demonstrated by the testimony of none other than William H. Rehnquist during the Genocide Convention hearings of 1971. As Assistant Attorney General in the Nixon administration, Rehnquist definitively repudiated all the various and spurious constitutional objections to the Genocide Convention and concluded that the treaty was "entirely constitutional."[17] Indeed, this author once told Mr. Justice Rehnquist that I routinely refer my fairly conservative law students to his testimony in the event they believe my analysis that these international human rights treaties are fully constitutional with respect to the Tenth Amendment has been tainted by some form of liberal bias. As Rehnquist himself responded: "Yes, it is rather difficult to be more Catholic than the Pope."

The disingenuity of the "states' rights" objections to some of these human rights treaties is further evidenced by the explicit constitutional grant of authority to Congress "to define and punish piracies and felonies committed on the high seas, and offenses against the law of nations" found in article I, section 8, clause 10 of the U.S. Constitution. Hence, where an international human rights treaty establishes the existence of specific international criminal offenses for individuals, Congress may directly define and punish those same offenses through the enactment of domestic implementing legislation. Thus, articles 3 and 4 of the Genocide Convention and article 3 of the International Convention on the Crime of Apartheid specify international crimes which can be committed by individuals. Congress may properly define and punish those crimes pursuant to its power under this "law of nations" clause of the Constitution.[18] The same would hold true for any other treaty creating an international crime.

---

17. *Genocide Convention: Hearings on Executive O, 81st Cong., 1st Sess., Before a Subcomm. of the Senate Foreign Relations Comm.*, 91st Cong., 2d Sess. 147-61 (1970) (testimony of Assistant Attorney General William H. Rehnquist).

18. *See, e.g.*, L. Henkin, *Foreign Affairs and the Constitution* 73 (1972) (the Genocide Convention may be implemented under the "law of nations" clause).

Nevertheless, for example, in regard to the protection of human rights during time of armed conflict, Congress has completely failed to enact the domestic implementing legislation long ago required by the four Geneva Conventions of 1949.[19] In particular, these Conventions require that individuals alleged to have committed "grave breaches" thereunder must be prosecuted (or extradited) in the event they enter upon the territory of a high contracting party such as the United States irrespective of their nationality.[20] Yet, it would be unconstitutional as a violation of due process of law to prosecute or punish any individual pursuant to the terms of such treaties that have not yet been implemented by a specific congressional statute that precisely defines the nature of the offense, fixes the penalty, establishes proper venue for the prosecution, etc.[21]

Clearly Congress would have the power to define and punish such offenses against the law of nations (i.e., war crimes) under article 1, section 8, clause 10 of the U.S. Constitution. Yet both the executive and legislative branches of the federal government have so far failed to discharge this most elementary obligation under the four Geneva Conventions since the time of their ratification by the United States government in 1956. And the primary reason has always been because their respective members fear the legal, moral and political implications of rendering U.S. civilian government officials, perhaps including themselves, subject to mandatory prosecution in U.S.

19. Geneva Convention for the Amelioration of the Condition of the Wounded and Sick in Armed Forces in the Field of August 12, 1949 (First Geneva Convention), *opened for signature* Aug. 12, 1949, *entered into force* Oct. 21, 1950, 6 *U.S.T.* 3114, *T.I.A.S.* No. 3362, 75 *U.N.T.S.* 31; Geneva Convention for the Amelioration of the Condition of Wounded, Sick and Shipwrecked Members of Armed Services at Sea of August 12, 1949 (Second Geneva Convention), *opened for signature* Aug. 12, 1949, *entered into force* Oct. 21, 1950, 6 *U.S.T.* 3217, *T.I.A.S.* No. 3363, 75 *U.N.T.S.* 85; Geneva Convention Relative to the Treatment of Prisoners of War of August 12, 1949 (Third Geneva Convention), *opened for signature* Aug. 12, 1949, *entered into force* Oct. 21, 1950, 6 *U.S.T.* 3316, *T.I.A.S.* No. 3364, 75 *U.N.T.S.* 135; Geneva Convention Relative to the Protection of Civilian Persons in Time of War of August 12, 1949 (Fourth Geneva Convention), *opened for signature* Aug. 12, 1949, *entered into force* Oct. 21, 1950, 6 *U.S.T.* 3516, *T.I.A.S.* No. 3365, 75 *U.N.T.S.* 267.

20. *See, e.g.,* Article 146 of the Fourth Geneva Convention which provides:
    The High Contracting Parties undertake to enact any legislation necessary to provide effective penal sanctions for persons committing, or ordering to be committed, any of the grave breaches of the present Convention defined in the following Article.
    Each High Contracting Party shall be under the obligation to search for persons alleged to have committed, or to have ordered to be committed, such grave breaches, and shall bring such persons, regardless of their nationality, before its own courts. It may also, if it prefers, and in accordance with the provisions of its own legislation, hand such persons over for trial to another High Contracting Party concerned, provided such High Contracting Party has made out a *prima facie* case.

21. *The Over the Top Case*, 5 F.2d 838, 845 (D. Conn. 1925).

courts for ordering, participating or at least complicity in the commission of war crimes.

Of course these same civilian government officials have no problem whatsoever with holding U.S. military personnel fully accountable for the commission of war crimes under the Uniform Code of Military Justice.[22] But when it comes to their own behavior, Congress and the executive branch of the federal government, including the President, wish to remain free to violate the terms of the Geneva Conventions with impunity in the event the United States government becomes a party to another international armed conflict such as Vietnam, Nicaragua, Grenada, and Lebanon; or to a non-international armed conflict such as El Salvador and Guatemala. The American peoples' failure to insist upon the prosecution of their civilian government officials responsible for actual commission or at least complicity in the commission of such monstrous international crimes against innocent people around the world provides yet another glaring example of the rank hypocrisy behind the formulation of U.S. human rights foreign policy.

Returning now to the domestic level of analysis, the so-called cause of "states' rights" was used to impede the institution of formal racial equality in the United States of America from the time of the seminal decision by the United States Supreme Court in *Brown v. The Board of Education* (1954),[23] until the adoption of the major pieces of civil rights legislation by Congress in the mid-1960s. "States' rights" was always the battle cry of those who opposed the institution of formal racial equality in this country by means of the adoption of civil rights legislation by the United States Congress or the invalidation of state discriminatory laws and practices by the United States Supreme Court. Today we still hear the same advocates of "states' rights" opposing the ratification of these human rights treaties on the same fallacious constitutional grounds. Yet the real reason behind this specious claim of "states' rights" has always been and continues to be racism and the desire to preserve the last vestiges of racial discrimination against Blacks in America today.

As a matter of law, the argument of "states' rights" has absolutely no validity whatsoever under the United States Constitution as in-

---

22. Uniform Code of Military Justice, 10 *U.S.C.* §§ 801-940 (1986).
23. *Brown v. Board of Education*, 347 U.S. 483 (1954).

terpreted by the Supreme Court when it comes to the formulation of American foreign policy. Almost two-thirds of a century ago, and three decades before *Brown v. The Board*, the United States Supreme Court decisively repudiated the "states' rights" argument when it was used to attack the constitutionality of a treaty that had received the advice and consent of two-thirds of the Senate. In the pathbreaking case of *Missouri v. Holland* (1920),[24] the Supreme Court held that the Tenth Amendment could not stand as a bar to the conclusion of a treaty or international agreement by the federal government so long as its subject matter palpably fell within the foreign affairs concerns of the United States of America. To be sure, as the Supreme Court made clear almost four decades later in *Reid v. Covert* (1957),[25] the federal government could not enter into a treaty or international agreement that violated other terms of the United States Constitution which provided expressly to the contrary. But, once again, even in this later case, the Supreme Court reaffirmed the classic teaching of *Missouri v. Holland* that the Tenth Amendment (i.e., the claim of "states' rights") could not stand as a bar to the federal government's conclusion of a treaty or international agreement on matters affecting the foreign affairs of the United States of America.

Some two decades after *Missouri v. Holland*, the United States government sponsored the foundation of the United Nations Organization during the course of the Second World War. The Charter of the United Nations was a treaty that received the advice and consent of two-thirds of the membership of the United States Senate.[26] For that reason, the United Nations Charter was and still is entitled to claim the benefits of the so-called Supremacy Clause found in the United States Constitution. Article 6 thereof provides in relevant part that "all treaties made, or which shall be made, under the authority of the United States, shall be the supreme law of the land; and the judges in every state shall be bound thereby, anything in the con-

---

24. *Missouri v. Holland*, 252 U.S. 416 (1920).

25. *Reid v. Covert*, 354 U.S. 1, 18 (1957) (holding that civilian dependents of American servicemen overseas could not be tried in U.S. military courts, pursuant to executive agreements with Great Britain and Japan, without the right to jury and other Bill of Rights protections):

> There is nothing in *Missouri v. Holland* . . . which is contrary to the position taken here . . . To the extent that the United States can validly make treaties, the people and the States have delegated their power to the National Government and the Tenth Amendment is no barrier.

26. United Nations Charter, *signed* June 26, 1945, *entered into force* Oct. 24, 1945, 59 *Stat.* 1031, *T.S.* No. 993, 3 *Bevans* 1153 (1969) (79th Cong., 1st Sess., 1945).

stitution or laws of any state to the contrary notwithstanding." In other words, in the event of a conflict between a United States treaty and a state law or constitution, the provisions of the treaty must prevail.[27] Needless to say, the revolutionary implications of the Supremacy Clause when applied to the Charter of the United Nations were quite clear to both the proponents and opponents of eliminating all forms of racial discrimination against Blacks in the United States of America at that time.[28]

For example, the Preamble to the United Nations Charter states that the peoples of the United Nations are determined "to reaffirm faith in fundamental human rights, in the dignity and worth of the human person, in the equal rights of men and women and of nations large and small." Likewise, Charter article 1(3) states that one of the purposes of the Organization is to promote and encourage "respect for human rights and for fundamental freedoms for all without distinction as to race, sex, language, or religion." Furthermore, article 55 of the United Nations Charter provides in relevant part that the United Nations shall promote ". . . universal respect for, and observance of, human rights and fundamental freedoms for all without distinction as to race, sex, language or religion." Finally, Charter article 56 specifically states that all members of the United Nations "pledge themselves to take joint and separate action in cooperation with the Organization for the achievement of the purposes set forth in article 55." These express commitments that were undertaken by the United States government when it ratified the terms of the United Nations Charter in 1945 created a glaring inconsistency between articles 1, 55, and 56, on the one hand, and the practice of blatant racial discrimination against Blacks in America before *Brown v. The Board*, on the other.

More significantly, the ratification of the United Nations Charter raised the following political and constitutional issues: Since articles 1, 55 and 56 of the United Nations Charter are part of a treaty that has received the advice and consent of two-thirds of the United States Senate, could they be used to strike down racially discriminatory legislation and practices established or permitted by the states of the Union or even by the federal government itself by means of invoking

27. *Fairfax's Devisee v. Hunter's Lessee*, 11 U.S. (7 Cranch) 603 (1813).
28. *See, e.g.*, Lockwood, "The United Nations Charter and United States Civil Rights Litigation: 1946-1955," 69 *Iowa L. Rev.* 901 (1984).

the Supremacy Clause in a suit brought in a U.S. federal court? Therefore, could not the United Nations Charter be wielded as a sword to cut away all types of state or federal legislation and practices that would promote, condone, or even tolerate any form of racial discrimination against Black Americans?

Shortly thereafter, when President Truman signed the Convention on the Prevention and Punishment of the Crime of Genocide in 1948, a similar but far more concrete legal issue emerged: Could American Blacks and their supporters use the provisions of the Genocide Convention to strike down racially discriminatory state legislation and practices by means of invoking the Supremacy Clause in U.S. federal courts on the ground that the latter promoted genocide? Moreover, later on, would it not be true for any multilateral international agreement entered into by the federal government for the promotion and protection of human rights that it could be used to strike down racially discriminatory legislation and practices by the states of the Union by invoking the Supremacy Clause in a federal court suit? In essence, the proponents of "states' rights" could not continue to maintain their system of racial discrimination against Blacks on a state-by-state basis in America when the federal government was busy concluding international human rights treaties and agreements that would ultimately require the states to abolish these various forms of racially discriminatory laws and practices.

This issue was joined squarely in the by-now celebrated case of *Sei Fujii v. California* (1950),[29] decided by the California District Court of Appeal. In that case a Japanese national who was ineligible to become a United States citizen under the U.S. naturalization laws then in existence sued for a determination of whether or not an escheat of land he bought could occur under the provisions of the California Alien Land Law which prohibited aliens ineligible to become citizens from acquiring real property in the state of California. Around the turn of the century, federal immigration and naturalization laws as well as this California legislation and other statutes like it adopted by states near the Pacific coast of this country were clearly intended to discriminate against individuals of Asiatic descent, particularly Japanese and Chinese.

---

29. *See Sei Fujii v. California*, 217 P.2d 481 (Cal. Dist. Ct. App. 1950), *aff'd on other grounds*, 38 Cal.2d 718, 242 P.2d 617 (Cal. 1952).

In *Sei Fujii* the plaintiff relied upon the human rights provisions found in the United Nations Charter, specifically its Preamble and articles 1, 55, and 56. He argued that under the terms of the Supremacy Clause, these provisions of a United States treaty must take precedence over the discriminatory state law. The District Court of Appeal agreed with his argument and held that the Alien Land Law was unenforceable because it violated both the letter and the spirit of the United Nations Charter.

Of course, this part of the holding by the District Court of Appeal was rejected by the California Supreme Court in *Sei Fujii v. State* (1952). The California Supreme Court held that these particular provisions of the United Nations Charter were not self-executing, but required implementing legislation by Congress to bring them into force as domestic law. For this reason, these provisions of the U.N. Charter could not be used to invalidate inconsistent state legislation. Nevertheless, the California Supreme Court struck down the California Alien Land Law on the ground that it violated the Equal Protection Clause of the Fourteenth Amendment to the United States Constitution.

Moreover, the Court did this despite the fact that in the landmark decision of *Terrace v. Thompson* (1923),[30] the United States Supreme Court had previously upheld as constitutional against attack under the Equal Protection Clause a piece of legislation adopted by the state of Washington that likewise discriminated against Japanese by prohibiting landholding to any alien who had failed to file a declaration of intention to become an American citizen, when Japanese were ineligible to become citizens under U.S. naturalization laws in effect at that time. Indeed, in *Porterfield v. Webb* (1923),[31] issued on the same day as its *Terrace* decision, the United States Supreme Court had upheld the constitutionality of the California Alien Land Law involved in *Sei Fujii* on the grounds that the issue was controlled by *Terrace*. Nevertheless, the California Supreme Court in *Sei Fujii* refused to rely on these earlier cases, declaring that subsequent U.S. Supreme Court cases were irreconcilable with *Terrace* and *Porterfield*, and concluding therefore that the California statute did violate

30. *Terrace v. Thompson*, 263 U.S. 197 (1923).
31. *Porterfield v. Webb*, 263 U.S. 225 (1923).

the Equal Protection Clause of the Fourteenth Amendment to the U.S. Constitution.

Yet, even though it was ultimately overruled on the international law point, the decision by the District Court of Appeal in the *Sei Fujii* case incredibly disturbed the proponents of "states' rights" for the purpose of maintaining racial discrimination against Black Americans on a state-by-state basis in this country. There was no guarantee that other state or federal courts would agree with the decision by the California Supreme Court that articles 1, 55 and 56 of the U.N. Charter were non-self-executing and therefore could not be used to strike down racially discriminatory state legislation and practices. Furthermore, if the United States government went ahead and ratified the Genocide Convention, it was conceivably possible that a federal or state court would find that either the Convention itself or at least some of its provisions were self-executing and therefore could be relied upon to strike down racially discriminatory state legislation and practices by means of the Supremacy Clause on the grounds that the latter promoted genocide against Black Americans. A similar principle would hold true for any other international human rights treaty that the federal government might conclude on behalf of the United States of America.

Thus, while the defenders of racial discrimination were fighting a heated battle in the domestic arena to oppose and impede Congress's adoption of federal civil rights legislation, the executive branch of the federal government could be concluding international treaties or agreements that might accomplish the exact same result. So the defenders of racial discrimination had to broaden their attack from the domestic front to the international level in order to prevent the executive branch of the federal government from concluding any international human rights treaties that could possibly be used in a manner that would undercut so-called "states' rights" for the purpose of continuing to permit discrimination against Black Americans. From a constitutional perspective, the way they sought to do this proved to be most insidious and quite effective.

In order to accomplish this objective, they turned to Senator Bricker, who at that time represented the state of Ohio, where the Ku Klux Klan was quite active and powerful. Senator Bricker introduced what came to be known as the Bricker Amendment to the

United States Constitution.[32] The proposed Bricker Amendment attempted to solve this problem created by the ratification of international human rights treaties by the federal government in a manner favorable to the advocates of "states' rights" for the purpose of continuing to allow states to practice or permit racial discrimination against Blacks. There were six sections to the proposed Bricker Amendment, two of which are most relevant to the analysis presented here.

Section 3 provided that a "treaty shall become effective as internal law in the United States only through the enactment of appropriate legislation by the Congress." This provision would have prevented anyone from bringing an action in federal or state court to strike down racially discriminatory state legislation or practices on the grounds that the latter were inconsistent with the terms of a ratified human rights treaty by means of invoking the Supremacy Clause. Traditionally it has been the case that some types of treaties do not require domestic implementing legislation to be entitled to the benefits of the Supremacy Clause; or at least that some provisions of a treaty might be deemed self-executing and therefore do not require implementing legislation to be effective.[33] Hence, in theory, such treaties or at least specific articles thereof could be used to strike down some forms of inconsistent state legislation and practices by directly invoking the Supremacy Clause.

Section 3 of the Bricker Amendment would have prevented that from happening. No court would have been able to use the terms of any human rights treaty to strike down state legislation or practices that were inconsistent with the terms of that treaty in the absence of specific congressional authorization to the contrary in the form of implementing legislation. And since the defenders of "states' rights" and racial discrimination were, at the time, effectively impeding Congress from adopting any domestic legislation to promote civil rights and racial equality, it could be expected that implementing legislation

---

32. S.J. Res. 1, 83d Cong., 1st Sess., 99 *Cong. Rec.* 160 (1953). *See Treaties and Executive Agreements: Hearings on S.J. Res. 1 and S.J. Res. 43 Before a Subcomm. of the Senate Judiciary Comm.*, 83d Cong., 1st Sess. 7 (1953) (statement of Senator Bricker citing the District Court of Appeal's decision in *Sei Fujii* as a justification for adopting the Bricker Amendment) [hereinafter *Treaties and Executive Agreements*]; 96 *Cong. Rec.* 5,994-6,000 (1950) (statements of Senators Donnell and Malone in the Senate debates on the implications of the District Court of Appeal's decision, just four days after it was rendered).

33. *Cook v. United States*, 288 U.S. 102, 119 (1933); *Foster v. Neilson*, 27 U.S. 253 (2 Pet. 253, 314) (1829).

for human rights treaties as required by the Bricker Amendment would never be passed by Congress. Hence, under the terms of the Bricker Amendment, even if these international human rights treaties were ever ratified by the federal government, they could not be enforced against the states of the Union to terminate racially discriminatory legislation and practices against Black Americans.

The real heart of the Bricker Amendment, however, was found in section 4, which provided that all "executive or other agreements between the President and any international organization, foreign power, or official thereof shall be made only in the manner and to the extent to be prescribed by law" and that such "agreements shall be subject to the limitations imposed on treaties, or the making of treaties, by this article." In other words, according to this provision of the Bricker Amendment, all such "executive agreements" would have required some type of formal approval by Congress in order to be effective both internationally and domestically.

It was section 4 of the Bricker Amendment that constituted the heart of the threat to the executive branch of the federal government in order to coerce the cessation of its support for the negotiation, conclusion, and signature of fundamental human rights treaties on behalf of the United States of America. This was because the vast majority of international agreements entered into by the United States government with other governments, international organizations, or foreign officials never receive the advice and consent of two-thirds of the Senate. Rather, they are entered into by means of executive agreements concluded by the President or his delegated authority on behalf of the United States of America.[34]

With respect to some issue areas, these international agreements require specific prior congressional authorization, or explicit subsequent congressional approval; with respect to other subjects, the President is free to enter into these agreements under his own independent powers in accordance with the terms of the Constitution as interpreted by the United States Supreme Court.[35] Section 4 of the

---

34. Between 1946 and 1972, the U.S. entered into 5,590 executive agreements, in comparison with only 368 treaties. H. Steiner & D. Vagts, *Transnational Legal Problems* 589 (2d ed. 1976).

35. *See, e.g., United States v. Belmont*, 301 U.S. 324 (1937) (distinguishing treaties from executive agreements, where in this case the President entered into an executive agreement under his independent powers as granted in the Constitution). *See also* H. Steiner & D. Vagts, *supra* note 34, at 590-94 (discussing the factors which may influence when a President requires congressional approval).

Bricker Amendment would have made it almost impossible for the executive branch of the federal government to conduct any form of business with other foreign states without receiving some form of express and almost daily approval by the Congress.[36] Such a requirement would have literally brought the conduct of foreign affairs by the United States government to an abrupt halt, and the proponents of the Bricker Amendment knew this quite well. That, then, was the real club held over the head of the executive branch of the federal government by the defenders of "states' rights" and racial discrimination when they brandished the Bricker Amendment.

Succumbing to the undoubtedly serious nature of this threat, Secretary of State John Foster Dulles appeared to testify in opposition to the Bricker Amendment during the congressional hearings on the resolution.[37] Dulles explicitly promised that if the Bricker Amendment were defeated, then the executive branch of the federal government would not become a party to any human rights convention or present it as a treaty for consideration by the U.S. Senate.[38] Partly as a consequence of that promise given by the Eisenhower administration, the Bricker Amendment was ultimately defeated in the Senate. But the concession still remained: Namely, that the United States government would not sign international human rights treaties and present them to the Senate for its advice and consent. That compromise was essentially continued by subsequent administrations, both Democrat and Republican.

To be sure, at the request of the Kennedy administration the Senate did eventually give its advice and consent to the Supplementary Slavery Convention (1956),[39] while rejecting the contemporaneously

36. On the stifling effect of such an amendment, see *Treaties and Executive Agreements*, *supra* note 32, at 823-24, 837-38 (statement of Secretary of State Dulles).

37. *See id.* at 823-900 (statement and testimony of Secretary of State Dulles at the 1953 Senate Judiciary Committee hearings on the Bricker Amendment).

38. The present administration intends to encourage the promotion everywhere of human rights and individual freedoms, but to favor methods of persuasion, education, and example rather than formal undertakings which commit one part of the world to impose its particular social and moral standards upon another part of the world community, which has different standards . . .

. . . We therefore do not intend to become a party to any such covenant or present it as a treaty for consideration by the Senate.

Id. at 825 (statement of Secretary of State Dulles). *See generally* L. Sohn & T. Buergenthal, *International Protection of Human Rights* 964-66 (1973).

39. Supplementary Convention on the Abolition of Slavery, the Slave Trade, and Institutions and Practices Similar to the Slave Trade, *opened for signature* Sept. 7, 1956, *entered into force* Apr. 30, 1957, 18 *U.S.T.* 3201, *T.I.A.S.* No. 6418, 266 *U.N.T.S.* 3 (*entered into force* for U.S. on Dec. 6, 1967).

transmitted Convention on the Political Rights of Women (1953)[40] and the Convention on the Abolition of Forced Labor (1957).[41] Nevertheless, the Convention on the Political Rights of Women was finally approved by the Senate in 1976. And in 1968 the U.S. government ratified the U.N. Protocol Relating to the Status of Refugees (1967).[42]

The Nixon administration supported the ratification of the Genocide Convention,[43] but without success in the Senate. Later on, the Carter administration finally signed the two U.N. Covenants on Economic, Social, and Cultural Rights (1966) and on Civil and Political Rights (1966), in addition to the American Human Rights Convention (1965). The Carter administration then transmitted these three treaties as well as the previously signed International Convention on the Elimination of All Forms of Racial Discrimination (1965) to the U.S. Senate for its advice and consent to ratification.

Nevertheless, these latter four covenants have yet to receive the advice and consent of the Senate. Moreover, when it transmitted these four treaties to the Senate for consideration, the Carter administration recommended that the Senate adopt a declaration along the lines of section 3 of the Bricker Amendment to the effect that these four covenants, or at least portions thereof, cannot become binding as internal law in the United States without the enactment of appropriate implementing legislation by the Congress.[44] Such an exemption of these four covenants from the benefits of the Supremacy Clause would gut a great deal of their meaning and effectiveness in the event that the United States Senate eventually does give its advice and consent to them.

Most recently, it superficially appeared that the Reagan administration was successful in finally convincing the Senate to give its advice and consent to the 1948 Genocide Convention. Quite frankly,

40. Convention on the Political Rights of Women, *opened for signature* March 31, 1953, *entered into force* July 7, 1954, 27 *U.S.T.* 8289, *T.I.A.S.* No. 8289, 193 *U.N.T.S.* 135 (*entered into force* for the U.S. July 7, 1976).

41. Convention on the Abolition of Forced Labor (ILO No. 105), *adopted* June 25, 1957, *entered into force* Jan. 17, 1959, 320 *U.N.T.S.* 291 (U.S. has signed but not ratified).

42. Protocol Relating to the Status of Refugees, *signed* Jan. 21, 1967, *entered into force* Oct. 4, 1967, 19 *U.S.T.* 6223, *T.I.A.S.* No. 6577, 606 *U.N.T.S.* 267 (*entered into force* for U.S. Nov. 1, 1968).

43. *Genocide Convention: Hearings on Executive O, 81st Cong., 1st Sess., Before a Subcomm. of the Senate Foreign Relations Comm.*, 91st Cong., 2d Sess. 12 (1970) (message to the Senate from President Nixon).

44. *See* the Reports of Deputy Secretary of State Warren Christopher on Dec. 17, 1977 explaining the proposed reservations, understandings, and declarations, 72 *Am. J. Int'l Law* 620-631 (1978).

it is shocking and inexcusable that the United States government has not yet become a party to this pathbreaking treaty that represented the first of the post-World War II international covenants designed primarily to protect human rights. The Genocide Convention was originally formulated to prevent a repetition of Adolph Hitler's attempt to exterminate the Jewish people and for that reason its ratification by the United States government has always been a critically important issue for American Jews and their sympathizers. Nevertheless, today's defenders of "states rights" and racial discrimination successfully fought a rear-guard action to amend the Genocide Convention out of existence in a variety of ways that flew in the face of the fact that the International Court of Justice had already held in a 1951 Advisory Opinion that amendments or reservations which are incompatible with the purposes of the Genocide Convention were invalid.[45]

Thus, when the U.S. Senate finally gave its advice and consent to the Genocide Convention on February 19, 1986 by a vote of 83 to 11, it attached two reservations, five "understandings" and one "declaration."[46] I will not bother analyzing these pieces of legal sophistry in any detail here. Suffice it to say that the one "declaration" provided that the President cannot deposit the instrument of ratification for the Genocide Convention until after the implementing legislation required by article 5 thereof has been enacted into law by both Houses of Congress.[47] In other words, the United States government is still not a party to the Genocide Convention and probably will not become a party for quite some time, if ever.

Historically, the primary reason for such vigorous and longstanding opposition to the ratification of the Genocide Convention in this country has always been and continues to be founded in considerations of pure racism and racial discrimination directed primarily against Black Americans. In particular, conservative southern Senators have always possessed the fully-warranted fear that Black Americans might thereunder gain the legal right and standing to allege that

---

45. *Reservations to the Convention on Genocide*, 1951 *I.C.J.* 15 (Advisory Opinion).

46. 132 *Cong. Rec.* S1377-78 (daily ed. Febr. 19, 1986) (statement of the resolution of ratification, including its reservations, understandings, and declaration).

47. While this provision is entitled a "declaration," one of its authors explains that it in fact represents a requirement to ratification and "is in the nature of an executory contract between the Senate and the administration." 132 *Cong. Rec.* S1273-74 (daily ed. Febr. 18, 1986) (statement of Senator Hatch).

the United States government or the states of the Union have committed acts of genocide against them. In theory, such allegations could be properly raised at the United Nations or before some other international organization;[48] or in an appropriate lawsuit brought in either a federal or a state court;[49] or in the International Court of Justice by another state party to the Convention,[50] etc.

Certainly in the past history of this country, Black Americans have been subjected to genocidal practices inflicted upon them with either the active participation or at least the tacit acquiescence of our state, local and federal governments. In my opinion, however, after *Brown v. The Board* and its progeny as well as the enactment of the major pieces of civil rights legislation in the 1960s, it cannot accurately be said that either the federal or state governments in this country today pursue or tolerate anyone's pursuit of policies tantamount to genocide against Blacks. I realize, of course, that many Black Americans inhabiting the ghettoes in Chicago, New York, Los Angeles and Philadelphia, among others, would vigorously contest the validity of this latter proposition.

But even if the United States government were to someday ratify the Genocide Convention, let alone without the two reservations, five "understandings" and one "declaration" attached by the Senate, this act would not open up to political or judicial scrutiny and adjudication the monstrous crimes of the past that have been undeniably perpetrated against Black Americans with the active participation or at least tacit acquiescence of our state, local and federal governments. This would be pursuant to the basic doctrine of customary international law enunciated in article 28 of the 1969 Vienna Convention

48. Article VIII of the Genocide Convention provides:
Any Contracting Party may call upon the competent organs of the United Nations to take such action under the Charter of the United Nations as they consider appropriate for the prevention and suppression of acts of genocide or any of the other acts enumerated in article III.

49. Article VI of the Genocide Convention provides:
Persons charged with genocide or any of the other acts enumerated in art. III shall be tried by a competent tribunal of the State in the territory of which the act was committed, or by such international penal tribunal as may have jurisdiction with respect to those Contracting Parties which shall have accepted its jurisdiction.

50. Article IX of the Genocide Convention provides:
Disputes between the Contracting Parties relating to the interpretation, application or fulfillment of the present Convention, including those relating to the responsibility of a State for genocide . . . shall be submitted to the International Court of Justice at the request of any of the parties to the dispute.

on the Law of Treaties[51] to the effect that unless specifically provided otherwise, a treaty does not "bind a party in relation to any act or fact which took place or any situation which ceased to exist before the date of the entry into force of the treaty with respect to that party." Nevertheless, the serious problem created by the policies our federal and state governments currently pursue toward indigenous peoples in this country would still need to be examined in light of both the letter and spirit of the Genocide Convention and any other international human rights treaties we might ratify.

For example, in its definition of the crime of genocide, the Convention provides that "genocide means any of the following acts committed with intent to destroy, in whole or in part, a national, ethnical, racial or religious group as such: . . . (c) Deliberately inflicting on the group conditions of life calculated to bring about its physical destruction in whole or in part. . . ." The federal government's longstanding treatment of American Indians and Inuits certainly raises legitimate concerns under this provision of the Genocide Convention, among others. If the U.S. government's ratification of the Genocide Convention and the rest of these international human rights treaties can somehow be used to improve the deplorable and lamentable condition of American Indians and Inuits, all U.S. citizens would be far better off for the success of such an endeavor. Yet today there are some Americans located in certain regions of this country where indigenous people live who opposed the ratification of the Genocide Convention in its pristine form for that very reason.

Hence, there is a direct continuity between those who originally opposed the institution of racial non-discrimination and equal rights and liberties for all Americans in the name of "states' rights" and those who are still opposing the U.S. ratification of international human rights treaties today. Their opposition has nothing at all to do with principles of constitutional law; the sovereignty of the United States of America; or the protection of the basic human rights of the people living in the particular states of the Union—an argument that really turns the entire issue on its head. Rather, the motivating force behind such opposition is racism, bigotry, and hatred against Amer-

---

51. Vienna Convention on the Law of Treaties, *adopted* May 22, 1969, *opened for signature* May 23, 1969, *entered into force* Jan. 27, 1980, U.N. Doc. A/CONF. 39/27, at 289, *reprinted in* 8 *I.L.M.* 679 (1969).

ican Blacks, Indians, Inuits and members of other racial minority groups in this country.

It seems that the same group of powerful conservative southern Senators, now joined by some Western colleagues, are still able to exercise enough influence on the Senate as a whole to keep these international human rights treaties from ever being brought to a vote on the Senate floor. Remember that a treaty requires the advice and consent of two-thirds of the Senate. All that is required to defeat any one of these treaties is one-third-plus-one of the members of the U.S. Senate (i.e., 34 Senators). The Senators who have consistently opposed the ratification of these human rights treaties in the name of "states' rights" have always exercised enough power to cast serious doubt upon whether or not these treaties would ultimately receive the advice and consent of two-thirds of the Senate. Consequently, many such treaties have continued to languish in the Senate Foreign Relations Committee; many others, the executive branch of the federal government has never even bothered to sign in the first place.[52]

This, then, is the explanation for the fact that the United States government is not a party to most of the major multilateral covenants for the protection of human rights. This is also the reason why other foreign states and peoples simply do not take our protestations about their violations of human rights seriously. It is only when we clean up our own record by ratifying these major international human rights treaties and eliminating the last vestiges of racial discrimination in America today against Blacks, Indians, Inuits, Hispanics, and other racial minority groups that we can then obtain any right or standing under international law to preach to other countries how they should treat their own citizens. Until that day comes, the rank hypocrisy and racism behind the formulation of U.S. human rights foreign policy

---

52. The U.S. has neither signed nor ratified the following treaties: the International Convention on the Suppression and Punishment of the Crime of Apartheid; the Convention on the Reduction of Statelessness; the Convention Relating to the Status of Stateless Persons. In addition, the following treaties have been signed, but still have not been ratified: the International Covenant on Economic, Social and Cultural Rights; the International Covenant on Civil and Political Rights; the International Convention on the Elimination of All Forms of Racial Discrimination; the Convention on the Elimination of All Forms of Discrimination Against Women; the American Convention on Human Rights; the Convention on the Abolition of Forced Labor; and of course most shamelessly of all, the Convention on the Prevention and Punishment of the Crime of Genocide. Finally, the United States government has failed to enact the domestic implementing legislation required by the Four Geneva Conventions of 1949 and therefore stands in breach of its solemn international legal obligation to do so.

will continue to mock and undercut whatever good-faith efforts we might make to promote and protect human rights around the world.

In the opinion of this author, it is highly unlikely that the U.S. Senate will someday give its advice and consent to any of the afore-mentioned international human rights treaties without attaching so-called amendments, reservations, and understandings that will completely gut the significance of their ratification by the United States government. Nevertheless, that is not the end of the matter. Just because various members of the Senate and of the executive branch of the federal government possess a distinctly regressive attitude toward the promotion of human rights cannot prevent state and local governments around the country from undertaking progressive measures in this field.

For example, this chapter's substantive critique of U.S. human rights foreign policy was originally delivered as a public address in Burlington, Iowa, on October 25, 1985 at the request of the United Nations Association of Iowa in honor of the 40th anniversary of the United Nations Organization. Afterwards, a member of the audience rose from the floor and asked this author a question along the following lines: "In light of the intransigence by the United States Senate on these international human rights treaties, what can the people of Burlington, Iowa do about the situation?" My response was to suggest that the city of Burlington consider enacting into law as a municipal ordinance the Genocide Convention, then the International Convention on the Elimination of All Forms of Racial Discrimination, then the Convention on the Elimination of All Forms of Discrimination Against Women, and then the two U.N. Human Rights Covenants of 1966. In other words, I said, they could turn Burlington, Iowa into an "international human rights zone" similar to the "nuclear-free zones" that have already been established at the local government level all around the country.

Due to subsequent developments with respect to the Genocide Convention that have been discussed above, the people of Burlington decided to focus their efforts upon enacting into local law the U.N. Racial Discrimination Convention. For that purpose, they contacted my friend and colleague Professor Burns H. Weston at the University of Iowa College of Law. Professor Weston kindly agreed to draft a series of amendments to Burlington's extant Human Rights Ordinance in order to bring it into compliance with the U.N. Racial Discrimination Convention. The text of these amendments as drafted by Professor Weston can be found at the end of this chapter.

Today, the United Nations Association of Iowa is undertaking an effort to introduce analogous ordinances in numerous small towns and cities around Iowa. Eventually, this movement should culminate in the introduction of a bill into the General Assembly of the state of Iowa that will enact the U.N. Convention on the Elimination of All Forms of Racial Discrimination into law for the entire state of Iowa. At that point, it would then be possible to point to the progressive state of Iowa as a model and an example for the rest of the nation to emulate when it comes to the implementation of the U.N. Racial Discrimination Convention at the state and local level. Hopefully, this initiative could then take off and be replicated by state and local governments around the entire United States of America, and perhaps someday culminate in the U.S. Senate giving its advice and consent to the Convention in its undiluted form.

Furthermore, that same task could also be performed for the U.N. Convention on the Elimination of All Forms of Discrimination Against Women. This would be one device whereby state and local governments could circumvent the national effort that had been mounted to defeat the Equal Rights Amendment to the U.S. Constitution. This author has already been in contact with the National Conference of Christians and Jews (NCCJ) to discuss the possibility of their support for this initiative on a state and local government level across the United States of America.

In the event that your community or organization is seriously interested in sponsoring legislation that would bring into effect on a state or local level the U.N. Convention on the Elimination of All Forms of Racial Discrimination, or the U.N. Convention on the Elimination of All Forms of Discrimination Against Women, or any of the aforementioned international human treaties, please feel free to contact Professor Weston or me. We will be happy to work with you and the members of your community in order to pursue such worthwhile grass-roots endeavors. You must not allow the rank hypocrisy and racism behind the formulation of U.S. human rights foreign policy at the federal level to interfere with the basic sense of humanity, compassion, decency, fairness, and justice that are so intrinsic to the American people.

* * * *

ORDINANCE NO. 2807
CAN ORDINANCE AMENDING CHAPTER 9.12 CITY CODE BY ADDING
THERETO BY REFERENCE CERTAIN PROVISIONS OF THE
UNITED NATIONS INTERNATIONAL CONVENTION ON THE
ELIMINATION OF ALL FORMS OF RACIAL DISCRIMINATION
(1966), AND MAKING CERTAIN EDITORIAL CHANGES NECES-
SARY TO
IMPLEMENT THE INTERNATIONAL CONVENTION

BE IT ORDAINED BY THE BURLINGTON, IOWA CITY COUNCIL:
Section 1. Subsection 9.12.010A is hereby repealed, and the following adopted in lieu thereof:

To secure for all persons within the City freedom from discrimination because of race, color, religion, creed, sex, national origin,
age, or mental or physical disability in connection with employment, public accommodations, housing, and credit; and thereby
to protect the personal dignity of these persons, to insure their full
productive capacities, to preserve the public safety, health, and
general welfare, and to promote the interests, rights and privileges
of citizens within the City.

Section 2. Subsection 9.12.010B is hereby repealed, and the following adopted in lieu thereof:

To provide for the execution within the City of the policies em-
bodied in the Federal Civil Rights Act (1964), the Iowa Civil Rights
Act (1965) and the preamble and Part I (Articles 1 through 7) of the
International Convention on the Elimination of All Forms of Racial
Discrimination (1966); and to promote cooperation among the City,
State, and Federal agencies which are charged, presently and in
the future, with enforcing these instruments; and

Section 3. Subsection 9.12.020 is hereby repealed, and the following
adopted in lieu thereof:

Construction. This chapter shall be construed broadly to effectuate
its purposes, and shall be enforced by the City Attorney and the

Commission on Human Rights consistent with the intent, language and spirit of the Preamble and Part I (Articles 1 through 7) of the International Convention on the Elimination of All Forms of Racial Discrimination (1966), made a part hereof by reference; provided, however, that the construction and enforcement of the Preamble and Part I of said International Convention shall in no event operate to diminish the protections that otherwise exist under this Chapter, the Federal Civil Rights Act, the Iowa Civil Rights Act, the Constitution of the State of Iowa, or the Constitution of the United States of America.

Section 4. Subsection 9.12.030N is hereby repealed, and the following adopted in lieu thereof:

"Public accommodation" means each and every place, establishment, or facility of whatever kind, nature, or class that caters or offers services, facilities, or goods for a fee or charge to non-members of any organization or association utilizing the place, establishment, or facility, provided that any place, establishment, or facility that caters or offers services, facilities, or goods to the non-members gratuitously shall be deemed a public accommodation if the accommodation receives governmental support or subsidy. Public accommodation shall not mean any bona fide private club, or other place, establishment, facility which is by its nature distinctly private except when such distinctly private place, establishment, or facility caters or offers services, facilities, or goods to the non-members for fee or charge or gratuitously, it shall be deemed a public accommodation during such period.

Section 5. Subsection 9.12.030 is hereby amended to adopt the following new subsection:

Subsection R. "State," "State Party," and "State Parties" as used in the Preamble and Part I of the International Convention on the Elimination of All Forms of Racial Discrimination (1966) shall mean the City.

Section 6: This ordinance shall be in full force upon publication as provided by law.
APPROVED and ADOPTED this 2nd day of September, 1986.
ATTEST:
Kathleen P. Salisbury   Marcia Walker
City Clerk   Mayor Pro-Tem

APPENDICES

Appendices

1. Boyle, "The American Society of International Law: 75 Years and Beyond," 75 *Am. Soc'y Int'l L. Proc.* 270 (1981).
2. Boyle et al., "Conclusions and Judgment of Brussels Tribunal on Reagan's Foreign Policy (Sept. 30, 1984)," *N.Y. Times*, Oct. 7, 1984, at 77, and in International Progress Organization, *The Reagan Administration's Foreign Policy* 459 (H. Koechler ed. 1985).
3. Boyle et al., "Violations of International Law," *Middle East International*, Sept. 3, 1982, at 11.
4. The Lawyers' Committee on Nuclear Policy, *Statement on the Illegality of Nuclear Weapons.*
5. Anderson & Verr, *Draft Brief on Behalf of the Washington Rabbis* (1986).

1. Boyle, "The American Society of International Law: 75 Years and Beyond," 75 *Am. Soc'y Int'l L. Proc.* 270 (1981).

The theme of this Seventy-Fifth Anniversary Convocation of the American Society of International Law is *Order, Freedom, Justice and Power*. These remarks will address the last element of this quadrumvirate—power—and its relationship to international law. During the past one hundred days of the Reagan administration we have heard repeated calls for American foreign policy to return to a "realist" or "geopolitical" approach to foreign affairs, one premised on a "grand theory" or "strategic design." Proponents of this viewpoint, such as Henry Kissinger and his protégé, Secretary of State Alexander Haig, invariably endorse a power politics approach to foreign policy decision-making. This attitude consists of nothing more sophisticated than a refined and superficially rationalized Machiavellianism that is qualified only by the stark reality of massive nuclear weapons installations on the part of both superpowers. A cardinal tenet of this "realist" approach to international relations is that international law and organizations are irrelevant to conflicts between states over matters of "vital national interest." Nations are hypothesized to survive precariously in a Hobbesian state of nature, where life is "solitary, poor, nasty, brutish and short." Statesmen who disobey the "iron law" of power politics and proclaim instead the need for more international law and organizations are said to invite destruction at the hands of aggressors and facilitate the elemental disruption of the extant world public order.

From the short-term perspective, however, Machiavellian power politics offers no substantive prescriptions for the day-to-day conduct of foreign affairs. It simply recommends a series of ad hoc calculations of national self-interest and power aggrandizement at the expense of other states in order to win the supposed "zero sum game" of international relations. Yet Machiavellianism provides no indication how these decisions should be integrated into a unified, coherent and consistent foreign policy except for its vacuous injunction that the "balance of power" must be "preserved" at all costs. For the long-term course of international relations, the practice of Machiavellianism tends to undermine the balance of power because it demands the constant threat and use of force by states in their mutual relations. As a theory, power politics prescribes the purposeful institution of hostilities between major actors, and even a general systemic war itself, in order to "uphold" or "restore" the "balance." Power politics and war are essentially inseparable because Machiavellianism is nothing more than a transparent philosophical justification for a foreign policy that basically consists of waging a permanent and universal war of aggression. Thus, because of both its impracticability and its suicidally dangerous nature in a nuclear world, power politics must be definitively repudiated as a theory for the conduct of foreign policy. Yet the reality of power must never be ignored in the formulation of a constructive alternative.

One alternative to power politics as a basis for the conduct of international relations by the world's governments can be found in the principles of international law. Here law must not simply be interpreted in its Hobbesian legal positivist sense as the making, breaking and enforcement of rules. A system of international law is more properly understood as creating a facilitative framework of rules that permits and enhances the quality of interaction among its participants. Analyzed in accordance with the Aristotelian doctrine of the mean, international law enunciates those rules which the actors in the international system have found to be indispensable for international life, and that which is essential to international life becomes enshrined in the rules of international law. Therefore, the requirements of international law should substantially, albeit imperfectly, coincide with the dictates of "vital national interests" and vice versa. The principles of international law have been created by states for the express purpose of serving and advancing their respective national interests in the first place.

These considerations apply especially to the conduct of American foreign policy. The United States is the outstanding example of a status quo power in the post-World War II system of international relations. American national security interests must include the promotion of obedience to international law by the United States and other governments because such conformity encourages the peaceful preservation of the political, economic and military status quo heavily weighted to America's advantage by virtue of its victory in that war. Phenomenologically, law is the instrument par excellence for the peaceful preservation and transformation of any political or economic status quo, whether domestic or international. By its very nature, the international legal order represents an attempt by advantaged international actors to legitimate and consolidate existing and proposed power relationships. To the degree a state enjoys the benefits of the existing configuration of international relations, the greater should be its commitment to upholding international law and organizations. Leading status quo powers such as the United States and its Allies have the greatest stake in upholding the integrity of the contemporary international legal order.

The foremost concern of American foreign policy decision-making that demands the pursuit of more reliance on international law is in the area of nuclear weapons. The strategic nuclear assumptions of the Committee on Present Danger (e.g., the "window of vulnerability"), which have come to predominate the defense and foreign affairs policies of the Reagan administration, do not possess substantial merit. Their outlandish scenarios do not justify the enormous conventional and nuclear weapons buildup currently proposed by the Reagan administration, which, it quite callously admits, will be financed directly by huge cuts from scarce resources previously allocated to social welfare programs and human services. Nothing could constitute a greater present danger to the peace, stability, security and prosperity of the United States at home and abroad than starting another wasteful and unnecessary arms race with the Soviet Union.

Upon assumption of office the Reagan administration should have moved immediately into formal negotiations with the Soviet Union to forestall the modernization of theater nuclear weapons in Europe. The Reagan administration should have also called for an immediate opening of formal negotiations to prevent the deployment of strategic nuclear systems not prohibited by SALT II. The Reagan administration should officially disavow Jimmy Carter's Presidential Directive 59, which naively contemplates the possibility of fighting a limited nuclear war. The Reagan administration should take an affirmative decision against deploying any land-based MX missile system or sea-based Trident II system that possesses a theoretical first-strike capability against the Soviet ICBM force. The life of the 1972 U.S.-U.S.S.R. Anti-Ballistic Missile Systems Treaty must not be terminated when it comes up for review in 1982. The Reagan administration should work assiduously towards conclusion of the partially completed Comprehensive Test Ban Treaty. Finally, the Reagan administration must stridently resist the further proliferation of nuclear weapons technology and materials.

To sustain movement in this direction, the Reagan administration must continue to adhere to the terms of the unratified SALT II Treaty and the expired SALT I Interim Accord. Ultimately American ratification of SALT II or of some cosmetic substitute negotiated by the Reagan administration will prove to be a precondition for further progress in reaching nuclear arms control and reduction agreements with the Soviet Union. The Reagan administration must also repudiate its adoption of Kissinger's theory of "linkage" between considerations of Machiavellian power politics and nuclear weapons control. If the highly politicized treaty ratification procedure in the U.S. Senate proves a major obstacle to the realization of the foregoing agenda, the Reagan administration must submit future arms control agreements for approval by a joint resolution of Congress. Failure by the Senate to support the Treaty of Versailles and the Covenant of the League of Nations was in part responsible for World War II. Senate obstinacy over a revised SALT II or SALT III must not be permitted to pave the way for World War III.

The principles of international law exercise a critical bearing upon other monumental issues of American foreign policy decision-making. One of the most pressing is the U.S. government's current posture towards Iran and the overall security of the Persian Gulf oil-producing region. There are several indications from the public record that the Carter administration tacitly condoned, if not actively encouraged, the Iraqi invasion of Iran in September 1980 because of its shortsighted belief that the pressures of belligerency might expedite the release of U.S. diplomats held in Iran as hostages since November 1979. In any event, American efforts to punish, isolate and weaken the Khomeini regime over the hostages crisis paved the way for Iraq to invade Iran. The American policy of "neutrality" towards the Iran-Iraq war, first announced by President Carter and then continued by the Reagan administration, misrepresented fact if not the law. A substantial body of opinion believes that the American government has consistently "tilted" in favor of Iraq despite its public proclamation of "neutrality." Even if the United States has been factually as well as legally "neutral" in the Iran-Iraq war, that position is itself shocking and indefensible under the most rudimentary principles of international law. When before in the post-U.N. Charter world has the

United States been "neutral" in the face of outright aggression? In a thermonuclear age, aggression per se is the most dangerous threat to world peace. The U.S. government cannot possibly be consistent in condemning the Soviet invasion of Afghanistan without likewise condemning the Iraqi invasion of Iran.

With the hostages crisis now behind it, the Reagan administration must officially label Iraq as the "aggressor" in the Gulf war, and publicly call for an immediate cease-fire and Iraqi withdrawal from occupied Iranian territory. The Reagan administration should move to restore normal diplomatic relations with Iran as soon as possible and without any prior conditions. The United States should work towards the establishment of a strong and stable government in Teheran that is able to repel the Iraqi invasion and to undertake the military measures necessary to offset Soviet divisions massed on Iran's borders. Nevertheless it is crucial to emphasize that the Iranian people possess the exclusive right to determine their own form of government without any more overt or covert U.S. intervention, even if this means the continuation of an Islamic fundamentalist regime in Teheran.

The Reagan administration should completely disavow the so-called Carter Doctrine as the foundation for U.S. security policy in the Persian Gulf. Even if supported by a creditable rapid deployment force, the Carter Doctrine is a dangerous bluff whose potential for nuclear confrontation and escalation with the Soviet Union is incalculable. As an alternative the Reagan administration should encourage the efforts of six local states to form a viable Gulf Cooperation Council that could metamorphosize into an effective Gulf Security Organization affiliated with the United Nations under Chapter 8 of the Charter. A Gulf Security Organization would be far more successful at the pacific settlement of local disputes, opposition to intra-regional aggression and the suppression of externally fomented disturbances than the Carter Doctrine and the rapid deployment force ever could.

The success of any American foreign policy in the Persian Gulf cannot be divorced from the establishment of peace between Israel and its Arab neighbors. The United States and Israel must finally recognize the international legal right of the Palestinian people to self-determination. Both the U.N. General Assembly and the League of Arab States have determined that the P.L.O. is the legitimate representative of the Palestinian people. That determination must be respected by Israel and the United States for the purpose of negotiating an overall settlement on the ultimate disposition of the West Bank, the Gaza Strip, and Jerusalem. Mutual and simultaneous recognition of their respective rights under international law by Israel and the PLO must be the next stage in the development of the Middle East peace process. This can occur by means of an appropriate revision of U.N. Security Council Resolution 242 (1967) that could then be formally accepted by both sides as a prelude to the start of diplomatic negotiations. In the meantime the U.S. government must continue to oppose the Israeli annexation of East Jerusalem as well as any proposed annexation of the Golan Heights, and the United States must stridently resist the establishment of Israeli settlements on the West Bank and the Golan Heights. Such Israeli actions violate the Geneva Conventions of 1949 and the customary international law of belligerent occupation. As a party to the Geneva Conventions of 1949 the U.S. government has an obligation to respect and to ensure respect for their observance by all other contracting powers.

For the same reason, the United States must also prevent Israel from using American weapons in Lebanon for the purpose of launching preemptive and retaliatory military strikes, all of which explicitly violate the U.N. Charter and the terms of U.S. domestic statutes applicable to arms transfer agreements. The United States should employ its tremendous arms leverage over Israel to secure the dismantling of the Lebanese Christian enclave that has been illegally created along the border with the collusion of the Israeli government. Such territory must be turned over to troops from the U.N. Interim Force in Lebanon. A renewed and strengthened mandate for UNIFIL will continue to maintain peace across the border until the Lebanese army is reconstructed as an independent military force under the control of an effective central government. The latter objective can be achieved within the context of an overall settlement of the Palestinian question. The Arab Deterrent Force, composed primarily of Syrian troops, could then be removed from Lebanon by the League of Arab States in accordance with the wishes of the Lebanese government. The creation of peace in the Middle East demands forthright American leadership acting in strict accordance with the rules of international law and in full cooperation with the relevant international institutions.

Another area of overriding concern to the Reagan administration is the influence exercised by the Castro government throughout Central America and the Caribbean. The best way to "neutralize" Castro as an alleged anti-U.S. actor in international relations excludes the means hitherto used: military invasion, naval blockade, covert operations, or economic and political destablization measures, all of which undoubtedly violate international law. The Reagan administration should seek to reestablish normal diplomatic relations with the Castro government; to remove U.S. economic sanctions imposed against Cuba; to prosecute Cuban refugee groups located in the United States that prepare armed expeditions against the Castro government in violation of 18 U.S.C. 960 (1976), and under 22 U.S.C. § 461 (1976) to employ U.S. military forces to thwart such expeditions whenever detected; finally, to reverse the 1962 Punta del Este Resolution by the Eighth Meeting of Consultation of the Ministers of Foreign Affairs of the American Republics that excluded the Castro government from participation in the inter-American system. Such measures would free Castro from Cuba's burdensome, and at times, counterproductive and unwanted reliance on the Soviet Union for military defense and financial subsistence. In addition, such a new Cuban policy would help the search for a peaceful settlement to the conflict in El Salvador negotiated by all internal parties under the auspices of the Organization of American States, or the United Nations, or both. In conjunction with a much needed improvement of U.S. relations with the Sandinista government in Nicaragua, this new Cuban policy would set the stage for restoring a modicum of peace and stability to Central America. Current intimations that the Reagan administration will employ overt or covert military operations against Cuba and Nicaragua are illegal, irresponsible and counterproductive.

U.S. initiation of a rapprochement with Castro could bring such other tangible benefits as the gradual withdrawal of Cuban troops from Angola. This result depends upon a renewed and strengthened U.S. commitment to the independence of Namibia along the lines of the plan approved by the U.N. Security Council in Resolution 435 (1978). Meanwhile, the Reagan administration should establish normal diplomatic relations with the MPLA government in Luanda, obey the terms of the Clark Amendment, 22 U.S.C. § 2293 note (1976), prohibiting assistance of any kind for military or paramilitary operations in Angola without explicit congressional authorization, and participate in the resolute condemnations by the U.N. Security Council of all South African military raids mounted from Namibia into Angola. The Reagan administration's myopic concentration on the Cuban presence in Angola will only lead the United States farther into the deadly embrace of the apartheid regime in South Africa. The Reagan administration's failure to actively support the independence of Namibia will undermine the good political and economic relationships with Black African states that were successfully promoted by the Carter administration, and will contravene the principles of international law and resolutions of international organizations concerning Namibia and South Africa. The right of the Namibian people to self-determination had been firmly established under international law before the American, South African, and Cuban governments decided to intervene in the Angolan civil war. The Reagan administration must not obstruct the achievement of Namibian independence by conditioning it on the withdrawal of Cuban troops from Angola.

* * * *

The rules of international law and the procedures of international organizations do not constitute a general panacea for all the problems of American foreign policy. But they do point the direction out of the rotting morass of Machiavellian power politics that has engulfed the American foreign policy decision-making establishment for at least the past generation. Yet too often the members of the American international legal community have wittingly served as mouthpieces for the Machiavellian foreign policy pronunciamentos of the U.S. government by manufacturing legal arguments as ad hoc or ex post facto justifications for decisions taken on the grounds of power politics. In the process, both the vital national security interests of the United Sates and the strength of the international legal order, which was originally designed to uphold them, have grievously suffered. The members of the American Society of International Law must organize themselves into the vanguard of a revolution against the hegemony of Machiavellianism over the conduct of American foreign policy. Otherwise the future of this planet will be left in the brutal hands of geopolitical practitioners of power politics such as Kissinger, Brzezinski and Haig. The present danger is power politics. The only antidote is international law and organizations. The choice is that stark, ominous and compelling. As international lawyers we must not hesitate to apply this imperative regimen.

2. Boyle et al., "Conclusions and Judgment of Brussels Tribunal on Reagan's Foreign Policy (Sept. 30, 1984)," *N.Y. Times*, Oct. 7, 1984, at 77, and in International Progress Organization, *The Reagan Administration's Foreign Policy* 459 (H. Koechler ed. 1985).

The International Conference on the Reagan administration's foreign policy convened in Brussels from 28-30 September, 1984 under the auspices of the International Progress Organization. Reports were submitted by international jurists and foreign policy specialists on various aspects of the Reagan administration's foreign policy. Among the participants of the conference were Sean MacBride (Nobel Laureate, Ireland), Prof. George Wald (Nobel Laureate, Harvard University), General Edgardo Mercado Jarrin (Peru), General Nino Pasti (former Deputy Supreme Commander of NATO) and Hortensia Bussi de Allende (Chile). The reports were presented before a panel of jurists consisting of Hon. Farouk Abu-Eissa (Sudan), attorney, former foreign minister, secretary-general of the Arab Lawyers Union; Prof. Francis A. Boyle (U.S.A.), professor of international law from the University of Illinois, Chairman; Dr. Hans Goeran Franck (Sweden), attorney, member of the Swedish Parliament; Hon. Mirza Gholam Hafiz (Bangladesh), former speaker of the Bangladesh Parliament and currently a senior advocate of the Bangladesh Supreme Court; Hon. Mary M. Kaufman (U.S.A.), attorney-at-law, prosecuting attorney at the Nuremberg War Crimes Trial against I. G. Farben; Dr. Jean-Claude Njem (Cameroon), assistant-professor at the Faculty of Law, Uppsala University, and a consultant of the government; Prof. Alberto Ruiz-Eldredge (Peru), professor of law, former president of the National Council of Justice; and Dr. Muemtaz Soysal (Turkey), professor of constitutional law, University of Ankara. An accusation against the international legality of the Reagan administration's foreign policy was delivered by the Honorable Ramsey Clark, former U.S. Attorney General. The defense was presented by a legal expert of the Reagan administration.

Based upon all the reports and documents submitted and the arguments by the advocates, the Brussels Panel of Jurists hereby renders the following conclusions concerning the compatibility of the Reagan administration's foreign policy with the requirements of international law.

A. Introduction

1. General Introduction. The Reagan administration's foreign policy constitutes a gross violation of the fundamental principles of international law enshrined in the Charter of the United Nations Organization, as well as of the basic rules of customary international law set forth in the U.N. General Assembly's Declaration on the Inadmissibility of Intervention in the Domestic Affairs of States and the Protection of Their Independence and Sovereignty (1965), its Declaration on Principles of International Law Concerning Friendly Relations and Cooperation Among States in Accordance with the Charter of the United Nations (1970), and its Definition of Aggression (1974), among others. In addition, the Reagan administration is responsible for complicity in the commission of crimes against peace, crimes against humanity, war crimes and grave breaches of the Third and Fourth Geneva Conventions of 1949.

B. Western Hemisphere

2. Grenada. The Reagan administration's 1983 invasion of Grenada was a clear-cut violation of U.N. Charter articles 2(3), 2(4), and 33 as well as of articles 18, 20 and 21 of the Revised OAS Charter for which there was no valid excuse or justification under international law. As such, it constituted an act of aggression within the meaning of article 39 of the United Nations Charter.

3. Threat of U.S. Intervention. In direct violation of the basic requirement of international law mandating the peaceful settlement of international disputes, the Reagan administration has implemented a foreign policy towards Central America that constitutes a great danger of escalation in military hostilities to the point of precipitating armed intervention by U.S. troops into combat against both the insurgents in El Salvador and the legitimate government of Nicaragua.

4. El Salvador. The Reagan administration's illegal intervention into El Salvador's civil war contravenes the international legal right of self-determination of peoples as recognized by article 1(2) of the United Nations Charter. The Reagan administration has provided enormous amounts of military assistance to an oppressive regime that has used

it to perpetrate a gross and consistent pattern of violations of the most fundamental human rights of the people of El Salvador.

5. Nicaragua. The Reagan administration's policy of organizing and participating in military operations by opposition contra groups for the purpose of overthrowing the legitimate government of Nicaragua violates the terms of both the U.N. and O.A.S. Charters prohibiting the threat or use of force against the political independence of a state. The Reagan administration has flouted its obligation to terminate immediately its support for the opposition contra groups in accordance with the Interim Order of Protection issued by the International Court of Justice on 10 May 1984.

6. International Court of Justice. The Panel denounces the patently bogus attempt by the Reagan administration to withdraw from the compulsory jurisdiction of the International Court of Justice in the suit brought against it by Nicaragua for the purpose of avoiding a peaceful settlement of this dispute by the World Court in order to pursue instead a policy based upon military intervention, lawless violence and destabilization of the legitimate government of Nicaragua.

7. Mining Nicaraguan Harbors. The Reagan administration's mining of Nicaraguan harbors violates the rules of international law set forth in the 1907 Hague Convention on the Laying of Submarine Mines, to which both Nicaragua and the United States are parties.

C. Nuclear Weapons Policies

8. Arms Control Treaties. The Reagan administration has refused to support the ratification of the Threshold Test Ban Treaty of 1974, the Peaceful Nuclear Explosions Treaty of 1976, and the SALT II Treaty of 1979, in addition to renouncing the longstanding objective of the U.S. government to negotiate a comprehensive test ban treaty. As such the Reagan administration has failed to pursue negotiations in good faith on effective measures relating to cessation of the nuclear arms race at an early date and to nuclear disarmament as required by article 6 of the Nuclear Non-Proliferation Treaty of 1968. Similarly, the Reagan administration's "Strategic Defense Initiative" of 1983 threatens to breach the Anti-Ballistic Missile Systems Treaty of 1972.

9. Pershing 2 Missiles. The deployment of the offensive, first-strike,

counterforce strategic nuclear weapons system known as the Pershing 2 missile in the Federal Republic of Germany violates the non-circumvention clause found in article 12 of the SALT II Treaty. The Reagan administration is bound to obey this prohibition pursuant to the rule of customary international law enunciated in article 18 of the 1969 Vienna Convention on the Law of Treaties to the effect that a signatory to a treaty is obliged to refrain from acts that would defeat the object and purpose of a treaty until it has made its intention clear not to become a party.

10. The MX Missile. The MX missile is an offensive, first-strike, counterforce strategic nuclear weapons system that can serve no legitimate defensive purpose under U.N. Charter article 51 and the international laws of humanitarian armed conflict.

11. No-First-Use. In accordance with U.N. General Assembly Resolution 1553 of 24 November 1961, the Panel denounces the refusal by the Reagan administration to adopt a policy mandating the no-first-use of nuclear weapons in the event of a conventional attack as required by the basic rule of international law dictating proportionality in the use of force even for the purposes of legitimate self-defense.

12. ASAT Treaty. The Panel calls upon both the United States and the Soviet Union to negotiate unconditionally over the conclusion of an anti-satellite weapons treaty.

D. Middle East

13. Lebanon. For the part it played in the planning, preparation and initiation of the 1982 Israeli invasion of Lebanon, the Reagan administration has committed a crime against peace as defined by the Nuremberg Principles. Likewise, under the Nuremberg Principles, the Reagan administration becomes an accomplice to the crimes against humanity, war crimes and grave breaches of the Third and Fourth Geneva Conventions of 1949 that have been committed or condoned by Israel and its allied Phalange and Haddad militia forces in Lebanon. Such complicity includes the savage massacre of genocidal character of hundreds of innocent Palestinian and Lebanese civilians by organized units of the Phalangist militia at the Sabra and Shatila refugee camps located in West Beirut that were then subject

to the control of the occupying Israeli army. The Reagan administration has totally failed to discharge its obligation to obtain Israel's immediate and unconditional withdrawal from all parts of Lebanon as required by U.N. Security Council Resolutions 508 and 509 (1982), both of which are legally binding on Israel and the United States under U.N. Charter article 25. This includes Israeli evacuation of southern Lebanon.

14. The Palestinian Question. The Reagan administration's policy towards the Palestinian people as well as the Reagan "Peace Plan" of 1 September 1982 violates the international legal right of the Palestinian people to self-determination as recognized by U.N. Charter article 1(2). As recognized by numerous General Assembly resolutions, the Palestinian people have an international legal right to create an independent and sovereign state. The Palestine Liberation Organization has been recognized as the legitimate representative of the Palestinian people by both the United Nations General Assembly and the League of Arab States. The Reagan administration's nonrecognition of the PLO and its attempt to brand the PLO a "terrorist" group contravene the Palestinian people's right to liberation. The panel denounces the negative attitude of the Reagan administration towards the call by the United Nations' Secretary General for the convocation of an international conference under the auspices of the United Nations, with the United States and the Soviet Union as cochairmen, and with the participation of all parties involved in the conflict including the PLO, for the purpose of obtaining a just and lasting peace in the Middle East.

15. Israeli Settlements. The Reagan administration's declared position that Israeli settlements in the Occupied Territories are "not illegal" is a violation of U.S. obligations under article 1 of the Fourth Geneva Convention of 1949 to ensure respect for the terms of the Convention (here article 49) by other High Contracting Parties such as Israel.

16. Libya. The Reagan administration's dispatch of the U.S. Sixth Fleet into the Gulf of Sidra for the purpose of precipitating armed conflict with the Libyan government constitutes a breach of the peace under article 39 of the U.N. Charter. The Reagan administration's policy to attempt to destabilize the government of Libya violates the terms of the United Nations Charter article 2(4) prohibiting the threat or use of force directed against the political independence of a state.

E. Africa, Asia and the Indian Ocean

17. Apartheid. The Panel denounces the Reagan administration's so-called policy of "constructive engagement" toward the apartheid regime in South Africa. This specious policy encourages discrimination and oppression against the majority of the people of South Africa; it hampers effective action by the international community against apartheid, and facilitates aggressive conduct by the South African apartheid regime against neighbor states in violation of the U.N. Charter. As such, the Reagan administration has become an accomplice to the commission of the international crime of apartheid as recognized by the universally accepted International Convention on the Suppression and Punishment of the Crime of Apartheid of 1973. The Panel also denounces the cooperation between the Reagan administration and South Africa in military and nuclear matters.

18. Namibia. The Reagan administration has refused to carry out its obligations under Security Council Resolution 435 (1978) providing for the independence of Namibia, as required by article 25 of the U.N. Charter. The right of the Namibian people to self-determination had been firmly established under international law long before the outbreak of the Angolan civil war. The Reagan administration has no right to obstruct the achievement of Namibian independence by conditioning it upon or "linking" it to the withdrawal of Cuban troops from Angola in any way. Both the U.N. General Assembly and the Organization of the African Unity have recognized SWAPO as the legitimate representative of the Namibian people and the Reagan administration is obligated to negotiate with it as such.

19. Angola. Cuban troops are in Angola at the request of the legitimate government of Angola in order to protect it from overt and covert aggression mounted by the South African apartheid regime from Namibia. There is absolutely no international legal justification for South African aggression against Angola in order to maintain and consolidate its reprehensible occupation of Namibia. The Angolan government has repeatedly stated that when South Africa leaves Namibia it will request the withdrawal of Cuban troops, and Cuba has agreed to withdraw its troops whenever so requested by Angola. According to the relevant rules of international law, that is the proper sequence of events to be followed. The Reagan administration's "linkage" of the presence of the Cuban troops in Angola with the in-

dependence of Namibia encourages South African aggression against Angola, and thus it must share in the responsibility for South Africa's genocidal acts against the people of Angola.

20. Indian Ocean. The Reagan administration's continued military occupation of the island of Diego Garcia violates the international legal right of self-determination for the people of Mauritius as recognized by the United Nations Charter. The Reagan administration has accelerated the rapid militarization of the U.S. naval base on Diego Garcia as part of its plan to create a jumping-off point for intervention by the Rapid Deployment Force into the Persian Gulf. As such the Reagan administration's foreign policy towards the Indian Ocean has violated the terms of the U.N. General Assembly's Declaration of the Indian Ocean as a Zone of Peace (1971).

F. Conclusion

21. United Nations Action. From the foregoing, it is clear that the Reagan administration has substituted force for the rule of international law in its conduct of foreign policy around the world. It has thus created a serious threat to the maintenance of international peace and security under article 39 of the United Nations Charter that calls for the imposition of enforcement measures by the U.N. Security Council under articles 41 and 42. In the event the Reagan administration exercises its veto power against the adoption of such measures by the Security Council, the matter should be turned over to the U.N. General Assembly for action in accordance with the procedures set forth in the Uniting for Peace Resolution of 1950. In this way the Reagan administration's grievous international transgressions could be effectively opposed by all members of the world community in a manner consistent with the requirements of international law.

Both the Security Council and the General Assembly should also take into account the numerous interventionist measures taken by the Reagan administration, whether direct or indirect, seeking to impose financial and economic policies which are contrary to the sovereign independence of states, especially in the developing world, and which severely damage the quality of life for all peoples.

Farouk Abu-Eissa
  Mary Kaufman
  Francis A. Boyle, Chairman
  Jean-Claude Njem
  Hans Goeran Franck
  Alberto Ruiz-Eldredge

Mirza Gholam Hafiz
Muemtaz Soysal
Brussels, Belgium
30 September 1984

3. Boyle et al., "Violations of International Law," *Middle East International*, Sept. 3, 1982, at 11.

The invasion of Lebanon by the government of Israel constitutes a violation of UN Charter article 2(3), mandating the peaceful settlement of international disputes, as well as the article 2(4) prohibition on the threat or use of force in international relations against the territorial integrity or political independence of any state. Despite the assertions of Israeli Prime Minister Begin before the General Assembly, the invasion cannot be excused as a legitimate exercise of the right of self-defense recognized by article 51 of the Charter and accepted principles of customary international law concerning the use of force.

The PLO is likewise bound by the article 2(3) and 2(4) obligations, and the Lebanese government must not allow its territory to be used in a manner violative of international law. Nevertheless, the PLO cannot be held legally responsible for every act of violence perpetrated against Israel that occurs anywhere in the world, but only to the extent that the Israeli government can produce clear and convincing evidence of specific actions sanctioned by the PLO. The evidentiary record establishes that during the preceding year, the PLO has in good faith adhered to the terms of the cease-fire applicable to the Lebanese-Israeli border that had been successfully negotiated last summer by President Reagan's special envoy for the crisis. Consequently, the PLO has not launched any "armed attack" upon Israel as required by article 51 before the latter can resort to the use of force to defend itself. It is Israel that has "attacked" Lebanon and the PLO in violation of its international legal obligations.

Even assuming the contemporary international legal order still recognizes the regressive doctrine of pre-emptive self-defense, the Israeli invasion of Lebanon fails to meet that test as well. As definitively stated by U.S. Secretary of State Daniel Webster in the case of *The*

Caroline, the "necessity of that self-defence [must be] instant, overwhelming, and leaving no choice of means, and no moment for deliberation". Furthermore, Israel cannot invoke the antiquated doctrines of intervention, protection and self-help to justify the invasion, because these were soundly repudiated by a decision of the International Court of Justice in the *Corfu Channel Case* (1949) as totally incompatible with the proper conduct of international relations in the post–World War II era.

Three seminal U.N. General Assembly resolutions have firmly established the fundamental proposition that non-consensual military intervention by one state into the territorial domain of another state is prohibited for any reason whatsoever: The Declaration on the Inadmissibility of Intervention (1965); The Declaration on Principles of International Law concerning Friendly Relations and Cooperation among States in accordance with the Charter of the United Nations (1970); and the Definition of Aggression (1974). At least the Arab Deterrent Force, composed primarily of Syrian troops, had been stationed in Lebanon with the consent of the Lebanese government and conducted its peacekeeping operations with the approval of the League of Arab States, which is the appropriate regional arrangement under Chapter 8 of the U.N. Charter for sanctioning such activities.

Finally, the Israeli invasion of Lebanon has violated the basic principle of customary international law dictating proportionality in the use of force, applicable to even a legitimate exercise of the right to self-defense. The massive scale of death, destruction, dislocations and suffering inflicted by the Israeli army in Lebanon is egregiously disproportionate to any harm that has been perpetrated upon Israel or to any serious threat to its legitimate national security interests posed by the presence of the PLO in Lebanon.

The four Geneva Conventions of 1949 apply in their entirety to the conduct of hostilities by Israel in Lebanon. Additional Protocol I (1977) indicates that the members of the PLO who have been captured by the Israeli army should be treated as prisoners of war within the meaning of the Geneva Accords. At the very minimum, captured members of the PLO and other individuals affiliated with them together with all Lebanese and Palestinian civilians, are entitled to the full panoply of protections set forth in the Fourth Geneva Convention and the customary international law of belligerent occupation. Statements by the Israeli government that captured PLO members will be treated as "terrorists" and thus presumably deprived of their protected status under the Geneva Conventions would, if acted upon, constitute a grave violation of the humanitarian laws of armed conflict that have been universally accepted by all civilized states.

As a party to the Geneva Conventions of 1949 the United States government has an obligation to respect and to ensure respect for their observance by all other contracting powers. This obligation becomes irresistibly compelling in a situation where Israel has been enabled to invade Lebanon by means of weapons, munitions and supplies provided primarily by the United States government at concessionary rates. To the extent the US government does not prevent Israel from using American weapons in explicit violation of international law and of U.S. domestic statutes applicable to arms transfer agreements, it must assume full legal responsibility before the international community for such proscribed activities committed by Israel in Lebanon. Under the circumstances the United States has an absolute duty to employ the tremendous leverage over Israel afforded by its arms supply relationship in order to secure the latter's strict obedience to the laws of war and its immediate and unconditional withdrawal from Lebanon as required by U.N. Security Council Resolution 508 (1982) and Resolution 509 (1982), which are legally binding on Israel under Charter article 25.

The Israeli government has no right under international law to intervene in the domestic affairs of Lebanon by dictating the terms of some future government as a condition for the withdrawal of its troops. The future of the Lebanese government must be determined by the Lebanese people without interference or compulsion from any external source. The most effective means to ensure the success of this endeavor is for Israel immediately to withdraw its troops from Lebanon and to turn over evacuated territory to the Lebanese army, where possible, or to the United Nations Interim Force in Lebanon (UNIFIL). The ultimate disposition of the Arab Deterrent Force should be determined by the League of Arab States in accordance with the wishes of the Lebanese government expressed after an Israeli military withdrawal.

The United States must actively oppose any proposals by the Israeli government to establish some type of international police force in Lebanon that is not under the jurisdiction of the United Nations Security Council. Israeli charges that UNIFIL cannot be trusted because the U.N. is biased against Israel obfuscate the fact that UNIFIL operates under the auspices of the Security Council (where the United States can, if necessary exercise a veto power) not under the General Assembly. The evidentiary record clearly establishes that UNIFIL has proven to be quite effective at preventing the large-scale infiltration of PLO fighters across the Israeli-Lebanese border. A renewed and strengthened mandate for UNIFIL will continue to perform this task until the Lebanese army is reconstituted as an effective and independent military force under the control of the central government. In this regard Israel must also dismantle the Lebanese Christian enclave it has created along the border, whose members have so far illegally resisted the interposition of UNIFIL troops with the collusion of the Israeli government.

A long-term solution to the problems of Lebanon can only be found when Israel is willing to recognize the international legal right of the Palestinian people to self-determination. Neither Egypt, Israel, the United States, nor Jordan have any right under international law to negotiate on behalf of the Palestinian people. Both the U.N. General Assembly and the League of Arab States have determined that the PLO is the legitimate representative of the Palestinian people. That determination must be respected by Israel and the United States for the purpose of negotiating an overall settlement on the ultimate disposition of the West Bank, the Gaza Strip and East Jerusalem. Mutual and simultaneous recognition of their respective rights under international law by Israel and the PLO must be the next stage in the development of the Middle East peace process.

Francis A. Boyle (University of Illinois), Richard A. Falk (Princeton University), C. Clyde Ferguson, Jr. (Harvard Law School), Roger Fisher (Harvard Law School), Stanley Hoffmann (Harvard University), W. Thomas Mallison (George Washington University).

4. The Lawyers' Committee on Nuclear Policy, *Statement on the Illegality of Nuclear Weapons.*

Humanity has entered a critical period in its history as a species. Today's nuclear arsenals have the potential for annihilating a large segment of the world's populations, for devasting and contaminating vast areas of the earth's surface, and for producing unpredictable and uncontrollable biological and environmental consequences. In short, nuclear weapons threaten human survival itself.

Yet, the use of nuclear weapons once considered unthinkable is increasingly being contemplated by U.S. policy-makers. In fact, with Presidential Directive 59, the United States has officially adopted a counterforce strategy that envisions the use (including the first use) of nuclear weapons in a variety of conventional as well as nuclear settings. This shift in nuclear strategy is all the more troubling given the Reagan administration's position that the United States must be prepared to intervene, using nuclear capabilities if necessary, to protect U.S. interests wherever threatened. Thus there has developed in U.S. official policy a dangerous acceptance of the legitimacy and efficacy of using nuclear weapons to reverse international situations considered adverse to U.S. national interests.

Rather than preserving international peace as claimed, this nuclear strategy is likely to bring us closer to nuclear war. The insistence on a limited nuclear war option increases dramatically the prospect that nuclear weapons will be used in a crisis situation. Furthermore, the notion that the use of nuclear weapons can be kept from escalating into an all-out nuclear exchange is, as many experts have argued, highly questionable. Consequently, we believe there is a growing spectre of nuclear war, which requires us to undertake a fundamental rethinking of the status of nuclear weapons under international law.

The prevalent belief among the general public as well as policy-makers is that nuclear weapons are legal. This belief is based on the assumption that a state may do whatever it is not expressly forbidden from doing. The legality of nuclear weapons, however, cannot be judged solely by the existence or non-existence of a treaty rule specifically prohibiting or restricting their use. Any reasonable legal analysis must take into account all the recognized sources of international law—international treaties, international custom, general principles of law, judicial decisions and the writings of the most qualified publicists. Of particular relevance to the legality of nuclear weapons are the many treaties and conventions which limit the use of any weapons in war, the traditional distinction between combatant and non-combatant, and the principles of humanity including the prohibition of weapons and tactics that are especially cruel and cause unnecessary suffering. A review of these basic principles supports a conclusion that the threat and use of nuclear weapons is illegal under international law.

A basic source of the laws of war are the Hague Conventions of 1907, particularly the Regulations embodied in Hague Convention IV. The United States Air Force, in its most recent official publication (1976) on international law and armed conflict, states that these Regulations "…remain the foundation stones of the modern law of armed conflict." A fundamental tenet of these Regulations is the prohibition of wanton or indiscriminate destruction. The Regulations forbid, for example, "the attack or bombardment, by whatever means, of towns, villages, (and even individual) dwellings or buildings which are undefended."

The universally accepted Geneva Conventions of 1949 updated and greatly strengthened the 1907 Regulations. In particular, the Convention on "the Protection of Civilian Persons in Time of War" imposes additional detailed obligations on all belligerents to ensure the essential requirements for the health, safety and sustenance of the civilian population. A primary objective of these Conventions is to assure that "disinterested (outside) aid (can be) given without discrimination to all victims of war including members of the armed forces who on account of their wounds, capture or shipwreck cease to be enemies but become suffering and helpless human beings." The use of nuclear weapons of any type would inevitably result in massive violations of both the 1907 and 1949 rules.

Furthermore, restraints on the conduct of hostilities are traditionally not limited to those given explicit voice in specific treaty stipulations. Aware of the continuous evolution of war technology, the 1907 Hague Regulations contain a general yardstick intended exactly for situations where no specific treaty rule exists to prohibit a new type of weapon or tactic. In such cases, "the inhabitants and the belligerents remain under the protection and the rule of the principles of the laws of nations, as they result from the usages established among civilized peoples, from the laws of humanity, and the dictates of public conscience." In short, this general rule, known as the Martens Clause, makes civilized usages, the demands of humanity, and the dictates of public conscience obligatory by themselves—without the formulation of a treaty specifically prohibiting a new weapon. Any specific Convention solemnly prohibiting a specific new weapon or tactic, of course, would serve to reconfirm and strengthen the existing body of law.

Historically, the principles of humanity have been one of the primary sources of law limiting the violence permissible in war. Ever since the Declaration of St. Petersburg of 1868, the principles of humanity have been asserted as a constraint upon military necessity. The Declaration embodies what may be the twin ground rules of the laws of war: that "the right to adopt means of injuring the enemy is not unlimited" and that "the only legitimate object which States should endeavor to accomplish during a war is to weaken the military forces of the enemy."

The protection of civilians and neutral countries flows logically from the elementary distinction between combatant and non-combatant. The commitment to protect civilians and neutral countries also implied that weapons must be used selectively, and only against military targets. As stated by the International Red Cross Committee in its commentary on the 1949 Geneva Conventions, "the civilian population can never be regarded as a military objective. That truth is the very basis of the whole law of war." Without differentiating between military and nonmilitary targets, the fundamental distinction between combatant and non-combatant becomes meaningless.

It is clear that the use of nuclear weapons in populated areas would result in the indiscriminate and massive slaughter of civilians. Moreover, even if nuclear weapons were used only against an enemy's strategic nuclear forces, the annihilation and extermination of the civilian population of the enemy would be an inevitable by-product. As the experiences of Hiroshima and Nagasaki amply demonstrate, the effects of nuclear weapons because of their very awesome nature cannot be limited to military targets.

The 1949 Geneva Conventions were adopted four years after the advent of the "nuclear age." It would therefore be illogical to assume that their provisions are not applicable to nuclear weapons from their provisions. Nor did any nuclear-weapons state or any of the 130-odd other states that ratified or acceded to the Geneva Conventions make any reservation to such effect. However, it would be impossible under conditions of nuclear warfare to carry out the obligations of the Geneva Conventions, just as it would also be impossible to live up to the universally binding rules of the Hague Conventions of 1907, all of which aim at preserving the minimum requirements for the continued survivability and viability of all societies involved in armed conflict. Hence, the use of nuclear weapons would inevitably result in the commission of war crimes on an enormous scale. This fact alone is sufficient to prohibit the use of nuclear weapons.

The use of nuclear weapons would also result, directly or indirectly, in the indiscriminate destruction of people of a particular nationality. If, for example, the stated objective were the destruction of a nation-state, then the threat or use of nuclear weapons toward this end would violate at least the spirit of the Genocide Convention of 1948 - which made the destruction of groups on racial, religious, or nationality grounds an international crime. To assume the legality of a weapon with the distinct capability to terrorize and to destroy an entire civilian population would make meaningless the entire effort to limit combat through the laws of war. As fragile as the laws of war may be, they must be supported, especially in the present setting where the risks to human survival are so great.

One of the most important law-making treaties, the United Nations Charter, establishes a legal duty for all states to refrain from the threat or use of force in their international relations except in self-defense or under the authority of the United Nations. Furthermore, the principle that a war of aggression warrants the highest degree of international opprobrium, namely, to be branded as an international crime, was affirmed by the Nuremberg Tribunals. These two principals have so often been unanimously reaffirmed by the General Assembly as to have become undisputed axioms of international law.

On the basis of these unquestioned principles of international law, the United Nations has repeatedly condemned the use of nuclear weapons as an "international crime." On November 24, 1961, for example, the General Assembly declared in Resolution 1653 (XVI) that "any State using nuclear or thermonuclear weapons is to be considered as violating the Charter of the United Nations, as acting contrary to the law of humanity, and as committing a crime against mankind and civilization." In Resolution 33/71-B of December 14, 1978, and in Resolution 35/152-D of December 12, 1980, the General Assembly again declared that "the use of nuclear weapons would be a violation of the Charter of the United Nations and a crime against humanity." As evidenced by these actions of the General Assembly, a consensus has been clearly emerging that the use of nuclear weapons contradicts the fundamental humanitarian principles upon which the international law of war is founded.

Yet, there is an influential school of thought which would deny the applicability of the existing laws of war to nuclear warfare. This school asserts that in an era of "total war" even the most fundamental rules can be disregarded if this enhances the chances for victory. This argument was urged in another context by some of the Nuremberg defendants, and indignantly rejected by the International Tribunal. The Tribunal's judgment warns that this "nazi conception" of total war would destroy the validity of international law altogether. Ultimately, the legitimacy of such a view would exculpate Auschwitz.

In sum, if the goal of the laws of war - to set limits on permissible violence - is to be realized to any serious degree, and if the fundamental principles of humanity are to be of continuing relevance to their interpretation, then it must be concluded that any threat or use of nuclear weapons is illegal. Global "survivability" is so elemental that the prohibition can be reasonably inferred from the existing laws of war. To conclude differently would be to ignore the barbaric and nefarious character of the use of nuclear weapons. As the laws of war embody the minimum demands of decency, exempting nuclear weapons from the body of laws would be abandoning even this minimum standard.

The genetic and environmental effects resulting from the use of nuclear weapons, alone, provide a compelling moral and humanitarian argument against their legality. But, as indicated above this is not the only basis for concluding that the threat or use of nuclear weapons is illegal. The unnecessary and disproportionate suffering resulting from their use; the indiscriminate nature of their effects for civilians and combatants alike; the uncontrollable radioactive fallout they set off; and their similarity in terms of effects to poison, poison gas, or bacteriological weapons (all of which are prohibited by the Hague Convention of 1907 and the Geneva Gas Protocol of 1925)—each is a sufficient basis for concluding that the threat or use of nuclear weapons is prohibited under existing international law. When taken together, these arguments provide overwhelming support for the conclusion that any threat or use of nuclear weapons is contrary to the dictates of international law.

So too, these arguments provide a sound legal basis for delegitimating and criminalizing the manufacture, possession, and ownership of nuclear weapons. If a course of action is illegal, then the planning and preparation for such an action are, by legal and moral logic, also forbidden. Moreover, the attack on the legality of manufacturing and possessing nuclear weapons is all the more necessary given the increasing prospects for the "accidental" use of nuclear weapons arising out of today's dangerous first–strike strategies.

Our intention is not to score points in a battle of legal wits. What we wish to present to fellow lawyers, to governmental decision-makers, and to the public is the view that nuclear warfare would lead to results incompatible with fundamental rules of international law, elementary morality, and contrary to any rational conception of national interest and world order. In short, the very nature of nuclear warfare is destructive of all the values which law obligates us to preserve. While it is accurate to say that international law has not been as effective as it should have been in regulating state acts, international law is important to preserve our sense of humanity and to enhance the prospects for peace.

Reducing the likelihood of nuclear war must obviously, then, be the highest priority of our profession. To this end, the legal community needs to give its urgent attention to the study and implementation of the international law relating to nuclear weapons.*

5. Anderson & Verr, *Draft Brief on Behalf of the Washington Rabbis* (1986).

IN THE SUPERIOR COURT OF WASHINGTON,
DISTRICT OF COLUMBIA
CRIMINAL MISDEMEANOR DIVISION

UNITED STATES OF AMERICA,	)	
	)	
Plaintiff,	)	
	)	
v.	)	Consolidated Cr. Nos: M8185-8194-85
	)	

---

*For a more extensive discussion of the legal arguments presented in this statement, see Richard Falk, Lee Meyrowitz, Jack Sanderson, "Nuclear Weapons and International Law," Center of International Studies, Princeton University, World Order Studies Monograph, 1981 and John Fried, "First Use of Nuclear Weapons - Existing Prohibitions in International Law," *Bulletin of Peace Proposals*, January 1981, pp. 21-29.

NINE PROTESTERS AT THE
EMBASSY   )
   OF THE UNION OF SOVIET   )
   SOCIALIST REPUBLICS,   )
)
          Defendants.   )

DEFENDANTS' MEMORANDUM OF LAW
IN SUPPORT OF THEIR MOTION TO ALLOW THE
INTERNATIONAL LAW DEFENSE AT TRIAL

Now come the defendants, NINE PROTESTERS at the Embassy of the USSR, by their attorneys, who submit this Memorandum of Law in support of their pending Motion to Allow the International Law Defense at Trial, and respectfully advise the Court as follows:

I. OVERVIEW OF THE INTERNATIONAL LAW DEFENSE

Defendants posit the following points: 1.) International law is incorporated into domestic law; 2.) International law is informed by various treaties, conventions and other multi-national agreements, decisional domestic law, customary international relations and the learned treatises of international legal scholars; 3.) The Soviet regime is a systematic and persistent violator of international law; 4.) Defendants possessed a privilege, if not an obligation, to prevent serious human rights violations, which under the peculiar instant facts, serve as a complete defense to the charged ordinance infraction; and 5.) The necessity defense can be invoked along with, and attendant to, the international law defense.

II. STATEMENT OF FACTS

The following facts are undisputed. All of the instant defendants, whose cases have been consolidated for trial, were arrested by the District of Columbia Police Department on May 1, 1985, and charged with violating D.C. Code (1973), ch. 22, § 1115, to wit, "Interference with foreign diplomatic and consular offices, officers, and property." Defendants, all U.S. citizens, were peaceably protesting in front of the Soviet Embassy with various placards and signs. At no time did the protesters trespass or threaten to intrude on Embassy grounds, nor did they threaten or actually interfere with Soviet officials, Embassy visitors, or the conduct of ordinary diplomatic and consular business. Specifically, the defendants, sponsored by the Washington Board of Rabbis, were protesting certain official Soviet domestic policies which they strongly and sincerely believed violated the internationally recognized human rights of Soviet Jews not to be tortured or arbitrarily imprisoned, and to be allowed to worship, emigrate, freely associate, and maintain their cultural identities, inter alia. Also protested were various repressive acts by the Soviet government, such as racial discrimination, religious persecution, wrongful imprisonment, physical reprisal, etc., all in violation of international law. The defendants have invoked the international law defense to their criminal misdemeanor charges as a complete defense to said charges, and on that basis have asked this Court to dismiss said charges with prejudice, or in the alternative, to permit the introduction of this defense at trial.

III. INTERNATIONAL LAW IS INCORPORATED INTO GOVERNING DOMESTIC LAW

It is well-settled that international law must be accorded full force in domestic American courts. In the landmark case of *The Paquete Habana*, 175 U.S. 677, 700 (1900), the Court affirmed that,

> International law is part of our law, and must be ascertained and administered by the courts of justice of appropriate jurisdiction, as often as questions of right depending upon it are duly presented for their determination.

See also, The Neveide, 13 U.S. (Cranch) 388, 422 (1815).

The precept enunciated in *Paquete Habana*, that international law is embraced by local law, has been unswervingly followed. American courts have scrutinized the complaints of conduct of foreign sovereigns and individuals to determine whether they had engaged in violations of international law. *Letelier v. Republic of Chile*, 488 F.Supp. 665 (D.D.C. 1980) (foreign nation's acts found to be violative of international law); *Filartiga v. Pena-Irala*, 630 F.2d 876 (2d Cir. 1980) (alien defendant held liable for Paraguay torture-death in part on human rights violation under international law). Additionally, international law has been examined to determine the propriety of American actors' conduct. *Haitian Refugee Center v. Civiletti*, 503 F.Supp. 442 (S.D. Fla. 1980) (international law consulted to determine constitutional deprivation); *Lareau v. Manson*, 507 F.Supp. 1177 (D. Conn. 1980), *mod.*, 651 F.2d 96 (2d Cir. 1981) (international standards on prison conditions examined for constitutional claim); *Fernandez v. Wilkinson*, 505 F.Supp. 787 (D. Kan. 1980), *aff'd*, 654 F.2d 1382 (10th Cir. 1981) (U.S. prison conditions held to internationally recognized standards).

IV. SOURCES OF INTERNATIONAL LAW

Having demonstrated the authority of international law in American jurisdictions, the next step is ascertaining the sources for that law. In *U.S. v. Smith*, 18 U.S. (Wheat) 153, 160-61 (1820), the Court held that international law includes "the work of jurists, the general usage and practice of nations, and judicial decisions recognizing and enforcing international law." The Statute of the International Court of Justice, Art. 38, delineates the sources of international law in greater detail, as comprising international conventions, customs, general principles of law recognized by civilized nations, and judicial decisions and the teachings of the most highly qualified publicists of the various nations.

1. COVENANTS, DECLARATIONS AND TREATIES

An increasingly utilized international law source are treaties which are regarded as evidence of customary international law. The various United Nations agreements, covenants and declarations, formally signed and ratified, are equivalent to treaties.

> The concept that international custom constitutes a primary and most important means of creating norms of international law was certainly correct for the 19th century, but ... it no longer reflects the present day situation in international law. In contemporary conditions the principal means of creating norms of international law is a treaty.

Tunkin, *Co-Existence and International Law*, p.23 (1959).

Many treaties are not self-executing and this fact has caused no little confusion over the effect to be given such treaties in domestic courts. A self-executing treaty provides rights to individuals without the necessity of implementing legislation. The issue of the non-self-executing nature of some of the international treaties upon which defendants rely is immaterial to the instant controversy. The instant criminal defendants are not bringing any treaty-based claim or civil action, nor are they petitioning this court for any affirmative or equitable relief. The defendants merely seek to introduce evidence about customary international law and the Soviet government's flight from it in order to show the justification for their peaceful protests. The defendants' efforts are purely defensive. American courts routinely accept non-self-executing treaties for offensive evidentiary purposes. *Re Alien Children Education Litigation*, 501 F.Supp. 544, 591 (S.D. Tex. 1980).

The *Filartiga* court examined many treaties of a non-self-executory nature, including international agreements to which the United States was never a party, in order to ascertain customary international law as to state-sanctioned torture. The *Filartiga* court admitted as evidence of customary international law, the Universal Declaration of Human Rights, General Assembly Resolution No. 217(III)(A) (1948); the United Nations Charter (1945); the United Nations Declaration Against Torture, General Assembly Resolution No. 3452 (1975); the American Convention on Human Rights, Art. 5, *O.A.S. Treaty Series* No. 36 (1975); the International Covenant on Civil and Political Rights, General Assembly Resolution No. 2200 (1966); the European Convention for the Protection of Human Rights and Fundamental Freedoms, Art. 3, Council of Europe, *European Treaty Series* No. 5 (1968), etc. In short, the *Filartiga* court recognized that these treaties were valid evidence of customary international law.

Similarly, the *Haitian* court, at 510-32, reviewed international documents to determine refugee treatment standards. The *Lareau* and *Fernandez* courts also employed various international treaties and covenants to evaluate international standards of prisoner treatment, at 1187-93 and 795-98, respectively. The instant defendants, likewise, submit below many of those same treaties, but in the capacity of criminal defendants. Surely evidence which is permitted civil plaintiffs to assist the prosecution of their complaints ought to be available to a criminal defendant. Whether the United States signed or ratified any of the following treaties and covenants is of little moment since the key issue defendants raise is whether the Soviet Union adheres to customary international law based on treaties it had signed and ratified. Under these circumstances, a given treaty's American domestic status, or whether it is self-executing, is immaterial. On this point, the *Filartiga* court, at 882, n.9, stated:

> We observe that this Court has previously utilized the U.N. Charter and the Charter of the Organization of American States, another non-self-executing agreement, as evidence of binding principles of international law. (citations omitted)

2. INTERNATIONAL LAW SCHOLARS

Another source of international law which is to be considered are the treatises of international legal scholars. Learned works about international human rights are given added weight because of the limited decisional law pertaining to them. The writings of qualified legal scholars were cited as authoritative evidence about the customary international law of human rights throughout the *Filartiga* decision. The *Laveau* court approvingly cited the *Restatement of Foreign Relations Law of the U.S.* (1980), at 1187-89, n.9, and a host of international law scholars, at 1193, n.18, as did the *Fernandez* court, at 787, 795-98.

Since both the International Court of Justice and weighty American decisional law hold international legal scholars to be a key source of international law, expert testimony about international human rights law ought to be admitted. As the Supreme Court ruled in *The Paquete Habana*, at 700, evidence of what international law is may be obtained from:

> ... jurists and commentators, who by years of labor, research and experience, have made themselves peculiarly well acquainted with the subjects of which they treat. Such works are resorted to by judicial tribunals, not for the speculations of their authors concerning what the law ought to be, but for trustworthy evidence of what the [international] law really is ...

V. THE UNIVERSAL DECLARATION OF HUMAN RIGHTS: AN INTERNATIONAL TOUCHSTONE

The Universal Declaration of Human Rights has become the most important and widely accepted formulation of the basis of international human rights law, a point judicially recognized in *Filartiga*, at 883:

> Accordingly, it has been observed that the Universal Declaration of Human Rights "no longer fits into the dichotomy of 'binding treaty' against 'non-binding pronouncement,' but is rather an authoritative statement of the international community." (Citations omitted.) Thus, a Declaration creates an expectation of adherence, and "insofar as the expectation is gradually justified by State practice, a declaration may by custom become recognized as laying down rules binding upon the States" 34 U.N. ESCOR, Supp. (No.8) (1962). Indeed, several commentators have concluded that the Universal Declaration has become, in toto, a part of binding, customary international law. ... The (U.N.) General Assembly has declared that the Charter precepts embodied in this Universal Declaration 'constitute basic principles of international law.' G.A. Res. 2625(XXV) (1970).

Other internationally recognized provisions may be resorted to in order to define with precision what constitutes international human rights. For example, the human rights provisions contained in the United Nations Charter, have been found to be evidence of binding customary international law for United States courts. *U.S. v. Toscanino*, 500 F.2d 267 (2d Cir. 1974). Much earlier in *Oyamav. California*, 332 U.S. 663 (1947), four concurring Supreme Court justices indicated the significance of the U.N. Charter to domestic law.

In sum, American courts must give deference to binding international law. To fulfill this obligation in the instant context, the Court must evaluate actions and policies of the Soviet state complained of by the defendants against the backdrop of international law as determined by the case-law, treaties and agreements, generally accepted customs, and the works of qualified legal scholars.

VI. PERSISTENT AND SYSTEMATIC SOVIET VIOLATIONS OF INTERNATIONAL LAW

While the Soviet regime possesses a horrendous and harrowing record of human rights violations running back to its inception, space limitations preclude a detailed chronology of this history. The enormity of the excesses of the Bolshevik and Stalinist periods, in which tens of millions of Russians and other nationals were murdered, starved, forcibly relocated, and marched into slave labor camps, among other grim fates, has been well-documented. Notorious events and places such as the liquidations of the Kulaks, Lapps, Balts, Tartars, and Volga Germans; the induced Ukrainian Famine; the Katyn Massacre; the giant Arctic labor camp, Vorkuta; the dread Moscow prisons, Lefortovo and Lubiyanka; the extensive Gulag Archipelago, among many others, mark frightful crimes on a scale difficult for Americans to comprehend.

Soviet outrages against international law are not things of a dark past however. The Soviet Union, as a matter of state policy and official action, persists to this day in the systematic and brutal violation of the human rights of its own citizens, not to mention its millions of subjects in Soviet-occupied and controlled areas.

Soviet abuses have been roundly condemned throughout the world. For example, after extensive hearings and research, the European Parliament:

1. Condemns the systematic violation by the Soviet government of the civil, social, cultural and religious rights of the Soviet citizens;
2. Condemns the Soviet government's institutionalized discrimination against various national minorities and racial groups, in particular the Crimean Tartars and those of Polish, Jewish and German nationality;
3. Denounces detention in psychiatric hospitals ....;
4. Condemns the official penal regime ...;
6. Condemns the Soviet government's arbitrary interference with their citizens' privacy, family, home and correspondence, which contravenes Article 12 of the U.N. Universal Declaration on Human Rights and Article 17 of the International Covenant on Civil and Political Rights;
7. Condemns the Soviet government's refusal to grant their citizens freedom of movement and residence within their borders and the right to emigrate from the Soviet Union, as laid down by Article 13 of the UN (UDHR) ....

Resolution of May 17, 1983, "Human Rights in the Soviet Union," 4 *Hum. Rights L.J.*, p. 13, July, 1983.

High ranking American governmental officials regularly underscore the poor Soviet record for human rights, and denounce criminal violations of international law. *E.g.*, Statement of President Reagan, July 30, 1985, *Dept. of State Bull.*, Oct., 1985, p. 31-3.

The instant defendants, mostly Jews and some of them rabbis, took offense to the treatment many of their co-religionists receive in the U.S.S.R. While the defendants in no way wish to de-emphasize the terrible mistreatment accorded to many other oppressed groups and people within the U.S.S.R., for the purposes of the instant action, Soviet anti-Jewish policies will be highlighted. Official Soviet anti-Jewish misconduct includes, but is not limited to:

1. Torture and wrongful imprisonment for Jews whose only crime was the practice of their faith; application, pursuant to Soviet regulations, for emigration; or the teaching of the Hebrew language;
2. Wrongful confinement to psychiatric facilities for the above mentioned conduct;
3. Illegal prohibition of emigration from the U.S.S.R.;
4. Banning the teaching and study of the Hebrew language, and rabbinical training;
5. Separation of spouses via the aforementioned custody or through the sanction of internal exile;
6. Proscription of religious observance, to include the denial of Jewish marriage, circumcision, Bar Mitzvah ceremonies, as well as ordinary Sabbath and holiday services;
7. Discrimination and removal from employment, professional licensure, and housing;
8. Widespread dissemination by the state-controlled media of false and defamatory information about Jews in an overt attempt to whip up popular anti-Jewish sentiment;
9. Withholdance of state-controlled medical and dental care to those in need;
10. Denial of advanced academic training to qualified Jewish personnel on the sole basis of their creed;
11. Prohibition of association and assembly of Jews for the purpose of maintaining their cultural and social traditions.
12. Imposition of fines or severe punishment for protesting or attempting to ameliorate the foregoing state actions.

[See attached exhibits.]

VII. SPECIFIC INTERNATIONAL AGREEMENTS BREACHED

The foregoing actions by the Soviet government manifestly violate various human rights in contravention of standing international law. A considerable corpus of international law, embodied in written conventions and agreements, specifically condemns such governmental maltreatment:

A. The Universal Declaration of Human Rights, United Nations General Assembly Resolution No. 217(III) (1948). This declaration, for which incidentally the U.S.S.R., and its alter ego U.N. Member "states" Byelorussian S.S.R. and Ukrainian S.S.R. voted approval, expressly prohibits deprivations of such basic rights as freedom of movement (art. 13(1)), non-interference with the family unit (art. 12), and liberty (art. 3), on the basis of "religion" or "national origin" (art. 2). The Soviet media broadcast and print attacks on Jews that also violate the Declaration's article 7, which prohibits "any discrimination in violation of this Declaration and against any incitement to such discrimination." The U.S.S.R.'s utter refusal to permit voluntary emigration violates article 13(2) which guarantees that right, as well as article 14, which affirms the right of asylum from persecution. Article 18 mandates freedom of religion to include "teaching, practice, worship and observance." Article 5 prohibits "torture" and "cruel, inhuman or degrading treatment," while article 9 bans "arbitrary arrest, detention or exile." All of these rights have been persistently violated for many Jews in the U.S.S.R.

B. The International Covenant on Civil and Political Rights, General Assembly Resolution No. 2200A(XXI) (1966), to which the U.S.S.R. is a signatory is another internationally recognized human rights document. This Covenant holds that individuals have the right to freely pursue their "social and cultural development", (I)(1), cannot be discriminated against solely on religious grounds, (II)(4), and cannot be subject to torture or other degrading punishment, (III) (7), among other safeguards trampled in fact by the Soviet government. Under this agreement, Soviet citizens are "free to leave" the USSR, (III)(12), possess freedom to worship, (III)(19), and, if they are an ethnic or religious minority, they have the right to "enjoy their own culture, to profess and practice their own religion, or to use their own language", (III)(28). Furthermore, under this Covenant, advocacy of "national, racial or religious hatred that constitutes incitement to discrimination, hostility or violence shall be prohibited by law," (III)(20). All of the foregoing provisions have been violated with regard to tens of thousands of Jews.

C. The United Nations Charter (1945), which the U.S.S.R. also signed, calls for "respect for human rights and for fundamental freedoms for all without distinction as to race, sex, language or religion," (I)(3). The Soviet Union also "pledged" to achieve that goal, (IX)(55-6). That pledge has been broken.

D. The International Covenant on Economic, Social and Cultural Rights, General Assembly Resolution No. 2200(A) (1966), signed by the U.S.S.R., recognizes that "All peoples have the right of self-determination." "By virtue of that right they freely determine their political status and freely pursue their economic, social and cultural development," (I)(1). Religious discrimination is prohibited, (II)(2), and the "right" to "take part in cultural life" is affirmed, (III)(15). The best available medical attention is guaranteed, (III)(12). In this Covenant, the U.S.S.R. also promised to make higher education equally accessible to its citizens, (III)(13), and expressly "recognized" that conditions fostering all citizens' enjoyment of "economic, social and cultural rights," must be maintained. (Preamble).

E. The International Convention on the Elimination of All Forms of Racial Discrimination, 660 *U.N.T.S.* 195 (1966), which the Soviet Union duly signed, requires signatories to condemn and renounce racial discrimination which is defined as "any distinction, exclusion, restriction, or preference" premised on, inter alia, "national or ethnic origin," and to take affirmative measures to combat and eliminate this ill, (I)(1)(2). The Convention also prohibits signatories from engaging in any propaganda which incites, encourages or promotes discrimination, (I)(4). This Convention also guarantees the right to emigrate, free domestic travel, to associate, and to obtain proper medical care, (I)(5), and is routinely violated.

F. The Final Act of the Conference on Security and Cooperation in Europe (1975), the so-called Helsinki Accord, signed by the Soviet Union, requires party states to "respect human rights and fundamental freedoms, including freedom of … religion or belief, for all …," (Basket VI). Moreover, the Accord mandated of all signatories that:

> In the field of human rights and fundamental freedoms, the partic-

ipating States will act in conformity with the purposes and principles of the Charter of the United Nations and with the Universal Declaration of Human Rights *supra*. They will also fulfill their obligations as set forth in the international declarations and agreements in this field, including inter alia the International Covenants on Human Rights, by which they may be bound.

VIII. DEFENDANTS' HELD PRIVILEGES, IF NOT DUTIES, TO PREVENT GRAVE HUMAN RIGHTS ABUSES, WHICH JUSTIFY THEIR MINOR OFFENSES

Defendants possess an affirmative duty, or at least a privilege, to act in order to prevent bona fide breaches of international law. As such, the acts committed by the defendants are justified under international law.

Since international law is incorporated into domestic law, and, secondly, given the fact of the ongoing and serious Soviet breaches of international law, the third and final leg of the international law defense is ready for elaboration, namely that on the basis of the foregoing two truths the instant defendants possessed a privilege, if not an outright duty to attempt to prevent violations of international law.

The Universal Declaration of Human Rights (UDHR) is the chief exponent of customary international law with regard to fundamental human rights. Key language in the Declaration's Preamble bears close scrutiny here:

> The General Assembly proclaims this Universal Declaration of Human Rights as a common standard of achievement for all peoples and all nations, *to the end that every individual* and every organ of society, *keeping this Declaration constantly in mind, shall strive by teaching and education to promote respect for these rights and freedoms and by progressive measures, national and international, to secure their universal and effective recognition and observance, both among the peoples of Member States themselves and among the peoples of territories under their jurisdiction.* (Emphasis added.)

This court is obligated to follow valid international law, and as such, the nonviolent defendant protestors' privilege, if not duty, under the UDHR, to effect adherence by the Soviet Union to the UDHR's precepts should be recognized. The UDHR creates an obligation or elective right to act in a progressive manner to promote compliance with the UDHR. The defendants were merely taking up that labor on behalf of their persecuted co-religionists in Russia. Their protests were intended to educate people about the egregious human rights abuses in the U.S.S.R., as well as hopefully effect positive change in the U.S.S.R. itself by dramatizing the violations. These orderly defendants' "crime" was to take international law seriously, and peacefully picket on public property, perhaps within 500 feet of the Soviet Embassy. For their efforts in highlighting religious persecution, imprisonment and discrimination in a distant land, they stand on trial. Their nonviolent civil resistance was directed half a world away, and was truly the only effective means to draw attention to the plight of their persecuted brethren. The defendants believed their protest would help correct the Soviet human rights violations by carrying out the hortatory instructions of the UDHR. As such these defendants deserve to be protected by that customary international law.

Since customary international law is part of American domestic law, the District ordinance the defendants have been charged with violating ought to be harmonized with international law. Since the defendants were acting in accord with international law, as embodied in the leading international pronouncement on human rights, the UDHR, the 500 foot zone of silence commanded by the District Code ought not frustrate that higher end. Had defendants been actual interlopers, noisy, abusive, protesting matters unrelated to international law, insincere, or unable to demonstrate genuine international law abuses, then they would not be clothed with a suitable excuse to break the municipal ordinance. The defendants had engaged in precisely the sort of protest which is protected by international law from prosecution by the District. The allowance of the international law defense in this special case throws open no door to unrestricted protesting in Washington. The defendants' manner and focus of constructive dissent is to be encouraged, not punished on the whim of the very object of their protest. On a small scale, but quite ironically, the instant situation affords the Soviet government the chance to punish protesters it disapproves of in the Capital, much as it would in Moscow.

Additionally, the defendants invoke the Nuremberg Charter which requires individuals to act in order to prevent the commission of crimes recognized under international law. Justice R.K. Jackson, 6 F.R.D. 69, 100 (1946); 22 *Trial, supra*, 411, 466 (1948). Defendants contend under this Charter that they had a duty to act reasonably to attempt to prevent the Soviet Union from its ongoing course of violating human rights.

IX. NECESSITY DEFENSE RESULTING FROM INTERNATIONAL LAW

The necessity defense, under the instant circumstances, can be raised along with, and attendant to, the international law defense. Assuming arguendo that the defendants did penetrate the invisible 500 foot restricted zone surrounding the Soviet Embassy, they were justified in doing so by the necessity of focusing international public attention on the Soviet pattern of human rights violations. Since the Soviet human rights abuses greatly transcend the public injury, if any, of breaking the 500 foot magic circle surrounding the Embassy, and since the defendants certainly had no hand in the violations they protested, the elements required for the necessity defense are met. *Cf., U.S. v. Bailey*, 585 F.2d 1087 (C.A.D.C. 1978); *cert. granted,* 99 S.Ct. 1497 (1979); *cert. denied,* 99 S.Ct. 1509 (1979).

1. ELEMENTS OF THE NECESSITY DEFENSE

The first element, clean hands, is easily satisfied since the defendants were never responsible for the violations they protested. Secondly, they sincerely believed that terrible human rights violations were continuing apace in the U.S.S.R., and also that their actions in coming within 500 feet of the Soviet Embassy caused less harm than the underlying violations in the U.S.S.R. They also believed their actions were necessary to halt the Soviet violations:

> As rabbis we are trained to hold the law in high regard. As Americans we appreciate most deeply the blessings of freedom. The decision to demonstrate in front of the Soviet Embassy, knowingly breaking the law, was not a decision easily reached. It came only

after extreme Soviet provocation required of us a demonstrable reaction.

An additional element of the defense was met because the defendants possessed no reasonable legal alternative to picketing the Embassy. It would be unreasonable to expect them to fly to the U.S.S.R. to lodge their protests—such a move would only endanger them given the very human rights violations the U.S.S.R. was repudiating. Their efforts at letter writing had proved totally unavailing. Finally there is no existing law which precludes the use of the necessity defense in these cases. The U.S. government has already gone on record castigating human rights violations as illegal under international law. *E.g.*, Ambassador Schifter's Statement before the U.S. Subcommittee on European Affairs of the Senate Foreign Relations Committee, Nov. 14, 1985, *Dept. of State Bull.*, Jan. 1986, p. 64. In *U.S. v. May*, 662 F.2d 1000 (9th Cir. 1980), *cert. denied*, 449 U.S. 984 (1980), defendant protesters were allowed to fully develop their necessity defenses. These protesters were opposing U.S. military policies. The instant defendants, however, are opposed to certain Soviet practices, a position *supported* by the U.S. government.

Wherefore, defendants pray that they be allowed to present at trial a defense based on principles of international law, and further that the testimony of an expert witness on international law be allowed at trial.

> Respectfully submitted,
> 132 Washington Board of Rabbis, Defendants
> By their Attorneys:
> Kimberly M. Anderson
> University of Illinois College of Law Class of 1987
> Steven Robert Verr
> University of Illinois College of Law Class of 1986
> To: Professor Francis A. Boyle
>   Final Examination
>   International Human Rights Law
>   May 21, 1986

BIBLIOGRAPHY

Recent Publications by Associates of the Lawyers' Committee on Nuclear Policy

(some reprints available upon request)

Treatises and Books

Falk, Richard A., *The End of World Order;* New York, Holmes and Meier: 1983.

Falk, Richard A. and Robert J. Lifton, *Indefensible Weapons;* New York, Basic Books: 1983.

Feinrider, Martin A. and Arthur S. Miller, *Nuclear Weapons and Law;* Westport, Connecticut, Greenwood Press: 1984.

Roling, Bert V. A., *The Impact of Nuclear Weapons on International Relations and International Law;* Netherlands, Publication of The Polemological Institute of Groeningen: 1982.

Weston, Burns H., ed., *Toward Nuclear Disarmament and Global Security: A Search for Alternatives;* Boulder, Colorado, Westview Press: 1984.

Law Review, Policy Journal and Newspaper Op-ed Articles

International Law

Daniel J. Arbess, "The International Law of Armed Conflict in Light of Contemporary Deterrence Strategies: Empty Promise or Meaningful Restraint?" (1984), 30 *McGill Law Journal* 90.

Daniel J. Arbess, "International Law Revisited: Meeting the Legal Challenge of Nuclear Weapons" (1985), 16 *Bulletin of Peace Proposals,* 105 (Norway).

Richard Bilder, "Distinguishing Human Rights and Humanitarian

Law: The Issue of Nuclear Weapons" (1982), 31 *American University
Law Review* 959.

Richard Bilder, "Nuclear Weapons and International Law" in Feinrider and Miller, *Nuclear Weapons and the Law* (1984), op. cit.

Francis A. Boyle, "Nuclear Weapons and International Law: The
Arms Control Dimension" (1983), 4 *New York Law School Journal
of International and Comparative Law* 257.

Anthony D'Amato, "The Purposive Dimension of International Law"
(1983), 9 *Brooklyn Journal of International Law* 311.

Richard A. Falk, Elliott L. Meyrowitz and Jack Sanderson, "Nuclear
Weapons and International Law" (1981), Occasional Paper No. 10,
Center for International Studies, Princeton University 80 *Journal of
International Law and Diplomacy* (Japan: 1982); 20 *Indian Journal
of International Law* 541 (1981).

Richard A. Falk, "Fulfilling the Nuremberg Obligation" (interview)
(1983), 2 *Ground Zero* 2.

Richard A. Falk, "Is Nuclear Policy A War Crime?" (1983), 11 *Human
Rights* 18.

Richard A. Falk, "The Spirit of Thoreau in the Nuclear Age" (1983),
14 *Forum for Correspondence and Contact* 83, revised and retitled
as "The Spirit of Thoreau in the Age of Trident" *AGNI,* forthcoming.

Richard A. Falk, "Toward a Legal Regime for Nuclear Weapons"
(1983), 28 *McGill Law Journal* 519.

Richard A. Falk, "The Quest for World Order: The Legacy of Opti-
mism Re-Examined" (1984), 9 *Dalhousie Law Journal* 132.

Richard A. Falk, "Environmental Disruption by Military Means and
International Law" in Arthur H. Westing, ed., *Environmental War-
fare: A Technical, Legal and Policy Appraisal,* SIPRI Publications,
London and Philadelphia, Taylor and Francis: 1984.

Martin Feinrider, "International Law v. Nuclear Weapons," *The
Miami Herald,* January 29, 1983.

John H. E. Fried, "The Positive Messages of 'Nuremberg' for the
Nuclear Age," *Proceedings of the XIth World Congress of the International Political Science Association,* Moscow, 1979, 17 pp.

John H. E. Fried, "First Use of Nuclear Weapons: Existing Prohibitions
in International Law" (1981), 12 *Bulletin of Peace Proposals* 21
(Norway).

John H. E. Fried, "International Law Prohibits the First Use of Nuclear
Weapons" (1982) 1 *Revue Belge de Droit International* 33.

John H. E. Fried, "Law and Nuclear War," *Bulletin of the Atomic Scientists,* June - July, 1982, reprinted No. 443 of *Promoting Enduring Peace,* 2pp.

John H. E. Fried, "Would a First Use of Nuclear Weapons be Permissible under Existing International Law?," *Proceedings of the XIIth World Congress of the International Political Science Association,* Rio de Janeiro, 1982, 20pp mimeo.

John H. E. Fried, "The Preparations for Nuclear War in the Light of International Law" *Proceedings of the International Nuremberg Tribunal Against First Strike and Mass Destruction Weapons in East and West,"* February 1983, 18pp mimeo.

Peter Goldberger, "Defenses that Keep Issues at the Fore," *Guild Notes,* November, 1983.

Saul Mendlovitz, "Filing Out the Right to Peace: A Basic Change in the Nation-State System" (1983), 4 *New York Law School Journal of International and Comparative Law* 419.

Elliott L. Meyrowitz, "The Status of Nuclear Weapons Under International Law" (1981), 38 *National Lawyers Guild Practitioner.*

Elliott L. Meyrowitz, "The Laws of War and Nuclear Weapons" (1982), *Proceedings of the American Society of International Law.*

Elliott L. Meyrowitz, "Nuclear Weapons Policy: The Ultimate Tyranny" (1983), 7 *Nova Law Journal* 93.

Elliott L. Meyrowitz, The Laws of War and Nuclear Weapons" (1983), 9 *Brooklyn Journal of International Law* 23.

Elliott L. Meyrowitz, "Are Nuclear Weapons Legal?" *Bulletin of the Atomic Scientists,* October, 1983.

Elliott L. Meyrowitz, "Nuclear Weapons are Illegal Threats," *Bulletin of the Atomic Scientists,* May 1985.

Jeffrey M. Kaplan, "First Strike Nuclear Weapons Violate International Law," *St. Petersburg Times,* August 15, 1983.

Jeffrey M. Kaplan, "Nuclear Attack: The Ultimate War Crime," *Newsday,* July 26, 1984.

James Munvies, "Nuclear Arms, the Law and You," *Nuclear Times,* April, 1983.

Ved P. Nanda, "Nuclear Weapons and the Right to Peace Under International Law" (1983), 9 *Brooklyn Journal of International Law* 283.

Bert V. A. Roling, "International Law, Nuclear Weapons, Arms Control and Disarmament" in Feinrider and Miller, *Nuclear Weapons and Law* (1984), op. cit.

Allan Rosas, "International Law and the Use of Nuclear Weapons," in *Essays in Honor of Erik Castren,* the Finnish Branch of the International Law Association, no. 2, 1979.

Burns H. Weston, "Nuclear Weapons Versus International Law: A Contextual Reassessment" (1983), 28 *McGill Law Journal* 542. Reprinted: U.S. Department of Defense, *Current News* (No. 1094), Special Edition: January 4, 1984.

Burns H. Weston, "Nuclear Weapons and International Law: Prolegomenon to General Illegality" (1983), 4 *New York Law School Journal of International and Comparative Law* 227.

Burns H. Weston, "Nuclear Weapons and International Law: Illegality in Context" (1983), *Denver Journal of International Law and Policy.*

Constitutional Law and Democracy

Mark C. Cogan, "Portland Should Support the Nuclear Free Zone Plan," *The Oregonian,* November 28, 1984.

Richard A. Falk, "A Response: Waging the Struggle Against Nuclearism" (1984), 1 *Religion and Intellectual Life,* 56.

Richard A. Falk, "Leaders Need Restraint of International Law," *Seattle Post Intelligencer,* August 22, 1982.

Richard A. Falk, "The Spirit of Thoreau in the Nuclear Age," *The Boston Globe,* August 4, 1983.

Richard A. Falk, "Nuclear Weapons and the End of Democracy" (1982), 2 *Praxis International* 1; also published in modified form in 4 *Gandhi Marg* 196 (1983); 5 *Harvard International Review* 21 (1983).

Richard A. Falk, "Nuclear Weapons and the Renewal of Democracy" in Lee and Cohen, eds., *Nuclear Weapons and the Future of Humanity,* Roman and Allenheld, 1984.

Martin Feinrider, "International Law as the Law of the Land: Another Constitutional Constraint on the Use of Nuclear Weapons" (1982), 7 *Nova Law Journal* 103.

Jeffrey M. Kaplan, "If Deterrence Doesn't Stop Crime, Will it Stop Bombs?" *The Des Moines Register,* April 19, 1984.

Jeffrey M. Kaplan and Daniel J. Arbess, "Not the President Alone"

(Presidential First Use is Unlawful), *St. Louis Post-Dispatch*, November 20, 1984.

Arthur S. Miller, "Nuclear First Use," *The Miami Herald,* August 12, 1984.

Arthur S. Miller, "The Constitution and Nuclear Weapons," *Bulletin of the Atomic Scientists,* June, 1982.

Arthur S. Miller, "Law, the Constitution and Nuclear War," *The Miami Herald,* June 20, 1982.

Arthur S. Miller, "Nuclear Weapons and Constitutional Law" (1982), 7 *Nova Law Journal* 21.

Claire Sherman Thomas, "U.S. Deliberately Plans First Use of Nuclear Weapons," *The Journal American,* September 8, 1984.

Claire Sherman Thomas, "What Does Weinberger Mean By 'First Strike?'," *The Journal American,* February 15, 1985.

Peter Weiss, "Nuclear War in the Courts," in Abdul Paliwala, ed., *Nuclear Weapons, the Peace Movement and the Law,* forthcoming.

Environmental Law

Simeon A. Sahaydachny, "New York Challenges Homeporting," *Blind Justice,* April, 1984.

Simeon A. Sahaydachny, "Harboring Nuclear Weapons: The USS Iowa Comes to New York Harbor," New York Public Interest Research Group Agenda for Citizen Involvement, November/December, 1984.

Arms Control

Daniel J. Arbess and William Epstein, "Disarmament Role for the United Nations?" *Bulletin of the Atomic Scientists,* May, 1985.

Daniel J. Arbess and William Epstein, "Stand Against Star Wars Could be a Beacon for Others," *The Globe and Mail,* (Toronto), Tuesday, April 9, 1985.

Francis A. Boyle, "Star Wars vs. International Law: The Force Will be Against Us," *ACDIS Bulletin,* Volume V/Number 6, May, 1985.

William Epstein, "A Periled Nuclear Pact," *The New York Times,* July 7, 1985.

Martin Feinrider, "Star Wars and International Law," *Proceedings of the American Society of International Law,* forthcoming.

Allan Rosas, "Comments on a Draft Declaration," in Lodgaard, Sverre, and Thee, Marek, eds., *Nuclear Disengagement in Europe,* SIPRI/Pugwash, London, 1983.

Allan Rosas, "Conventional Disarmament—A Legal Framework and Some Perspectives," in Tuomi, Helen, and Vayrynen, Raimo, eds., *Militarization and Arms Production,* London, 1983.

Allan Rosas, "The Militarization of Space and International Law," *Journal of Peace Research,* (1983).

Allan Rosas, "Negative Security Assurances and Non-Use of Nuclear Weapons," in *German Yearbook of International Law,* Berlin, 1982.

Allan Rosas, "Non-Use of Nuclear Weapons and Nuclear-Weapon-Free Zones," in, Lodgaard, Sverre, and Thee, Marek, eds., *Nuclear Disengagement in Europe,* SIPRI/Pugwash, London, 1983.

Allan Rosas, "The Nordic Region as a Nuclear-Weapon-Free Area—Legal Aspects," the *Second Scandinavian Seminar on Nuclear-Weapon-Free-Zones,* Helsinki, August, 1984.

The Role of Lawyers in Preventing Nuclear War

Francis A. Boyle, "The Role of Lawyers in Preventing Nuclear War," *Proceedings of the 76th Annual Meeting of the American Society of International Law,* April 21-24, 1982.

Robert F. Drinan, "The Role of Law and Lawyers in the Debate Over Nuclear Arms" (1983), 4 *New York Law School Journal of International and Comparative Law* 405.

Elliott L. Meyrowitz, "Nuclear Weapons: An Area of Professional Responsibility," *The California Lawyer,* April, 1982.

Peter Weiss, "Commentary," (1983) 4 *New York Law School Journal of International and Comparative Law* 427.

Burns H. Weston, "Clergy, Doctors and Now the Lawyers," *The Des Moines Register,* March 27, 1982.

Burns H. Weston, "The Nuclear Arms Race: Lawyers and the Professional Responsibility," a project of the 1983-84 *Seminar on Problems in International Law and Policy: Arms Control, Disarmament and the Law,* College of Law, University of Iowa.

Articles, Manuscripts and Working Papers of the Lawyers' Committee on Nuclear Policy

I. Research and Education

The Lawyers' Committee on Nuclear Policy, "Statement on the Illegality of Nuclear Warfare" (1982; Updated, 1984).

Project on the First Use of Nuclear Weapons

"Constitutional Duty to Control Nuclear First Use" *Lawyers Committee on Nuclear Policy Working Paper,* forthcoming.

Jeffrey M. Kaplan and Daniel J. Arbess, "Not the President Alone" (Presidential First Use Is Unlawful), *St. Louis Post-Dispatch,* November 20, 1984.

Arthur S. Miller, "Law, the Constitution and Nuclear War," *The Miami Herald,* June 20, 1982.

Arthur S. Miller, "Nuclear First Use," *The Miami Herald,* August 12, 1984.

Claire Sherman Thomas, "U.S. Deliberately Plans First Use Of Nuclear Weapons," *The Journal American,* September 8, 1984.

Claire Sherman Thomas, "What Does Weinberger Mean By 'First Strike?'", *The Journal American,* February 15, 1985.

Project on Alternatives to Nuclear Deterrence

"Beyond Deterrence: The Political and Technological Challenge," A Roundtable discussion with Thomas Powers, Theodore Draper, Herbert Scoville Jr., Leon Wieseltier, Richard Garwin, Saul H. Mendlovitz, Robert Johansen, Gregory Fossedal and Robert Jastrow, reproduced as "Is There A Way Out?," a Forum of *Harper's* Magazine, June, 1985.

Daniel J. Arbess, "The International Law of Armed Conflict in Light of Contemporary Deterrence Strategies: Empty Promise or Meaningful Restraint?" (1984), 30 *McGill Law Journal* 90.

Daniel J. Arbess, "International Law Revisited: Meeting the Legal Challenge of Nuclear Weapons," (1985), 16 *Bulletin of Peace Proposals,* 105 (Norway).

Daniel J. Arbess and William Epstein, "Disarmament Role For the United Nations?" *Bulletin of the Atomic Scientists,* May, 1985.

Richard A. Falk, "Toward A Legal Regime for Nuclear Weapons" (1983), 28 *McGill Law Journal* 519.

Project on the Strategic Defense Initiative

Daniel J. Arbess and William Epstein, "Stand Against Star Wars Could

be a Beacon for Others," *The Globe and Mail* (Toronto), Tuesday,
April 9, 1985.
Francis A. Boyle, "Star Wars vs. International Law: The Force Will
Be Against Us," *ACDIS Bulletin,* Volume V/Number 6, May 1985.
Martin Feinrider, "Star Wars and International Law," *Proceedings of
the American Society of International Law,* forthcoming.

II. Advisory Programs

Nuclear Free Zones Project
*Planning for a Nuclear Free Environment: A Handbook of Legal Is-
sues,* The Lawyers' Committee on Nuclear Policy; contains "Model
Nuclear Free Zone Legislation and Commentary," Lawyers' Com-
mittee on Nuclear Policy Paper, Mark C. Cogan, July 6, 1984 (re-
vised), and "Recent Court Decisions That May Bear on Nuclear Free
Zone Laws," Lawyers' Committee on Nuclear Policy Memorandum,
Mark C. Cogan; May 10, 1984 (revised).
"Prospects for a Nordic Nuclear Weapons Free Zone: Naval War-
Fighting Strategies and International Law," Report by Simeon A. Sahaydachny to the Second Scandinavian Seminar on Nuclear Weap-
ons Free Zones, Helsinki, Finland; September 1, 1984.

Homeporting Program

"Public Safety Implications of the Navy's Plan to Homeport a Surface
Action Group in New York and Other Major Coastal Cities," a man-
uscript of the Lawyers Committee on Nuclear Policy; November,
1983; Revision, forthcoming.
*Nuclear Trojan Horse: The Navy's Plan to Base Nuclear Weapons
in New York Harbor,* a manuscript of the Lawyers' Committee on
Nuclear Policy, Simeon A. Sahaydachny, November, 1984.
Simeon A. Sahaydachny, "Harboring Nuclear Weapons: The USS
Iowa Comes to New York Harbor," *New York Public Interest Re-
search Group Agenda for Citizen Involvement,* November/December,
1984.
Simeon A. Sahaydachny, "New York Challenges Homeporting,"
Blind Justice, April 1984.

Litigation Project

Enforcing International Law in Domestic Courts: A Handbook, The Lawyers' Committee on Nuclear Policy; forthcoming.

Richard A. Falk, "Fulfilling the Nuremberg Obligation" (interview) (1983), 2 *Ground Zero* 2.

Richard A. Falk, "The Spirit of Thoreau in the Nuclear Age," *The Boston Globe,* August 4, 1983, retitled as "The Spirit of Thoreau in the Age of Trident," *AGNI,* forthcoming.

Peter Weiss, "Nuclear War in the Courts," in Abdul Paliwala, ed., *Nuclear Weapons, the Peace Movement and the Law,* forthcoming.

The LAWYERS' COMMITTEE ON NUCLEAR POLICY, established in 1981, is a nonpartisan research and educational organization supported by attorneys, foundations, and the public at large. Its purpose is to assist policy makers, scholars, the media, and the public by providing analysis and information concerning legal aspects of arms control and deterrence policies. The Committee's scholars have published widely on matters of international law; arms control and defense policy, and are currently collaborating in the development of a long term legal agenda for controlling, minimizing, and ultimately eliminating reliance on nuclear weapons. Views expressed in the Committee's publications are those of the authors and do not necessarily reflect those of the Lawyers' Committee on Nuclear Policy, Inc., its directors, advisory panels, members, or staff. The Committee is a tax exempt, educational organization under section 501(c)(3) of the Internal Revenue Code and is classified as a publicly supported organization under the Tax Reform Act of 1969. ■

225 Lafayette Street
New York, NY 10012
(212) 334-8044

INDEX

Abortion, 240, 248
Abu-Eissa, F., 328, 335
Act of state defense, 48, 54, 61
Affirmative defense, 25, 26-27, 31, 35, 39, 148, 280
Aggression, xiv, 102, 146, 197, 198, 226, 232-233, 246, 267, 276, 321, 323, 329
Aimen, J., 253
Allende, H. de, 328
Allende, S. de, xv
Allison, G., 84
American Civil Liberties Union, 192
American Law Institute Model Penal Code, 54
American Society of International Law, 117, 320, 327
Amnesty International, 117, 192
Anderson, K.M., 358
Angola, 212, 213, 226, 234, 258, 267, 326-327, 333-334
Anti-Apartheid Movement, 8
  Clark Amendment, 181, 326
Anti-Ballistic Missile System (ABM) Treaty (1972), U.S.-U.S.S.R., 149-153, 283-287, 322, 330
Apartheid (anti-apartheid), xix, 2-3, 10, 34, 39, 46, 211-280, 296, 327, 333
  Bantustan policy, 245
Application of Yamashita, 47, 63, 136-137, 170, 171, 206
Arab Deterrent Force, 325, 336, 337
Arab Lawyers Union, 328
Arkin, W., 78, 89, 92
Armed conflict, humanitarian, 52, 70-106, 116, 120-122, 199, 203, 331, 337, 338-344
Assassination, 46, 158, 173, 188, 206
Assimilative Crimes Act, 112, 144
Asylum, political, 3, 190, 191
Azrael, J., 289

Ball, George, 90, 97
Battlefield nuclear war, 95-100, 133-134
Baxter, Richard R. 75-79, 127, 205, 206
Bentham, J., 265
Berlin Airlift, 85
Berman, H., 289
Bishop, M., 179
Blocker, C., 59
Booth, H., 217
Boston Tea Party, xx
Botswana, 258, 268
Bowett, D., 96
Bracken, P., 89, 100
Brezhnev, L., 87, 151, 180
Brownlie, I., 62, 102
Brussels Tribunal, 328-334
Brzezinski, Zbigniew, 92, 135, 327
Builder, C., 86
Burlington, IA, 313-316
Butler, W., 94

Carter administration, 59, 92-93, 134-136, 213, 266, 269, 273, 292-293, 308, 323, 327. See also Nuclear weapons
Central America. See Policy, U.S.; individual countries
Central American Defense Council Pact, 167-168, 181
Central Intelligence Agency, 158, 169, 173, 184, 188-189, 197, 198, 203, 204
Chayes, A., 181
Chicago, IL, 218-219, 244, 252
  City of, Municipal Code, 10, 218-219
Chicago v. Streeter, 9-11, 211, 216-254, 280-281
Choice of evils defense, 24, 49, 137-138, 161
Chomsky, N., 185
Christopher, W., 308
Churchill, W., 122
Civil Disobedience, 5, 7-8, 16-17, 272

Civil resistance, ix, 1-12, 13, 28, 35, 40,
    41, 51, 85, 107-147, 201, 255-256,
    272-273, 284, 286, 287, 295
  Distinction from civil disobedience, 5-8,
    16-7, 272
  Rules for defense, 13-50
Civil rights, 314-316
  Demonstrations, ix, 164
  Movement, xx, 17, 272
Clark, Ramsey, 6, 328
Clarkson, J., 98
Clarridge, D., 204
Cochran, T., 78
Committee on the Present Danger, 93, 290,
    322
Common law defense, 17, 24-5, 35, 112,
    143, 221
Common law privilege to prevent the
    commission of a crime, 237-239. *See
    also* Prevention of a crime defense
Comprehensive Test Ban Treaty, 320
Compulsion defense, 24, 138
Constitution, U.S., x, xviii, 1, 5, 7, 11, 31,
    32, 46, 50, 108, 110, 119, 158, 159,
    183, 187, 194-196, 208, 218, 221,
    224, 237, 275, 296, 297, 298, 306,
    316
  Bricker Amendment, 304-308
  Equal Rights Amendment, 314
  States' rights, 296-314
  Supremacy Clause, 31, 32, 37-38, 119,
    128, 222, 300-301, 302, 304, 305,
    308
  War Power Clause, 160
  First Amendment, 1-12, 14, 33, 49, 147-
    148, 192
  Fourth Amendment, 3, 14
  Fifth Amendment, 14, 26
  Sixth Amendment, 7
  Tenth Amendment, 296, 300
  Fourteenth Amendment, 7, 14, 26, 303
Conyers, J., 251
Counter-ethnic targeting, 91-93, 134-136
Criley, R., 185
Crime(s) against humanity, 9, 31, 46, 47,
    48, 52, 53, 61, 62, 63, 64, 81, 82, 83,
    101, 102-103, 109, 123, 124, 125,
    127, 128, 131, 136, 137-138, 139-
    140, 146, 149, 178, 198, 205, 218,
    220, 221-222, 226, 228, 230-231,
    235, 236, 237, 238, 258, 259, 260,
    265, 274, 329, 331
Crime(s) against peace, 9, 31, 46, 47, 48,
    52, 53, 61, 62, 63, 64-65, 81, 82, 83,
    101, 103, 109, 123, 124, 127, 128,
    137, 139, 146, 149, 178, 198, 205,
    235, 237, 238, 258, 267, 268, 274,
    329, 331
(Criminal/unlawful) trespass, 10, 28, 29-31,
    49 110-113, 144, 218, 220, 239, 240,
    244, 253, 257, 273-274, 281
Crocker, C., 269
Cuba, 172-173
  Castro government, 326-327
  Missile Crisis, 85, 141, 180
  Troops in Angola, 212, 213-214, 333-334
Culen, S., 217

Dachau, 144
Davis, K., 253
Declaration of London (1909), 73-74
Delf, G., xvii-xviii
Dickey, C., 204
Diego Garcia Island, 334
Diminished capacity, 28-29
Divestment, 2-3, 11-12, 211, 249, 250,
    273 *See also* University of Illinois
    Student Divestment Protest Case.
Dixon, M., 185
Dmytryshyn, B., 91
Dominican Republic, 180
Dore, I., 181
Duffy, G., 59
Dulles, J. F., 66, 307
Dunn, L., 104
Duress defense, 54
Dycus, S., 185

Effects of Nuclear War, The, 141-142
Eichmann, A., 62
Eisenhower administration, 307. *See also*
    Nuclear weapons
El Salvador, 3, 10, 168, 171-172, 184, 189-
    196, 299, 326, 329. *See also* Policy,
    U.S., on Central America
Enders, T., 204
Entebbe, 178
Erwin, S., Jr., 296
European Convention for the Protection of
    Human Rights and Fundamental
    Freedoms (1950), 223, 224, 277, 348
European Parliament, 351

Falk, Richard, vii, xv, xvii-xxii, 51, 60, 64,
    181, 186, 336, 342
Federal Rules of Evidence, 20, 36, 44, 112
Feinrider, M., 181, 185
Ferguson, C.C., Jr., 181, 338
Fine, J.D., 182
Finlay, L., 182
Fisher, R., 338
Foote, M., 87
Ford, G., 151
Franck, H.G., 328, 335
Freedman, L., 59
Freedom of Information Act, 130
Fried, J., 344
Friedman, L., 237

Gaitskill, N., 254

Gandhi, M., 164
Garry, C., 185
General intent crimes, 27-31
General Principles of Law Recognized by Civilized Nations, 139
Geneva Conventions, 4, 9, 28, 31, 39, 41, 46, 53, 62, 80, 108-109, 116, 118, 127-128, 137-139, 160, 170, 171, 173, 193, 195, 197, 198, 207, 209, 226, 233, 239, 298, 299, 312, 325, 329, 331, 332, 336-337, 339, 340, 341
    Additional Protocol (1977), 193, 195, 336
Geneva Protocol (1925), 76, 99, 121, 142, 343
Genocide, 31, 46, 53, 92, 101, 103, 137, 138, 139, 140, 145, 194, 201, 213, 225, 234, 239, 259-260, 274, 302, 308-309, 310-311. *See also* United Nations, Convention on the Prevention and Punishment of the Crime of Genocide
Genocide Convention. *See* United Nations, Convention on the Prevention and Punishment of the Crime of Genocide
George, J., 185
Graubard, M., 86
Gray, I., 91, 98
Great Lakes Naval Training Center/Base, 9, 157-158, 161, 164
Greenham Common Women, 2
Grenada, 8, 160, 165-168, 175, 202, 299. *See also* Policy, U.S.
Gross, B., 185
Guatemala, 190-195, 299

Hafiz, M.G., 328, 335
Hague Conventions, 71, 76, 109, 113, 120, 122, 123, 134, 138, 330, 339-341, 343
Hague Peace Conferences, 120, 176
Hague Regulations, 28, 41, 121, 124, 126, 127, 131
Haig, A., 320, 327
Hanford, WA. *See* PUREX facility
Hasenfus, E., 205
Hay, J., 187
Hellie, R., 289
Helms, J., 296
Helsinki Accord, 354-355
Henley, R., 217
Hitler, A., 46, 123, 125, 128, 135, 139, 164, 170, 258, 259, 306, 308
Hobbes, T., 320-321
Hoenig, M., 78
Hoffmann, S., 338
Hoft, J., 114-144, 155-157

Illegal orders, 79-83

Illinois Criminal Code, 25-26, 111-112, 273-274
Illinois Revised Statutes (1983), 9, 255, 273
    Necessity Statute, 239-243
In limine, motion, 33-36, 107-114, 129, 155-164, 192, 211, 253
Inter-American Human Rights Convention, 200, 277
International Court of Justice, 9, 37-38, 70, 113, 159, 160, 176-177, 183-184, 186, 199, 202-210, 215, 216, 226, 232, 266, 309, 310, 330, 336, 349
    1984 Interim Order of Protection (on behalf of Nicaragua), 9, 176, 197, 199, 330
    Statute, 139, 174, 213, 222, 234, 347
International law defense, 14-17, 23
International Military Tribunal for the Far East, xxi, 136, 139, 237, 268-269
International Nuclear Warfare Tribunal, 117
International Peace Bureau, 117
International Progress Organization, 116, 328-334
International Red Cross Committee, 341
Iran, xv, 323-324
Iran/contra affair, 6, 205
Iraq, 323-324
Israel, 322-323, 329-330, 333-336

Jackson, R.K., 64-65, 109, 237, 357
Jarka case. *See People v. Jarka*
Jarrin, E.M., 328
Jervis, R., 91
Johnson, L., 180
Joint Strategic Target Planning Staff (JSTPS), 90, 132
Judiciary
    State and municipal, 19-21, 37, 38. *See also* United States of America, judiciary
Jury, 7-11, 15-50, 107, 111, 113, 143, 255

Kaplan, M., 56
Kaufman, M.M., 328, 333, 335
Keenan, E., Jr., 289
Kellogg, F., 69
Kellogg-Briand Peace Pact (1928), 69-70
Kennan, G., 87, 99
Kennedy administration, 307. *See also* Nuclear weapons
Kennedy, D., 185
King, M.L., 272
Kinoy, A., 185
Kissinger, H., 320, 321, 323, 327
Knoll, S., 185
Korean War, 215
Krugerrands, 2, 249, 252

Law of Land Warfare, The (U.S. Army Field Manual 27-10; 1956), 47-48, 56-57,

58, 60, 61, 62-63, 67, 68, 75-79, 93, 121, 126-130, 137, 145-146, 164, 171, 173, 205-207
Law of Naval Warfare, The (Department of the Navy Field Manual NWIP 10-2; 1955), 57, 58, 61, 67, 68, 75, 76-77, 127
Lawful orders, military obedience to, 79-83
Laws of Armed Conflict, 80, 120
Lawyers Alliance for Nuclear Arms Control, 129, 285-287
Lawyers' Committee on Nuclear Policy, vii, ix-xi, xviii, 10, 13, 50, 115, 129, 283, 287, 338, 369
League of Arab States, 324, 336, 337
League of Nations, 266
  Covenant, 68-69
Lebanon, 325, 331-332, 335-338
Lesotho, 212, 234, 258, 268
Libya, 332
Lieber, F., 80
Limited Test Ban Treaty (1963), 151
London Agreement on War Criminals (1945), 109, 122, 231, 234
Lotus case, 58, 67-72, 75
Lotz, W., 218
Love, Kary, 107, 113, 114-144
Lucas, R., 217

MacBride, Sean, vii, xiii-xvi, 117, 328
Mallison, W.T., 338
Martens Clause, 70-72, 75, 340
Martin, L., 59
Mauritius, 334
McGrath, S. & W., 196-197
McKinley, J., 187
McNamara, Robert, 59, 96, 99
Measures otherwise authorized by law defense, 49
Mendlovitz, S., 184
Meyers, L., 254
Meyrowitz, L., 51, 60, 64, 76, 344
Middle East. *See* Policy, U.S.
Miller, Alex, ix-xi
Miller, Arthur, 184
Miller, D., 70
Mob action, 156, 177
Moller, A., 68
Mozambique, 234, 258, 268
Murphy, J., 96
Muther, J., 69
Mutual and Balanced Force Reduction (MBFR), 97, 104-105

Namibia, 212, 213-214, 226, 232-233, 247, 265-267, 273, 326-327, 333-334
  U.N. Security Council Resolution 435 (1978), 214
National Conference of Christians and Jews, 312

Nazi (government/leaders), 46-47, 48, 65, 70, 109, 122, 125, 128, 139, 144, 163, 175, 198, 220, 258-259, 268, 343
Necessity defense, 9, 10, 12, 24, 35, 54, 111-113, 137-138, 143-144, 149, 156-164, 177, 219, 222, 239-252, 254, 273-274, 279, 281, 357
Neely, D., 253
Negroponte, J., 204
Nicaragua, xi, xv, 3-4, 10, 24, 113, 117, 157, 158,159-160, 168-171, 175, 181, 183-184, 186-187, 189, 197-210, 299, 326, 330
  Contras, 169-171, 178, 189, 197-210
  Intervention in. *See* Policy, U.S., on Central America
  Mosquito Indians, 200-201
Nicaragua Must Survive Campaign, 201
Nixon, R., 141
Nixon administration, 297, 308
Njem, J.-C., 328, 335
Nonviolent resistance. *See* Protest, nonviolent
North, O., 204
North American Air Defense Command (NORAD), 85, 112, 140
North Atlantic Treaty Organization (NATO), 57, 65, 66, 79, 86, 96-100, 105, 133-134
Nuclear arms race, ix, 330
Nuclear Freeze Movement, 2, 8
Nuclear Non-Proliferation Treaty (1968), 330
Nuclear power, 252
Nuclear weapons/warfare, ix, xix-xxii, 2, 9, 10, 28, 31, 39, 51-105, 107-153, 283-285, 290, 319, 322, 323, 338-344
  "Counterforce" targeting, 89, 90, 93, 103
  Deterrence, paradox of, 52-105, 129
  Deterrence policy, strategic, 52, 64, 66-67, 81-104
  "Flexible response," 59, 85, 86, 87, 88
  "Launch on warning," 84, 86, 103
  "Massive retaliation," 59, 66, 79, 88, 91
  "Mutual assured destruction (MAD)," 59, 66, 87, 86, 87, 88, 104
  Nevada weapons test facility, x, 2
  Presidential Directive 88, 93, 131-132, 134-136, 322, 339
  "Protracted nuclear war-prevailing" capability, 67, 86-88, 91, 104
  "Schlesinger doctrine," 59, 88
  Single Integrated Operational Plan (SIOP), 89-93, 105, 131-132
  Weinberger Five-Year Defense Guidance Statement (1982), 59, 131-132
  See also Policy, U.S.
"Nuclear winter," 141-142
Nunes, K., 181

"Nuremberg Defense," 23
Nuremberg Principles, xvii, 28, 39, 41, 46,
    47, 48, 52, 61-67, 75, 81, 101, 109,
    118, 122, 124, 125, 126-127, 128,
    131, 133, 134, 135, 164, 194, 198,
    205, 206, 218, 220, 222, 226, 231,
    235, 236, 237, 255, 257, 258, 259,
    260, 261, 268, 331
Nuremberg Tribunal, xxi, 47, 53, 65, 70,
    80, 83, 110, 122-123, 128, 138, 163,
    175, 237, 259, 269, 328, 342, 343
    Charter, 47, 61, 62, 64, 81, 109, 123,
        124, 146-147, 163, 183, 205, 226,
        234, 235, 236, 237, 260, 357
    Judgment, 62, 70, 83, 124, 139, 198,
        205, 235-237

Oak Park, IL, 189-196
Offenses against the peace and security of
    mankind, 235, 236, 238
Organization of African Unity, 331
Organization of American States (O.A.S.),
    118, 176, 179-183, 324
    American Convention on Human Rights
        (1965), 292, 308, 312, 348
    Charter, 4, 9, 160-161, 165-177, 179,
        180, 182, 197, 329, 330, 350
    Punta del Este Resolution (1962), 326
Organization of Eastern Caribbean States,
    179, 181, 182
Outer Space Treaty (1967), 151

Palestinian people, 324-325, 331-332, 338
P.L.O., 324-325, 332, 335-338
Palmer, E., 217
Paquete Habana, The, 31-32, 38, 120, 128,
    139, 143, 146, 147, 149, 159, 183,
    222-223, 346, 349
Pasti, N., 328
Pauling, L., 185
Pax Christi, 2
Peeters, P., 59, 66
Peaceful Nuclear Explosions Treaty (1976),
    330
Peeters, P., 59, 66
People v. Jarka, 9-11, 25, 43, 49, 107,
    149-153, 155-178, 253, 257, 273
Peremptory norm of international law (jus
    cogens), 103, 261
Perle, R., 152
Permanent Court of Arbitration, 187
Permanent Court of International Justice, 58,
    60, 67-68
Permanent Peoples Tribunal, xviii, 117
Permissive theory of international law, 57-
    60, 61
Persian Gulf, 323-324, 334
    Carter Doctrine, 324
Pipes, R., 289-300
Piracy, 103
Platt, T., 185

Pledge of Resistance Movement, x, 3-4, 8,
    201, 208
Plowshares, x
Poison, 121, 142
Policy, U.S., 15, 279
    Apartheid, 13, 40, 41, 284
    Central America, x, 3-4, 5, 8, 9-11, 13,
        24, 31, 34, 39, 40, 41, 49, 116-117,
        155-210, 286, 329
    "Constructive engagement," 2, 212-216,
        218, 222, 233-234, 235, 239, 243,
        266, 267-268, 270, 277-290, 333
    Cuba, 325-327
    Grenada, 8, 178-183, 329
    Human rights, 292-314
    Middle East, 8, 13, 116-117, 175, 324-
        325, 331-332
    Nuclear weapons, xi, xvii, 2, 5, 8, 9-11,
        24, 34, 39, 40, 41, 49, 54-105, 110,
        115, 117, 130-144, 330-331
    Racism, 296
    South(ern) Africa, x, 2-3, 5, 8, 10-11, 13,
        31, 34, 39, 40, 41, 117, 211-281,
        286
    Soviet Union, 5
    See also Nuclear weapons; United States
        of America
Prevention of a crime defense, 24, 25, 35,
    49, 138-139, 178, 192-195, 255, 353-
    356
Prevention of a public catastrophe defense,
    24, 49
Pringle, P., 89, 92
Privilege, defense of, 143-146, 355-356
Prohibitive theory of international law, 57-
    60, 67-68, 71
Protest (nonviolent), ix-xi, 2, 3-4, 5, 28, 34-
    50, 211, 279
    See also Civil resistance
Puerto Rico, 172-173
PUREX facility (Hanford, WA), 2

Quigley, J., 184

Ramsey, J., 217
Reagan, Ronald, 4, 87, 89, 91, 93, 94, 99,
    104, 149, 151, 160, 180, 182, 183,
    186, 187, 189, 204, 249, 335
Reagan administration/government, 1-12,
    15, 17, 19, 20, 39, 40, 42, 44, 45, 46,
    48, 50, 63, 67, 85-105, 107, 118,
    132, 150, 152, 160, 167-177, 178,
    209-210, 212-282, 284, 287-314, 318-
    334
Reasonable mistake of law defense, 40
Reciprocity of reservations, 70
Redekopp, O., 217
Refugee, 3, 348
Relevance, defined, 20
Rehnquist, W., 297

Rhinelander, J., 150
Risley, J., 68
Rock Island Arsenal, 133, 147
Rocky Flats nuclear arsenal, 12
Roosevelt, F.D., 122, 261
Roosevelt, T., 176, 180, 187
Root, E., 176, 187
Rosenne, S., 101
Ross, A., 68
Royce, T., 254
Rubin, Alfred, 83
Ruiz-Eldridge, R., 328, 335
Rule of Law, xiii-xv
Russel, R., 69

Sagan, Carl, x
St. Petersburg Declaration (1868), 121, 341
SALT I Interim Accord (1972), 150, 151, 284, 323
Salt II Treaty, 94, 104, 113, 151, 284, 322, 323, 329, 330, 331
Sanchez, N., 204
Sanctuary, xix, 189-196
Case, 6, 192
Sanctuary Movement, 3, 6, 8, 20, 21, 189, 192, 201
Sanders, J., 185
Sanderson, J., 51, 60, 64, 344
Savage, B., 211
Savage, T., 217, 254-274
Scheer, R., 59, 132
Schindler, D., 120-122, 125-128
Schwarzenberger, G., 61, 71
Scoon, P., 182
Scott, J., 71
Seychelles, 212, 234, 268
Shultz, G., 91
Singh, N., 71
Segal, J., 186
Slavery, 103
Smith, D., 150
Snow, D., 59
Sofaer, A., 152
Solf, W., 75
South(ern) Africa, x, xv, 2-3, 5, 10, 12, 211-281, 296, 326-327, 333-334
Azanian Peoples Organization, 248
Banning, 246-247
Constitution, 247-248
Internal Security Act (1982), 246, 248
United Democratic Front, 247
See also Policy, U.S.
Southwest Africa Peoples' Organization (SWAPO), 214, 333
Sovereignty, 57, 58, 60, 68, 160
Soviet Union, 5, 52, 57, 62, 65, 66, 80, 81, 83, 84-105, 112, 123, 131, 133-136, 141, 150, 184, 215, 234, 283, 284, 285-287, 288-289, 290, 291, 322, 323-324, 326, 332

Association of Soviet Lawyers, 283-287
Government, 53
Human rights (violations), 13, 287, 290, 291, 294, 295, 351-353, 355-357
Invasion of Afghanistan, 180, 324
Invasion of Czechoslovakia, 180
Jews, 345-358
Soysal, M., 328, 335
Spaeth, J., 156, 158
Specific intent, 27-31, 275-276
Speech, political
Nonviolent, symbolic, ix
Spock, B., 185
Stalin, J., 122
Star Wars. *See* Strategic Defense Initiative
Statutory defense, 17, 24-5, 35
Steiner, H., 304
Stender, M., 185
Strategic Air Command, 78, 132
Strategic Arms Reduction Talks (START), 104
Strategic Defense Initiative (SDI), 67, 88, 104, 107, 149-153, 284
Streeter, A., 217
Study Commission on U.S. Policy Toward South Africa, 250
Suffragettes, 164
Superior orders defense, 48, 54-56, 62, 80, 81, 128, 206, 231, 235, 257

Terrorism, xiv-xv
Thermonuclear weapons/war, 77-78, 100, 323
Thomas, A., 96, 99
Thomas, A.J., Jr., 96, 99
Threshold Test Ban Treaty (1974), 330
Thurmond, S., 294
Tokyo Tribunal. *See* International Military Tribunal for the Far East
Toman, J., 76, 120-123, 125-8
Torture, 46, 170, 193, 221, 223, 226, 230-239, 248, 263-265, 274, 346, 353. *See also* United Nations, Declaration on the Protection of All Persons From Being Subjected to Torture and Other Cruel, Inhuman or Degrading Treatment or Punishment (1975)
Treaty of Versailles, 323
Treaty of Washington, 172
Truman, H., 184, 302

Ulam, A., 289
United Nations, 3, 117, 244, 310, 326, 340, 342
Charter, xiii-xiv, 4, 9, 28, 37-38, 39, 41, 52, 57, 68, 95, 118, 128, 133, 138, 159, 165-175, 179, 182, 190, 197, 212, 214-215, 220, 222, 223, 224, 228, 233, 238, 262-263, 296, 300-303, 307, 309, 323, 325, 329-334,

335-338, 342, 348-358
Convention on the Abolition of Forced Labor (1957), 308, 312
Convention on the Political Rights of Women (1953), 291, 308
Convention on the Prevention and Punishment of the Crime of Genocide (1948), 28, 39, 41, 92, 125-126, 131, 134-136, 145, 193-194, 195, 201, 225, 226-227, 234, 259-260, 261, 291, 292, 296-314 *passim*, 342
Convention on the Reduction of Statelessness, 312
Convention Relating to the Status of Refugees (1951), 190, 191
Convention Relating to the Status of Stateless Persons, 312
Declaration of the Indian Ocean as a Zone of Peace (1971), 334
Declaration of the Inadmissibility of Intervention in the Domestic Affairs of States and the Protection of Their Independence and Sovereignty (1965), 329, 336
Declaration on Principles of International Law Concerning Friendly Relations and Cooperation Among States in Accordance with the Charter of the United Nations (1970), 329, 336
Declaration on the Protection of All Persons from Being Subjected to Torture and Other Cruel, Inhuman or Degrading Treatment or Punishment (1975), 223, 226, 230, 348
Definition of Aggression, 329, 336
Draft Code of Offenses Against the Peace and Security of Mankind (1954), 235, 236
General Assembly, xxi, 62, 123, 125, 145, 160, 180, 214, 215, 216, 232, 233, 234, 235, 247, 251, 261-262, 263, 265, 266, 267, 324, 329, 332, 334, 342, 350, 355
Interim Force in Lebanon, 325, 337-338
International Convention on the Elimination of All Forms of Discrimination Against Women (1979), 291, 292, 308, 312, 313, 314
International Convention on the Elimination of All Forms of Racial Discrimination (1965), 291, 292, 308, 312, 313, 315-316, 354
International Convention on the Suppression and Punishment of the Crime of Apartheid (1973), 227-229, 261, 291, 292, 297, 312, 333
International Covenant on Civil and Political Rights (1966), 200, 223,

224, 226, 230, 263, 291, 292, 308, 312, 313, 348, 353
International Covenant on Economic, Social and Cultural Rights (1966), 200, 291, 292, 308, 312, 313, 354
International Law Commission, 163, 235
Protocol to the Convention Relating to the Status of Refugees (1967), 3, 190-191, 195, 307
Security Council, 160, 179, 180, 181, 214-215, 226, 232, 258, 261-262, 266, 267, 273, 277, 325, 326, 332-334, 337-338
Standard Minimum Rules for the Treatment of Prisoners (1977), 224
Supplementary Convention on the Abolition of Slavery, the Slave Trade, and Institutions and Practices Similar to the Slave Trade (1967), 307
Treaty on the Non-Proliferation of Nuclear Weapons (1968), 56, 102, 104
United Nations Emergency Force, 215-216
Uniting for Peace Resolution of 1950, 215-216, 334
Universal Declaration of Human Rights, 223, 224, 226, 229-230, 239, 262-264, 348, 350, 353, 355-356
Vienna Convention on the Law of Treaties (1969), 103, 310, 331
United States of America, xiv, xviii, 117, 140-141
    Army Field Manual. *See Law of Land Warfare*
    Congress, xx, 4, 142, 194-195, 196, 208, 245, 250-251, 297-298, 299, 305-306
    Foreign policy, Reagan administration, 1-5, 7, 8, 10, 15, 16, 18, 40, 117, 161, 189-195, 212, 328-334. *See also* Nuclear weapons; Policy, U.S.; Reagan administration.
    Federal Alien Tort Statute, 264-265
    Federal Assimilative Crimes Act, 18
    Federal Criminal Code, 18
    (Historical) commitment to rule of law, 4, 5, 8, 11, 94, 113, 118-9
    Immigration and Naturalization Service, 191-195, 197
    Judiciary, xviii, 4, 19-21
    National Security Council, 204, 288
    National Security Decision Directive 17, 204
    Office of the President, 20
    Refugee Act (1980), 3, 190, 195
    Senate, 183-84, 186-187, 194, 204, 209, 222, 295, 300, 301, 306-314, 323, 358
Separation of powers doctrine, 4-5, 6, 7

States' rights, 283-314
Supreme Court, 26, 31-32, 38, 47, 136-137, 148, 159, 162, 171, 176, 183, 194, 206, 219, 265, 299-300, 303, 306, 346, 350
Uniform Code of Military Justice, 80, 299
United Nations Participation Act, 262, 267
War Powers Act, 181
Withholding of Deportation, 191
See also Carter administration; Constitution, U.S.; Nuclear weapons; Policy, U.S.; Presidents, by name; Reagan administration
United States v. Schweiters, 107-153
University of Illinois Student Divestment Protest Case, 43, 211
Urbana, IL, 196
US Out of Central America, 183, 201
Ustinov, D., 87

Vagts, D., 306
Verr, S.R., 358
Vietnam, 202, 299
Vladivostock Agreement (1974), 151
Von Rauch, G., 91, 98

Wald, G., 185, 328
Walters, F., 69
War crime(s), 9, 31, 39, 46, 47, 48, 52, 53, 61, 62, 63, 64, 81, 82, 83, 101, 103, 109, 123, 124, 127, 128, 136-138, 139, 146, 149, 170, 171, 178, 188, 193, 198, 205, 206, 226, 235, 236, 237, 255, 268-269, 274, 298, 299, 329, 331
German industrialists, 268-269
War criminals, 54, 61, 65, 70, 81, 109, 123, 125, 136, 139, 140, 175, 183, 189, 198, 206, 258, 268
Warsaw Pact, 97-99, 105
Washington Board of Rabbis, 344, 358
Webster, D., 335-336
Welch, H., 211
Weston, Burns H., 64, 95, 182, 313, 314
Wilson, Woodrow, 74
Winograd, B., 185
Witt, Alphonse F., 9-10
Woetzel, R., 62
Wortman, R., 289
World Court. *See* International Court of Justice
World Politics and International Law (1985), 14, 115, 284
World War I, 72-75, 91, 98, 99, 177, 266
Unrestricted submarine warfare, 72-75
World War II, 46, 65, 70, 71, 91, 98, 99, 118, 122, 125, 170, 177, 236, 268, 269, 292, 300, 309, 321, 323
World War III, 65, 99, 118
Wright, T., 211, 253

Yamashita, 175. *See also Application of Yamashita*
Yom Kippur War, 85, 141

Zimbabwe, 212, 234, 258, 268

AFTERWORD FROM THE PUBLISHER

The Center for Energy Research is a non-profit, tax-exempt corporation concerned with energy and peace issues.

We are pleased to make this book on the legal bases for civil resistance activities available for the use of those whose consciences impel them to take personal responsibility for bringing justice to areas where the United States Government has failed.

The Center for Energy Research and the American Peace Test have enjoyed a fruitful partnership producing educational materials relating to the testing of nuclear weapons and the nuclear arms race. This is our first joint venture related to international law. We hope it will be useful to many activists.

Please address questions and/or tax-exempt contributions to:

> The Center for Energy Research
> 333 State Street
> Salem, OR 97301   Phone: (503) 371-8002

Contributions to the American Peace Test may be sent to:

> P.O. Box 26725
> Las Vegas, NV 89126   Phone: (702) 363-7875

NOTES